I Do It All

DON BOZARTH

ISBN 978-1-0980-6605-5 (paperback)
ISBN 978-1-0980-6606-2 (hardcover)
ISBN 978-1-0980-6607-9 (digital)

Copyright © 2020 by Don Bozarth

All rights reserved. No part of this publication may be reproduced, distributed, or transmitted in any form or by any means, including photocopying, recording, or other electronic or mechanical methods without the prior written permission of the publisher. For permission requests, solicit the publisher via the address below.

Christian Faith Publishing, Inc.
832 Park Avenue
Meadville, PA 16335
www.christianfaithpublishing.com

Printed in the United States of America

I DO IT ALL

There it was! I heard it again! It was distinct and clear, but was it audible or was it just in my head? It was early morning, still dark with an orange hue from the streetlamps. I was getting tired from running and, quite frankly, a little frustrated that my efforts were not producing what I wanted. First it was "Help you?" now it was "I Do It All." I somehow knew this moment would change my perspective on how I would be living my life!

Life from Two Perspectives

Two people seeing the same event can have two completely different perspectives or accounts when recounting the incident to their friends. It is also true when a person views their own life, even as it plays out right in front of them. Their life can take on a positive, encouraging outlook when looked on from the best perspective. The other more depressing perspective is also there to focus on given a poor viewpoint and in the company of negative individuals. How is that possible? Two opposing points of view given the same information.

When retelling my story, some will say what an amazing life I have had with so many exciting and wonderful adventures coming my way. One positive opportunity after another, seamlessly unfolding right before me through the years. Others will say, "How could I have had so much bad luck, with so many seemingly unlucky and disappointing setbacks taking place in my life?" Again, one life, two completely different perspectives, neither one coming close to recounting my actual life's story.

My older brother was visiting me in Australia, during a particularly difficult period of his life. We had a tense debate sitting out on a balcony with the sound of the Gold Coast waves in the background. He glibly said I could not possibly understand his situation as everything had worked out so perfectly and wonderfully for me during my life. In his mind, this was especially true right then with me living on the beautiful and idyllic Gold Coast in Australia. I was living in an apartment with an ocean breeze waking me up each morning, next to one of the world's most beautiful beaches, hardly a stone's throw away. His statement was made in spite of him being aware of almost every painful detail of my life. How could he have had that viewpoint, even though he knew I was living with spinal cord damage and going through a number of uncomfortable therapies each week. Dealing with various pain issues in my back was obvious to him as he sat there with me on that Gold Coast balcony. Again perspective plays a huge role in determining someone's outlook on a situation.

But how could he possibly think that way? He couldn't imagine any situation being as bad or worse than his present condition. It was impossible for him to see clearly from his clouded perspective. My life looked idyllic to him in comparison. Maybe it was because I loved living on the Gold Coast and saw all the beauty around me, feeling like I was one of the lucky ones to live there. I didn't choose to complain or comment about my various pains or uncomfortable body. It was easy for him to discount my present situation when making his statement. He was watching me go out for a run, bike, swim, or walk over to the beach for a relaxing time of body surfing in the inviting Gold Coast's wonderful blue ocean. I believe our countenance plays a huge role in how people view our lives in general. My Father once said I was blessed with a "blessing" and a "curse." When I asked him why, he stated, "When you are sick or injured, you still give the appearance of being happy and well. Nobody is ever going to feel sorry for you." I don't know if that was part of my DNA makeup or something I had unknowingly developed over the years because of my family grounding. When working out with my dad and taking a bad fall or a hard knock left me on the ground, my dad would always say, "Get up. Brush it off and keep going."

I have come to believe that we have only two choices in life: we can either get up and be positive, or stay down in the dirt, grime, and mud of life and be negative. Depending on those two perspectives, the same incident will appear completely different in the minds of those involved. One person will see the obvious roadblocks, while another person will only see new opportunities. I was raised to believe in a loving God who has our best interests at heart. I have also met people who believe they are completely on their own, living in a dark and foreboding world where they have no choice but to fight and scrape for everything. From their viewpoint, roadblocks seem to be looming large and foreboding everywhere they look. With no promise of outside help to achieve their life's dreams, these individuals can be overwhelmed when life's inevitable bumps, potholes, or roadblocks suddenly appear.

From my perspective, there is always an expectancy of a better day even if it is a change of direction. I am far from perfect, but I do my best to look for the serendipity factor when seemingly "bad" things take place. This attitude keeps me upbeat about life in general. My parents filled my childhood with an eternal perspective, so the end result in this world is something far better than we have here in this life on earth. I was taught to enjoy this wonderful gift of life and get ready for the best to come. When there is no eternal perspective, and life isn't working according to our plan, life can become bleak and foreboding. This leaves no light at the end of a dark tunnel. Negativity can easily creep in, clouding your entire perspective. You will eventually view the negative side of life in every situation.

I have made many mistakes and take full responsibility for them. However, I don't believe we should be identified by our mistakes. This was what my brother was really saying. He was viewing my life through all the positive, miraculous episodes I had gone through, totally ignoring my past mistakes, trials, and present physical limitations. My mistakes are many when itemized out in a list. I was once charged by a Hong Kong colleague as being a dreamer. He couldn't understand how I could be so positive when a horrible life-altering accident altered my life. Being a dreamer or having a positive vision is a good thing when it keeps us up, moving forward, positive and in a hopeful frame of mind.

Have I had a perfect life like some have said, born with a silver spoon in my mouth? Or has life dealt me a bad deck of cards no one would wish for? You can determine for yourself, as you view my life and others, in the pages ahead. Decide from your own perspective, hopefully seeing there is always hope and light at the end of every seemingly dark tunnel.

JOURNEY TO A COOL HARD PAVEMENT

For the first time in years, I woke up late! This should have been an omen. It was clear, beautiful, and with stars dotting the dark early morning sky. Rushing to get up, I was too busy to talk with God, even to say good morning. It was too beautiful of a day, and I couldn't wait to get up and head out of our Hong Kong country park home for my bike ride.

It was 1992, and for six months, I had been committed to a very disciplined training program. I was preparing for the first professional Asian Triathlon Championship in Japan and the Fourth Triathlon World Championships in Muskoka, Canada, later in September. That morning of April 22 was also just two days before the Clearwater Invitational Tennis Tournament. I had been invited to enter and compete with some of the top professional doubles teams in Asia. My triathlon training was keeping me extremely fit, and I was looking forward to the tennis tournament. Since I was tapering for the tennis event, I was looking forward to an easy early-morning bike ride with my two sons, Donnie and Brian.

It was a beautiful warm and balmy Wednesday morning, still dark with stars sparkling in the clear dark ebony sky shining above the skyline. This was promising to be one of those many spectacular days we enjoyed in Hong Kong.

My two sons had both taken up triathlon training and racing eight months earlier. They had been watching how the sport of triathlon was keeping me fit and healthy, and they were also viewing my travels to many wonderful and exotic places around the world to compete. Both had received new Klein racing road bikes in the fall and were in the habit of training with me in these early-morning hours through the challenging hills of Clearwater Bay. This area provided a serious and perfect training route for our cycle training. Our cycling was excelling after negotiating Clearwater Bay's steep hills, descents, and technical corners at high speed.

My sons had also unexpectedly slept in, which should have been "another omen" for me. When I woke them, they decided not to go on my shortened ride. This was the first time in months they had decided to stay in bed. I found this unusual, but I was still focused to go on my ride. A "third omen," but I was too single-minded and focused on my goals to notice or pay attention.

I had a new racing bike myself and wanted to test it out that morning. So I headed out for a "relaxing" tour around the hills of Clearwater Bay. There was only going to be time for one lap of our usual multilap thirteen-kilometer bike route. Very little traffic was seen on the roads this time of morning, except for the occasional mini bus going to the bottom of a steep hill called Clearwater Bay Beach 2. I warned my sons many times to "be careful" coming around the final sweeping left-hand bend at the bottom of this hill. It was the most dangerous section of our route, with entrance and exits of two parking lots located at the bottom. This was where we would be flying our fastest when exiting that last sweeping corner.

Starting my ride down the hill from our Chinese village house, it felt great being on my bright new multicolored bike. The first kilometer from our house was completely downhill and always got my adrenaline pumping in the early-morning darkness while passing the university, just visible on my left. The sharply banked sweeping left corner at the bottom of this hill never failed to make my heart rate jump. It was almost eerie in the early-morning dark, with the amber orange streetlights and jungle growth on both sides of the road and the occasional Chinese village peeking through the foliage.

I loved it, the feeling of being out on the road when everyone else was still catching their last few hours of sleep. It felt like I was stealing a little bit of paradise while they slept through this magical time of day. I cruised along the road until it turned sharply upward for a few hundred meters. This hill was a short climb but very steep. I would always remember the first time going up this hill, which looked like a wall in the darkness. That time, I was forced to stop and walk my bike to the top because of my lack of strength and fitness. Now I was able to ride to the top with confidence, even though it still looked like a wall and required serious effort.

Once reaching the top, this section of the road ended at a country park after another two kilometers in the pitch-black darkness. The amber orange streetlights disappeared on this area of our route as the road remained undeveloped. It was actually spooky as moonlight provided the only light amid the dark shadows outlining the trees and the few homes hidden in the jungle. With village dogs barking in the distance and sounds of the waking jungle, there was never any lack of goose bumps and adrenaline as I flew down this dark country road. Other than the occasional early-morning couples still celebrating the end of a late-night date in a parked car, I was alone with my bike, the whir of my wheels on the road and the wind rushing past my face. I loved being out there, energized and excited!

When there was no moon to provide a hint of light, this section could also be dangerous. One morning, I had almost had a bad accident when a group a six young Chinese chose to walk side-by-side right down the middle of the road in my direction. I didn't see them until the last moment and somehow slipped between a small gap without incident. They screamed out in fright as I zipped by them, and goose bumps increased on my arms as I realized how fortunate I had been to still be on my bike without a serious fall.

With this on my mind, I always took it easy when there was no moon to light this section of the road. This morning was moonlit and spectacular as I turned back at the country park. Coming back from the park and eventually picking up speed down the short hill, I turned left to start my descent down the steep 600 meter Clearwater Bay hill. Picking up speed, I could feel how solid my new bike frame felt. Feeling wonderful on that beautiful morning, I picked up speed through a couple of sweeping curves. My mind was wandering, thinking about the upcoming tennis tournament to be held at the end of this very road at Clearwater Bay Country Club in two days and how excited I was to be included. At forty-five years old, I was fortunate to still compete with the top professionals in the region and felt honored to be invited to play this doubles invitational. Triathlon had done wonders for my fitness as I was feeling the best physically I had felt in my entire life.

I will admit, it felt great to have people think I was in my twenties and my sons were my brothers. Most of all, it was just exhilarating to be so healthy and compete with those half my age. Excitement about life can barely express how I felt at that moment.

My cycle that morning was to be an easy, relaxed ride, but the exhilaration of the moment got the better of me. I loved the feeling of speed when cycling. As I started down toward Clearwater Bay Beach 2, I pushed hard, accelerating fast and preparing to sweep past their two huge parking lots at the bottom of the hill. Often my sons and I would race each other down this steep descent reaching speeds of over 80 kph. I remember pushing my speed and loving how solid my new bike felt. First a sweeping right, then an easy left as I picked up more speed. Coming into the final sweeping left bend, which I had many times warned my sons about, I could just see into the two parking lots to the left. This morning they were empty of cars or buses, so I laid my bike over to take the last curve at full speed. I was feeling great! Everything was perfect when suddenly, something was out of place…

BECOMING CONSCIOUS
(And Random Thoughts on Childhood and Raising a Racket)

Suddenly, thoughts rushed through my mind in rewind, as I first wondered where I was and how did I end up here, lying on a cool early-morning road in Hong Kong. Asia was a world away from where I had been born and raised. No rich parents in the world's glittering, successful economic eyes—just an ordinary kid who had opportunities to explore life. I always took every opportunity to reached out and embraced all that was available. This adventurous spirit took me to exciting, wondrous, and challenging places around the world. I was blessed with many incredible people in my life who spoke positivity and energy into everything I did. This gave me the feeling I could accomplish anything! If I only put all my mind and effort into these endeavors, I felt I could succeed at anything. I felt like I could *do it all* if I followed my dreams and not give up. I felt I could overcome life's bumps even when apparent roadblocks would suddenly appear.

Did every plan work out perfectly? Certainly not, especially now as I lay completely motionless, on the cool hard asphalt road of Clearwater Bay Road. In the process of dreaming big and living life to the fullest, things always had a way of sorting out, giving me an enriched life. I had already experienced more exciting journeys than I could have ever dreamed as a young Idaho boy. My dreams evolved and grew as I embraced the many opportunities that seemed to drop in my lap, even with the obvious setbacks and roadblocks.

Dreaming of a wonderful life began early

My brother Ken and I were born in a small quiet college town of Nampa, Idaho. Our dad was attending Northwest Nazarene College, a Christian college, after serving our country during World War II. He was stationed at Guadalcanal. Many stories had been told and retold about the horrors of Guadalcanal. Some of the fiercest battles in the worst conditions were fought and lives lost in this region of the South Pacific. A general was once asked where he would put a prison for the worst criminals on earth. He didn't hesitate when he recommended Guadalcanal because his experience of its remote location in the Pacific Ocean. Intolerable conditions of heat; humidity; and every creepy, crawly bug imaginable would make Guadalcanal ideal. Now at war, my dad with other Americans was in Guadalcanal fighting an army of Japanese soldiers willing to die for their emperor. This was where my dad served and fought the Japanese for two years.

I couldn't have asked for a better father. Like so many of that great generation, he didn't have it easy growing up during the Great Depression. The Great Depression had devastated the US economy, so he, like so many other teenagers, had to work when not in school to help keep food on the family table. He quit high school, lied about his age to join the military at seventeen, and served in the United States Army during World War II. These difficult times left him little time to enjoy playing the many sports he loved. My dad always seemed positive, even though he could have been bitter about the many trying situations that altered his ambitions as a youngster. Once leaving Guadalcanal, my dad was sent to Hawaii to rest, relax, and recover. Enjoying the beaches and tropical sun would hopefully wash the memories of war away. Arriving back to the States, he was discharged because of his injuries at Guadalcanal. He also suffered from PTSD (Posttraumatic Stress Syndrome). A backfire from vehicles driving by would send him scrambling under a table, behind a couch, or under a church pew. He had also contracted a severe case of malaria in the South Pacific.

When he arrived back home, he was very ill and suffered daily. A small group of friends and family gathered together at his parents' home one evening and prayed for his recovery. One of the many miracles I heard growing up took place right then when they prayed. My dad recovered from malaria, and the effects of his PTSD had disappeared. Having left high school early to join the army, he had no high school degree when he was discharged after the war.

It wasn't long before he married his sweetheart Lila and decided to use his GI bill to get a college education. He was determined to be a great husband and father, so he started college with the understanding from the school; he would finish his high school degree during his first year at Northwest Nazarene College. Married and starting a family while at college was not easy, but he was still able to graduate in four years with a degree in history and education. He became a schoolteacher and coach after graduating college, spending all his free time with his family. There were four of us—Ken, Kathy, Jon, and myself. All of us children became grounded in a strong Christian home with American ethics and respect. Our parents were wonderful models to follow with positive character traits. Looking back on my childhood, my parents were a perfect example of a loving couple. They made our home a safe and welcoming environment as we grew up.

My older brother, Ken, was two days less than a year older, and we were inseparable. When I was three and a half and Ken was four and a half, he saved my life when I fell into an irrigation ditch near our home in Fruitland, Idaho. We had snuck out of the house before church one Sunday evening, and I fell into the fast-flowing irrigation ditch. Ken ran to my rescue, reaching down with some branches for me to hang onto. He and I held on until our parents arrived to safely pull me out.

Ken and I were always into something, keeping our parents busy and alerted to our next adventure. One day, our parents heard the car attempting to drive down the street. Thinking someone might be stealing the car, they rushed out, only to find Ken standing up in the driver's seat, holding onto the steering wheel. *Where was Donnie?* they thought as they watched the car lurch down the street. When they finally arrived to the car, there I was lying on the floor, simultaneously pressing the starter and gas pedal to make the car go. The starter back then was on the floor next to the gas pedal. While Ken handled the steering, I was in charge of moving the car forward.

Shortly after that, we moved from Fruitland, Idaho, to Boise, Idaho, when Ken and I were five and six years old. Our home was in an area where there were no fences separating the backyards. Backyards were like a local park where all the neighborhood kids would gather and play games. That is, when we were not playing out in the mostly empty streets. Ken and I were the youngest of the neighborhood kids and stuck together like glue to stop being bullied. One day, walking out of the house, Ken saw me being beaten up by a larger kid from the neighborhood. He immediately raced over and joined me, as we fought off the bully together. Our mom and dad witnessed what was happening. My mom wanted to rush out and rescue us, but my dad said we needed to work this out ourselves. We did sort it out, and from then on, none of the other kids bullied us as they knew they had to fight both Bozarth boys if they started a fight with either one of us.

A traumatic incident happened to me when one of our backyard neighbors decided to kill three chickens for their family meal one afternoon. Ken and I, being our normal curious selves, walked out to see what was about to transpire. To our horror, in quick succession, he chopped the heads off all three chickens. The chickens immediately started running and rolling around headless for fifteen to twenty seconds, spraying blood out of their headless necks. I was hardly able to sleep for weeks without this image playing over and over in my mind.

Ken and I were inquisitive and never stopped exploring and trying new things. One of the neighbor kids came by one day with an old broken-down bike, which could still be ridden. Of course, we all wanted to try riding it. The bike was sized for eleven- or twelve-year-olds, much too large for Ken and I. The bike only had one complete pedal on the left side. The other pedal only had the round post or peg sticking out with a sharp edge at the end. Ken, being older and a little bigger than me, gave it a try first. He was able to ride it a-ways down the street and back. It was now my turn, and I could barely straddle the crossbar when getting on the bike. I needed to have a push to get moving, so they shoved me forward.

Sitting on the crossbar, I slid back and forth and was able to start riding without falling. It was a great success until I pushed down too hard on the right side with just the post peg sticking out. The post spun, throwing me off balance and headlong into the sharp end with my chin. The bottom of my chin sliced open and hung down, looking like a fresh steak from the supermarket. Mom was shocked when I walked into the house, seeing this rather large gash hanging down and wiggling in front of my neck. This was my first in many visits to doctor's offices in the years ahead. This time, it required fourteen stitches to put my chin back together.

Ken and I definitely kept our parents busy with the usual cuts, scrapes, broken bones, broken teeth, and bruises. We learned how to take our lumps and get up running. Our dad would always say, "Just brush it off!" With his remembrance of Guadalcanal, our injuries were just minor bumps in the road of life. I had been forever grateful for my dad and mom's attitude to make us as strong as possible, and at the same time, knowing we were deeply loved in a strong Christian environment. We may not have been rich in the world's eyes, but we were rich with love and the things that really counted.

Ken and I were always busy organizing the neighborhood kids to form teams and play games. We were continually active, never bored like so many children nowadays, staring at their phones and computers, keeping them trapped in front of these mesmerizing screens. Living life digitally and remotely is not really living, and I am forever grateful for our childhood experiences.

Ken and I found ways to make money by mowing lawns and picking cherries from our backyard trees, selling them in small buckets to local neighbors to make cherry pies. Our most memorable job was delivering newspapers in the early-morning dark before school. Delivering papers in the early morning was not easy for me.

First, I had to wake up! I had the uncanny natural ability to sleep through anything, especially a loud alarm clock without even stirring. More than once I awoke to loud knocking at our upstairs front door. It was the newspaper man, wanting to know where I was and why I wasn't at the local market folding papers to be delivered. I would dress faster than any fireman, race up the basement stairs, out the back door, through a few backyards, and continue running as fast as I could, eventually beating him back to the little market. Maybe this was where I got some of my quickness and speed while growing up. My dad was never happy to be woken up this way and would let me know it at breakfast, when I would innocently smile and saunter in from my paper route.

Secondly was how dark it could be with cloud-covered skies, no moon or stars to help light the streets, and the different weather conditions when delivering those newspapers. In the winter, it was even worse because of snow blanketing everything—roads, grass, bushes, and trees. This left all the neighborhoods and streets in an eerie quiet. The streets where I delivered papers were located in some of the older sections of town, where the older trees were huge. The branches from one side of the street would sometimes reach out and touch the branches of the trees in the yard on the opposite side of the street.

Those early-morning dark streets looked like eerie black tunnels where a young boy's imagination could run wild. In the winter with no leaves covering the branches, it was even worse for me. Those large limbs looked like huge arms extending outward with numerous fingers reaching down to capture any unsuspecting paperboy. With my newspaper vest securely attached, carrying all the day's latest news in pockets front and back, I would take off running with goose bumps all over my body, trying to finish my route as quickly as possible. I would think to myself, *Maybe I can outrun these imaginary monsters?*

When arriving back from delivering papers on a cold snowy morning, I noticed the back door of our family car slightly ajar. Walking past the car, I casually opened and threw the door closed to shut it correctly. Back then in the late fifties, it was still so safe; we didn't worry about locking our cars at night. For some reason, the door didn't close properly. I again opened it slightly, this time slamming it, to make sure it was tightly shut. Again it didn't shut all the way. I wondered, *What is going on?* This time, I opened it completely to see what was blocking the door, then I froze with fright. I saw a man lying on the back seat. The door would not close properly because his head was in the way. *Oh no*, I thought, *I had been slamming the door armrest on his head.*

I just knew he had to be dead, after him not waking up and the door hitting him so hard. My imagination again ran wild, and it got the better of me, as I bolted into the house. I startled both my mom and dad, yelling, "There is a dead man in the back seat of our car."

As usual, my dad said, "Calm down, I will check it out." I needed to get ready for school, so still shaking, I headed downstairs. When Ken and I came back up for breakfast, we found the same "dead man" sitting at our table with a hot cup of coffee in his hands. Thankfully, he was not dead as I had thought, just dead drunk with a sore head. He had passed out in our car after a long hard night of drinking. He was known to my parents as a respected local businessman. He had become so drunk, he lost his way home and found refuge in the back seat of our car. How he survived on a freezing cold snowy night without freezing to death, I don't know.

In spite of all the happenings around the Bozarth household, we were just a typical American family during the fifties, sixties, and seventies. Mom, Dad, my two brothers, and one sister lived in Boise, Idaho, until 1962. This was when my dad found what he thought was a dream teaching position in Marin County, California. He had always wanted to live in California, which came as a surprise for us children. We all loved living in Boise. Our friends, school, and church activities were in the Treasure Valley. We thought we would live in that part of Southern Idaho forever. "Why would we ever want to leave?" we questioned? It was our world!

It was 1962 when California was known as the land of sunshine, with white-sand beaches, where dreams come true. Many families around the country were making the same journey to California during the sixties, and we were about to join this great migration train. Uprooting from Boise, we started our so-called dream adventure in the summer of '62.

Until that move, we had lived what felt like an idyllic life in Boise, Idaho. The Treasure Valley was identified as one of the top 10 places in the US for children to grow up during the fifties and sixties. Boise was all we knew, except for my one adventure alone back east to Michigan to play a national junior tennis tournament. Our friends, schools, church, and the comfort of knowing our neighbors and community made Boise perfect for us kids.

Ken and I couldn't have agreed more as we continued to do everything together. In Boise, it seemed like any and every activity was available. In the winter, we would spend our Saturdays and holidays skiing up at Bogus Basin. Our days around home were spent in snowball fights, building snowmen or some illegal hooky-bobbing.

Hooky-bobbing was grabbing onto the rear bumper of unsuspecting vehicles when they slowed down for a stop sign on our snow-covered roads. We would whoop it up as we'd hold onto their bumpers and slide on the slick roads until we were thrown off into some snowbank or hit an unsuspecting manhole cover, rolling and sliding down the same soft, slick snow-covered streets. This activity was illegal and dangerous but a great thrill for us kids in the neighborhood, when we didn't get caught!

At the beginning of each school year, our dad would coach our football team. The fall practices were held every afternoon until dark. We played basketball and wrestled in the winter and then onto baseball and track as springtime warmed the air. It seemed like we were always busy doing some sport with our dad. Our father always emphasized proper technique while practicing in our backyard. He did this so we could do our best and enjoy each sport to its fullest. I have met many athletes who just lived on their natural athletic ability and ignored technique. Athletic ability only takes a gifted athlete so far, and sadly, they eventually find it difficult to reach their true potential. We were always thankful our dad understood dedication and technique and how it would make our lives more interesting and fulfilled. This became evident as our futures continued to unfold.

Summers in Boise were perfect. The weather was wonderful. Hot days were followed by warm balmy evening where we didn't want any day to end. There was never a lack of activities to keep us going from sunrise to sunset. We played little league baseball; swimming at the South Junior High School pool; rafting or inner tubing down the Boise River; or just hanging out with friends throwing a football, Frisbee, or baseball at Julia Davis Park. Ken and I would often get on our bikes at sunrise and head down South Vista Avenue toward downtown. This route would take us past the iconic train station, then onto South Capitol Boulevard. We would then pick up speed going down this steep hill looking directly at the Capitol Building in the distance. Crossing over the bridge spanning the Boise River, we would head into the park on our right for another full day of fun. Our parents expected us to be home in time for dinner, well before dark, as sunset in Boise during the summer was very late. No cell phones back then, so we and our friends were all on the honor system to be home on time.

All of this was happening until Ken forced me out onto a hot, steamy tennis court to help him practice his tennis. I had very little interest in tennis, as the South Junior High School swimming pool, where I would rather be spending my time, was right beside the tennis courts. Our parents always arranged a summer swim pass for us so we could swim as much as we wanted. I loved being able to swim every day in a cool pool during those never-ending hot summer days. After many other activities such as baseball or tennis practice, it was straight to the pool for more fun and games. Diving and splashing around with our friends was always more inviting than playing tennis on a hot court. To make matters worse, we could hear everyone playing and splashing in the cool pool while we were sweltering playing tennis just outside. Ken loved tennis and could be very insistent. Before long, I found myself practicing with him on a regular basis. South Junior High School tennis courts in the 1960s were not of the best quality. They were made of old rough, worn-out gray asphalt. You could expect many inconsistent bad bounces. To make things even worse, chain-link fence material were installed as nets. There couldn't have been a less conducive atmosphere for me to get started or interested in tennis.

Ken loved tennis and was the city tennis champion for seventh grade. He wanted my help to give him some extra practice. This unlikely scenario started my tennis playing experiences and eventually encouraged me to enter the No-Champions Tennis Tournament at the end of that summer. Ken was ineligible to play as he was already the city champion. Without him in the tournament and all of our practices together, I improved enough to win the tournament. I was excited at having won, but even better, being given two trophies. One was a large traveling trophy; the other was a small trophy for me to keep. I loved the large traveling trophy, but it had to be returned after a year. The traveling trophy would be awarded to the winner of the No-Champions Tournament the following year. I treasured the small trophy, as it would always be mine to keep. I wanted more of this sport! All other sports we had participated in, the coach or sponsor received the trophies for the team's championship results. It wasn't like nowadays where kids get trophies for anything, including participation trophies. Awards back then really meant something. This tournament excited me, and I ended up with the same tennis bug that had infected Ken. Ken used to drag me onto the court, but now I wanted to practice with him. I started playing as much as I could, which wasn't much considering how fall and winter usually came early in Boise.

When school started and fall arrived, I was again the starting quarterback on our football team. I loved playing football, as my dad had always been our coach since we started playing in the second grade. Back in the '50s and '60s, all little league football games and leagues were played with full tackle equipment. We felt like giants putting on our uniforms.

Little league football as quarterback

Another successful season as champions was highlighted when our football team was selected to play in the Pop Warner National Playoffs. We lost the semifinal game to a team from Northern California called Little Redwood Giants from Marin County. It was a crazy game as our team was made up of mostly seventh graders, while their team was made up of eighth graders, a year older and bigger. The difference in maturity and size was significant, as they really did look and feel like giants when we went on the field to face them. We came up just short of scoring three times to lose 34 to 14. Being bigger and faster, our fastest halfback was run down from behind three times, keeping us from those three scores and the much-needed eighteen points.

Pop Warner Championship team

We were still happy as a team, as we had played our best. We had played well and held our own on a big stage, which is now the Boise State University Stadium. Although we lost, I was presented with the game ball by the opposing team at the awards banquet. The other team had signed it, "To the Little Magician." This honor was really for all of us in the backfield. Our backfield would get-together in our backyard during the summers and practice every play over and over until we worked together like clockwork. This practice allowed us to completely fool other teams with fake handoffs. I just happened to be the quarterback and was honored with the game ball.

This was just part of my crazy childhood. Every team I played on, with one exception, won every league championship. The only exception was the season when my dad was sent to the hospital for an operation. I, along with an older teenager, tried to coach our little league team. As can be imagined, it was a joke, and we were totally disorganized, losing most games. My dad was discharged from the hospital two weeks before the end of the season. When he saw what we had done with the team, he worked hard with us so we would be ready to play our final game against the eventual league champion. We were so inspired to have my father back; we worked really hard and won that last game by the lopsided score of 56 to 14. Even with that one losing season, I grew up not knowing what it meant to lose. This is unusual, looking back on it. That winter, the winning continued as I won the city wrestling championship for my grade, skied at Bogus Basin almost every weekend and public holidays, and played basketball at South Junior High School.

Snow skiing was different for the Bozarth boys, as we didn't have the money to afford skiing. But as usual, our parents found a way for us to ski. My dad had missed out on so much during his childhood, he was not about to let us miss out on anything. None of these activities were just given to us, as we would work doing odd jobs for much of what we had. Through a friend, our dad found out we could work off our winter ski passes. We traveled up to Bogus Basin in the summer and worked a few times to prepare the slopes for the upcoming winter snow. This allowed us a ski pass to ski as much as we wanted during the winter, as long as we could obtain a ride up the mountain on a ski bus. We bought used skies at the fall ski swap sale for next to nothing and improvised when it came to ski clothing.

Since we couldn't afford fancy ski clothing like our friends, we figured a way to stay warm while using what we had available. We would layer our clothing and ski in Levi's. Ken and I might have been the first ever to ski in Levi's. Levi's were not windproof or waterproof, so we put on long johns (thermal underwear), then took large plastic bags, slipped them over our first layers of socks and long johns. We would then use large rubber bands to secure the top of the plastic bags on our upper thighs. A second pair of knee-high wool socks would be slipped over the plastic bags before putting on our final layer of Levi's. This kept us warm, windproof, and dry. No one figured out how we did it, skiing in Levi's while staying warm and dry. Our bottoms were not waterproofed, so if we fell too much, we would have cold and wet backsides. This, however, provided extra incentive to ski our best and stay upright. If we wanted to do something, we always found a way, with our parents' help. They always encouraged us while making everything a fun challenge.

With all this going on, there was very little time to practice tennis outside in the winter, especially with the snow and cold. No indoor tennis courts in Boise back then like the nice Boise Tennis Club nowadays. Learning from my parents, I improvised and did the best thing I could think of.

Ken and I shared the same basement bedroom with our sister Kathy occupying the other bedroom. The basement had a large common room with a furnace on one side. Against one large wall was a couch and a small basement window high on the wall, next to the ceiling at ground level. This flat cement wall between the basement window and the couch became my tennis practice court during the winter. I hit tennis balls against that wall until it drove my parents crazy with the sound of *boom-boom…boom-boom…boom-boom.* Since there was very little room in the basement, I was restricted to hitting volleys and half volleys over and over. I would continue hitting until my forearm and grip would become so weak, I could barely hold onto the racket. By springtime, I had hit tens of thousands of tennis balls against that concrete basement wall, increasing my timing and building up strength in my grip and forearm.

Baseball and tennis season conflicted in the spring. I tried to juggle both sports as I had always played shortstop on baseball teams growing up. Since I liked *doing it all,* I didn't want to give up either sport. I was finally forced to choose when both coaches met with me and made me decide. The decision was an easy choice for me. It was tennis. With tennis, I was hitting the ball continuously. In baseball, you get to bat four or five times per game and maybe field a dozen or so balls playing shortstop. It was an easy decision I never regretted. Tennis is a lifetime sport, baseball not so much, unless you call going to a ballgame, eating hot dogs, and slurping down a drink as exercise.

When the city tennis championships arrived, I was a little nervous but still entered to play. The best tennis players in the Treasure Valley would be playing this event, unlike the No-Champions Tennis Tournament event I had won the previous summer. I was fortunately paired in doubles with the best singles player in Boise. I somehow was able to win not only the doubles but also the singles event, defeating my doubles partner Chris Coughlin in the singles final.

This was the start of a very surprising summer of tennis as this tournament qualified me for another event where I also won singles and doubles. I won singles and doubles at the district qualifying me for the state championships. When arriving at the state championships I was scheduled to play the number 1 seeded player in Idaho in the first round. The other players were surprised to hear me say, "I am excited to be on the other side of the net from the best fifteen and under tennis player in Idaho." Maybe I was stupid, but I sincerely wanted to see how good he played. I surprised myself and everyone else when I defeated him and then went on to win both the Idaho state singles and doubles championships. Each tournament, I was paired to play doubles with Chris. This was very fortunate for me to have such a good doubles partner. I also played Chris in the finals in almost every singles event.

I had played tennis for one year and had not lost one single tournament match. Everything was a whirlwind as the Idaho Tennis Association informed my parents I was now qualified for the National Jacee Championships back in East Lansing, Michigan. I had played tennis just over a year and was given the honor to represent Idaho at the nationals. Brad Humphries was the state eighteen and under champion, and every Idaho junior tennis player looked up to him. He was a tall gentleman and possessed languid, beautiful long strokes. He made tennis look easy, and I always wanted to hit a tennis ball like him.

That summer, I had won against much more experienced tennis players. I always told my parents, "I was just lucky," as the other juniors had nice strokes and looked great on the court. I had no coaching and was relying on my speed around the court and ability to serve big, hit volleys, half volleys, and overheads. Being a quarterback throwing a football over the years really helped my serve, and our basement wall paid huge dividends for my volleys and half volleys. I continued to hit on that basement wall every chance I had while living in Boise.

The national championships was a different story. I was the total outsider from potato country. I was shy and wanted to slink away into some unnoticed dark corner. Not only was I "new" to tennis and had no idea what I was doing, I was also from Idaho. Junior tennis players from Idaho, as far as most of the national juniors were concerned, was the black hole of tennis. Many of the other junior players felt we probably didn't deserve to be there. I was a nobody and felt lost on the national scene. I was also treated that way by many of the other juniors when they realized where I was from. It seemed like most of them already knew one another. I felt lost!

Suddenly, something very special happened to me when a tall eighteen and under junior, stepped up in front of me and asked my name and where I was from. I must have looked shy and forlorn to him. When I looked up, I found a rather tall and thin Arthur Ashe standing in front of me with a big smile, making me feel welcomed and right at home. He took a fair amount of time talking with me before wishing me luck, then faded away in the crowd of the other junior tennis players. Arthur was always a gentleman even when he was a junior player. He had no idea how great he made me feel. He had allowed me to relax and enjoy the experience of playing at the nationals.

My winning streak was over after that tournament, but I did have the opportunity to play a seeded player in the first round and win a number of games before being bundled out and sent home. My serve, volleys, and overheads had allowed to do well. I knew then what the top players hit like and wanted more than ever to come back and win a few matches the following year. In hindsight, maybe a little ambitious but a great goal to work toward. You can always dream, and I still had my friendly basement wall, inviting me for a volley workout.

Everything about my life was going great as far as I was concerned. Fall and winter went by with the usual football, skiing, and the Boise snowstorms. I kept up my routine, of hitting balls against the basement wall, as I wanted to qualify for the nationals again. They were to be held in Corpus Christi, Texas, the following summer. Whenever I had the chance to be on a tennis court, I would pretend I was playing Rod Laver and winning great rallies again the best. I did have a bump in the road as I lost one match in the spring. Even while losing, it turned out to be a positive as I was still featured with a huge article and a large photo of me in the Boise paper. After that, things went like the previous summer winning the Idaho state boys sixteen and under titles in singles and doubles. This time, the state tournament was held in Rexburg, Idaho.

Idaho Singles & Doubles Champion—
Idaho Statesman Newspaper

This was also the same year when the USTA (United States Tennis Association) made the change in the age group events. The previous year, the age groups were eighteen and under, fifteen and under, and thirteen and under categories. The USTA changed this in 1962 to two-year increments—eighteen, sixteen, fourteen, and twelve and under events. So I was the fifteen and under state singles and doubles champion in '61 and the sixteen and under state singles and doubles champion in '62. I was enjoying tennis, meeting more and more players at each tournament. This gave me a better idea of what to work on to improve my game. I was finally developing some groundstrokes trying to copy what I had seen of Rod Laver playing on TV. I was looking forward to improved results at the nationals, which I had again qualified to play.

I was excited when I arrived back from Rexburg, Idaho, to let my parents know I had again qualified for the nationals, this time in Corpus Christi, Texas. When arriving back home and giving them my good news, my dad had some news of his own. He was excited as an opportunity had opened up for him to teach school in Marin County, California. He had always wanted to live in California, so he had immediately accepted the job. Secretly, I thought, *Without my permission?* My life was perfect in Boise! It seemed everywhere I went, somebody knew me. I couldn't believe it. How could he do this to me? Even the high school coach, Troxel, said he was priming me to eventually be the varsity quarterback on Borah High School's state champion football team.

To make matters worse, we would be moving right away. "What about my national tournament in Corpus Christi, Texas," I asked? Sadly, I was informed that our move was right in the middle of the national tournament. I would need to pull out of the tournament I had been looking forward to competing in for months. We had no extra money to allow me to go to the nationals and then pay for extra flight tickets, allowing me to fly alone to San Francisco. I was devastated, but I had no choice in the decision. Until then, my life had been a dream-come-true. We were moving. I had to accept it and get used to the idea that I would be living in the dream State of California instead of playing my dream tournament at the nationals in Corpus Christi, Texas. Not knowing it then, this would be my last chance for a trip to any national junior tournament. After the hard life my dad had growing up, I knew he deserved to live his dream too!

Many other thoughts of my growing-up years rolled through my head as I tried to figure out where I was, there on that dark morning in Clearwater Bay. The journey of my life had led me to arrive on this very section of road in Hong Kong. The move to California was the first major move of my life, and without knowing it then, directly led me to Hong Kong.

How this move to San Anselmo would affect our family or me personally would only be completely felt as the years unfolded. California was reported to be the Sunshine State where people could build their dreams. I felt my dreams were shattered! I cried myself to sleep more than once after we arrived in Northern California, thinking about the other junior tennis players playing tennis in Texas at that very moment. We did our best to settle in the small community of San Anselmo. This was a secluded bedroom community for mostly rich families. One section was called Sleepy Hollow where my uncle's family lived, and it seemed perfectly named. That's how my dad found his new job—through my uncle.

Sleepy Hollow was far from our first home, which was located in a less affluent area of San Anselmo. Our rented house was so small, Ken and I slept on the outside front deck until it started to rain. Then we moved under the kitchen table in what seemed to be the world's smallest kitchen. To say it was a small house would be an understatement. We stayed there for a few months until my dad found a larger rental home closer to Drake High School.

I would fall asleep crying for the first time in my life other than my broken leg in football. When first arriving in California, I realized my somewhat starlike status in Boise where I appeared in newspaper articles was gone for good. California was like a foreign country for Ken and me. My sister Kathy was four years younger, so it was even tougher on her, as Ken and I were at least together at Drake High School. Our younger brother, Jonathan, was only four years old, so it did not affect him at that time. Ken and I did our best to get involved in a similar routine by joining the football team. For some unknown reason, Ken was bullied so much on the team that he eventually quit, even though he was doing well. I was more stubborn and stuck with it, even though my aspiration of quarterbacking was cut short when I injured my elbow. I finished the season and lettered, but other than making a few acquaintances, it was not a positive experience.

Ken and I both played in the band, which turned out to be an amazing experience. The band was made up of some extremely talented musicians. Three of our band members played professionally in San Francisco during the summer even though they were still in high school. This inspired all of us to play our best and try to keep up with their amazing abilities. Our band concerts were so well attended that they would add an extra night to our scheduled performances. Our band director would point to one of these three talented musicians, let them take the stage, and play adlib solos. Until then, I thought I was an okay trumpet player. Being in the presence of real talent was inspiring and humbling at the same time. These kind of experiences always kept me humble while still inspiring me do whatever it took to improve. Being part of the band was one of the most positive experiences at Drake High School. You wouldn't know that these high school band students were that talented when watching them melt into the crowds of other students walking down the hallways. I was just learning then not to judge a book by its cover, certainly not these exceptionally talented musicians.

Tennis proved to be better than football for both Ken and me. However, we didn't start out on the best footing with the tennis coach. We were from Idaho! Before the coach had seen either Ken or me hit a tennis ball, he gave us a lecture in front of the entire team about how good California tennis players were. He also let us know how much better Californians were than any players could possibly hope to be coming from Idaho. He also said not to expect too much as the top two varsity players, pointing at two of them, were returning from the previous year. The top players and coach thought we wouldn't even make the varsity team, much less be a challenge to them. This was before the tryouts and challenge matches began. I was only a sophomore, so I had no idea what to expect from these California seniors, especially after the coach's disheartening speech.

When the challenge matches were completed, I ended up playing number 1 on varsity as a sophomore and Ken played number 4 as a junior—not the way to win friends and influence people, especially with the tennis coach losing face. He liked having us on the team but felt like he had lost face after saying we wouldn't make the team.

Playing in a Californian tennis league was a great experience for us. I had the opportunity to play against two nationally ranked eighteen and under juniors in the dual matches. One player was ranked eighth, and the other was ranked twelfth in the nation. Although I lost to both of them, I played well enough to earn three and four games a set. I found pictures of them in the Marin County newspaper to put them on my closet doors. Below the pictures, I put, "Beat (inserted their name)," so I could visualize winning every time I went to bed.

Ken and I found a seminary within walking distance from our home containing two isolated nice tennis courts. We practiced our tennis at these courts with no one else around. The seminary courts were tucked in on three sides by high cliff walls, making it even more secluded. We had a great time playing tennis there. The loud echo of hitting the ball coming off those cliff walls made us sound like tennis pros. This was one of the reasons we both had a good tennis season at Drake High School. In the summer, I won a doubles tournament against the same two nationally ranked juniors from the school season. The opportunity to play with one of their younger brothers made this possible. So my tennis was still okay. These top-ranked juniors said my volleys and half volleys were the best they had ever played against. That wall in Boise had really done wonders for my net game.

This turned out to be my last USTA tournament as a junior, even though I had two and a half years left to compete. The summer of 1963 was between my sophomore and junior year of high school. We suddenly made another major move as my dad was hired with a more favorable teaching position in San Jose, California. I didn't know it then, but this would turn out to be a pattern for my life. Before we moved again to San Jose, I had the opportunity to watch Whitney Reed, former US number 1, play a tournament in San Rafael. Watching him continued to inspire me to play tennis.

Ken was now a senior, and I was a junior. New school, new students to get to know. This school was different than Marin County, as this was newly built and in a less uppity but very nice suburban neighborhood. Leigh High School was only in its second year built in the fast growing area of South San Jose and Silicon Valley. Everyone was somewhat new to Leigh High School. Many of them had gone to different junior high schools. When the district divided, the students were sent to three different high schools. Ken and I, as with everyone else, was getting settled into this new environment. It immediately felt more comfortable than the uppity area of Marin County, where many graduating seniors received cars as graduation gifts.

Family photo—Bottom row, Jon, Mom, and Dad; Top row, Kathy, Me, and Ken

We both decided to forego football for the first time since second grade in Boise, but we still played in the band. The band at Leigh was more relaxed than the high-octane sessions at Drake High

School, but still positive with some excellent musicians. Being in the stands watching every football game instead of being on the field playing football was a new experience for me. Not an experience I enjoyed! The band played at every home football game. I didn't know I would miss football as much as I did. Sitting in the stands was not nearly as fun or exciting and fulfilling as being on the field. I made up my mind sitting there in the band section to sign up and play football my senior year.

Church was the one unexpected blessing when moving to San Jose. There was a vibrant large youth group who accepted us immediately. Ken was looked on as one of the leaders right away and instrumental along with a few other key teens for the spiritual growth of this youth group. It was a large youth group with some amazingly talented individuals. I was becoming more reserved after my experience in Marin County. After trying hard to be accepted at Drake High School for nine months, I had not made one real friend. The church youth group in San Anselmo was very small. There were two pastor's daughters, Ken, our sister Kathy, and me making up the bulk of the group. With that experience behind me, I managed to cruise through my junior year at Leigh High School without meeting many students or making many friends. I kept my head down and did my best to remain invisible. I was always the first student to leave at the end of the school day and race walk the mile home.

When arriving back for my senior year, a senior girl came up to me and asked if I was a new student. I was astonished, as I had sat one seat behind her in history during our junior year. With my head down on the desk sleeping half the time, it was no wonder she didn't recognize me. If I had shown her the top of my head, she might have realized who I was.

Bozarth Wins League Title

Don Bozarth, number one singles tennis player at Leigh, won the West Santa Clara Valley Athletic League Tennis championship Monday and Tuesday, May 4 and 5, by defeating the representatives from Camden, Campbell, and Saratoga in the

Tennis League Champion

I did, however, play number 1 singles on the varsity tennis team my junior year and won the league singles championship, after being down seven match points in the first round to the number 1 seeded player. Part of my miracle sports experiences continued through high school. Even with my picture in the school newspaper as league champion, nobody seemed to recognize me when our senior year began. Tennis was not looked on as a real sport in the midsixties, and the tennis courts were at the far end of the school property. Few students would venture out near the tennis courts without a special reason. That area of the property was all orchards, so very few homes were south of the school. I actually liked being anonymous and being the first student to leave school at the end of every school day, unless of course, there was tennis practice. Racewalking home probably helped keep me in shape. I had gone from being an outgoing class president in Boise who seemed to always be in the spotlight to retreating into invisibility. It seemed an easier way to cope than putting myself out there and finding out it didn't work. I was forever thankful for the church youth group. I made friends there, who have remained true friends through the years, no matter the distance or time interval.

Ken immediately got involved with Youth for Christ Club at Leigh. It didn't take long before he became the club leader and see Youth for Christ grow to over one hundred students by the middle of the year. The classroom designated for us to use soon became too small. Without getting approval from the administration, Ken took it upon himself to move the club to the outdoor corridor. I was amazed to see the growth, as it was only a small group of a dozen or so when Ken arrived. It wasn't long before Ken received a call to visit the principal's office. The principal informed Ken the group had to disband as it had become too large and was blocking the walkway. Ken's response was classic, "If you were me, who would you listen to, you or God?" Back then, the mention of God still had influence and meaning in public schools. Youth for Christ continued on campus and flourished the rest of the year as the principal provided a much larger room for the Youth For Christ club. Ken always had an air of boldness about him I admired. Ken was a true Christian and bold with his witness and conviction. I was jealous of Ken's strong relationship with God, but I was more interested in being good at sports than to spend the time he did with God.

Ken had graduated and was off to college after graduation, so my senior year started before school began with preseason football practice. I was barred from spring football practices, along with another student who was a varsity swimmer. Our respective swim and tennis coaches did not want us playing football for fear we would get injured and keep us from competing in tennis and swimming our senior year.

We checked the league rules during the summer and discovered they could not ban us from trying out for football. My friend Al, unlike me, had not played football before but wanted to give it a try as he was big, fit, and a good athlete. Al was a tall fit swimmer, one of the best in the school league. He, being a lot bigger than me, tried out for defensive tackle. I was fairly strong but only about 145 pounds soaking wet. I knew football inside and out after having a dad who coached and myself playing quarterback and defensive linebacker for a number of years in Idaho. As quarterback, I had been required to learn all the positions and their relative assignments. My dad and I continually talked and lived football at home. We sat around the house watching football games, sometimes over a meal at the dining table.

Al and I didn't have the ideal start to the football season. Our head coach, Adams, sent both Al and I down to the junior varsity team, with the idea we wouldn't be injured. Our tennis and swim coach had obviously talked with Coach Adams. We both liked Coach Adams, and he turned out to be an excellent coach. He was only doing what he thought would keep us uninjured and ready for our respective swim and tennis seasons. Al and I were disappointed at first, but we came up with a plan to work our way back up to varsity.

Al was a defensive tackle, and I was set to play outside linebacker. This placed me just outside of Al's position. I was small, but from my years of playing football in Idaho, I knew how to read plays, stick a tackle, and bring down a ball carrier. Al and I worked together to understand and read the plays. We had fun, combining on tackles—Al hitting them low and me right behind tackling them up high or reversing roles with me tackling them down low and Al lowering the boom on them up high.

Our plan only took a week before the junior varsity coach insisted Coach Adams take Al and I back on varsity. The JV coach said, "Too many JV players were being injured." We were both thrilled. Al earned a starting position at tackle and I playing special teams and defensive linebacker at times. I didn't care what position I played as long as I was able to play football again. I had spent an entire season watching from the band section, missing being on the field. I loved hitting as hard as I could and tackling anybody and everybody that came in my direction. I loved practice as much as the games, as long as I could put on the pads, feel the contact, and make another tackle. I loved playing football again. I don't think Coach Adams ever knew I played quarterback on almost every team before. I was happy to keep it that way, as our quarterback Larry Daniels was terrific and had earned first team on the All Central Coast Section the year before. Larry went on to have an excellent career playing NCAA football at San Jose State University, along with our end, Ron Carruthers who started for Arizona.

One day, when my dad showed up at practice, Coach Adams took him aside and asked if my parents fed me tiger meat for breakfast? I laughed when I heard my dad relay that to me. I had so much fun being on the field again. I hit as hard in practice as I did in the games. With so much experience in Idaho playing quarterback, I could read plays quickly and put myself in the right position, often making the tackles. One day, after making a couple tackles in a row against our first team offense, Coach Adams came up, grabbed my face mask, pulled me forward to the first string offence, and said, "This guy is the smallest guy on the field, and I had better see him blocked on the next play." Needless to say, I was taken out by three players on the next play but loved it just the same.

Preparing to go on the field for our Thanksgiving Day game, coach Adams asked, "Who is going to make the first tackle on the kickoff?" This was usual for him to get us ramped up and energized before heading out onto the field. The eleven of us on the special team would usually yell out, "I am!"

This time, when he asked, I yelled, "I am," but quite a few of my teammates yelled, "Bozarth will," and luckily, I did!

Leigh High League Champions #44

Coach Adams surprised me one more time at the student assembly when he awarded us our varsity football letters. When he presented me with my varsity letter, he shook my hand like everyone else, but when I started to walk away, he didn't let go of my hand. He instead pulled me back announcing for everyone to hear, "Pound-for-pound Don Bozarth was the surest tackler in the league." It surprised and embarrassed me, as I felt I didn't really do that much for our team during the season. We had all-league players, a few of them up for All Central Coast Section. Two went on to start on major university football teams, so I was a minor component of our league championship team. I was honored he felt that way but mostly just thankful I had the opportunity to play one more season of football before college. Coach Adams and I reconnected after a number of years, only for me to find out he had taken up tennis and plays regularly in senior events in Northern California.

In spite of the trauma of leaving Idaho where I was well known in the sporting community and was a class president, I was seeing that you can still have a great time making the most of every moment. I still run into players from Leigh High football team, and to my surprise, they remember the slight-built guy who just loved to hit, tackle, and also play tennis. It was wonderful meeting up with my former classmates at our twenty-fifth high school reunion. The reunion was very special after spending years overseas and coming in from Hong Kong for the event.

Keeping a fairly low profile my senior year, my plan was to leave school as soon as the bell rang, when not playing on a sports team. Thanks to Donna McDougal, one of the teens from church who went to Leigh High School, I started to meet many of my classmates my senior year. I still played on the varsity tennis team but had a horrible record in our dual matches as number 1 singles player. I lost almost every dual match, losing badly, only winning a few games. Since I only played a few months in the spring, I was pretty rusty when our high school tennis season arrived. Going up against seasoned tennis players who played USTA junior tournaments year around and belonged to expensive clubs with professional coaches was not an easy task for me. My opponents arrived ready to play, as most were working out three or four times a week, year-round. As returning league champion, it was embarrassing losing so much and so badly. I knew I was letting our team down, but there was nobody else good enough to take my place at number 1 position. I just had to take my losses and bear it.

Playing no USTA junior tournaments since arriving in San Jose added to the difficulty of match play. What could I expect playing against ranking juniors who regularly played the USTA tournaments? The year-end league championships were coming up, and I had no one to practice with. I definitely wanted to produce better than what I had been playing in the dual matches. Brother Ken was off at college, so unlike the year before, where he had been there to practice with during the season, I was on my own this time around.

Two weeks before the finals, I found another wall to practice against, and I hit a couple hundred or so serves a day. I didn't know how much it would help, but I wanted to give my best effort as the returning league champion. My record was so dismal during the season, I wasn't seeded as the returning league champion. Surprising myself but also everyone else, I somehow worked my way through the draw and won the league tournament again without the loss of a set. I had the honor to represent our league at the CCS (Central Coast Section) again. This year, I had much better results, beating some well-known ranking USTA juniors. I eventually lost a close match in the semifinals to the eventual Central Coast champion, which made it a memorable and successful week. It was a great way to finish off my senior tennis season.

How did I do it? I didn't deserve it with my lack of play and practice for ten months. So, how did it happen? I had been raised to believe anything was possible and I had been fortunate to play on a winning team every time, in every sport, except that one time, through my senior year in high school. I had an inner belief that I could win when it counted, and I never gave up trying. This didn't make me special. I knew there were millions around this beautiful planet with the same character trait. I was thankful my mom and dad had been instilling this in us children since my dad first started coaching us.

It wasn't just the winning that built the confidence. Positive character traits are instilled at an early age. Difficulties and trials were looked on as an opportunity to embrace. You build strength by moving forward, believing the best results will eventually come. Winning isn't always the score line at the end of a competition. When you have a winning attitude and have done the best you know how to do on the day, you have won! No person or score line can take that away from you. This attitude will inspire you to look for more ways to improve and keep you getting up early, striving to always do your best. I was fortunate to be surrounded by individuals who spoke uplifting and positive motivation into my life. These people allowed me to dream big and

Leigh High Graduation Photo

always have a vision. I would also get up early and try to work harder than anybody else to achieve my dreams. There is no way to properly thank all these individuals for their positive input into my life.

Years later, a club manager said I was a dreamer, indicating it was a negative attribute. I surprised him and myself when I took it as a compliment. At that time, I was dreaming of being normal again back at work and learning how to walk and run. Without a vision, the people perish. I always had a vision of where I wanted to go and spent very little time dreaming of where I had been. This club manager had confused my vision with dreaming. I had been raised to stay positive by accomplishing the little goals right in front of me and not worrying about the eventual larger outcome. I completely believed the "wins" would take care of themselves.

TENNIS SHOES OR ARMY BOOTS AND HAVING INDEPENDENCE

After graduating from at Leigh High, I had no time for tennis. I worked for a local builder as a laborer and carpenter to earn money for college. It was a wonderful time growing up during the sixties, as everyone seemed hopeful and positive. We all believed the future would be bright except for the cloud of Vietnam hovering over our heads. Vietnam was still so far away; it felt like it wouldn't or couldn't touch us. I was no different as I didn't worry about Vietnam or college. Our church denomination had some excellent colleges around the country, and my brother Ken was already attending one, Northwest Nazarene College in Nampa Idaho, where he and I were born and our dad had attended. I wanted to go where it was warmer and I would have a chance to play tennis. I checked out Pasadena Nazarene College in Southern California. I fortunately received a tennis and basketball scholarship. This, plus a small discount for being a member of the Nazarene Church and my summer jobs, made college affordable.

A few other high school graduates from our church had also made the decision to head south for Pasadena. It was the only decision for me, so I was off to beautiful Southern California. Pasadena College was a small, intimate campus located in an older developed residential neighborhood, unlike their campus nowadays located in San Diego, California. It is now known as Point Loma Nazarene University, a NCAA Division II school. PLNU is one of the most beautiful campuses in the country, sitting high on the bluffs of Sunset Cliffs on the Southern California Coast, looking out over the blue Pacific Ocean.

Pasadena College, high on Hill Avenue, was only a short distance from Colorado Boulevard, where the famous Rose Parade is held each year on New Year's Day. The campus was tucked into a quaint neighborhood of homes, with huge old trees lining the quiet streets. The Pasadena tennis coach recruited heavily before my freshman year, and I was fortunate to be on a team with other very good tennis players. A well-known National Public Parks Champion Pat Robinson and some excellent Southern California players rounded out the team. This was one of the reasons I improved so much in my two years of studying there. College was cut short when I was unceremoniously drafted for the Vietnam War.

I was honored to be selected as one of the Freshman 24 when I arrived at Pasadena. Freshman 24 was unknown to me and awarded to twenty-four of the incoming freshmen after reviewing their high school achievements and extracurricular activities. These activities included music, class officers, sports, and such. As Freshman 24, we were required to run for class office, and I ended up being elected as freshman class treasurer. I had grown up believing in the idea of everyone having the opportunity to compete fairly. It bothered me that the rest of the freshman class were barred from running for these class offices. I wanted to end what I viewed as an inequity.

Our freshman class was proving to be a real pain in the neck for the administration. Pasadena College had an intramural sports organization set up, so all the competitions were separated by class. Seniors were on one team, juniors, sophomores, and freshmen were on the other three teams respectively. This was usually a sizable handicap for the freshman and sophomore classes. Juniors and seniors being older, more mature, therefore won most, if not all the competitions. This system also encouraged separation between the classes in other activities and the friendship groups around campus.

A group of us felt it would be better for the college community to have teammates from different classes on each team. Seniors would get to know the freshmen as well as sophomores and juniors when placed on the same team. With this in mind, I ran for intramural president for the sophomore class during the spring elections. Once I was elected, a meeting was organized between the other class intramural presidents. A plan was formulated for changing the system starting in the fall.

My mom and dad had taught us to be fair in all we did. When I saw something that promoted division rather than unity, it rubbed me the wrong way! I always wanted to be part of a solution. Our plan was simple but would take some work. Instead of four intramural teams for competition the following year, there would be five teams under the Greek alphabet names of alpha, beta, delta, epsilon, and gamma. The problem was how to decide who would be on each team. We agreed to arrive back to school a few days early and do an entire school draft, much like the drafts for major league teams. Each round we were allowed to pick one boy and one girl for our designated team. The incoming freshman were unknown to us, so we did a blind draw to decide their team placements.

Intramural competition took on a completely different atmosphere the following year. The mix of different classes allowed everyone to easily meet students from different grades, developing friendships and bonding, which had not easily been developed in the past. It was great to be part of this process and see the positive atmosphere it inspired. For some reason, the administration went along with some of our crazy ideas.

Playing varsity tennis my freshman year was wonderful, as our coach had lined up some excellent competition for our team. We had a great season winning one match against Pepperdine University, a Division I school. They were not happy losing to a NAIA division college. They actually walked off the court with the score tied at 4 to 4. My partner and I were leading 6–4, 5–2 in the final match. Suddenly, they angrily picked up their gear and walked off the court, defaulting the match. At the end of the season, my tennis had improved enough to easily win the Flight 4 Southern California Championships in singles and Flight 2 in doubles.

Three of us qualified for the NAIA national championships in Kansas City but found ourselves without transportation. It was not in the school's budget to send our players back to the Midwest that year. They had not anticipated we would qualify. A quick call home and I talked my dad into letting us use his huge DeSoto automobile for the trip. I lost to the number 4 seed in three long sets at the nationals after leading 6–4, 4–1. Just when I was poised to win, our coach came up to the fence and said, "Don't blow it." The worst coaching advice I could have heard. Until then I was playing relaxed, with total confidence. I suddenly thought about losing and changed my game. I started playing conservatively, allowing my opponent to gain confidence. He raised his level of play with mine lacking direction and self-doubt creeping in. My opponent eventually won 10–8 in the third and final set. It was a disappointment, but I learned a valuable lesson about losing focus and worrying about the outcome. If I had been able to keep my focus on the ball and keep moving my feet, I might have moved deeper into the tournament.

I learned that in life, it is the same. If we stay focused on what is really important, we will accomplish far more than if we worry about what people think or we unnecessarily worry about the final outcome. My coach was not wise to break my momentum, but it was still up to me to keep doing what was working—a very long trip to learn a valuable lesson. When the unexpected happens and we don't seem to know why, we can choose to stay positive or get bitter and give up. I have always done my best to stay positive and move forward. Most times I succeeded, other times falling short of keeping things simple, uncomplicated, and positive.

During the fall of my sophomore year, I was in the gym watching the wrestling team practice and casually mentioned to a friend, "I could out wrestle that one," pointing to one of the varsity wrestlers. My big mouth was overheard and was passed on to the coach.

The coach came over and heatedly said, "If you are so good, come out and prove it." I tried to decline, but he made such a big deal in front of the whole team, I went on the mat and pinned his wrestler in less than a minute. My dad had taught us to wrestle when I was in grade school to get us fit for football. We spent hours in the living rooms going over every move and countermove possible. This had led me to be the city wrestling champion for my grade at junior high school. At Pasadena College, they thought I was only a tennis player. We should never judge a book by its cover.

Never Judge a Book by Its Cover

Junior high teacher

Home from college and back in San Jose, my dad asked me to drive him over to a fellow teacher's home to have a tool made. I didn't think too much about it as I had met his teaching friend before when picking my dad up from the middle school where they taught. My dad's friend was a quiet man in his late thirties. There was nothing about him that seemed unique or remarkable. It didn't take us long to arrive at his single-level home in an average residential neighborhood with a detached garage in San Jose. My dad's friend warmly greeted us when we arrived, taking my dad directly into his garage.

He asked me to wait for them inside his house while he and my dad took care of business in the garage. I headed inside to an amazing catalog of photos. My dad's friend was in every photo, which was not surprising; it was his home. But the context of each photo held my gaze, as I stayed fixated longer on each photo than I would have expected.

I had thought he was just an unmarried middle school teacher with a very boring life of going to school each day, giving tests, spending his evenings at home grading papers and preparing for his next day's lessons. What I witnessed before me was a life well-lived, and he was still so young. One of the first photos showed him in the winner's circle in a race car. He was a race car driver? Then a photo of him standing on top of one of the world's highest mountains. A mountaineer? Then there was him standing on top of Mount Kilimanjaro with more photos of him walking across hot deserts. Who was this guy? He was also an athlete with photos showing him running some distance races. More photos showing him on beautiful beaches looking out at surf breaks for him to catch a wave. He was also a scuba diver? I stood transfixed and amazed at how I had completely misjudged my dad's friend by the cover of his life's book, showing him to just be a simple middle school teacher. The cover of his life's book was nothing like leafing through the exciting pages inside.

I walked out of his house and entered his garage with a newfound respect for this teacher. I was surprised again when I opened the garage door to be even more amazed. What opened before me was a complete machine shop of grinders, lathe machines, and large tooling equipment to make and machine your own tools. My dad had come over so his friend could make a tool my dad needed for a repair at home. His friend also had much to share with those willing to listen. He took some time to share with me a valuable lesson he learned when he was very young. This one lesson he shared with me has proven invaluable through the years when simply applied. I was forever thankful I had the opportunity to encounter this individual and look beyond the cover of his life's book.

*****

Back to Pasadena College and how this moment of being misjudged by the wrestling coach and my big mouth would change my future was to be seen clearly in the spring. At the coach's request and urging, I joined the wrestling team and wrestled for half the season. I did not enjoy wrestling, as the coach only wanted me on the team to save points, helping with the team's overall results. The wrestler I had replaced was inexperienced and had been pinned every match before I joined the team. This meant a loss of five points every time he wrestled in his weight division. If I could just avoid being pinned, the team would only lose three points or gain two points in the overall results. If I could win, it was a bonus as the team would gain five points for winning or a ten-point gain for the team results. I was very quick and was never pinned but only won a few matches. I was wrestling against some of Southern Cal top NAIA wrestlers. Me and my big mouth!

With the season only a little more than half over, I let the coach know I would not continue wrestling on the team. I was not enjoying it, and it was cutting into my court time to practice tennis. I was on a tennis scholarship, not a wrestling scholarship. I was on the wrestling team as a favor to the coach, so I let him know I would not continue wrestling. This didn't seem like a big deal to me at that time, as I hadn't planned on wrestling in the first place. When the spring term began, our tennis coach suddenly called me into his office and notified me I was ineligible to play tennis. I knew that was impossible, as my grades were fine. He then notified me I had an F on my transcript. I went to the administration office to find out how they had made such an error.

When I looked at my records, sure enough, there it was, an F. It was for wrestling! I had never formally or personally signed up for a wrestling class, so how could this be? I let them know it was a mistake. They also let me know it could not be changed. Someone had signed me up for the wrestling credit and had also signed my signature. I would be ineligible during the entire tennis season, which I was looking forward to. I would also lose my scholarship money for that term. My pleading was to no effect. The wrestling coach had, without my knowledge or permission, signed me up for a wrestling credit and given me an F because he was upset I quit the team. Looking back, it is easy to see God's hand in our lives, but at that moment in time, I was devastated.

One of our other best tennis players had also been declared ineligible, so it wasn't a total loss. We practiced together almost every day but weren't allowed to play any of the team's dual matches, the season-end tournament, or the nationals again. Before the season started, we were expected to be one of the top NAIA teams in the country, so this was a big disappointment, for us personally, our coach, and our team.

My time at Pasadena was cut even shorter because of the Vietnam conflict and the operation on my right leg to repair a previous injury. My big toe tendon was severed when I broke my leg in the fifth grade. The severed tendon had reattached itself to my shin bone. Big plans in our lives can be sidelined when unexpected events from our past seem to change everything. If we learn to relax, God has a way of directing us to destinations both exciting and challenging. I had a hard time seeing this clearly then and other trying times in my young life.

The operation to repair my tendon led me to meet my first and only tennis coach while recuperating in San Jose. Dick Skeen was a prominent tennis pro at one of the local clubs. He had put a challenge in the San Jose *Mercury* newspaper. He claimed, "No one was willing to put in the necessary effort to really succeed in tennis now days." My dad had noticed the article and found it provocative. Setting the article in front of me, he said I should go over to Los Gatos Swim and Racket Club and meet this Mr. Skeen. Dick Skeen had taught thirty-nine world and national champions during his career, with an amazing personal playing résumé himself. When we met, he was over sixty years old and immediately took me on the court for an assessment. I thought I hit really well and believed he would be impressed. Dick was always direct and was very blunt with me when he said, "You don't have much of a game!" I was stunned.

This could have ended our relationship right then. But knowing he had taught the likes of Jack Kramer, Louise Brough, Pauline Betz, and thirty-six other notable players, I took his assessment as a challenge. I spent that year out of school making mortar shells at FMC for Vietnam at night and working on my tennis skills with Dick Skeen during the day. Dick arrange a membership for me at the club where I strung rackets in exchange for the membership and free time on the court with Dick. I was relearning my tennis game from the ground up. It was frustrating, challenging, and exciting. For the first time ever, I was getting used to having a coach. I was determined to go through the process to improve. Hopefully I would improve enough to someday compete at the pro level. My ego took a beating as my match results were getting worse. Even with these poor results, I could sense my game was developing and my skills were improving. Developing new skills was still exciting and inspired me to work even harder to follow Dick's instructions and examples.

Working with Dick was very much like working with my Father in different sports through the years. I was willing to put in the tedious, hard workouts because I could see results. Through my early years, with my dad's help, I had developed a goal oriented work ethic. I tried to stay focused on my short-term goals to achieve long-term results. I had no idea that these very character traits instilled in me by the likes of my father and Skeen would bring me through some of my most trying and challenging days in the future.

Dick never complimented his students. He only pointed out any and every minute flaw. Dick was meticulous and had a way of seeing every little detail of your game. Being a perfectionist himself, he was able to demonstrate and play tennis with the same perfection.

Dick Skeen on left with Fred Perry

He was classy and dressed for the occasion, whether teaching or playing a match. He was uniquely Dick Skeen, and the minute you saw him strike a tennis ball, you knew you were watching an immensely gifted athlete. The most vivid memory of watching Dick compete was his ability to move effortlessly around the court. Age never seemed to catch up to him as his movements resembled a wizard floating over the court rather than running. He made everything look breezy, balanced, and effortless. He also left the impression of a person who had no emotions when playing a match. This was true, whether he was winning or losing, although it was difficult to remember him losing many matches.

When Dick was sixty-four years old, I saw him win two practice matches in one week. One against the US National 35 champion Don Gale and then against the National 45 champion Butch Krikorian, just two days apart. Both were Northern Californian Hall of Fame tennis players. Dick would only play matches if the other players agreed to play three out of five set matches. This particular week, he completely destroyed these two national champions, many years his junior, losing only one game in three sets to both players. He made it look effortless as he ran them ragged, hitting what seemed like impossible angles on the court. Dick taught me to play an intelligent game by example when we finally started playing sets together. I learned very quickly to play smart shots or quickly lose a point. Even when I thought I had played a point perfectly against Dick, he often found ways to put me under pressure. At times, I felt he truly was a wizard, as he would find impossible angles on the court to steal another point from me and his other opponents. Because of my time with Dick, I was able to enjoy playing open-level tennis. Later on, I was able to play the Italia Cup in Australia and some success in doubles with wins over world-class players like Jeff Borowiak and Torbin Ulrich.

Dick and I became close friends and would sometimes head over to his house for a quick lunch. Dick was married to Pauline, a lovely lady who had a serious medical condition. She had failed kidneys and was required to be on dialysis a few times a week. Dick's insurance had run out years before, so he paid for all of her in-home treatments out of his tennis lesson income. Pauline and Dick never complained, and Dick never mentioned their situation as a hardship. Dick and I shared much together, practically living at the club.

When I couldn't get off the court for lunch, Dick would sometimes bring me a snack. Once he brought me a specialty sandwich to get me through the afternoon. With his quizzical little smile, he said it was a treat that Pauline had prepared for us. I was hungry and took a huge bite into a liver sandwich. I never had a taste for liver and practically threw up. I forced myself to finish that bite, only to see a little smirk on Dick's face. He then gave me a lecture on the nutritional value of liver. Even when Dick joked around, it was usually with a deadpan face. He treated me like his son, once inviting me to play an open doubles event with him in Stockton, California. We drew Whitney Reed and Don Kirbo, one of the top seeds in the first round. We made a respectable showing before losing, even though Dick was more than thirty years older than any other player in the draw. It was an honor for me to partner one of the greats of tennis.

The military was still doing their best to track me down and draft me. They wanted to send me off to that faraway conflict in Vietnam. Every time I was contacted for a physical, I somehow had something wrong. First was my leg operation, then I severely burnt my right forearm working at the FMC factory, making motor shells for Vietnam. This third-degree burn again left me with a 1Y (temporary medical deferment). The Army continued to chase me back and forth from California to Idaho where I ended up going to Northwest Nazarene College (NNC) for my junior and senior years.

When the Army eventually caught up with me in Idaho, I knew my day of reckoning had finally come. By this time, Vietnam had become a national nightmare, with newscasts regularly showing horrendous images of war on the evening news. This was coupled with the sight of protesters spitting on our soldiers returning to the States. I started having visions of myself trudging through a hot, humid jungle dodging sniper fire when I tried to sleep at night. I had more of these visions as I took the twenty-mile ride to Boise for my final physical. Several of my friends had been unceremoniously pulled out of their everyday lives with the notice, "Greetings, you have been invited to serve in the Armed Services of the United States of America." For many of my peers, this meant they were sent to an Army boot camp for eight weeks and then quickly off to Vietnam. One member of our high school football team, Daniel Hayes, and member of my graduating class had gone to Vietnam, only to come back to California to be buried. This was a huge wake-up call for us during the idyllic '60s. Vietnam was real, and a friend of ours had given his all in this out-of-the way Southeast Asian country.

The usual process of going from room to room and having one military doctor after another, probe and poke me inside and out was familiar by then. However, this time was different, as I was eventually led into the private office of the Army doctor. At this point, I was resigned to the outcome, imagining the worst. More visions flooded my mind of soldiers marching in and taking me directly off to some military base, inducting me without having a chance to even go back to NNC and retrieve my belongings. These thoughts completely occupied my negative mind-set. When the doctor finally arrived to greet me, I was ready for any bad news he might bring, except for what actually occurred. The doctor sat down on the other side of a large desk without so much as a greeting and started writing. The suspense was thick in the air for me. After writing for a bit, he slowly raised his head saying I needed to sign a document he shoved in my direction. What was this? Was I signing my future and life away? I thought, *Finally the Army has caught up with me.* Even with my negative outlook and fast-beating heart, I had enough coherence to ask, "What am I signing?"

Looking up again from his paperwork with no emotion, he calmly said, "This is your permanent 4F deferment classification."

"What is 4F?" I asked. For the first time, there was a slight expression of a smile on his face.

He calmly said, "You will never need to worry about the military again."

The 4F classification was a permanent disability status. What was I hearing? How could this be happening? He explained that the huge lump on my lower right leg, left over from my tendon operation, would make it impossible for me to wear Army boots. He had determined I would not be able to make it through boot camp, much less marching through some hot, humid jungle in those same boots.

Wow, I had received a 4F classification because of the results of the operation on my leg to repair my big toe tendon. This was all because I broke my leg in the fifth grade? My chance to continue playing tennis and attending Pasadena College had been cut short because of losing my scholarship. Then while at home, I had decided to have my tendon operated on and repaired, leaving the huge lump! During that time, many—including myself—had thought, *What bad luck!* But again, God's ways are not man's ways, and man's ways are not God's ways.

Because of the seemingly bad luck of breaking my leg in the fifth grade, then the subsequent operation during my college break, I was not being sent to Vietnam. I had not evaded the draft, but the Army's 4F classification meant I would be free to concentrate on my studies and tennis. The worries of Vietnam and the draft hanging over my head were finally over. I found the doctor's decision strange as I was skiing twice a week and still played varsity tennis for NNC.

The realization that I would not be in the Army, marching through some sweltering humid jungle, fighting and dodging the enemy while avoiding landmines made me realize how truly fortunate I was. As I walked up the steps to the sidewalk, to an even more beautiful sunny crisp day, the sunlight seemed to be brighter, filtering through the large maple trees lining the road in front of the Army facility. Part of me felt like I was going to miss out on a rite of passage. My dad was a decorated World War II veteran serving in Guadalcanal, and I always assumed I would someday be in the military. The way Vietnam was going and the horrible hate so many Americans had toward veterans returning to the States, I was truly thankful to be staying in school.

The 1968–69 school year suddenly became wonderful without the weight of Vietnam hanging over my head. The tennis team at NNC was enjoyable, and the coach allowed me to arrange some of the scheduling. Playing number 1 on the NNC team allowed me some excellent competition. I was able to help organize a one-weekend tournament against three of the powerhouses of the Pacific Northwest. The match was scheduled in Boise against Boise State University, University of Idaho, and Weber State University.

That weekend, I learned another important lesson in how our mind determines the outcome of competitions. The best tennis player in this two-day event was the number 1 player from University of Idaho. He had not lost a match during the season against some strong schools. We were scheduled to play University of Idaho on Friday afternoon. Matches with the other two schools were scheduled for all day Saturday. This was a very long weekend of tennis, as back then, we didn't have tiebreakers to end sets quickly.

I unexpectedly beat the top player from Idaho in straight sets, his first loss of the season. I was puzzled as I knew I wasn't playing that much or even felt great about my game. When the match was over and we were shaking hands, he said, "You don't remember me, do you?" I really had no idea who he was or how I would have known him. It turned out we had played each other back in Boise when we were younger. That was when I had won the Idaho State singles and doubles titles two years in a row. I had beaten him a few times during my time in Boise more than six years earlier. Remembering our previous matches caused him to be intimidated and played below his normal level.

I then lost to the number 1 players from Boise State and Weber State in long three-set matches while the Idaho player went on to claim wins against both of them. I was always learning valuable life lessons no matter where I was. This was another of those lessons for the books: learning to stay focused on what is important and divorcing ourselves from past experiences or the surrounding environment allows us to do our very best whether on a tennis court or living life to the fullest.

At the end of the season, I lost in the semifinals of the Pacific Northwest NAIA tournament to the eventual champion. I had a great tournament beating two of the previous Pacific Northwest NAIA champions on my way to losing in the semifinals. Still a disappointing result as a finals appearance would have qualified me for the national NAIA championships again back in Kansas City.

My major at NNC was psychology. With only a semester left to graduate, I was fortunate to receive counseling from a very wise educator. Helen Wilson let me know that work opportunity with a degree in psychology was limited without obtaining a master's or doctor's degree. She had received an award as Pacific Northwest Educator of the Year the previous year and I was always grateful for her honest counseling that morning.

At the same time, I received an offer to teach tennis professionally with Dick Skeen back in San Jose, California. Skeen was going to be general manager and head pro at the new Blossom Hill Tennis Club, which was getting ready to break ground. He wanted me to be the assistant manager and assistant tennis pro, working directly with him. When Mrs. Wilson found out how much I would be making, and it would be more than twice her yearly salary, she asked, "Why are you staying in school?" I left NNC with no regrets and never looked back. I have never been asked about my college or university degree when interviewing for work positions. Dick was a wealth of information and taught me much more than just being on the tennis court. Playing and teaching tennis alongside Dick was a real gift. Dick had designed a number of well-known clubs in California including the Newport Beach Tennis Club and the new Blossom Hill Tennis Club, where I was set to work.

Blossom Hill Tennis Club was approved and ready for its groundbreaking ceremony when I arrived. Opportunity to learn many of the intricacies involved in the designing and building of sports clubs was literally handed to me under Dick's tutelage. Also discovering the details of tennis court surfacing, and managing a club all under Dick's supervision was invaluable for me through the years. Having the honor to teach, manage a club as assistant manager, and work on my game with Dick Skeen was a true blessing. This was the final reason for leaving college. Not only would I have extra time to workout with Dick, but I was also able to watch him play national age group champions and dominate them. He was twenty to thirty years their senior, but his skills and strategy proved to be superior. Skeen was also coaching some current tour level players, which gave me an opportunity to workout with a number of them. Honing my game against some of the best allowed my game to significantly improve. Some of Dick's students were either preparing for or coming back from Grand Slam events.

I DO IT ALL

Stranded with an English RoadBlock

Another tennis professional from California unexpectedly contacted me about traveling to Europe as his doubles partner. Thinking this might finally be my opportunity, I made arrangements to accept his offer. George was the same player who had bundled me out of a tournament years before when he dominated the Central Coast section high school tennis championships. He had a sponsor who was willing to include his choice of a doubles partner in the agreement. I considered this an honor as George was a quality tennis player. Finally, a chance to play consistently against the best and maybe make it on the major circuit. I was excited to finally have this opportunity to play with a sponsorship and not constantly worry about my finances. My tennis aspirations could finally be handled properly. Even with this opportunity, it was a difficult choice for me. I was recently married and, for the first time in my life, needed to think of someone other than myself.

After much thoughtful discussion and consideration, we decided to take the opportunity and headed to England to begin playing tennis seriously. Arriving in England was a journey in and of itself, but the story of what happened after we arrived was disheartening and devastating for us and my tennis plans. It was not easy for me to gracefully accept this setback when newly married.

Arriving at our first scheduled grass court tournament in the small town of Chingford on the east coast of England, we found ourselves in the middle of a typical, heavy English rainstorm. My partner George and the promised sponsorship were nowhere to be found. An available British bed and breakfast was close by to stay the night and wait out the pouring rain. Rain continued for two days straight, and still no doubles partner or sponsorship in sight. It was beginning to be desperate times, as I was relying on George's sponsorship money and finances to live and play the spring tournaments. We had arrived on one-way tickets and needed George to show up. I hadn't hit a tennis ball in ten days since leaving California. I was anxious to get on a court to get a feel of my racket again and feel for the grass courts.

We had arrived without the necessary funds to even enter England properly. Flying into Luxemburg, we had taken a train to the English Channel before boarding a ferry to cross the channel to England. Immigration for England was organized on the boat. Waiting in the immigration line, we saw they were checking to make sure each passenger had the necessary funds to live while visiting England. Everyone had to show return tickets or enough funds to be able to leave England without being stranded. We knew we were in trouble as we had no way to show enough finances or a round-trip ticket to get past these immigration officials. When it was our turn, I made sure the officer saw my many tennis rackets. He immediately asked if I was playing the upcoming professional grass court circuit. When I said yes, there were no more questions as he stamped our passports and wished me good luck.

Waiting out the rainstorms, we found ourselves with dwindling funds in our wallet. Our plight didn't improve as I was finally able to get a phone call through to George, still in California. Not the good news I was hoping for! He had injured himself and was not coming! Also absent was his sponsorship money! This was not the age of cell phones, so communication was difficult and limited. With very little left in our pocket, no credit cards, and arriving on a one-way ticket, I knew we were in trouble. We had taken this trip on faith, and now nothing seemed to be going right. That Bible verse again, "Plans are in men's minds, but God directs your steps."

Dick Skeen had shared a similar memory happening to him when traveling to his first professional event years before we met. Now on the east coast of England, I prepared myself to win some matches to earn some money like he had done. I was desperately hoping to get us out of this situation. My disappointment, however, was far from over. When the rains finally let up and play could begin, I went to the tournament desk to check in. There in front of me, I found a new draw with my name missing. I, along with many of the first-round matches, were deleted. The tournament officials had eliminated thirty-two of the lesser or unknown players from the draw. I was obviously one of the lesser and unknown. They had made this determination so they could complete the tournament on time.

My name was gone from the draw, and nothing could be done to change the officials' decision. How was I to explain this to my new wife?

Stranded in England

Here I was, feeling stranded, very little money left and no tickets to get us back to the US. Having my wife with me on this adventure made the situation even more complex. Talk about feeling like a loser, we were basically stranded in a foreign country with no apparent options. I put on my very best face for my wife as we boarded another train back to London. The deluge of the heavy rain met us again in England's largest city. Packed into an iconic red English phone booth with our luggage for an hour to stay dry, we listened as the rain pounded on the roof, showing no signs of letting up. We eventually located another bed and breakfast for the night, luckily nearby. This left less money in our very thin wallet. To say we were feeling desperate would be an understatement.

The following day, we decided to find the US embassy. The embassy turned out to be a waste of time. Their only solution was to call our parents and have them send money to fly us home. I was too proud and stubborn to call for help. We had spent time with one of our church leaders before we left the US, talking and praying about this trip. I felt strongly that it was no accident we were in England. I felt God had something in store for us, that we couldn't see at that moment. I was determined to figure a way out of this apparent disaster. We felt we were on our own when we left the embassy. My wife had left the States with me, along with her dream job, to accompany and support me on this adventure. I desperately wanted to make this work out right for her, as well as myself. I wasn't sure what options we had left. Then we thought of the Nazarene Church and wondered if they had churches in London. We were fortunate when we found some in a phone directory.

The next day, we traveled by the Tube to Clapham Junction for the closest Nazarene Church. We planned to attend their Wednesday-evening service. We needed to find an answer to the predicament we found ourselves in. By this time, we were completely living on a blind faith. I could see the wide-eyed look of my wife as she was hoping "I" might have all the answers. I didn't really know it at that time, but blind faith is where God wants us to live, learning to trust Him completely. We had no choice, given our present predicament, but to trust Him as we were out of options. We had enough money left for two more night's stay in a bed and breakfast and a few cheap meals. Except for my many tennis rackets, playing tennis was the furthest thing from my mind. We lugged my tennis rackets, gear, and large suitcases everywhere we went. We were exhausted!

We attended a Nazarene Church in San Jose, California, so it was natural for us to look for a familiar environment. God was definitely leading as we found ourselves close to the pastor's home or The Manse, as they called it in England. We walked out of Clapham Junction Train Station only a short distance from the pastor's home. For some reason, his manse was listed as the church address and was just across Clapham Common. A quick call to the number listed also lead us to their home.

Kenneth Staniforth and his wife, Rosemary, were very gracious and invited us to stay for dinner. We experienced a wonderful dinner and conversations around the table, making new and lasting friends. Ken was a real character and fun to be around. He and I hit it off immediately. They felt like family and insisted we stay on for a few more days. We stayed with them for four days, at their continued insistence and hospitality. We never shared our dire predicament, so they had no idea the extent of our financial situation. Going to church with them on Sunday allowed us to meet a young widowed mother with two well-behaved and cute children, initially from Barbados. She shared with us her need to find someone to take care of her flat for the next five months. Her husband had recently passed away, and she and her two daughters were heading off for Canada to stay with relatives for the rest of the spring and summer. They needed to be around her family to help recover from their terrible loss.

She inquired about our trip and asked if we would be open to watching her flat while they were away. From not knowing what we were going to do, we were being asked to house sit a flat and have a

I DO IT ALL

place to live for free. We were starting to see God's hand in leading our life. We were learning how God takes care of us and directs our paths, even though our plans have felt like a train wreck.

With all this going on, I was still hoping to get in a few tennis tournaments. The idea of playing tennis never completely left my mind. I was able to play a little tennis after meeting the number 1 junior tennis player from England. He invited me to the famous Cumberland Lawn Tennis Club to workout and play a few sets one perfect afternoon. With all the apparent bad things happening, I had the opportunity to play on some of the finest grass courts in all of England. This was a great experience to be in the staid traditional atmosphere of old London. Some of the oldest club directors were looking on, and I played well enough to receive their approval.

Still doing what I could to be ready for any opportunity to play tennis, my wife agreed to feed me tennis balls on the Clapham Common grass courts. These courts were nothing like the Cumberland Club, but they were available. I would do my exercises, stretching and running around this beautiful Common trying to stay fit enough to compete, if the chance to play a tournament ever arrived.

One of our scheduled tournaments was coming up. Somehow it was arranged for me to play this warm-up grass-court tournament before Wimbledon in Halifax. Halifax was a small tournament but still featured a number of Wimbledon entrants, making the field of players very strong. Halifax is an industrial city north of London located near some of England's more beautiful green countrysides. We were invited to stay with one of the club's members who turned out to be wonderful hosts. Both husband and wife were very gracious, making the tournament extra special. Richard looked very British, but his wife, Betty, looking like Doris Day was the clubs squash champion. She enticed a number of the tennis pros to play squash with her during the tournament. Then with a disarming smile, she would humiliate them into submission with her squash ability. Halifax was my first grass court event and taught me a lot about that surface and difficulty of competing on grass. I lost to a big hitting New Zealander who eventually qualified for Wimbledon. A few doubles wins still made it a memorable tournament. I was asked if I was playing Wimbledon but thought it was a joke. Only later to learn about the boycott of Wimbledon by most of the top players. That protest had made it possible for many lesser players to play that year. There was a good chance of my being able to play at the All England Club, had I known about the boycott.

    We had a wonderful experience by coming to Halifax when our hosts invited us to stay on for a few days following the tournament. They took us on a sightseeing trip up to York. York is an incredible city and contains one of the finest Cathedrals in all of England. The York Cathedral was going through its last stage of renovation when we arrived. Entering the Cathedral, we were treated to a children's choir, who sounded like angels singing with the incredible acoustics amplifying their angelic voices. A short distance walk took us back a few centuries in time, as we came upon the Shambles. The Shambles is an area several blocks long, which was preserved so you feel like you have stepped backward in time to ancient England. The street is so narrow, the second floors jut out far enough in places, so the occupants literally would be able to hand items back and forth without leaving their flat. Another item, which was startling, was the doorways. They were very low, so even with my height at that time of almost six feet, I had to duck under the door frames to enter the houses. Inside one of the dwellings was a preserved coat of armor worn by one the knights of that time period. To fit inside that armor, you would have been five feet five inches tall or less to wear it. I suddenly had a vision of these little Knights of the Round Table running around England in these tiny little suits of armor.

    Our tour-guide couple from Halifax were wonderful and even tried to convince us to stay on for another week to experience the North Country, as they called it. Reluctantly, we declined, as we needed to get back to London. We were still house sitting in Tooting Bec. Tooting Bec turned out to be only a short train ride to Wimbledon. We decided to experience the All England Club, even if I didn't have the opportunity to play in the tournament. We saved up some money from odd jobs to buy tickets so we could experience Wimbledon's Centre Court magic. We stood in line for hours to get what was back then standing-room area of Centre Court. They

I DO IT ALL

have since eliminated this standing-room area to make it safer for the players.

We were able to stand in the front row, right next to Centre Court and watch Ilie Nastase play the opening match. Family back home said they saw me at Wimbledon in the local San Jose paper—not the way I had hoped it would be. It was a large photo of Nastase reaching for a volley with me standing in the background. Although I was only able to play in one tournament in those five months, the experience of finding work to survive and live in London taught me a lot about not giving up and the miraculous way life works out when we trust God completely, do our best to stay positive, embrace the moment and not get discouraged.

We embraced the experience, found work, and discovered a way to enjoy the entire adventure. We washed dishes, mopped floors, helped at the cash registers, and served food. The most interesting job happened when I rolled tea trolleys around corporate offices, working at Trust House Forte. I was offering biscuits and making tea for the executives. Finding it strange for an American to say, "Tea up," and serving them tea, one of the executives offered me a job making sample boards for their hotels worldwide. What an unforgettable experience. After working all summer, enjoying one of their driest years on record and making the sample boards, we were loving our English experience. We were able to do some sightseeing during our last week in London, making it even more memorable.

After five months of living and working in London, we did make enough money to fly back to the States. On our flight back, the unexpected continued as we were delayed on our stopover in Reykjavik, Iceland. This delay in Iceland caused us to miss our onward flight back to California. Although Icelandic Airlines put us up in a hotel for the night in New York, we were required to pay extra to board the onward flight to the West Coast. Here we were again, short on funds. We did our best to look forlorn and explain our situation. God provided a very understanding employee who made arrangements for us to board without having to pay the extra dollars required. The craziness of this trip never seemed to stop. Even the taxi ride back to the airport in New York was interesting. Icelandic

Airlines had paid for the taxi, but our driver was a big New York taxi driver who made it clear he expected a tip. He stood with his hand extended! Being a tennis player, I cheekily gave him a tennis tip "take an early backswing," as we ran for our lives into the terminal.

Home and New Directions

England was an amazing life time adventure, but we were happy and relieved to finally arrive back home in San Jose. The timing was perfect again, as I received a call from the owner of a new club, just ready to have their grand opening. Their tennis director and head pro had decided to accept a different offer and left them stranded without a teaching pro for their grand opening scheduled to happen in two weeks. With this unexpected offer, I was immediately able to work, teach tennis, and start a family. This stop-gap position was perfect, as I was able to save enough money to head out and play more tennis tournaments. My eldest son, Donnie, was born just before I was scheduled to travel to Florida and play on the WATCH (World Association of Tennis Champions) circuit. I then turned to the Southern states to play on the Southern circuit. This was another effort at making it to the ATP, or WCT, as it was called then. I didn't have the promise of a sponsorship this time but had saved up enough money from tennis lessons to play tournaments for four or five months. This was only possible, if we were careful with our expenses and received accommodation help from many of the tournaments. Most people thought I was crazy, and maybe I was.

During the WATCH circuit and the Southern circuit, I was able to improve my game enough to compete well against some world-ranked players, four times playing top 50 ranked players, losing twice in tournament play in closely contested matches and twice winning in practice and exhibition matches. My doubles results were much better winning a number of matches but hardly ever with the same partner. My experience from playing consistently for six months did wonders for my game and tennis teaching skills. This proved invaluable for me for years to come.

Life is funny or even strange at times, as things don't often work out as we plan in our mind or on paper. I knew I could play against the very best and hold my own, but it always seemed like something would happen to thwart my efforts. How was it possible to lose in the last round of qualifying so many times and never have my name drawn out in the lucky loser pool for the main draw? Or getting to match point and see it drift away on a lucky shot dribbling over the net by my opponent? Or getting in the best shape of my life for a tournament and see it disappear with a sprained ankle? Then watch as others seem to fall on their backside and have grapes drop in their mouths or attain a three-year sponsorship because of the right family connections or right acquaintances? Is this bad luck or God's perfect plan for a life?

Some things were meant to be, and we can only do the best we know at the time. In spite of the frustrations of not getting the chance to achieve my original goals on a tennis court, life had proven to be amazing as I had the opportunity to meet and teach some amazing students who went on to achieve their dreams and goals and are to this day a success in their various lives. I also had an amazing life, which is different than I had planned, yet much more than I would have ever expected. All these amazing memories would surface whenever I slowed down enough to think about them! Right then, I had completely stopped and many of these memories came flooding back.

Sudden Darkness and Foreboding

With all these thoughts flashing through my mind, darkness like I was experiencing, was not a good sign because of my past encounters. This wasn't the first time I experienced a sudden darkness and everything seemed disoriented and out of place. First time I could remember it happening was when I was in the fifth grade playing tackle football. Playing quarterback, I had just been hiked the ball by my brother Ken. Suddenly, at eleven almost twelve years old, I found myself on the ground with a lightheaded darkness and searing pain. It didn't take but a moment to locate where the severe pain was coming from. The lightning-like sensation was coming from my right leg. My leg was broken, a spiral fracture covering almost the entire length of my lower leg. Our doctor said temporary blackout was normal when experiencing sudden trauma, like a broken leg.

Second time there was sudden blackness happened in college. I was on the wrestling team, competing during a dual match with another college. My opponent executed an illegal move throwing me head-first into the mat from a standing position, knocking me out. Again, sudden disappearance into a dark void as I blacked out. Disoriented when I came to, I felt lost as I tried to figure out where I was. Staggering to my feet, with vision still blurred and unable to focus, I walked straight into the visiting team's bench of wrestlers. The referee directed back to the center of the mat so I could continue the match. I was able to clear my head enough to finish the match and not be pinned. Not much fun being disoriented and pretend you are fine.

While owning the tennis club in Medford Oregon with my parents, I suddenly had severe pain in my lower back after arriving early at the club. I went straight to the restroom to try to relax, hoping to relieve the pain. But the pain continued to increase while I was sitting down. The pain became so intense, I thought, *This pain would cause some people to pass out.* Suddenly it was dark. *Where am I and what's happening?* I asked myself.

I found it impossible to orient myself. Everything was out of place as my head seemed stuck to the wall. I initially found it impossible to move. Finally, some hazy light came into view, and I understood where I was. My head was not leaning against the wall as I first thought; my head was on the floor. The other item of concern was the intense pain I had been experiencing. Pain was still evident, but I couldn't seem to locate it in my lower back. Still disoriented and not being able to locate the pain made it all the worse.

Now, knowing I was on the floor, I was able to roll over, sit up, and stagger to my feet. I moved to the vanity to rinse off my face and clear my head. Looking up with relief and dismay, I could see my head in the mirror. I was finally able to identify this new pain. My forehead was covered with blood with the skin peeled back. I had indeed passed out, pitched forward from a sitting position, causing me to land straight on my forehead, slamming it on the rough tile floor. I had passed a kidney stone, which caused a lightning bolt of excruciating pain.

That wasn't the last time I experienced a blackout while living and working in Medford. Riding my bike home at the end of a long day of teaching tennis from Hillcrest Club in Medford, I was running late, and it was getting dark. Coming down a slope past the first homes after the pear orchards, I picked up speed, trying to arrive home quickly. Out of nowhere, there was a blur to my right in the darkness. Suddenly darkness again was everywhere as I fought to come out of what was becoming a familiar foggy haze of unconsciousness. Weeds and dampness surrounded me as I forced the haziness to lift. Again the question, "Where am I, and how did I end up here?" The last thing I could remember was riding my bike. *I must have fallen off my bike!* I could hear people talking and just see the top of an ambulance with lights flashing. Thinking it was for me, it suddenly disappeared as it drove away. I slowly forced myself to a sitting position. Searing pain near my left shoulder made it impossible to use my left arm. Holding my left arm and leaning on my right side, I was finally able to sit up to get a better view of my surroundings. I was sitting in the bottom of a four-foot-deep ditch with high weeds practically covering me. I could hardly be seen from the road, especially in the now darkness of night. Just when I was wondering what I was going to do, I heard a car slowly approaching and thankfully stopped. Now that my head cleared up, I was high enough for the driver of the car to see me in the ditch. He quickly offered to take me to the hospital, where the full story of what happened finally emerged.

Unknown to me, an eighth grader living in the home across the road, from the ditch, had sprinted out of their driveway, shielded by a high hedge. He ran right in front of my bike. He had been completely hidden by their high hedge until he suddenly appeared in front of me. He went headlong into my left collarbone with his head. It was like being hit by a bowling ball at thirty miles an hour. I had flown off my bike straight into the ditch on the left side of the road.

The eighth grader was left lying in the road beside my bike. He had suffered a concussion and was attended to by the ambulance, then taken to the hospital. Everyone thought he had fallen off his own bike coming down the road. I was unconscious at that time, so no one knew I was lying in the ditch, buried by wet muddy weeds with a busted collarbone.

When the boy saw me come into emergency and knew I was the one riding the bike, he thought he had hurt Jesus. He recognized me from our church Easter play where I played the part of Jesus. His mother came in to see if I was all right. She then asked me to meet her son and let him know I would be okay and, most importantly, let him know I wasn't Jesus. My severely broken left collarbone healed fine in a couple of months but left a visible and sizable lump for years.

Sudden darkness followed with hazy, groggy awareness that something wasn't right was part of my past. Coming fully conscious on Clearwater Bay Road that fateful morning, I knew from past experiences, a serious event had taken place. Whatever was happening, this present event would most likely affect weeks or even a few months in my future. Somehow this present darkness, lying on a Hong Kong road was different and more difficult to get a handle on. I couldn't seem to do anything, even try to sit up. The only thing I could do was just lay still. I would have given anything to make this latest dark black-hole experience disappear.

LIMBO IN A FOGGY DREAMLAND

Everything was black, so unreal. What a horrible dream. Why do I feel superglued to the surface and cannot move? It was like the dream where I was falling and never seemed to reach the ground. Only, this time I was stuck to the ground and couldn't move or sit up. This had to be a dream; otherwise, I would be able to sit up and move! I let myself drift back to sleep, hoping this horrific dream will go away.

Becoming conscious of the same dream again, still very dark, can't move and definitely feel more superglued to the ground this time. *Why can't I move?* Hating the feel of this dream, I drifted off again. *I can't believe it, what is happening?* as the dream came roaring back again. Only everything was more real this time as the blackness was pierced by some amber-orange color. It seemed there were two shadows in front of the orange glow. Thoughts rushed through my mind, *Is this really a dream?* As I came into a more conscious state, the thought arose, *I may have had a bad accident.* I still couldn't move, but this time I realized, I not only feel like I was superglued to the road surface, but I really was! *Oh no, this is not a dream. This is real and actually happening!*

What is happening and how did I end up here? Another thought rushed in like a loud voice pounding through my head, *You must control your breathing!* I immediately started counting my inhale and exhale so they were even. I couldn't explain why that was my primary thought, but that was all I concentrate on as time faded in and out.

I continued to pass out a few more times as I had no recollection of the ambulance arriving, only awareness of being roughly lifted into the vehicle.

I had been involved in an accident with a Hong Kong minibus illegally reversing across the center of the two-lane road. I had been lying half dead in the middle of the road, in a bloody mess. A passing motorist going to the nearby Clearwater Bay Country Club, where I was to play the invitational tennis tournament in two days, stopped and asked what had happened. He was told by the bus driver, "This cyclist has just killed himself." The still unidentified concerned driver said he detected me still breathing and immediately called for an ambulance. This was the witness statement given to the police. I was grateful for whoever made that call.

Back home, it was getting close to our normal time to leave for school and work. I was unusually late coming back from my morning ride. My wife, Sally, with my oldest son, Donnie, got in the car and came looking for me. They followed our usual bike route to find out what had delayed me. They assumed I had encountered a flat tire or some other bike problem. They expected to find me walking back home, pushing my bike. However, when they started down the steep hill toward the accident site, they could see the many flashing lights from police vehicles at the bottom of the hill. My brightly colored bent bike came into view, still lying beside the road. Arriving at the scene of the accident, my wife told our son the obvious, "Your dad could not have survived the crash with the obvious impact and streams of blood running into the drain." I was already on my way to the hospital by the time they arrived at the accident scene.

My son could not believe that I was dead. Blocking out the evidence in front of him, he said, "Dad will be all right. He is tough!" He refused to believe the evidence even though he could see the crash scene spread out before him. Even though he found my bike pump some fifty feet from the road, he was in complete denial. No one is that tough!

I found out much later at the hospital, I had hit a minibus doing an illegal reverse U-turn across a solid double line just past a sign stating, "No buses beyond this point!" When the bus reached a diagonal point across the road, I slammed into his right-rear tail light at full speed. Many of my triathlete friends joked that I should not have tried to enter the bus through the right-rear tail light. My left handlebar, arm, and helmet covering my head had taken the full impact. The bike had recoiled, causing me to bounce backward forty feet or more. My injuries were extensive and life-threatening. As my doctor stated later, "Only a miracle could have saved you. At least one of four things should have killed you at the scene." He also said my fitness played a major role in my survival, stating, "Maybe your heart was just too stupid to stop beating." Whatever it was, for some reason, even with all the pain and helplessness, I was filled with a complete sense of peace about my situation. After all, what can you do when you are unable to move and you are completely relying on others to take care of you? The doctor was right when he said it was a miracle I survived and I was alive. Only a miracle could save a person from this kind of impact.

All of my dedicated months and years of getting up early, training so hard to be fit and ready to race at the Triathlon World Championship and also play tennis at the highest possible level, had disappeared in a microsecond! These thoughts were fleeting through my mind, as well as the pressing thoughts of how I was going to handle my present situation. How to survive and recover took precedence over all other thoughts.

I couldn't help but think how all the experiences of my life had led up to this very moment in time. How could I take charge and be in control when I couldn't even move?

How Did I Get Here?

As I lay there in the road and finally traveling in the ambulance to the hospital, I asked myself the question, "How did I end up here and what can I do now to get through this ordeal?"

Good questions, I thought. Firstly, how did I end up in Asia, on that piece of road in Hong Kong, that particular morning? It is amazing all of the thoughts we can come up with when we are helplessly relying on others and can't move. For me, it was my past that kept running through my mind. It played like a movie. Scene after scene of the various happenings leading me to this very moment in time. Any one of these past experiences being slightly altered could have saved me from this terrible helplessness I felt that morning in Hong Kong.

I brought up memories of my early growing up in Boise, Idaho. I was born in the small college town of Nampa, Idaho, just twenty miles from Boise. I was a typical Idaho kid in the fifties who did everything he could to stay active. Football, baseball, basketball, swimming, inner tubing down the Boise River in the summer, and hooky bobbing behind cars in the winter were the norm for my brother and me. Two main things changed the direction for my future, which ended me up in Hong Kong.

Number 1, my brother Ken had taken up tennis and was the Boise City tennis champion for his grade. Number 2, my dad, always wanted to live in California; and unknown to his children, he was actively searching for a teaching position there. There were many other things that happened over the years, but these two were the major happenings in my early life, which led me to where I was on that early morning stretch of road in Clearwater Bay.

Number 1, the summer between my seventh and eighth grade year, Ken started nagging me to play tennis with him so he could improve his game during our hot summer days of vacation. I was not easy to convince, but he was my brother. If you knew Ken, you would know how insistent he could be, and I finally gave in. I began playing tennis with him on the courts beside the South Junior High School swimming pool. Our summers were packed full with a lot of swimming, baseball, tennis, swimming, baseball, tennis, and more swimming. We were enjoying the usual idyllic summer days kids experienced in the fifties and early sixties.

This also got me daydreaming about some of the best times of my life, and there had been many. Good-time memories flooded through my mind with the one of me starting tennis in Boise looming big. This one single addition to my life was what eventually led me to Hong Kong and Clearwater Bay that morning. As I continued to daydream through my pain, I thought more about what tennis had meant to me and how tennis inspired me to stay active through the years.

IDYLLIC DAYS OF SUMMER

Many almost disconnected, and random thoughts rushed through my head during the next couple of hours and days as I lay paralyzed and trapped in a bed. With very little else to do, I spent most of my time reminiscing and daydreaming. Many of my thoughts were directed toward tennis and how this one sport had directed much of my adventurous life.

I was reminded about the evolution of tennis. Tennis has evolved through the decades and distinctly defines our present generation of tennis players. It also identifies what we deem to call truth about our sport today. I mean, how can today's youth even begin to understand the tennis culture when I began? We used heavy wooden rackets strung with lamb's gut needing to be treated with gut oil to last and play properly. Or having to use the exact center of the strings on a tiny head for any hope of controlling the white tennis balls with power and finesse. This was still a time when we considered ourselves lucky compared to the antiquated original wooden rackets used by the former greats of our game. Their tennis rackets were also made of wood but looked primitive with grooved wooden handles instead of finely wrapped leather grips or the finely manufactured synthetic grips dominating our rackets nowadays.

Our time in the late '50s and early '60s were idyllic, with not a care in the world. My brother and I would jump on our bikes and head down to Boise's main park in the early morning for the entire day. We would enjoy time with our friends running around the park and play some tennis or even play tennis all day. At the end of a long day at the park courts, after wearing our rackets and bodies out, we would still compete off the courts. There were no fancy tennis clubs around to play tennis and hone our skills back then in Boise, Idaho. There were, however, the wonderful bank of six slightly dirty Julia Davis Park tennis courts inviting us to savor another day out and about with our friends. This was where I won my first tournament. These same courts would turn our white tennis balls dark gray in no time at all. Our freshly oiled strings would capture some of the dirt, leaving a dark-stained circle to be closely compared with one another's racket. At the end of a long summer's day in Julia Davis Park, we would stand around and gage who had the smallest discolored stain or circle on our strings. That person would be declared the winner. We would then know who had watched the ball closest. We always wanted to increase our concentration and use the very center of our tennis racket.

As late evening approached, we had spent a long day under beautiful skies in a wonderful green park, playing a challenging sport with our friends. The park lagoon with huge lily pads floating on the water made rowing a boat there even more relaxing, watching the lily pads float around our boat as we would paddle through their field of bright green. How could life get any better than that? Sometimes taking a break, jumping in the Boise River to cool off or just laying down on the soft grass under one of the huge maple trees, gazing up at some billowing white clouds, is just what we needed. The smell of the fresh-cut grass was wonderful as we watched squirrels chasing one another around the huge trunks of large trees or racing through the myriad of leaf-covered branches. Our imaginations would run wild as we would see all kinds of figures in those ever-changing billowing clouds. To us kids, summer was perfect in Boise, even better once we discovered tennis.

Tennis for us back then was about making new friends and competing fairly in a welcoming environment. Signing up for a tournament meant entering three events and playing at least three matches a day. Some days, you could be scheduled to play five matches with the long summer daylight hours extending past 9:00 p.m. We had never heard of a tiebreaker in the early 1960s, so there was no such thing as an abbreviated point system for a third set. It was not unusual for sets to go to 8–6 or 10–8. No one complained about the weather being too hot or going on the court too soon after their last match. Everyone wanted to be on the court playing tennis instead of just standing around for hours, waiting for another chance to hit more tennis balls and compete. Points tended to be much shorter back then because of the wooden rackets, unlike the forgiving rackets today, which allow for longer, extended rallies.

We would sign up for singles, doubles, and mixed doubles. It was great to be playing in three events and meeting new tennis players. I don't even remember when junior tennis tournaments eliminated mixed-doubles events. Younger players today are missing out on the joy of playing mixed doubles. It was a much more light-hearted feeling than what you sense at today's tournaments. I was always paired with a girl in Idaho named Molly, who had a twin sister, Mary, playing in the same tournament. Part of my tennis development could be directly attributed to playing the extra mixed-doubles events.

There was very little tennis on TV then, so most of what we knew was from what we read in newspapers or rumored around the courts. In Idaho, we had heard about Budge, Kramer, Gonzalez, Segura, or the latest greats, Rod Laver and Ken Rosewall. Some of the older players would tell stories of the past greats, most of them probably true, but nobody really cared. We would be transfixed by the retelling of their exploits. These stories fueled our imaginations and excited us to play this crazy game. We would often pretend we were one of the greats, trying to emulate the stories we had heard so many times. My idol was Rod Laver, so I developed a serve-and-volley game while trying to imitate his fearsome backhand.

This seemed like such a long time ago but also felt like yesterday, while being stuck in a hospital bed. These memories provided me an escape from my present dark situation. I could hardly believe how much had changed in such a brief span of time. I was supposed to be playing an open tennis tournament instead of reminiscing about my past. My thoughts took me back again to how I ended up playing tennis.

Most of us started playing tennis with cheap Woolworth tennis rackets. Mine was called a Coronet. It was strung with some cheap nylon strings, which would fray and look like fine angel hair when the plastic coating started to wear off. We didn't care as long as we could be on a court pretending to be a great tennis player ourselves, winning as many rallies as possible.

Those who taught tennis back then weren't in it just for the money or fame. They loved their sport, offering to help promising young players so they could also learn to love the game. Barbara Chandler was one of those who had settled in Boise back then. She had incredible tennis credentials and would offer free advice to us young players at the junior tournaments. She was instrumental in the organization of tennis events in Idaho and went on to help form the Boise Tennis Club. She is largely responsible for the huge growth of tennis in the Treasure Valley. We were taught to believe in the integrity of tennis, and most us had a plaque on our wall reminding us, "It wasn't whether we won or lost but how we played the game." Another adult in Boise watched Ken and I play a tournament one day and took an interest in our tennis. He surprised my brother and me when he presented each of us with a high-quality Butch Buchholz Rawlings tennis racket. This racket was strung with gut, like the pros. We were surprised and honored. This tennis racket allowed us to enjoy tennis at a whole new level.

The '50s and '60s were an idyllic time to live and dream of one day being a great tennis player. If we were lucky enough to actually see a great tennis player in person. We would do whatever it took to be present and be entertained by their greatness. One day in Boise, it was announced that Pancho Gonzalez and Pancho Segura would be playing an exhibition match downtown at an indoor arena. This was huge for Boise. My dad, brother Ken, and I were able to get tickets and sit in the balcony. We watched in awe as they put their immense talents on display for everyone to enjoy.

It was amazing watching them glide around the court, making the seemingly impossible look effortless. Pancho Gonzalez—tall, elegant, and graceful—playing opposite Pancho Segura, who stood on a little bowlegged frame, scampering around faster than seemed possible. Gonzalez had one-handed smooth strokes, and Segura used two hands on both sides. Segura seemed to chop at every ball in comparison to Gonzalez's effortless-looking strokes. They couldn't have been more different gladiators, facing off against each other.

Just when you thought you couldn't be more dazzled, Segura suddenly yelled out in a heavy Mexican accent, "Hey, Pancho, my next return will be so hard you won't even see it go by!"

Not to be outdone, Gonzalez fired back, "Hey, Pancho, I will hit my serve so hard you won't be able to see it!"

Then Segura yelled back, "Hey, Pancho, I know you, and you are nothing compared to my return!"

Gonzalez, having one of the greatest serves ever, was not to be outdone with one last emphatic remark, "Okay, Pancho! Here comes another ace!" Both used exaggerated Mexican accents, bringing more laughter from spectators, never failing to be wonderful entertainers.

After more bantering back and forth, Gonzalez was set to serve. Everyone held their breath as the entire crowd of spectators thought Gonsales was surely going to ace Segura. Gonzales had the hardest and best serve in the world at that time, but Segura's return could also be breathtaking. We all held our breath as Gonzalez yelled out one more time, "Okay, Pancho, here goes!" Gonzalez went into his graceful, smooth service motion, tossing the ball high into the air, lifting his 6'3" frame off the ground to explode into the ball. It sounded like a gunshot piercing the air, echoing around the arena.

The sound made me jump inside, but almost as quickly, there was another deafening roar on the other side of the net as Segura's tiny frame exploded into Gonzalez's serve. Segura, having the best return in the game, rocketed the ball into the far corner of the court, untouched by Gonzalez. The stadium went wild with screams and applause. As soon as it quieted down, Segura screamed out one last time, "I told you, Pancho!" The crowd erupted again into more applause and laughter as these two legends of tennis did not disappoint. I doubt this was ever documented, but the truth is, I was there; I was enthralled, and it changed how much I loved the sport of tennis. We loved watching these two grown men entertain, exciting everyone there with their skills and love of tennis, acting like they were kids themselves. I wanted to be able to play and entertain the way they had, hopefully acquiring their amazing skill and ability. Maybe I would be able to inspire others to play tennis in the future.

I am sure there were those in the hospital who wondered why I was smiling at times with tears of joy in my eyes when nothing else was going on. With my condition seeming to be so hopeless, smiling wasn't a normal reaction. My memories almost always brought a smile to my face as my life left little to be unhappy, sad, or regretful about.

There were many stories of Gonzalez, which were fun to recount and share with anyone willing to listen. Gonzalez was a character, and approaching the end of his career, there were the usual young "guns" wanting to outplay him. They all wanted the opportunity to take the scalp against one of the game's greats. One particular match, Gonzalez was playing an up-and-coming young, promising player. This young pro was having an awesome start to their encounter. He seemed to have Gonzalez's number, surely heading for a memorable win. After winning the first set, Gonzalez looked sure to lose the match. During the changeover, he made a casual remark to the youngster as they passed by the net. Until that point in the match, this young pro had been hitting great forehands. But something changed after that brief encounter. His forehand fell apart, erratically spraying them into the net or beyond the sidelines.

Gonzalez went on to easily win the match. What had happened to turn the tide so quickly? A friend of Gonzalez later shared the causal question he had posed to the young pro. He had simply complimented this young professional, saying how wonderful his forehand was. But then as quickly, Gonzalez asked, "What is that little quirk you do in your preparation?" After that little remark and question, this young professional couldn't relax and hit his forehand without thinking, *What little quirk?*

I loved these old stories because they always added personality and psychology to a great sport. Gonzalez wasn't known for being the nicest player at times. He employed the psychological side of tennis, as well as his immense talent, to win matches.

Gonzalez's serve was so domineering in his prime. He hit 88 percent of his first serves in during a major final. He also won eight US Pro Championships in nine years, between 1953 and 1961. The other top players at that time were trying to figure out a way to blunt the dominance of Pancho's serve and his reign at the top. At a meeting with a number of pros, it was suggested to go to a one-serve format to hamper his game. This was debunked as ridiculous, when a well-known celebrity asked, "How would that help? Gonzalez is hitting 88 percent of his first serves in, so wouldn't it be even more to his advantage to go to a one-serve format?"

There were other greats like Kramer who could hit an outslice forehand deep into the opponent's backhand corner while gracefully moving forward. Covering the line, he would hit a forehand volley crosscourt for a winner time and again. His opponents were asked many times why they didn't hit the ball back crosscourt. Trying to hit a ball crosscourt, which was slicing away, using heavy wooden rackets was almost impossible. The greats of the past were doing all these remarkable things using these heavy small-headed wooden rackets. These rackets made it much more difficult to control a tennis ball than with today's scientifically designed marvels.

I loved listening to stories of these tennis players who traveled from tournament to tournament, barely keeping their heads above water financially. They were often relying on the hospitality of clubs or their members to keep playing the game they loved. Some earned their income more from private tennis lessons at each venue than from the little prize money available. For them, it was an adventure to see how long they could stay out there playing tournaments before their money ran out or win enough matches to reach the big time.

Thinking about tennis and my present physical condition, I realized how fortunate my coach Dick Skeen had been to stay healthy and play at a top level through his seventies. He had his hard times but never seemed to be phased by the hard knocks life threw at him. One of those times was in his first professional effort heading back east to compete against the very best. I loved to sit and listen to Dick recount this and other adventures for anyone willing to listen. Even then he only shared with his most intimate tennis friends.

Dick Skeen traveled back east to play his first professional tennis tournament, only to discover his current funds were not going to be sufficient to pay his way back to California. If he lost early in the tournament, he would find himself in a very difficult situation. Dick knew he had to win a few rounds. He ended up having blisters on both feet from running down every shot his opponent hit in his direction. His career allowed him to compete evenly and win matches against some of the greats and legends of tennis. One year losing to Fred Perry in the finals of the year-end Pro Championships. This only happened because of his love of the game, his amazing talent, and willingness to endure whatever hardships he faced. His perseverance allowed him to play the sport he loved at the professional level.

Dick related that the professionals back then were like a troupe of vagabonds going from city to city, similar to a carnival show. They would play an event anywhere they could draw a crowd to pay their way to the next tournament. They were a close-knit group, even if some personalities would rub others the wrong way. Dick said this always made it interesting, as he was the one who could definitely rub the other players the wrong way. They all had their own story to tell and intimately knew they could not live this tennis life without the other committed and talented tennis enthusiasts on the other side of the net. There was a respect and appreciation for the sport of tennis, not knowing then what their beloved sport would eventually become. These professionals were criticized for accepting money to play tennis by the amateur organizations around the world. The amateur and Grand Slam organizations somehow felt threatened by money compensation, even though most, if not all, the better amateur players received money under the table to play certain events. While the deans of the tennis world sat high in their ivory white towers, they couldn't help loving and watching the skills this marauding group of professional performers displayed. These professionals were taking the sport of tennis to a new level. Amateur organizations couldn't deny their positive influence of inspiring more and more people and youngsters like myself to take up tennis.

Listening to former tennis greats like Fred Perry, Don Budge, Bill Tilden, or Dick Skeen recount the early years of pro tennis always brought to life an idyllic softer time where tennis felt pure and unsullied by the mass marketing, huge money frenzy we see today. They were the pioneers who sacrificed and created what we now see at every tournament around the world. The dazzling talent displayed nowadays with the new equipment is great to watch. I am not sure if today's tennis would be everything these pioneers would have hoped for, but the evolution is here to stay. Sure, it is great to see the financial rewards players receive, but at what cost? Has the love of the sport of tennis been replaced by the love for the almighty dollar? Who knows, only time will tell.

The days are gone where you would see a player overrule a line call to favor their opponent. Fairness and honor have been replaced at times with an "anything goes, win" mentality. This can easily be seen in junior tennis all the way through lower-level open events where players can still call their own lines.

How has tennis evolved? In today's world, everyone is an expert as hundreds of thousands of parents around the world are encouraging their children to play from age four or five. Many are hoping their children will become fabulously rich tennis pros in the future. At the worst, they will have their university degree paid for. Maybe these young prodigies are their parents secret retirement program? Oh, for the days when life seemed simple!

Tennis is not a game of cookie-cutter mentality where someone's game can easily be stamped out perfectly like a factory. Tennis is one game with a thousand ways to play it. Tennis is played differently depending on each individual's body type and personality. It is sad when you see the pressure put on these youngsters nowadays to win and hit perfectly. The innocence of the pure sport of tennis seems almost gone at times until we witness the Federer types who still bring us back to the nostalgic days of the past where a player would make a call in his opponent's favor because it was the right and fair thing to do.

Lying paralyzed in the hospital bed, I couldn't help but think how lucky I was to have positive role models who taught me to enjoy the purity of fair competition. I think I competed as hard as anyone but never felt winning was more important than competing honestly. The exhilaration of playing well, when matched up against a player of equal ability, left me not really caring if I had won or lost the match. The respect for your opponent transcends the end result, no matter how much you desire to win. The best tennis players understand they need each other to enjoy the tennis abilities they have acquired. Life is the same as we all need each other to enjoy our God-given talents. Without those around us to share with, life would become very lonely and boring. At that very moment in the hospital, I was wondering, *Would I ever be able to experience my life as it was or my athletic abilities again?*

Where has the time gone where tennis players would sit around talking about matches and points, which seemed magical, recounting a partner diving for a shot to win an important point while sharing a drink courtside. Then there was a time where you saw a player hit an overhead off an overhead, reacting impossibly fast as the ball bounced at 100 mph right in front of him, hitting another overhead back to win the point or another time being thrilled watching as a player jumped over a courtside bench to reach and hit the ball over his shoulder, finding an impossible angle back over the net for a winner.

Nastase hit one of his many magical shots when playing on Wimbledon's Centre Court one year. He was in a close encounter and made one of the great efforts of his career. He had come to net, and his opponent hit what appeared to be a perfect topspin lob to win the point. I was standing in the front row of the standing-room-only area. I watched incredulously as one of the fastest tennis players ever turned and raced backward to retrieve the lob. It seemed crazy to even attempt, but what seemed like lightning speed, Nastase chased backward on that extralarge Centre Court and started sliding. While nearly doing the splits, he reached behind him and hit a perfect winner back down the line. He was facing backward to the court when he hit the ball, not knowing for certain if his ball went in. The crowd went crazy and erupted in applause, and his opponent had no resolve after losing this point. Nastase went on to win an inspired match.

These were the times when the real magic and mystery of a great sport really live. A similar experience happened to me when playing the Southern Circuit years ago. My partner Richie Cleveland made what seemed like an impossible shot to lift us over the number 1 seeds in our first-round encounter. We were playing on clay courts and found ourselves in a very hard-fought first set. When our opponents hit a seemingly perfectly angled drop shot, it looked to be a winning shot. Richie was near the baseline, and the shot was angled sharply away from me. When Richie took off running to reach the ball, I thought, *Impossible. The ball would surely bounce twice before he can reach it. Why is he even trying?*

I had a ringside seat to witness his near-impossible get and then hit a perfectly executed shot. With a final lunge forward, sliding on the clay, Richie reached forward getting his racket under the ball only a couple of inches off the ground. He was close to the net and outside the doubles sideline and net post. He then hit the ball perfectly back across the face of the net with the ball staying on our side until the last possible moment, right in front of me. Finally crossing to their side of the net, the ball landed on their doubles sideline only a foot from the net. This one shot changed the momentum of the match, allowing us to eventually win and defeat the number 1 seeds. It was these magical moments that made tennis worth playing and then retelling the encounter over and over again.

The days of Budge, Perry, Tilden, Skeen, Kramer, Laver, "Little Mo," Althea Gibson, Pauline Betz, Louise Brough, or Arthur Ashe are gone forever. But the memories conjured up by their past exploits should never be forgotten. It was a time of innocence, hard work, and great joy for a sport that deserves to be loved and remembered. Because everything nowadays is documented and cataloged so well, we tend to forget how important and powerful our imagination is. Roger Federer conjured up these same magical feelings nowadays, as we watched him glide effortlessly around the court, producing shots that captivate our imagination. This was why Roger was always a fan favorite year after year. He seemed to have developed the spirit of the past in today's high-pressured professional world of tennis.

What difference does it make if a story is embellished or changed slightly over time? Just the retelling, makes it come alive again. Instead of having young people live in a pressure cooker, we should teach them the integrity of honor and good sportsmanship while relating these magical moments to enliven and exhort more of them to play their best. We should inspire them to investigate and read about the past greats and live in a world of magical experiences so they too can recount to their kids and grandkids the magic they experience and the history behind it. This magic is still out there for those willing to take this priceless adventure.

Idyllic days of summer still exist in our fast-paced world. If you look close enough, you can still see your favorite tennis player in the billowing white clouds racing across a pure blue sky!

Now with a broken-up body bringing up magical thoughts of my past allowed my ever-present pain to almost disappear. Our imagination can give us strength to move forward. Positive memories and images of those accomplishing the seemingly impossible gave me inspiration to keep doing my best to improve and believe it was possible for me to do the seemingly impossible—walk and run again.

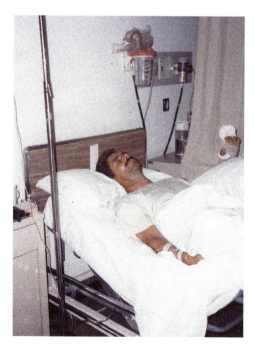

Paralyzed

I DO IT ALL

As I lay there with a broken body and continued daydreaming, I thought of my first summer of tennis and how I was encouraged to enter the No-Champions Tennis Tournament. I was surprised with my results of winning, thanks in no small part, to my brother Ken not being eligible. He was the returning city champion for the eighth grade. This simple tournament win was the catalyst for my love of tennis. In every other sport, only the coach received the trophy after we would win a championship. Winning this tennis tournament, I had been given my own trophy to keep!

Then my thoughts turned to my first big disappointment. Now years later and lying in a hospital bed, it didn't seem so big. It was, however, the second definitive moment in, not only my young life but also for our entire family.

Number 2. My dad was given the opportunity to teach school in Marin County across the Golden Gate Bridge from San Francisco. This happened right after I had won my second Idaho State singles and doubles titles. For a second consecutive year, I had qualified for the nationals. I was looking forward to again competing at the nationals in the sixteen-and-under event. This was the first year they changed from fifteen and under to sixteen and under for USTA events. I was looking forward to improving my results from the previous year.

Life continued to throw us curve balls, and this was a major curve ball for me personally. This sudden disruption took away my opportunity to play the national tournament in Corpus Christi, Texas. Moving to California only increased my love of tennis. California and Florida were the heartland of tennis in the States during the midsixties. We didn't have the money for me to play tennis tournaments, but I still played number 1 on my high school teams in California, beating some national-level players in league matches.

I ended up with a small college tennis scholarship in Southern California and was able to improve enough to play challenger-level professional events. Playing these events took me across the US, England, and later on to Asia.

I was very fortunate to earn enough of a reputation playing and teaching tennis to open up the opportunity to relocate my family to

Asia. That was the over simplified journey of how I physically ended up superglued to a road at the bottom of a steep hill on that fateful morning in Clearwater Bay in Hong Kong.

LIFE GETS... COMPLICATED

Ever since I can remember, I have wanted to be a good and respected father and husband like my dad had always demonstrated to me and my siblings. He had set a great example for us children to follow when growing up. My dad worked hard putting food on the table but never seemed to lack time to spend with us children. Ken and I benefited most as we were involved in one sport after another year around. Our dad loved sports and the opportunity to teach and work with us in every sport possible. He enjoyed watching us play different sports regardless of the season or activity. He deeply loved our mom, setting a wonderful example of a good husband. We went to church three times a week, which produced a positive spiritual and moral influence. This combination gave us a solid grounding and security with our family and life in general.

We knew we were loved, no matter what the circumstance. I always desired to create the same environment for my family. Lying there helpless, I thought, *Had I always done what was necessary to make my family unit strong?* Was I also making sure my family knew they were first in my mind, like my father had been for us? If I was honest, I would have to say my desire for recognition and success in the world's eyes became far too important for me.

When first married, I still had aspirations of playing tennis on the major circuit, and every activity was designed to direct me toward achieving that goal, no matter the sacrifices I needed to make. I was so focused on what I needed to do, I didn't notice my family might also be sacrificing. My attention to my family was less than my father had been for me and our family growing up in the fifties and sixties.

My desire for personal success led me to various jobs while still playing as much tennis as possible. These positions included director of tennis, tennis teaching, owning a club, running resorts, owning fitness centers, consulting on an ATP event, commentating for ATP, WTA, and the Olympics. These were just some of the activities, which took up time during my every busier days. All this was exhilarating, exciting, and challenging for me as I relished this lifestyle and the recognition that came with it. But how did this affect my family? Was it creating a better marriage? Was my lifestyle building a strong family unit for my children? Or was it slowly tearing my family apart at the seams under the guise of being a great provider? Buying my family off with worldly goods or holidays and summers back in the States for the sake of my exposure and reputation was actually creating a divided family. This was not a good tradeoff, but the busyness of my success blinded me completely.

Then when I thought I couldn't be any busier, triathlon came on the scene. It is amazing how much your mind can wander when you can do very little but lay paralyzed in bed, with nothing else to do but think. Had it really been six years since I arrived in Hong Kong from the States? I thought back to my arrival and the impact it had, not only on my life but also my wife and our children's lives.

BRIGHT LIGHTS AND LURE OF ASIA

My life seemed almost perfect after transferring to Asia on Thanksgiving Day 1986. In the twinkling of an eye, it seems life can change quicker than we possibly think. One month earlier, I would not have dreamed of heading out on a plane to Hong Kong. So much transpired so fast that it made my head swim thinking about how it had taken place so unexpectedly. A phone call from a stranger just three weeks before had changed everything for us as a family. An unexpected offer to accept a position in Asia sounded crazy. How could a person half a world away even know who I was? Just as crazy was how quickly I accepted what seemed like the offer of a lifetime. There I was on a flight by myself, which would completely change my life, my wife's life, and our children's lives forever.

After flying for fifteen hours and what seemed like halfway around the world, I—along with all the other passengers—was ready to touch down and finally experience Hong Kong personally. The approach into Hong Kong's Kai Tak famous airport was something every visitor to Hong Kong never forgot. It was like no other major airport approach in the world. Finally seeing land again, we could see Hong Kong island with its tall high-rise buildings stretching up toward the famous high point of the Peak Restaurant across the iconic Hong Kong Harbour before coming in low over the high-rise apartments on Kowloon side. Suddenly, the plane banked sharply to the right, instantly finding yourself looking straight into the apartment buildings on the approach path. You could see people watching TV, eating dinner, or doing their laundry inside their apartments stacked one on top of another. Then slipping by one restaurant named Near Miss, we breathlessly watched as the plane leveled out, passing over one of Hong Kong's many elevated roadways. The runway was very short by international standards. After touching down, the pilot hit full reverse thrusters coming to a quick stop. This only added to the excitement when finally touching down to earth again. Stopping what appeared just short of the watery edge of Hong Kong's Victoria Harbor made us feel like we had just avoided slipping into a watery grave.

Never really knowing why, I felt right at home the minute I stepped off the plane onto the Kai Tak tarmac. There were no gangways taking us directly into the terminal in 1986, so we exited the plane down the aircraft's stairs to the hot humid tarmac, with buses finally transporting us to the terminal. Hong Kong was one of those visually stimulating cities that captivates the imagination the minute you arrive. Canyon-like roads leaving the airport were gray and foreboding except for the myriad of clotheslines protruding from every apartment. Every type of colorful garment was waving from these lines like small national flags of their own. I felt like of small child with my face glued to the window wanting to take it all in at once. Kowloon gave off the old-world feeling of Hong Kong back then, passing near the Walled City, now torn down, on the way to our next destination. After traveling through the Harbour Tunnel, I found myself in a totally different environment of Hong Kong Island. A modern city with glitzy high-rises and new elevated expressways unfolded before my eyes.

I had the opportunity to stay in Hong Kong for a few days after I arrived. I enjoyed every new sight, sound, and smell, reveling in the mix of the old-world feeling and its new modern society. After living in the quiet country setting of Little Applegate Valley, Oregon, I had trouble sleeping the first few nights. I could actually feel the vibration of the city, which literally never sleeps. Even with the opportunity of staying in the relative quiet area of Repulse Bay on the south side of Hong Kong island, the vibration could still be felt. Staying with a fellow tennis pro, the setting was beautiful, looking out over the calm waters of Repulse Bay.

As much as I enjoyed Hong Kong, I had to leave for my intended destination of Macau. I had arrived in Asia to be the director of tennis and squash at Hyatt's Taipa Island Resort in Macau. Macau, a Jetfoil ride from Hong Kong, was the old Portuguese enclave that once served as the pirate haven of the South China Sea. When arriving there in 1986, there was little sign of Western civilization on Taipa or Macau for that matter, except for a few hotel casinos on the peninsula, and the Hyatt Hotel and Taipa Island Resort. As much different as Hong Kong was from the sedate country life I'd gotten used to living in the states, Macau was equally different from Hong Kong.

Macau, also known as the Monte Carlo or Las Vegas of the Far East, existed largely—if not completely—through the gambling money flowing through there daily. A million-dollars-a-day net profit for the Lisboa Casino was impressive back then, considering Macau consisted of only six square miles of land divided almost equally between a peninsula and two islands connected by a bridge and a causeway. There were 500,000 people living on that small plot of earth when I arrived. The census statistic made it the most populated country (territory) on earth per square mile. Macau was another culture shock for me, but just like Hong Kong, I loved it from the very beginning. I felt right at home, settling into life as tennis director and teaching pro running the tennis and squash programs.

Macau was an amazing experience for visitors, whether you stayed in the resort, which could have been anywhere in the world except for the stunning view of the Buddhist temple looking down from the hillside beside the resort or eating huge plates of shrimp in Taipa Village or curried crabs at the famous Fernando's Restaurant located at the far end of Coloane Islands' Black Sand Beach. Once I was assured my position was secure, I sent for my family, and we were all back together within six weeks of my arrival. We spent a few months living in a suite at the Hyatt Hotel, which my children loved. They were able to have access to the many activities and swim in the large tropical pool. We eventually transferred to the Baguio Court

Apartment complex on the Peninsula side of Macau, where the main population lived and worked.

Baguio Court was right next to the famous Macau Formula 3 Grand Prix race course and backed up to the hilltop park behind the apartment complex. From our rooftop apartment perched high on the hill above the Macau Ferry Pier, we could look out on the only blue waters of the Macau Reservoir, next to the Jai Alai Stadium. The ocean waters surrounding Macau were always brown because of the massive amounts of silt washing down from China, collecting pollution along the way. On the other side of Baguio Court was Macau's hilltop park where you would witness dozens of Chinese doing their early morning Tai Chi. Just beyond the park, you would discover the older, almost ancient sections of the peninsula.

The older restaurants and herbal shops were located in this area. My two sons found themselves wandering these streets and alleyways when they had free time or they were playing hooky from school. Don and Brian discovered places I would have never found on my own if it had not been for their inquisitiveness. They eventually introduced me to many of these historic sites and sounds. The old tunnels from World War II under the hill, the Lookout, the Macau Fort and gun placements, along with the famous Façade, were some of the haunts we were able to share and explore together. Macau contained many old, even ancient-feeling, districts to explore. You could easily get away and relax in their secluded, peaceful, and quiet hidden retreats. These were Chinese manicured gardens, which had not changed in hundreds of years, waiting to be explored. One of the memories remaining with every visitor were the aromas pungently wafting on any slight breeze from the numerous herbal shops with restaurants and incense sticks burning in front of each business.

When my parents arrived in Macau for a wonderful holiday, my dad asked my sons, "What is your favorite place?" After all their adventuring, you would have thought it would have been one of the many famous sites they had discovered, but with no hesitation, they responded, "McDonald's!" McDonald's had recently celebrated their grand opening in Macau eight months after our arrival. After eating only Chinese cuisine for a week, my dad understood why my sons said McDonald's. He, Brian, and Donnie would sneak out at times to take in a "McDonald's break."

My parents came to Macau to visit and spend a holiday with my family and experience this part of Asia. I had not known until they arrived that my dad's secret ambition in life had always been to visit Asia or "The Orient," as he used to call it. Both my parents loved visiting Macau and China, but my dad especially enjoyed his time delving into the Asian culture. He had the opportunity to ride bikes around Taipa with his grandsons, then we all visited rock quarries in China while taking a two-day trip to old Canton, now name Guangzhou. Most memorable for me was watching my dad play Santa Claus riding down Main Street in the center of Macau during their Christmas celebration. My dad's white hair glistened, and he had just the right amount of extra fat around his waist to convince numerous Macanese children he might actually be the real Santa. He couldn't stop smiling as he threw small gifts of candy and sweets to the crowds of children and adults lining the main boulevard. It really did turn out to be "his trip of a lifetime."

Conjuring up these wonderful memories of Macau while lying helpless on a hospital bed couldn't help but bring smiles to my face. I was blessed with so many amazing memories continually flashing through my mind to keep me company. I could raise my left arm high, wiggling my fingers, and flex my right arm for some exercise while continually making every effort to eventually move and feel my toes. Recalling each memory of Macau in vivid detail and colors made me realize my journey was filled with many wonders and blessings. My mind raced through the days and months we were privileged to live there, even though it was only a small dot of land nestled on China's southern border.

My family and I were living an amazing life melting into the Macanese community. Being Macau's only real resort at that time, Taipa Island Resort served most of the influential businesspersons. This gave me the opportunity to be the guest of honor at numerous functions around Macau. Being guest of honor at local Macanese restaurants provided many interesting eating experiences for this Idaho boy who grew up on meat and potatoes. Growing up in the

US, I had never been given the opportunity to encounter the variety of food this area of the world had available. Local restaurants and chefs never wasted anything. These amazing chefs used every part of an animal and found a way to cook and eat it all. I learned very quickly that what Westerners threw away was somehow considered to be a delicacy or had some medicinal or viral quality to be desired.

When my resort staff invited me to a local Chinese restaurant on The Peninsula one evening, we were warmly greeted and immediately ushered up to the private dining room. The owner rushed in to greet me and excitedly said he would cook a special delicacy in my honor. A sense of foreboding swept over me as I had been in Macau long enough by then to know what would arrive would most likely be unrecognizable by sight or smell. I also knew it was no choice whether to eat or not to eat. Eat or risk having the owner "lose face." While living in Macau, I ate many specialty dishes that I still have no idea what was served. Once while visiting China and enjoying an omelet, the owner remarked that he had never seen a Westerner eat the dish placed in front of them with such enjoyment. Suddenly looking closely at my breakfast, he informed me what I thought was a simple omelet was a worm omelet. Peering down at my plate, I could see what I had mistakenly thought were spices were actually tiny centipedes with their little legs visible on closer inspection. An abundance of these centipedes can be found in the local rice fields. Extra protein for a fit athlete is always a good idea, right? This breakfast may have been one of the reasons I became a vegetarian a few years later.

Smiles etched across my face as I called up many more wonderful memories. Late one evening, my Macanese staff again offered to take me to another unique Macau eatery. This time to a secluded garden restaurant not far from the Macau Hyatt. This restaurant was a local outdoor barbeque business. It was located in a heavily overgrown jungle-like setting. Over twenty of us were sitting at a long table, and it wasn't long before we were served some unusual dishes. After enjoying a few recognizable dishes, the unusual started to appear. I was taken aback when the next offering arrived. Looking down at my plate, I found a tiny sparrow squashed between two metal meshes. This tiny bird had been barbequed between this mesh without any preparation. Its feathers had burned away in the hot fires, charcoaling the meat to a dark brown and black. The tiny bird was then set before us to be eaten. I watched as my staff dug into this dish, devouring this tiny little sparrow in a few bites. This was one time I had to refuse, but one excited member of my staff jumped at the opportunity to gobbled my portion down.

Macau

The texture and fabric of Macau continued to surprise anyone staying longer than a few days for a holiday to gamble. Macau had been ruled or influenced by the Portuguese for five hundred years and thus the term Macanese. Everywhere you turn, you are surprised by the variety of cultures and nationalities represented. The upmarket stores or famous restaurants dotted around the maze of winding streets are some of the many wonders waiting for those willing to exit the main avenues and famous gambling establishments. Visitors are instead encouraged to head in the direction of the many casinos. It may be fun for some to gamble away their life savings, but you will only understand the real Macau once you take time to discover the variety of food found in many unique Portuguese restaurants. The A Lorcha following the Avenue da Republica far enough along the waterfront is just one I was able to enjoy. Then you could take the opportunity to stay in the Pousada De São Tiago Castle Hotel for a true feeling of years gone by.

Most people only judge Macau by its glitzy cover once arriving by Jetfoil. They are herded like cattle straight onto one of the many casino buses. Once aboard, they are driven to one of the various casino hotels, where they stay cloistered during their stay. As wonderful as it is to stay at the Venetian, you can easily miss out on experiencing the multilayered pages of Macau. Macau is a true living organism still containing a rich past, amazing present, and glitzy future.

Mr. Luk

Moving to Macau allowed me to view a kaleidoscope of cultures and individuals. The amazing colors of Macau were not limited to the different districts, islands, foods, and bewitching odors. The people who had chosen Macau home were just as varied and mesmerizing. One of the individuals I was honored to meet in Macau was a gentleman who surprised me when he voluntarily opened up the inside pages of his life for me and my family to experience.

Mr. Luk was a businessman whom I met as general manager of Taipa Island Resort and Head Tennis pro. Mr. Luk joined the club and signed up for a series of tennis lessons for himself and his sons. Mr. Luk was warm, engaging, and had been living in Macau for a number of years after escaping China during the Cultural Revolution. He was short, plump, and always looked rather jolly. Teaching him tennis allowed us to become good friends. We would often take a rest following our court time at the Poolside Flamingo Restaurant. I enjoyed his lessons but enjoyed our chats even more. The resort provided a wonderful environment to learn more of each other. Sitting poolside with a cold tropical fruit drink, watching the Mandarin ducks floating across the pond always allowed us to relax in the shade of an umbrella. He shared how he wanted to give his boys the opportunity to study in Canada when they finished their high school degree in Macau.

Even though Mr. Luk became very successful after his arrival in Macau, he wanted to give his boys the experience of Canada's western culture and worldview. Mr. Luk had journeyed to Macau at the right time and grabbed up the opportunity to acquire the rights to trade goods through Macau. He was a garment manufacturer with a very large business. The amount of garments a business could sell overseas were later limited. With his original allotment guaranteed, Mr. Luk was well-off. He would use a portion of his allotment for himself, then lease out the remaining allotments to other businessmen who needed to move their garments overseas.

This appeared to be pretty much Mr. Luk's story when we were first getting acquainted. I had definitely misjudged him during his

I DO IT ALL

first few tennis lessons. I thought he was just an average office worker as many local Chinese are. My initial impression of Mr. Luk had proven wrong, following our tennis lessons and poolside lunches. I was still only looking at the well-worn cover of his life's book.

Viewing some of the inside pages of his life, I stood amazed at how successful he had become. He had seen his garment business grow to a large international distribution. As with many others I met through my travels, with Mr. Luk, there was much more to discover. When my parents came to Macau, Mr. Luk and my father became friends. Watching them together, you would have thought they had been lifelong acquaintances. It was wonderful to see these two sitting poolside, chatting away like old school buddies.

One day Mr. Luk invited my family and parents for dinner at the famous Lisboa Hotel. When we arrived, Mr. Luk was already there leading us to a private dining room reserved for our evening meal. Surprisingly, we found another Chinese gentleman already seated at the large table. Once Mr. Luk showed us to our prearranged seating, he proudly introduced us to his childhood best friend, who would be sharing the evening meal with us.

Sharing dinner with Mr. Luk and his friend was when the more private inner pages of Mr. Luk's remarkable life's story opened up for us to view in all its wild splendor and heartbreak. Over dinner, Mr. Luk shared how he and his best friend had grown up in Mainland China during the start of the Cultural Revolution. They had both been part of the privileged upper class or academia in the Shanghai region. When the cultural revolution began gathering up all the academia for execution or sending them to reeducation camps, both Mr. Luk and his friend fled for Macau to escape persecution promised for them if they stayed in China.

Mr. Luk had been the fortunate one, making it across the border into Macau, just before the border closed to start his wonderfully successful career and new life. However, his friend had been detained before reaching the border and spent years in reeducation camps doing hard labor, forbidden to even read a book. Mr. Luk's good friend had wilted into submission with the abusive treatment. He now sat almost motionless, looking submissive as we listened to Mr. Luk recount how their lives had taken such unexpected and divergent paths. My heart ached for his friend. His misfortune had separated them, but it was obvious their friendship remained solid through the years. For myself, I sat in awe as I viewed Mr. Luk with a completely different perspective and respect. The pages of his life's book had fluttered open to reveal how little I really knew about my friend. This reminded me again to "never judge a book by its cover!"

Almost every successful person I have met seemed to have overcome severe hardships before becoming the successful achiever everyone ends up experiencing. I am always humbled when given the opportunity to learn their life stories.

What were the pages of my life's book going to look like now that I was paralyzed and helpless to even take care of myself. These memories made me smile, but there was still a deepening sadness as I realized my life might never be what it was before April 22, 1992. I still felt fortunate not to have endured the treatment Mr. Luk's friend had encountered. Even given my present injuries, I knew I was the fortunate one.

Macau surprises

Being the guest of honor during local Chinese celebrations also offered a chance to participate in their yearly festivals. Chinese New Year fireworks didn't last an hour or for one evening like the Fourth of July in the States. I had been told the celebration would last for ten days, but I had no idea what that actually meant. Fireworks could be heard nonstop for ten days, twenty-four hours a day! There seemed to be no end to the loud explosions and popping of fireworks. There was also no apparent control or regulations. When walking along Macau's waterfront, you felt like you took your life in your hands. Dozens of firework stalls lined the promenade with everyone buying fireworks and immediately firing off their purchase on the wide walkways. They seemed to be whizzing over your head every few seconds. Why there weren't multiple injuries, I don't know, but we were there as a family enjoying every minute of their celebration. One firework stall actually caught fire one evening from the mayhem. This provided extra excitement with fireworks shooting in every direction, causing everyone to scramble for cover. The locals hardly took notice as the fire was quickly extinguished. You could then continue ducking more fireworks as you walked along the waterfront.

    The Dragon Boat Festival provided another opportunity for members and staff at Taipa Island Resort to participate in one of Macau's yearly featured festivals. We had often seen the local fishermen practicing their dragon boat skills in a few inlets around Macau. We became intrigued. It wasn't long before we organized a Taipa Island Resort Dragon Boat team of our own made up of mostly Westerners. We thought we could show the local teams a thing or two as several of our team members had been on university rowing teams in Europe. One day, when we were out practicing in the brown waters near the ferry pier, a large wave from a Hong Kong ferry tipped our boat violently to the side, tossing our Australian coxman headlong into the brown silt. It was low tide, and the water was only a few feet deep, so his head went straight into the soft gooey silt at the bottom. Murray eventually worked his way free, coming up with brown sticky goo stuck to his skin from his shoulders up. Sewage treatment was not a major priority, or any priority, at that time in Macau. The seaside smelled like a sewer at low tide with rats darting back and forth amid the debris. You can imagine what this silt was made of. Once comments and laughs finished, there was an urgency to get ashore and help our Australian fitness director get scraped off and cleaned up. Murray was diagnosed with a serious health problem later that year. Maybe this was a factor in his health issues?

    We were all fired up and excited when the Dragon Boat Race day finally arrived. We were hoping to go for gold. Anticipation was in the air as we expected to show some serious speed on the course. We were probably the first *gweilo* team to ever enter in Macau and wanted to make a good impression on the locals and surprise the more experienced teams. We definitely made an impression and surprised the other teams, but speed not so much. When the gun fired off, our oarsman found our oar had been tampered with and came completely loose. Our dragon boat veered sharply to the right, narrowly missing the next boat. With this loose oar, he then overcompensated, sending us sharply to the left. Our boat was all over the course, weaving left and right instead of straight down the course. All of us were paddling like crazy as we watched the other boats stream away down their proper lanes. We were finally able to straighten out and edged our way past the two slowest boats to finish in seventh place.

We did make an impression as everyone along the waterfront and in the grandstands were laughing and cheering as hard as they could when we finally floated by. Except for one serious-minded member of our boat, we were laughing so hard at the finish line we could barely keep rowing. The local *gweilos*, as they called Westerners in this part of Asia, had learned some valuable and needed respect for the local dragon boat specialists.

Now, lying helpless in Hong Kong, I couldn't help smiling and laughing a little as more of these wonderful memories and experiences kept flashing through my mind. Were these good times all behind me now? What would happen with my life in the future? I had some wonderful memories and couldn't imagine a life without many more exciting and challenging experiences filling my weeks, months, and years ahead. More memories of my Asian experience filled my mind with positive images, as I was being "treated" at the Chinese hospital and waiting for my first diagnosis.

Career-wise, things started to go well within my first month in Macau. Hyatt Hotel International Asian Pacific asked me to become Taipa Island Resort manager. They had reviewed my resume and offer me the job when the position suddenly opened up. I was asked to keep my current position as director of tennis/squash and head teaching pro. I was now busy seven days a week, twelve or more hours a day, and loving every minute of it.

Hong Kong visitors were common in my teaching schedule. A couple of my more notable students were Brian Langley and Patricia Hy. Brian was the main presenter for sports at TVB, and Patricia Hy was one of the top WTA professional tennis players in Asia. Patricia wasn't really a student, but her father and coach would come to Macau now and then for me to workout with Patricia. Having Patricia and her father HyNy arrive for a hit was always great as it broke up my normal day and teaching schedule.

I DO IT ALL

Serving in Macau

TVB, where Brian Langley worked, was the main English language station in Hong Kong. After a few oncourt tennis lessons, Brian asked if I would consider hosting the French Open Grand Slam commentary with him. This was only one of the many unexpected opportunities that came my way in Asia. I accepted Brian's offer and had a wonderful time joining him for the French Open broadcast. Brian and I instantly connected, forging a lasting friendship. My French Open commentary was well-received in Hong Kong, so I was honored and blessed when he asked me to accompany him for the final two Grand Slams of the year. After successfully commentating on Wimbledon and the US Open, TVB again indicated my commentary was positive with the Hong Kong audience. This began a long-term relationship with TVB, Brian Langley, and then his replacement Andrew Sams. Brian was recruited to work for Star

TV as their main sports presenter. Andrew and I became very good friends and have remained friends through the years. Brian Langley had requested me to join him at Star TV, but famous Indian professional, Veja Amritraj had expressed an interest and was from Asia. Veja ended up with the Star TV position. I stayed with TVB and loved working with Andrew.

Memories of TVB and commentating on all major sporting events was a wonderful and cherished experience. The big question on my mind at that moment was, "Would Andrew and TVB still want me for more commentaries in the future, considering my present and future physical condition?" Everything about my future was a foggy blur as I lay there in pain. Somehow I remained positive while conjuring up more wonderful memories. These remembrances continued to bring a smile, even if it was only on the inside. I couldn't help smiling on the outside as well as I thought more about my introduction to Asia and my Macanese experience.

I loved teaching tennis to the local Macanese and began learning some Cantonese. One day, while teaching Mr. Luk, I used some of my newly acquired Cantonese. After a few attempts using the same phase, he came to the net, politely asking me to teach only in English. My pronunciation of some Cantonese words were causing a few ladies gathered courtside some embarrassment. In Chinese, the same word spoken with slightly different inflections can have completely different meanings. I never found out what I was saying, but to avoid embarrassing my students or spectators in the future, I made sure I taught only in English. Every time I thought of Mr. Luk, this incident brought a smile to my face. What had I been saying? Mr. Luk was also the one who had convinced my dad that McDonald's was the only way for a Westerner to comfortably eat in Macau. He had offered my dad snake or *sneck*, as he pronounced it, when my dad was guest of honor that one evening at the Lisboa Hotel and Casino.

I enjoyed my Macanese experience, as the famous five-hundred-year-old old-world side of Macau was still alive and vibrant. It was also just an hour's Jetfoil ride from the high-octane energy of Hong Kong.

I DO IT ALL

While I was resort manager, we had the opportunity to host Hyatt's Worldwide General Managers Meeting. For ten days, every general manager from Hyatt's top hotels and resorts worldwide converged on Macau and Taipa Island Resort. It was a great opportunity to showcase the resort and the uniqueness of Macau.

As resort manager, I arranged awards for many of the activities and competitions located in the resort. The most difficult award involved the top two directors of Hyatt International from Chicago. They both happened to be enthusiastic tennis players. Both executives scheduled tennis hitting sessions with me daily. One of the plaques to be awarded was for the most dedicated tennis player during the conference. This was proving to be a difficult task for me. I had to decide the winner of this award but did not want to offend either one of these tennis enthusiasts from Hyatt International Headquarters. I was dealing with two very motivated and powerful high-profile executives.

After much thought and a little creative thinking, there seemed to be a solution. With this, I commissioned a local trophy shop to make a special plaque for the awards ceremony. Everyone knew how much each executive wanted to win this simple but coveted award. Several of the general managers attending expressed how happy they were to leave that decision to me. Whoever won the award would be thrilled but not so much for the one who was left out. I didn't want to offend either as I had spent time every day hitting tennis balls and becoming friends with both of them.

I came up with a solution I thought would make both directors happy when I commissioned a fairly large winner's plaque. It was cut in two pieces and then glued back together to appear like one large winner's plaque. An inscription was engraved on each side and was identical except for the name of the winner. When I arranged the award speech, the ballroom went quiet in anticipation. Who would receive the award and who would be denied? The two company directors were called on stage as the award plaque was held high to be presented. Their expressed love of tennis and daily sessions were announced to be identical, so it was expressed how difficult it was to decide on a winner. There was a tense moment as the attributes of both tennis players were declared. The presenter said that I, as tennis director, had found it difficult to choose between them. So with this in mind, each director was declared a cowinner. With one loud snap, the plaque broke perfectly in half with each one receiving the coveted award. Whew, disaster averted. Each director was thrilled to have their engraved plaque to display in their executive office back in Chicago.

Many of the directors' activities took place in Macau's more scenic and famous districts. The activities varied from rickshaw rides for every GM, transporting them to famous secluded Macanese restaurants or the most memorable evening at the Old Fort. Macau Fort was elaborately decorated to resemble the centuries-old Pirate Haven of Macau. With perfectly attired male and female pirates hosting and serving the GMs and pigs roasting on huge spits, it felt like the Old Fort had spun hundreds of years back in time. The presentation was perfect for all the visiting Hyatt managers and directors. They were enthralled to be experiencing the past Old World side of Macau.

Climax of the evening came when fireworks were placed inside the huge old cannons and fired off without notifying the local authorities. Those in charge had grossly misjudged the huge explosion with fire barreling out of the antique cannons. They had sat dormant for centuries, positioned high on the old walls of the Macau Fort. This explosion sent local authorities scrambling. With sirens blaring, official vehicles charged up to the Macau Fort. There was an air of tension as a serious exchange took place before things were amicably settled. It was agreed that using the cannons for fireworks, which had sat dormant, was inadvisable as well as dangerous. This entire exchange only added to the Old World atmosphere of a "Pirate's Haven."

Macau was like that back then, as the Portuguese were happy to keep alive the pirate haven feeling, when pirates ruled this part of the South China Sea.

After a wonderful year as resort manager, I reluctantly moved to Hong Kong to take over as director of tennis and head pro of the prestigious Aberdeen Marina Club. This decision was partly made for my children's benefit, as schooling in Macau was far short of desirable. I loved living in Macau, but as good as it was for me, it was not the place for my family. My children could probably write a book about their adventures while playing hooky from their school, where they were harassed daily as the only *gweilos* (big-nosed ghosts).

The laid-back feeling of Macau was instantly replaced by the glitzy fast-paced society of Hong Kong. We were almost overwhelmed by the ever-present speed and energy of Hong Kong's society. Our lives felt like a VHS on fast-forward every time we left our apartment. I was immediately invited to play in their very competitive elite tennis league, where betting on matches made for exciting and serious play when matches were scheduled at the Chinese Recreation Club. League matches were also played at other prestigious clubs dotted around Hong Kong. Many of the foreigners playing at the Chinese Recreation Club said they felt uncomfortable, as spectator cheering could be notoriously biased for the local and regional Chinese players. For some reason, club members seemed to embrace me and my style of doubles. Playing matches at the Chinese Recreation Club was always something I looked forward to. I felt completely at-home competing in front of their billionaire members.

Loving the club's atmosphere, I enquired about joining CRC. They were very polite when they informed me that Westerners were not allowed to join. With a smirk on my face, I tried to explain I was part Chinese since my grandmother's lineage had some American Indian. "American Indians had some connection with Chinese ancestry, didn't they?" I asked. There was an awkward moment of silence until my friends realized I was not serious. I was fortunate as Hong Kong embraced me as much as I embraced the culture and its fast-paced society. Hong Kong always made me feel welcomed as I relished and enjoyed our cultural differences. Not being able to join the Chinese Recreation Club didn't stop them from inviting me to join their league tennis team a few years later. Playing league matches in Hong Kong led to wins over China's top professional doubles team and a number of other highly ranked regional players. I was having the time of my life embracing Hong Kong while playing some of the best tennis of my life.

So many good memories to conjure up when consciousness allowed me to think. There were so many positive memories. My life almost seemed like a fairy tale as I lay there reminiscing. Hong Kong seemed to make every experience exhilarating, and I couldn't get enough of the positive vibes and accolades coming my direction.

I wasn't in Hong Kong very long before I was approached to do TV sports promotional spots, then commercials and Print Ad modeling, which gained international exposure. I had the opportunity to model for United Airlines, Holiday Inn, and TV commercials for Salem Open Tennis. These all took place when I joined a couple of younger tennis pros at Victoria Park one late afternoon. I was watching them cast for a TV promotional video for the Salem Open ATP event.

When my friends finished their on-court camera shoot, the producer approached and said they were ready for me to cast for the part. I was still in my tennis clothes after leaving Aberdeen Marina Club, so he had mistaken me for one of those wanting the job. I was much older than the other tennis pros, so I was surprised they wanted me to cast for their commercial. He said it didn't make any difference in my age, as I looked midtwenties to him.

I went on the court for my casting and unexpectedly received the job for the Salem photos and video commercial. Watching the Salem Open commercial being filmed was the United Airlines representative. They had scheduled a United photoshoot in Taiwan for the following week at the famous Black Buddha Monument. They were searching for a model for their magazine advertisements. They approached me about the photoshoot. Visiting the Big Buddha of Baguashan, Changhua, was an opportunity I couldn't turn down. I was hired on the spot for this print-ad photoshoot as well. The photographer was in a bind as their previously hired US model had unexpectedly cancelled out. They happened to be in Hong Kong looking for a replacement. I seemed to constantly be in the right place at the right time in Asia until that minibus (the wrong place at the wrong time).

I DO IT ALL

Don in United Airline Ad

Suddenly, opportunities to consult for sporting events opened up. These included the same first Salem Open ATP event in Hong Kong and the Prince Asian Challenge Circuit for Asia's top junior tennis players. Salem Open ATP marketing arm contacted me to do some discreet consulting as they were having some big problems preparing for their inaugural event. Prince Racket Company asked me to put together a circuit for Asia's top junior tennis players, which had been talked about for ten years. When I agreed, I was immediately hired as Circuit Director and Administrator for the circuit. I was able to organized the first event in Thailand within one month.

The Prince Asian Challenge Circuit ran successfully for three years hosted by six different Southeast Asian countries. I then started a company, Silvereign Ltd., which hosted sporting events and consulted on the building of tennis courts and synthetic putting greens. Although most of these endeavors were not that profitable; they kept me busy and provided an avenue for me to build an excellent network of amazing friends and associates. It also kept my life busy, interesting, and exciting. I was like the Energizer bunny every single day. I then became involved with a Singapore sports consulting company as VP and partnered in a fitness center located at the Dynasty Hotel on the famous Orchard Road in Singapore.

My mind raced through all these thoughts, bringing me to that one defining moment on April 22, 1992, at 5:00 a.m. All these events led me to be lying paralyzed in a Hong Kong Chinese hospital.

Reeling backward in time again, I thought about how, through the Singapore Sports Company association and subsequent business meeting in Dasmariñas Village in Manila, I was intrigued into signing up for my first triathlon in Singapore. The other company directors and I met for a meeting in one of the most expensive housing estates called Dasmariñas Village. These villages, dotted around Manila, are secure high-walled housing estates where you are required to pass through imposing gates with armed guards. Once documented as an approved guest, you enter an almost fairy-tale quiet environment compared to the loud, busy, and polluted roads just outside the walls near downtown Manila. It felt like you had entered an area similar to what I found in Beverly Hills, California.

Once arriving at the director's home, we were approached by two additional armed guards. One guard was holding a sawed-off shotgun, the other, some kind of automatic weapon. A quick call to the main house allowed us to pass through into the elegant setting of landscaped gardens, swimming pool, and beautiful mansion-like interior. After business was discussed by the pool over a simple lunch, conversation quickly turned to recreational interests.

My fellow directors talked about competing in an upcoming triathlon in Singapore ten weeks later. They indicated it was best for me not to enter as they felt tennis players were not fit enough to attempt a triathlon. They also said, "At forty-one, it might be too difficult for you to even complete the event, especially since you have no triathlon experience." I had never trained for a triathlon, but triathlons had always intrigued me. Although not a competitive swimmer, I had grown up swimming in Idaho and felt fairly competent. I had ridden bikes my whole life and felt like I could run. After all, I was known to be very quick on a tennis court. That one insulting comment by the pool was just enough to entice me to enter the Singapore event. They had no idea I had finished the twenty-kilometer Pear Blossom Run in Medford, Oregon, years before, so why not give it a go? I am doing everything else. Why not "do it all" by entering my first triathlon?

Pat Dixon

My first foray into triathlon happened by accident because of that meeting in Manila with my associates. My fellow directors were judging my overall fitness because I was a tennis teaching pro. They weren't aware I was still playing open-level competitive tennis events in the region. They were, however, aware of my age and that I knew very little about what it took to complete a triathlon. Each one of them had at least some triathlon experience and thought it would be too difficult for me, a tennis teaching pro to even finish the event, being the oldest director. They were thinking, "What could Don possibly know about the effort required to complete a triathlon." And they were right.

I couldn't blame them as I had only completed one distant race in my life. I had entered the famous twenty-kilometer Pear Blossom Run in Medford, Oregon, a few years before moving to Asia. Just like triathlon, I hadn't known anything about long-distance running back then. I entered the Pear Blossom Run for almost the same reason. That was after being encouraged and egged on by one of my top junior tennis students, Will Forsythe. His entire family were runners, and he thought it would be good for me to sign up and give it a go. I guess he thought I could do anything.

In Medford, I was a novice distant runner, and my preparation was not adequate for what it took to complete the twenty-kilometer event. I was only able to do a few long-distance runs before the race but felt I would at least be able to finish given my excellent tennis fitness. I was completely surprised when I encountered thousands of dedicated running enthusiasts lined up for a few blocks to start the race. The Pear Blossom half marathon was one of the largest races of its distance in the States at that time. Many famous distance runners would travel to Medford to line up. Once the race started, I was fortunate to encounter an experienced distance runner twelve years older than myself. She and I were running about the same pace next to each other for the first few kilometers. I felt comfortable running her pace and we eventually introduced ourselves. I asked if it was okay for me to run alongside her? Due to my lack of experience, I thought it might help me to comfortably finish the event.

At first glance, she gave me the feeling she had been running her whole life. She looked very fit and very comfortably running with a nice cadence. It didn't look too fast for me to stay with her. It wasn't long before she agreed to run with me for the final seventeen kilometers "if I could keep up with her." Curiously, she asked if I was willing to carry her huge stopwatch, periodically requesting her time splits. I thought it was cute that she was keeping such close track of her time and didn't mind accommodating her requests. She was letting me feel comfortable with my run, pacing beside her. Running with her kept me moving down the road at a steady clip.

We continued running together when suddenly at eighteen kilometers, she started cramping up. She said she needed to stop. She also said she couldn't go on with the cramps affecting her legs. After running side by side for eighteen kilometers, I wasn't about to go on without her. We stopped a few times for her to stretch her legs, and I encouraged her to continue running after each short stretching session. She amazed me each time when she straightened up and kept running. The last few blocks to the finish line turned uphill, and she surprisingly took off for a strong finish. Charging up the final hill through the finishing tape, she left me behind, as I watched on in amazement.

I thought it was great she was so happy with her time as I watched well-wishers and media suddenly crowd around her. Crossing the finish line myself, I melted into the crowd of finishers and other people milling around. With the huge crowd crushing around her as she finished, my race number had not been taken or recorded. That was until a race official notice my number was still hanging on my race shirt. This mistake eventually led to my time being recorded some ninety seconds behind Pat. I had mistakenly thought she was just one of the thousands of recreational runners hoping to get a personal best time at the Pear Blossom Festival.

Everyone turned as a voice was yelling, "I want him, I want him." We all looked around trying to find out who sounded so desperate to find someone. Suddenly, forcing her way through the crowd, I saw Pat followed by many of the press, looking for me. She rushed up and gave me a big hug with cameras clicking away.

I had totally misjudged Pat Dixon as she was not only trying to record her personal best time, she was also setting a substantial world-record time for her age group. She exclaimed later that I was responsible for encouraging her to finish the race in a world-record time. You wouldn't have known it when seeing us together following the race. She looked great, and I looked like I was about to faint. There was a photo of us featured in the local paper and in *Runner's World* magazine recounting her world record Pear Blossom run. She looked wonderful in the photo while appearing to hold me up. We held onto each other celebrating her world record.

I was just beginning to learn not to judge a book by its cover.

The Island State

Now a few years later, was I going to let my fellow directors judge me? This one negative comment by my friends and business partners led me to get up early and train for this crazy sport of triathlon. Maybe my other directors were misjudging me, but maybe not? I was going to do everything I could to prove them wrong, even with the little time I had before race day.

I had no idea what I was getting into! We never know how one event can possibly change the course of our life. Triathlon would end up impacting my life in more ways than I could have ever imagined. Eight weeks weren't much time to train before Singapore, and I didn't even own a bicycle. Aberdeen Marina Club had a beautiful swimming pool available for my swim workouts, a stationary bike for cycle training waited for me in the gym, and, of course, the roads out and back to several beautiful inviting Hong Kong bays for my run training.

Following that Manila meeting, I arrived back in Hong Kong with the simple goal of making sure I finished this triathlon. The Singapore Triathlon consisted of a two-kilometer swim, seventy-one-kilometer bike, and a sixteen-kilometer run. It wasn't long before my triathlon training surprised me and I began finding it enjoyable. Getting out of the club during my noonday break for a run instead of sitting in the restaurant turned out to be refreshing and stimulating, even with the hot humid midday sun. I would head out from the club toward Deep Water Bay Road and then past the beach. I would continue along the waterfront of Middle Bay, around Repulse Bay or further on my long days before heading back along the same route to the club. I had always believed those I saw running must be crazy. How could just running for forty to sixty minutes be fun? After only three weeks, I began looking forward to the solitude of getting away from the club. I could feel my body adapting and responding to this new and different discipline. I was already in pretty good shape from hitting tennis balls with students for forty to fifty hours a week. I had a head start into my triathlon fitness, in spite of my fellow directors' concerns. After doing research into triathlon training, I knew I couldn't hope to be in proper shape to race this event. Even with this knowledge, I was still determined to do the best I could to at least finish. The directors' negative comments about tennis players were just enough to get me entered and consistently train.

Even with eight weeks of training, I still had a major problem: I didn't own a bike. My tennis workouts were ideal for developing the right muscles for riding a bike, even though I didn't know it then. I didn't know if I would ever do another triathlon, so I wasn't about to go out and spend a few thousand dollars on an expensive road bike. Calling ahead to our Singapore fitness center provided the answer. One of our directors living in Singapore arranged a used bike for me through a local bike shop. Now I was set to either prove my fellow directors wrong or fail miserably to finish the race.

Triathlon Initiation, 'the Little Engine That Could'

Having never lined up for a triathlon before, I had no idea what to expect on that beautiful Singapore morning. I knew nothing about arranging my gear in the transition area. I watched other experienced triathletes position their gear around their bikes in a detailed and organized fashion. I don't think I'd ever been so nervous or unprepared for an athletic event in my life. As I walked toward the water's edge with everyone else, I was hoping I had not made a mistake by entering. When the starter's gun finally sounded, I was still nervous and shaking with apprehension. I had been swimming alone in a twenty-five-meter pool and was completely unprepared for the rush of bodies trying to find their place in the Changi Channel swim course. I thought I was a competent swimmer and able to complete the two-kilometer course until the tidal flow started to flow against us. They said the race began at the most optimal time to take advantage of the tide.

The swim course was set out like a fat *T*. We swam straight out from shore for 100 meters and turned 90 degrees left for 400 meters. U-turning back along the top of the *T* was when the tide changed and began to flow with us. The tide slowly picked up speed but hardly noticeable as the increased flow was with us. We all knew our swim was feeling easy and fast. However, approaching the 1,500 meter turning buoy, I looked up and judged the U-turn buoy to be about ten strokes away. To everyone's surprise, mine included, after ten strokes, we found we had traveled some distance beyond the buoy. It was only then we realized the force of the increasing tide assisting our swim for the last 1,000 meters. Now the tide was directly in our face, and we still needed to negotiate the final 400 meters before heading for shore. I felt like I had been in the water far too long already. I, like everyone else, started to measure my advancement by glancing to the shoreline for encouragement. This was not encouraging, as my group didn't seem to be making much progress. In fact, I personally felt like I was on a swim treadmill, hardly moving. To make matters even worse, I was swimming alongside someone doing the breaststroke. I later discovered he had competed in the Olympics as a breaststroker and was swimming at a fast pace.

He and other swimmers alongside me were making the same progress. Our small pack of swimmers encouraged me to keep going. It seemed like it took forever before we finally rounded the last buoy guiding us to the bike transition. *What had I gotten myself into?* I questioned. I had excelled in other athletic endeavors, but here in Singapore, I was out of my element and comfort zone. Exiting the water, I was too daunted and tired to look around transition to notice how many bikes, if any, were still waiting for participants to come through transition.

Singapore Triathlon

I was steadfastly focused on my bike and what I needed to do to jump on and begin the seventy-one-kilometer bike course. I also had no idea how far seventy-one kilometers was on a bike, having never ridden that far in my life. I had been on a stationary bike in the gym for eight weeks. I was a true (no idea what I was doing) "newbie." How hard can it be? Ride a bike for seventy-one kilometers, then get off, and run to the finish line. Like they say, "Ignorance is bliss."

As I raced out of transition, there was no one down the road I could see, and I felt very alone. *Was I the last one out of transition?* I asked myself. I was still determined to finish and not end up in last place. After the directors' comments about tennis pros, I felt like I was racing for the reputation of all tennis players. I also believed the younger directors must be way out ahead of me, especially with their past triathlon experience. This thought made me peddle even faster. The bike course was three, twenty-four-kilometer laps on beautiful but hot, steamy undulating roads near Singapore's Changi International Airport. I hadn't been on a road bike for years other than getting on this rented Peugeot bike the day before.

An indoor-cycle trainer had been my friend leading up to Singapore. It took me a few kilometers before I felt comfortable cycling. Ten kilometers into the bike course, I finally saw another competitor down the road in front of me. I could see I was closing in on him. This gave me a little extra energy to cycle faster. *If I could only pass him,* I thought, *I will not be in last place.* It wasn't long before I passed him and started to ease past one cyclists after another. One kilometer after another rolled smoothly by under my wheels. This was actually fun being on a road bike again under clear blue skies. This encouraged me even more to increase my speed.

I was just into the third and final twenty-four-kilometer lap when I noticed the bike was not responding as it had the first two laps. I looked down trying to see if the brakes were rubbing or maybe I had a low tire. Nothing seemed to be wrong! Then the thought came flying into my head, *What if there is nothing wrong with the bike?* I had to come to the sobering realization, *My body was not responding…my energy was waning, so there was nothing wrong with the bike! It was my body!*

I still had to finish this lap before heading into transition. The sixteen-kilometer run loomed ahead, however far that was! I was still a novice with only eight weeks of training under my belt. I had no idea of pacing myself. I had gone as fast as I could since the beginning of the race. This was nothing like tennis. By now I was feeling the effects of the two-kilometer swim plus fifty kilometers already on the bike. With the hot heavy humid heat of Singapore's roads and air, it was taking a toil on my less than properly trained and prepared body. I still hoped my years of fitness from tennis would be there to fall back on. I was sincerely hoping the other directors' comments about tennis pros were not correct. The year around weather report for Singapore is Hot, Hotter, then even Hotter and Humid! There was no chance for a cool breeze to suddenly appear.

Finally finishing the 71k bike and arriving at the bike to run transition, I could barely keep my balance dismounting my bike. I tried running into transition, but my legs felt like two huge oil drums completely full of lactic acid. Right then, I began thinking, *How could I have let the other company directors entice, encourage, and egg me into doing this crazing sport?* Then I realized they had actually tried to discourage me from even attempting a triathlon. I had got into this on my own and my own huge ego! As bad as I felt, I was determined not to quit, even if I had to crawl across the finish line!

I put on my running shoes and headed out of transition for the final leg, the sixteen-kilometer run. Crowds of cheering spectators lined the road. Wanting to make a good impression, I decided to take off running fast. Just as I reached what I thought was a good speed, someone in the crowd yelled out, "Come on, start running." I couldn't believe what I'd heard. I was running! Looking down, I was astonished to find my legs hardly moving. My legs were, for the first time in my life, letting me down and barely shuffling me down the road. I picked up my pace as best as I could until the road turned left, away from the few discouraging and maddening hecklers. *Running looks easy from the grandstand*, I thought, *just let them come out on this road and try running after riding a bike hard for seventy-one kilometers.* I was not aware that it took a while before my legs would adjust from cycling to running. Finally adjusting, I settled into a pace, which suited me. Not fast but it suited me. I just hoped my legs would take me to the finish line. My legs and body felt terrible.

Missing the race briefing was not a smart move. Race briefings are designed to familiarize triathletes with course maps and transition rules and details to make the triathlete comfortable during the race. As it turned out, I was completely unaware of the run course. We knew there were plenty of course marshals to guarantee us triathlete wanna-bes would not get lost. So I was not too worried. I just kept running trying not to think too much. *Just keep my feet moving, and don't stop,* I kept saying to myself. The Changi running course was not flat. The roads were continuously undulating up and down. What happened next completely jolted me psychologically and physically, right to the center of my core.

After running what seemed like forever and my legs feeling like rubber, I came around a right-hand corner and saw the crowds again. Thankfully, I could see the finish line banner fluttering just two long blocks away. I couldn't believe it; I was going to finish a triathlon! It felt like I had been running forever, but it all seemed worthwhile seeing that finish banner beckoning down the road. I was going to prove the other directors wrong, even if I was finishing way behind them. Suddenly I felt a natural high kick in and began to run faster. Just as I came to the final twenty meters and celebration, an official stepped in front of me, pointing back down the same hot, humid road I had just come from, saying, "AGAIN."

What I had thought was sixteen kilometers was only eight kilometers? I wasn't sure I could keep running or do another lap. I was exhausted! Still determined not to quit, I found strength from somewhere to keep going. I headed out for another exhausting lap trudging down the same road I thought I would never, ever need to see again. After another arduous lap and what seemed like an eternity, I was relieved to finally turn the same right-hand final corner. Looking past the madding crowds of spectators, I saw the finish line banner again, calling for me in the hot breeze a few hundred meters away. I took off again with renewed energy when the worst thing that could have happened, happened! The same official stepped out again blocking my advance through the finish line, saying, "One more lap."

I stopped in my tracks and yelled out, partially pleading, "I can't do it!"

He looked completely rested and fresh in the heat, and with an unemotional look on his face, he casually replied, "Well, it's up to you!"

How could I have thought the first lap of five and one-third kilometers was sixteen kilometers and then thought it was eight kilometers? I obviously had no idea what running sixteen kilometers was all about, especially after swimming two kilometers and cycling seventy-one kilometers for the first time in my life. This was another reminder that I was a true novice. This last lap would prove how much I needed to learn about the sport of triathlon and, more importantly, about myself. After coming this far, I couldn't quit, so I dejectedly turned to head out for one final lap. I could only describe my condition as beyond exhausted. The worst I had ever felt in a sporting endeavor, period!

My body hurt, my legs hurt, and my feet and knees felt like they would explode and not hold me up for another one hundred meters, much less five kilometers. Maybe I was a little delirious as I started to think of the little children's book, *The Little Engine That Could*. This book had been read to me as a child, and I had also read it to my children. *The Little Engine That Could* kept coming into my head as I trudged down the road. I was determined not to stop for fear of not being able to start moving again. I kept saying over and over in my mind and, even out loud, words from the book, "I think I can, I think I can, I think I can," to the chug of the little engine. I kept my run cadence to that rhythm to keep myself moving and not stop. For the entire last five kilometers, I kept repeating out loud, "I think I can, I think I can, I think I can."

When finally seeing the same final right-hand corner come into view, I knew the finishing banner would finally be beckoning me to finish this maddening race. This time, I knew without a doubt, it really was the finish line! No man to pop up unexpectedly, only the bliss of knowing I could finally stop and rest my weary legs and body in the shade just beyond that banner. Winning a prize or finishing ahead of any of my fellow directors was the furthest thing from my mind. I was going to finish this triathlon and reach my goal. At least I was proving the other directors wrong. A tennis teaching pro can do a triathlon! What happened next completely took me by surprise. I was overwhelmed with a sense of accomplishment, different than I had ever experienced in my many other athletic endeavors. Euphoria filled me with energy and elation as I changed my chant from "I think I can" to "I thought I could, I thought I could, I thought I could!"

Once past the finishing banner and receiving my finishing medal, I walked around transition and recovery area looking for the other directors. I wanted to celebrate with them and let them know I had actually done it—finished the triathlon. A tennis player had actually done it! I assumed they had all finished long before me because they were nowhere to be found in the recovery area. *Had they already headed back to the hotel?* I thought. I couldn't believe they weren't there waiting for me to cheer me on though the finish line. I started the race along with 350 other much more experienced triathletes than me, and I had miraculously finished thirty-third overall. My finish time also turned out to be more than thirty minutes ahead of my closest associate. They didn't leave without cheering me on; they were still out on those steaming-hot, humid roads fighting demons of their own to finish. I ended up waiting for them for an hour or more, cheering them on one by one through the finish line.

When heading out that evening to Newton's Circus for some Singapore delights and celebration, I found my knees hurt so badly I could hardly climb the stairs going up and over one of Singapore's largest roundabouts. Taking one agonizing step and stair after another, I arrived ten minutes after my associates were settled into their seats for our evening celebration meal of delicious frog legs. My friends didn't feel a bit sorry for me after my surprising finish. To this day, I don't know how I did it. I paid a huge price jumping into triathlon racing with only eight weeks of training. I knew so little about proper triathlon training; it was a miracle I even finished the race, much less placing third in my age group.

My knees swelled up, and I limped around the tennis court for a few weeks after I arrived back to Hong Kong. I was thankful my tennis fitness allowed me to completely recover. It may have taken me weeks for my knees and body to feel normal again, but the euphoria I had completing that triathlon never left me. I was hooked on triathlon and researched proper training techniques to finish in much better condition for my next triathlon. Friends thought I was crazy when I began entering events wherever and whenever I could find them. I started racing much shorter events, allowing me to build a proper base of fitness. I then invested in a good race bike of my own. I was hooked on the sport of triathlon and the amazing community of triathletes. These triathletes never failed to encourage me to do my best and finish strong. There are never losers in triathlon, as everyone who finishes is a winner!

How could this one event so completely change my outlook and passion for life and my fitness level? I loved how I felt and even watched my tennis improve as my strength and flexibility increased. I was feeling younger and stronger every month.

How could my life get any better? I couldn't imagine! I was feeling healthier and fitter than I had ever felt. I couldn't wait for 3:45 a.m. to arrive each day so I could get up. I was energized for another full day of activities. This new addiction took me all over Asia, then to the US, representing Hong Kong in my age group at the second ITU World Triathlon Championships. In 1990, it was held at Walt Disney World in Orlando, Florida. Here was where I experienced world-level triathletes for the first time.

ITU World Championship at Walt Disney World with nieces

This exposure only inspired me more as everyone was fit and thriving with their positive enjoyment of life. I loved being in this environment as both men and women seemed to enjoy running more than walking. When the bus transporting us to the race venue that morning was caught in traffic, one age-group female jumped off the bus and took off running ahead of the bus. Everywhere I looked I was inspired by what I saw. I fell in love with being part of this community and quickly improved. Along with well over one hundred triathletes in my age group, I finished twenty-fifth. In Florida, I felt much better at the finish line than I did in Singapore. The same feeling of euphoria I had competing in Singapore was there at every single triathlon when crossing the finish line. This never seemed to change, and it inspired me to keep training and racing.

Only one player is considered the winner at the end of a tennis tournament. Every other tennis participant is classified as a loser. With triathlon, everyone's a winner and respected as a winner by every other triathlete for putting in the effort to cross that elusive finish line. Every triathlete knows the training and sacrifice required to line up at the start line and then finish the course. This is the reason for the profound respect every triathlete has for the effort of his fellow competitors. This respect is even shown by top professionals for age-group triathletes. The professionals I was fortunate to know often hung around to encourage and cheer on age groupers like myself.

I was still competing in tennis in 1991 and was fortunate to represent Hong Kong at the Italia Cup (world's over-thirty-five men's team tennis championships) held at the famous Kooyong Grass Court Club in Melbourne, Australia. I had dreamed of playing the Australian Open there when I was younger and now found myself playing number 1 singles and doubles in all four matches on those hallowed grounds representing Hong Kong. It was like a fairy tale come true for me when Hong Kong finished eighth, ahead of countries like the US and Sweden. I was honored to have the opportunity to play Australian legend Peter McNamara in both singles and doubles on those historic grass courts. He later said I was his toughest match and had a great game, which made the event even more special for me.

Italia Cup—World 35+ Team Championship Australia

ITU World Championship, Gold Coast, Australia

Later that same year, I went back to Australia to compete in the Triathlon World Championships on the Gold Coast finishing twenty-second. Again there were more than one hundred competitors in my age group. How lucky did I feel, traveling to two beautiful destinations in Australia while competing in two different sports? Doing two world championships in the same year on the east and south coast of Australia was almost more than I could have hoped for. I was in the best shape of my life, feeling younger and more alive each day! My times in triathlon were improving so much, I couldn't wait to wake up every day in Hong Kong and train. I knew life couldn't get any better. I was living my dream!

It was truly a real dream now, as the reality of my terrifying moment came rushing back!

Lying broken, in pain and paralyzed in Hong Kong, I realized my dream life might just be over for good. I wasn't ready to give in just yet. I had been on a great run, as many friends and acquaintances stated. I had been fortunate, but why did so many feel my active life was destined to be over? I wasn't about to give in to that kind of defeated attitude. I was still hoping and praying it wouldn't be long before I would be back on the road running, cycling, swimming and on a tennis court again, running around like nothing had ever happened.

I was on Clearwater Bay Road that morning because of my desire to be recognized as a world-class athlete. I slowly became opposite of my father who sacrificed his goals and dreams for the good of us kids and our family. The more I chased fame for myself, the more the world hung that glittering, elusive, unattainable, and never quite satisfying crystal ball of recognition out there in front of me, especially in Hong Kong.

It seemed everywhere I turned there was always more recognition and local fame, as opportunity after opportunity presented itself. These opportunities took up more and more of my time and resulted in less and less time with my family. I was working six days a week and up to sixty hours teaching tennis while at Aberdeen Marina Club. This all was happening while playing in the local open tennis league in the evenings. I was then competing in many Asian triathlons, mostly taking place around Southeast Asia on weekends. Besides this, I was in charge of the Prince Asian Challenge Circuit for Asian junior tennis players as circuit director and administrator for Prince Racket Company. These junior tournaments took me out of Hong Kong for one week every two months. Aberdeen Marina Club was very gracious and allowed me to be involved with these many activities. The press and notoriety I was receiving reflected positively for the Marina Club. How could I ask for anything more?

There is always a cost or trade-off in what we do. In my case, I could hardly see the trade-offs in the midst of this whirlwind of activities feeding my ever larger and growing ego. There was now less and less time for my family. What made it worse, I wasn't even aware it was happening! How could I have so slightly veered off my important life's course? I was leaving my family mostly alone to fend for themselves. The one blessing for me was my sons' sudden interest in triathlon. I wasn't sure their interest was really in triathlon or wanting to spend more time with their increasingly absentee father. Their interest in triathlon was wonderful for me. Our time spent together suddenly increased.

Both my sons, Donnie and Brian, took up triathlon in the fall of 1991. I promised to buy each one a nice triathlon bike if they kept up with their training program. They surprised me by religiously staying with their training schedule, so I kept my word and bought each one a nice bike. In December, they traveled with me to Rayong, Thailand, and competed in their first ever Olympic-distance race.

Continuing my dedicated training during the fall, I had seen my 10k run time improve significantly, dropping under forty minutes in training. I looked forward to racing with Donnie and Brian in this Olympic-distance triathlon. I also wanted to see if I could run ten kilometers under forty minutes, following a hot forty-kilometer bike course. By the end of 1991, I had been winning almost every race around Asia for my age group. There were still those around Asia who were doing their best to take my place on the top step of the podium. We all knew one another by then and had become friends. Triathlon had almost become an obsession for me. I was racing as

I DO IT ALL

much as I possibly could, even with my busy work schedule and other commitments.

Arriving in Rayong, the weather was the usual Thai forecast—blue skies and hot. Teaching on a hot tennis court six days a week made heat less of a factor for me. It was wonderful lining up on the water's edge beside my sons. I couldn't have been more proud to have them here with me. We dove in together when the gun went off, and I left them behind. This was to be one of the last times I would be able to finish a swim faster than either of them. My swim was consistently fast for my age group, so I came out of the swim first in my category. I then pulled ahead even farther with a strong forty-kilometer bike. I also found myself in second place overall, but not long after the twenty-kilometer bike turnaround, I saw another more than forty veteran my age coming down the road. He yelled out, "I see you!" Phil had been working hard to improve his bike time. He was Swiss but living in Thailand, staying fit. He loved racing triathlons. I had raced against him in the past, and he felt confident he could catch me on the run when he saw how close we were on the bike. I couldn't blame him for feeling that way, as my previous run times were not nearly equal to his best. This time was different as I knew my run had significantly improved in training. I was looking forward to seeing how my run would feel coming off the bike. I was able to take out fast from transition 2. For the first time in a race, I felt like I could actually run. It felt great to be running!

Run Start—Half Ironman, Thailand

This was unlike any other race I had competed in. My legs usually felt swelled with lactic acid and heavy. But it was different this time around. I was actually enjoying the run and found myself running side by side with the number 1 elite Thai triathlete. The race officials kept yelling out something in Thai, which I couldn't understand. At the same time, this Thai triathlete would look in my direction. He spoke a little English, so while still running, I finally asked, "What are they saying?"

He said they were yelling out, "Second elite, first vet." He turned to me and asked, "Who's the veteran triathlete?"

He thought I was way too young to be in the veteran category. This was a great compliment. I just smiled, letting him know I was the veteran. My run was feeling wonderful, and I ended up finishing second overall and first veteran. My fellow vet couldn't believe I had outran him but seemed happy with his sixth place overall and second veteran finish. He was one of the reasons I loved triathlon. Phil Guinand and I remained friends and in contact for the last twenty-five years.

Don, Ian Rayson, and Paul Terry—Thailand Triathlon

These wonderful memories filled my mind with positive encouragement knowing how I had started from scratch and become a triathlete. I was determined to start from scratch and learn how to walk again, even if it was against all odds. Conjuring up all these memories helped me to maintain my mental balance and stay positive without even realizing it.

Thailand Vacation

Thailand Bungee Jumping

Thailand on a bungee cord

Following Thailand, my energy level was higher than ever from my great-run finish. My daily schedule continued to be packed full as 1992 rang in. I would start at my usual 3:45 a.m. six-days-a-week schedule. I never used an alarm clock and never woke up late. By 4:00 a.m., I was on the road with my sons for a difficult forty-to-fifty-kilometer cycle through the hilly Clearwater Bay area of Kowloon. We would arrive back home just in time to change and I would drive our family into Hong Kong Island. After being dropped off, I would teach tennis for four or five hours, then would rush down to the locker room, change into my running clothes, and head out for a ten-to-fifteen-kilometer run. The always hot and humid air in the middle of the day in Hong Kong helped my triathlon racing results. I was acclimated to the heat and humidity. Never having much time, I would always run at a fast pace. Arriving back to the club totally soaked, I would rinse off and dive in the pool for a quick 1,500-meter swim. If time permitted, the club gym was waiting for some stretching and a short weight workout. Showering quickly, I would return to the courts for another three or four hours of tennis lessons.

My family would arrive back to the club after school and hang around for my lessons to end. We would leave for home at 6:00 or 7:00 p.m. A call home to our maid assured dinner would be hot and waiting for our family. After dinner, I would go to the computer to do any work or consulting waiting on my fax machine. There were many other work requirements happening with commentating, modeling, promotional commercials, consulting; and basically, life was on a super high. Life was definitely on fast-forward! I was not rich by any means, as living in Hong Kong was expensive, but I was living my dream. Most of my sporting activities, which took place outside of Hong Kong were sponsored. Nike and Prince were my main sponsors and were very good to me as I actively promoted their products. Hong Kong Triathlon Association provided free or greatly reduced flights and accommodations.

By spring of 1992, I was in the best shape of my life and had made plans to do everything I could to win the World Triathlon title for my age group in Muskoka, Canada. Everything was going as planned as I had just qualified to race elite (pro) men at the first

Asian triathlon championships in Japan, representing Hong Kong. I had also just competed in my first-ever official mile race with the Hong Kong Track Association on the Aberdeen Sports track in a time of five minutes thirty-two seconds. I was also invited to play in the Clearwater Invitational Tennis Tournament starting on April 24. This tennis tournament was reserved for the top tennis professionals in the region. I really was "doing it all!" Nothing could possibly dampen my spirit for life and the energy I felt each day.

Suddenly it was black like a bad dream.

Everything was pitch-black, surreal! What a horrible dream as I struggled to get a grip on what was happening. I recognized the darkness from my previous struggles of waking up from an unconscious state. The feeling of being superglued to a surface and unable to move or find my bearings was hard to accept. I was in the dream state where nothing seems real and yet at the same time too real! Unable to do anything for myself, I slipped in and out of consciousness until there was help.

I did my best to stay calm as I was being helped and eventually taken by ambulance to the nearest hospital. I found I could do nothing for myself and prayed the necessary treatment would have me up and running in no time at all. Pain seemed to be everywhere and yet nowhere at the same time, leaving me a little confused. I was finally lifted out of the ambulance and into the hospital to receive the help I so desperately needed. That comforting voice was always with me, making me feel calm, even with the ever-present pain and discomfort. I still had no idea of how I ended up there or the severity of my injuries. I just kept my breathing steady and even to keep myself calm. Now that I was at the hospital, I could relax and let the doctors do their magic.

I guess I won't be playing the Clearwater Tournament, I thought as I went back into dreamland again.

Again, How Did I Arrive Here?

As I lay there in the road and finally traveled by ambulance to the hospital, I kept asking myself these two questions: how did I arrive here, and what can I do to work my way through this?

Good question, how did I end up in Asia and on that piece of road in Hong Kong?

The first question was easy to answer. I was being carried away by my mesmerizing and unexpected successes. Why was I on Clearwater Bay Road that particular morning and at that exact time? That was easy to answer: I woke up late. My boys also woke up late and, for the first time in months, decided to stay in bed. I was too stubborn to listen or see the signs flashing right in front of me: "Stay Home Today!" It is so clear looking back in time. I wanted more fame and more recognition, even if it was only in my own mind. Recognition was like a drug where I couldn't seem to get enough. I was training hard to become the World Triathlon champion for my age group in Muskoka, Canada. I was willing to sacrifice even more time away from my family to achieve this single-minded goal. This would give me more recognition. The big question I was avoiding, "Who was sacrificing most from my pursuits?" I hardly noticed that my wife felt isolated in the male-dominated society of Hong Kong because I was thriving. She was not impressed with my fitness or my attempts to basically buy her off with clothes, jewelry, vacations, and summers being back home in the States with our children and her parents. Summers were her chance to feel normal again while I stayed in Hong Kong and worked harder than ever to make money and reach my goals. I was occupied making more money to support my children's schooling and our expensive sporting habits.

I was on Clearwater Bay Road that morning for myself and myself only. At that time, I was completely convinced I was doing everything so my family would be proud of me and enjoy life to the fullest! Looking back, the truth was all too clear. I was only thinking of myself and used triathlon as an excuse to keep traveling, feel younger, and compete in exciting venues and countries around the world. I thought I was living my life to the fullest! My eventual wake-up call was violent and abrupt. I would only come to realize the level of my selfishness as the years passed. Because of this obsession, I found myself paralyzed and stuck to the surface of Clearwater Bay Road that dark morning on April 22, 1992.

The second question was not so easy to answer. How was I going to get through this? Time, faith, and many people's prayers would eventually answer this question and other questions in profound ways. I may not have felt like I deserved all the help and prayers, but I still received more than my share.

HOSPITALS: NOBODY'S IDEAL VACATION

Passing in and out of conscientiousness while the ambulance transferred me to the hospital was surreal. Everything was a bit hazy, but once I arrived, I relaxed as they carried me inside to the emergency room. A Chinese hospital on the Kowloon side of Victoria Harbor was the closest available facility. Arriving at the hospital, the adrenalin rush from the accident had all but disappeared. Pain of being x-rayed was uncomfortable and unspeakably painful in some areas of my body as they laid me on a hard X-ray table. Intense pain shot through my head, neck, and upper back. I had obvious broken ribs, compound fracture of my left radius, shattered ulna, and smashed up bones in my left hand and knuckle. It was impossible for me to locate a definitive place to focus the pain. It felt like I hurt everywhere, but then the real mystery began. How come I could not feel anything from my lower chest down through my toes? Maybe I was injured in my lower body, but I couldn't tell if I was hurt there. Being placed out in the hallway until my family arrived only added more confusion to the pain.

Why was I in the hallway and not in the ICU, for my best chance of survival? I also had no idea how long they kept me in the hallway before I finally saw the wonderful familiar faces of my fam-

I DO IT ALL

ily. It lifted my spirit to see their faces. I knew they would do their best to look after me and see I was properly cared for. Unable to do anything for myself, they comforted me while trying to get credible information regarding my condition. It was an understatement to say how much encouragement loved ones impact you, following a mass trauma accident and in a life-threatening condition. Positive encouraging words and prayers are huge in helping you to stay positive yourself. They help you to relax knowing you don't need to take care of it by yourself. This allows you to feel you will eventually get through an awful moment and, for me, a terrifying situation.

My dad's experiences of serving in the military during WWII, while stationed at Guadalcanal, made my situation seem minuscule compared to his ordeal. One night, his position was overrun by a large platoon of desperately trapped Japanese soldiers. The Japanese had retreated up a box canyon, with only one way in and one way out. My dad and his men were holding their positions, blocking the only exit for the trapped Japanese. Running out of food and water, the Japanese made a desperate charge directly over my dad's position. The sudden rush of the enemy was on a pitch-black cloud-covered starless night with no moon, making it impossible to see their hand in front of their face. Perched on a small bluff, he and his few soldiers were knocked off the bluff, suddenly in a battle for their lives. While fighting to save his life, and those under him, he prayed the most sincere prayer of his life. Being shot and sustaining other grenade fragment injuries, he was thankful

My dad's medals

that he and those under him survived that nightmare of a night. He was decorated with several medals, including the third highest award for valor, the Silver Star, along with the Purple Heart for injuries sustained.

Here I was in Hong Kong, all banged up facing my own small battle to survive. Thinking of my father's experiences, I still felt very fortunate as I don't know how I would have dealt with his experiences. Why had my father grown up in a time of world war that changed his life? There is no way to explain one's journey as life is not guaranteed to be easy for anyone. How could I have been on that road at the exact wrong moment? Ten or twenty seconds, one way or the other, and I would have been at work at that very moment, looking forward to the tennis tournament on the weekend. If my father could make a way through his setbacks, I felt I would somehow find a way through my present situation. My father was always a great inspiration for me.

Having left high school early to join the Army, my dad came home from the war with no high school degree. He met our mom, Lila, at church and married her not long after his military discharge. He was determined to be a great husband and father, deciding to use his military benefits to obtain a college education. He was accepted at Northwest Nazarene College with the understanding he would complete his high school degree during his freshman year. Both Ken and I were born while he was studying in Nampa, Idaho. There was an area of housing next to the college that housed a number of veterans called Vet Ville. This was where Ken and I did our early growing-up years and dreaming. With support from my mom and the college, my dad was able to graduate with a degree in history and education. Our dad became a schoolteacher and coach after graduating and spent his free time with family. He and our mom did their best to pass on their many positive character traits to each one of their children.

Now lying in a hospital bed in Hong Kong, I needed to draw on all that faith, strength, and many positive attributes our parents had demonstrated to us. I leaned heavily on those traits for any hope of recovering from my accident.

As an athlete, I always looked on injuries as a timeline. Each injury requires an exact number of days, weeks, or months to fully recover. Sooner, if you have specialized treatment. A sprained ankle was a four-to-six-week injury. Broken leg was eight to twelve weeks plus another four weeks of rehab to fully recover. Pulled or torn muscles had their own timeline, depending on the severity. I never had anything this severe and found it difficult to get a handle on the kind of timeline needed for a complete recovery. I planned on looking for professionals and experts to advise me on the recovery process. I was thankful my dad was not alive to see me in this condition but also missed him terribly. He had always been a source of strength when unexpected injuries happened in my past.

The initial report from the first hospital was encouraging: "I only had a broken leg, with nothing else of any importance." Looking at me lying there with visible traumatic injuries to my left arm and no ability to move my lower extremities set off alarm bells with my family. Compound fracture of my radius and broken-off end of my ulna with severe fractures to my hand and knuckle were obvious. My family saw enough to move me to another hospital on the other side of Victoria Harbor. I couldn't help but be worried as I continued to have no feeling from my chest down and was unable to move or feel my legs. I was concerned and told my family I had terrific pain in my upper back, head, and neck. My upper ribs felt broken; and my left arm, wrist, hand, and knuckles were in a state of trauma. I knew I had to get out of that hallway and so did my family. I wanted to be moved to the American Adventist Hospital on the other side of Victoria Harbor. I felt I could receive proper treatment there and wouldn't be left out in the hallway. Donnie and Brian literally commandeered an ambulance and accompanied me on a very painful transfer through the Harbor Tunnel, up Stubbs Roads, and finally to the Adventist. Hong Kong that time of morning being very congested resulted in a jerking stop-and-go traffic the entire way. I was only half conscious during the trip but still excited to be arriving where I could relax and have confidence in a new evaluation process.

When finally rolled into the Adventist emergency room, I relaxed even more when I saw the very doctor who had led a fitness seminar at Aberdeen Marina Club the month before. Four weeks earlier, when finishing my fitness assessment, he remarked I was the fittest forty-five-year-old he'd ever met. At that time he stated, "I can't tell you anything you don't already know." During that earlier assessment, I felt great, as all my dedicated training was paying off. It felt even better to have it verified by a doctor. That was then! This morning, he was looking at a broken body. I relaxed when he informed me they had to take another series of X-rays. The ones from the original hospital were of such poor quality, they could not ascertain my injuries correctly. It had been well over three hours since the accident, and this new X-ray process was more painful. All the adrenaline from the accident had completely worn off.

The most comforting words spoken to me in the hours since the accident were "We are going to take you into surgery now."

I remember smiling, at least it felt like a smile, and saying, "That's great."

The following day, the doctor asked why I seemed so happy when told I was going into surgery. It seemed obvious to me. They would need to put me to sleep, and I could finally relax and rest. Taking a break from all that consuming pain was a luscious thought. I was also hoping for some good news when coming out from surgery. I just knew it would be good news and I would begin a quick road back to complete recovery. I was, after all, still alive, and that was a miracle.

Having undergone previous surgeries, I knew it wouldn't take but a moment to put me to sleep. I couldn't wait to escape this nightmare for a while. Maybe there would be a positive prognosis and I would be able to move my legs again after waking from the anesthesia? A previous operation to repair a tendon in my right leg, broken in the fifth grade, allowed me to have a complete recovery. I was positive there would be a similar prognosis when I awoke. Complete recovery would then begin. Before everyone would realize it, I would be back to my normal fit self! I was positive and couldn't wait to recover.

Coming out from under the anesthetic, I found myself connected to wires and tubes and what they thought was a successful operation to rebuild my left arm, wrist, and hand. My back was stabilized but no operation. This was a miracle again as X-rays and MRIs confirmed I had a complete blowout of my T5 vertebrae and hairline fractures throughout my T12 vertebrae. My helmet had saved my life, but the compression fracture left my T5 vertebrae crushed and almost powder. This was not the news I wanted, but it was still an amazing miracle I was alive. Another miracle was the fact the disks between my vertebrae were not damaged. Even better and more unbelievable, there was no dislocation of my vertebrae. Dislocation would surely have severed my spinal cord, leaving me permanently paralyzed with no chance of any recovery. Life as a paraplegic would have been my future. I still had no feeling from the chest down, and first prognosis was paralysis, where I would never walk again! Unless something even more miraculous happened, walking would only be done with great effort or with some sort of aid, i.e., a walker or crutches. According to all the initial tests, most likely a wheelchair would be my future.

I obviously had no idea what I was talking about when I blurted out to the doctor, "Don't worry, I will do another triathlon by the end of the year." He looked startled, let out a nervous laugh, and quickly left the room. He had just said I needed to get used to the idea of spending the next six to nine months in the hospital recovering while going through what rehabilitation I could endure. Somehow, I was going to do another triathlon by the end of the year, nine months later? He had probably heard this before when spinal cord patients were in denial, unable to accept their fate.

Trying to get around the idea of staying in bed for months was difficult enough. Thinking of the number of times I heard someone say, "I would love to sleep in for a week!" Now that statement sounded absurd, as I tried to come to grips with the idea of actually staying in bed for six months. Six months! Didn't the doctor know I always got up at 3:45 a.m. and went full blast for fourteen to sixteen hours a day? Like so many others who had gone through traumatic accidents, I refused to believe what was right in front of me. I was paralyzed, and life might never be the same. With all the evidence clearly in front of me, I somehow believed in the impossible. I couldn't allow any other thoughts to enter my mind. Being paralyzed was just too unimaginable. I just wouldn't believe it was happening to me!

I grew up in a family where I heard about miracles and witnessed some for myself. I knew miracles were real and also possible for me. I held onto that belief and thought back to how many times in my life where it seemed the impossible happened, even for me. Memories of past injuries and recoveries to compete again and win were in my spiritual DNA. I never lost hope and always believed for a complete recovery. There were those around me who thought I was crazy and a dreamer. But that was okay with me as this was my life, and I had to live it the best I could. Being negative never helped anyone, and I needed to stay focused on what I could to recover.

Lying there in my new quiet hospital room allowed me to introspectively take stock of my life and where I had been heading. In the world's eye, I was successful beyond my own expectations. It didn't seem like I could set a foot wrong. Everything was turning up roses.

It was so good that one day at the Marina Club, a member asked me, "Do you ever stop smiling?"

As I thought back just a few days, I asked myself, "Was I really that happy and full of joy?"

Sure it was easy to be caught up in the fast-paced routine of success and positive accolades that follow. Happiness and Joy, are they really the same? I knew happiness was the result of positive outward influences and is generally affected by our current circumstances and environment surrounding us. Joy, on the other hand, is defined as Inner Peace and Contentment, regardless of our outward circumstances. Not much around a hospital room or necessary exams will make a person happy. Would I be able to reach inside and find that Inner Peace and Contentment, which brings Joy?

I had been raised to seek God first but had allowed myself to be pulled away from that thought with all my recent successes. I had drifted so far away from my upbringing that I was being influenced more and more by the world's way of thinking. Many people would say, "If you are heavenly minded, you will be of no earthly good."

Is this really true? I thought as I lay there, unable to move my legs, which I had so heavily depended on for my success.

Famous author C. S. Lewis stated that you need to be aware of your heavenly destination if you are to be of any earthly good. All I knew right then was I needed help beyond my own ability to make things happen. With all my injuries, I was thankful for the ability to still move my uninjured right arm. Even with my severely damaged left arm, I was still able to raise it up, gently opening and closing my grossly swollen fingers.

"Seek ye first the kingdom of God and all these things shall be added to you." What were "these" things, and had I been seeking God first or only my way of doing things? Man's way of doing things! Were they what I had been striving for? Running after the security, fame, success, money, travel, and sense of worth—were they worth it? It didn't take long for me to realize the emptiness of that kind of thinking now that I was lying helpless in a hospital bed. Everyone of those items can rot, be stolen, or just disappear in an instant because of some careless minibus driver doing an illegal U-turn on a remote country road in Hong Kong. All those things had been stripped away from me in a split second! What were these things that God promised, and were they going to be added to me? Firstly, was I seeking first the kingdom of God in my everyday life?

The truth somehow becomes very vivid when everything you have put value on disappears in a heartbeat. Those truly permanent things, which are added to us, happen because of putting God first. Only then will the worries of this world tend to fade away. Food, clothing, and shelter occupy our thinking, along with the many pursuits of our modern-day world. As important as these items are, the real permanent items we desire are much deeper. Faith, Hope, and Love are the essence of most movies that capture our imagination and attention. Faith in something or someone, hope for a better future, and last but most important, Love, which is real and lasts forever, are the essence of a joyful life.

I knew deep down that the things that God adds to our lives were real and lasting. Without realizing it, men and women want and desire items that last. God gives love, joy, peace, patience, gentleness, goodness, faith, humility, and discipline. Who wouldn't want this shopping list of items as real and permanent parts of their everyday life? I knew this but had been distracted by the glittering and fleeting moments of success.

I lay there realizing I had been chasing dreams that could be destroyed in an instant or, like a puff of smoke, quickly disappearing high in a blue sky. Chasing these temporal dreams never brings permanent joy, peace, or love to one's life. Putting God first or to say it another way, heavenly thinking actually makes us more earthly good, not less. A list of these items reads like the following: a love that lasts, joy that no man can take away, peace that transcends any circumstance, patience that allows solid relationships, gentleness that creates intimacy, goodness that fosters hope, faith that gives life, humility that helps us see the best in everyone, and finally, discipline that fosters true success. Boiled down to three words—*Faith, Hope,* and *Love*. These three are intrinsically connected. Without faith, you cannot have hope. When hope is gone, you lose your faith. And finally, without faith and hope, love cannot exist; and faith and hope cannot exist without love.

Everyone wants real permanent quality character traits in their lives. As I lay there, inspecting my life, I found myself far short of God's ideal. I was still overwhelmed by the world's ideas but wanted to do much better once I was out of this bed and eventually leave the hospital. Was I always successful with my new commitment? No, but I was determined to be better and not give in to the allure and glitter the world had to offer and the life I had before. If I had been completely successful in what I was learning, my first marriage would not have collapsed in divorce.

Once out of surgery, I was placed in a fourth floor room with two other patients. It wasn't long before a flow of visitors, flowers, fruit baskets, and chocolate boxes started to arrive. I was well-known in Hong Kong because of the TV commentary and newspaper reports of my tennis and family triathlon exploits. News of my accident was carried on all the media outlets. Even with this, the number of get-well gifts and cards coming in were unexpected but gladly welcomed. The patient nearest the window was transferred out on the second day. Only two of us now occupied the room, with my bed nearest the door. My bed gave me a clear view of the hallway and the nurses station bustling with activity.

Here we were, two strangers placed in a quiet room by circumstances out of our control. Everything became almost eerily quiet when the hustle and bustle of the doctors, nurses, and visitors disappeared. We warily surveyed each other, with sideways glances, only a bed apart. Finally, after an awkward moment of introduction, we started a conversation. He asked about my accident and the prognosis. He said he felt fortunate after hearing my story, letting me know he was going in for a simple exploratory procedure using a small incision to insert a camera. Simply stated by his doctor, he would hardly notice the incision and be able to leave the hospital in a day or two. How little we really know about our future!

The following day, he was wheeled out early in the morning for his "simple" surgery. But after being gone for most of the day, he finally arrived back to our room, not looking well. This was not a good sign, after being gone for so long. His doctor removed his dressing the following day to view the incision. It was not a small incision like he had been promised. The incision turned out to be a nine-inch wound stapled back together. A large amount of his small and large intestines were removed during the operation. In obvious discomfort, both of us agreed to watch out if a doctor said, "You will hardly feel a thing, or this will be a simple procedure." Most likely, it would only be him, the doctor, who would hardly feel a thing. It may be simple for him because he would be at home having dinner with his family, not on some drip to ease the pain, allowing a semblance of sleep. We both started to laugh but found that wasn't so simple either.

My left arm had been shattered by the impact with the bus and needed a number of procedures to put it back together. A metal plate was inserted for my left radius, which was a compound fracture, twice exiting in slightly different locations on my outer forearm. The end of my ulna had to be winched back together after it completely broke off and tried to take up residence in my hand. Finally, three pins were inserted to stabilize broken bones in my hand and base knuckle of my index finger. The resulting plaster cast left my fingers and thumb showing. The only way I could get some relief from my blackened and grossly swelling fingers was to keep my arm raised high, then slowly and gently opening and closing my fingers.

I was fortunate having my bed by the door as the nurses station and the lift (elevator) doors in the large vestibule reception area were visible. Virtually everyone who visited the fourth floor arrived off those lifts, with many passing our open door on the way to visit other patients. Everyone seemed overly friendly, waving as they strolled by. This became wonderful therapy and kept me upbeat, as my second roommate finally asked to be moved. He was a good roommate and seemed to stay fairly positive after such bad news about his surgery. He was, however, becoming increasingly depressed as he watched more and more gifts arrive daily for me. Only one small plant had arrived for him in three days since he arrived. Only once did I see him with a visitor. Because of the nature of his operation, he wasn't allowed to eat any of the amazing fruits, biscuits, or chocolates in the cornucopia of gifts arriving for me. Again it was easy for me to see the brighter side, as I could indulge in the many eatable variety of gifts. My gifts made the room seem like a flower shop and started to fill up the empty spaces. One potted plant for my roommate did nothing to cheer him up. This was understandable as the doctor's news continued to be discouraging. In spite of him trying to stay positive, he struggled with depression. My condition may have looked desperate, but I realized he was in far worse shape. There were so many patients struggling with serious conditions in the hospital, I somehow found a way to feel more fortunate. I was still expecting to be on the mend, planning to prove the doctors completely wrong.

I was now alone in a room meant for three persons. It remained my private room, for the remainder of my stay at the Adventist Hospital. Friendly visitors passing by to other rooms kept waving. This felt wonderful and warmed my spirit as these visitors were strangers, having never met them before. Frequently these same people, when not in a rush, would stop, come in, and talk. This always helped the relentlessly slow days pass more quickly. One visitor came in and thoughtfully dropped by a book for me to read. This was a great gesture. But I discovered another problem from my accident:

I couldn't read! The words were a complete blur from the massive blow to the back of my head. My sight was fine from a distance, but everything up close was fuzzy. This became a huge concern as my eyesight before the accident had been twenty-ten. I had always taken my excellent eyesight for granted. It always allowed me to see the tennis ball early and clearly from a distance. Being able to cleanly hit tennis balls coming to me at high speed was an asset. First it was my arm, ribs, and legs. Now it was my eyesight. Would my eyesight improve or stay the same in the future? How many more irritating problems like this would pop up along the way? Being injured was proving to be more adventurous than I thought.

My eyesight was the least of my worries with everything else going on. Even though I couldn't read the book, I was grateful for the visitors and additional company. The fact that so many strangers were willing to drop in and be so friendly was wonderful. One day, I remarked to the nursing staff how friendly everyone was at the Adventist Hospital. The staff had also witnessed this happening from their nurses station across the hall. This brought out some laughs from the nurses as they explained, "The visitors are just waving back and responding to your friendly gesture." Until that moment, I hadn't realized that my exercises of raising my cast-covered left arm and opening and closing my fingers made it appear I was waving to everyone passing my room. They were just returning my friendly gesture. Another life lesson I relearned during my recovery—being friendly encourages others to be friendly.

I HAVE SOME CONTROL... RIGHT?

Three days lying still and in pain in a hospital bed felt like an eternity. It was about this time I became aware of nurses injecting something into my intravenous tubes. *What was being injected into these tubes?* I thought? I had been careful throughout my life not to take medicine or even an aspirin tablet unless it was absolutely necessary. I had always been concerned about the long-term effects of drugs and injections. When I was a young tennis teaching pro, the owner of Blossom Hill Tennis Club had developed a dependency on painkillers after being released from the hospital. He found it almost impossible to live without this addiction, negatively impacting his everyday life.

The nurse on duty let me know pain medication was being administered through the steady drip, drip, drip. With the little I had studied about painkillers, I requested to have all pain medication stopped unless they had my consent. She wasn't thrilled with my request, and her response was predictable, "All painkillers are authorized and ordered by your doctor." Her job required her to follow his instructions, especially now with me still listed in serious condition. She was just following the doctor's mandate. I still politely requested to have all pain medication stopped. It was, however, my body; and I wanted some say about painkillers or medication. Unless these medicines were keeping me alive or helping me to heal, I felt strongly to have the steady drip, drip, drip stopped.

I DO IT ALL

The same small distinct voice was in my head I first heard at that accident site was pounding again in my head: pain medication must be stopped if I was ever to walk again. I was thankful my doctor agreed to this request and stopped all pain medication after that last dosage. The nurses were wonderful, but at the same time let me know I would have difficulty getting much sleep without the medication. Giving up a month or two of sleep seemed like a small sacrifice if it meant I had a chance of walking and running again. I desperately wanted to go back to my normal life of constant activity. I had not given up on that happening. Imagining a life without physical activity and competition was unthinkable. I was willing to do anything, even put up with temporary pain or sleepless nights to gain back my stimulating and successful lifestyle.

Even with the few setbacks I experienced through life, I had been fortunate. I always seemed to encounter wonderful people and friends while on my surprising journey. During many of my sleepless nights, my thoughts would fleet backward to the number of these seemingly small and unexpected encounters. They all impacted my life and led to the day I was laid up and paralyzed.

Our father had spent countless hours teaching us not only the technical aspects of sports but also the value of sportsmanship. There was also my brother Ken forcing me onto a tennis court to start playing tennis, our sudden move to California and my fifth-grade broken leg indirectly leading me to Dick Skeen, then how this chance meeting changed the direction of my life. After Skeen became my coach and mentor, we spent hours together off the court, as well as hitting thousands of balls on the court. He shared his incredible life experiences with me. Listening to his encounters inspired me to continue to give my best and never give up.

I will never completely know how these small seemingly unrelated encounters instilled in me the necessary skills and faith I needed at this critical juncture of my life. I would only begin to understand the value, as the days, months, and years unfolded in front of me.

Dick was one of those unique individuals whom people could not easily forget. He could be abrasive and abrupt to some while engaging, inspiring, and being a wealth of information to others.

He never failed to polarize everyone he met into these two distinct groups. He seemed braggadocios to some but just plain honest to others while stating simple truths. This was especially true about his past tennis exploits and present tennis skills. Some of his stories seemed so outrageous, they were hard to believe. I read quite a bit about tennis, and his name had never come up in my brief searches. If his stories were remotely true, he would be an inspiration to anyone he worked with him and striving to reach goals of their own. It would only take a few minutes watching him play a tennis match to realize you were watching someone special and gifted.

Inside story of my friend and mentor Dick Skeen

Dick Skeen was of Irish descendants a little more than 5'8" tall, with a quizzical little smile he hid from those not in his closest circle of friends. Skeen's tennis attire was long cream-colored tennis slacks from bygone years, cream-colored long-sleeved shirt, and floppy Aussie hat when he played matches. When he was teaching tennis, he wore a large-brimmed gardening-style straw hat to protect his light-colored skin from daily sun exposure. He was not an imposing figure like many tennis players. That was until you saw him float effortlessly around a tennis court and almost magically control a tennis ball. He was a real character even though he was understated in most of what he was involved in.

Dick Skeen was born in Dallas, Texas, in 1906 to a wealthy family who moved to Hollywood, California, in 1918 when he was eleven. According to Dick, they owned a corner of Hollywood and Vine. His Father was a course hard-nosed, crusty businessman who thought playing sports was foolish. His father basically forbade any children in his family the opportunity to participate in sports. Dick started playing tennis secretly on three tennis courts, not far from their home. He loved hitting tennis balls the moment he held a tennis racket in his hand. Dick never ended up being very tall at under 5'9" but had long arms and strong huge hands. The moment he picked up a racket, he began using it like a magic wand. To say he was a natural would be a gross understatement.

Dick would head down to those three tennis courts every chance he had to play tennis with whoever was available to hit a few balls. Dick and his friends would keep a wary eye out for Father Skeen's limousine coming down Hollywood Boulevard. Once Dick was alerted to his father's approach, he would race off the courts and hide his rackets in the hedge surrounding the courts. He would quickly sit down and pretend to just be watching when his father arrived. His dad would take his rackets away and burn them if he caught Dick playing tennis. This did not deter Dick from his love of tennis. With any money he could obtain, he would buy more tennis rackets and keep playing every chance he had.

Because of his father, Dick was not able to play junior tennis tournaments like other friends his age. He only really started playing tournaments once he was old enough to leave home. In 1931, Dick turned professional while teaching tennis in Pasadena, California. His tennis teaching is legendary as he coached three world champions—Jack Kramer, Louise Brough, and Pauline Betz along with thirty-six other national champions. These included many great tennis players like Billy Talbert, Gussie Moran, Kathleen Harter, Carol Caldwell, Dave Ranney, Mike Caro, Julius Heldman, Ted Olewine, Eleanor Harbula, Jimmy Wade, George Richards, Connie Jaster, and Barbara Winslow. His legendary teaching was confirmed by the likes of Bill Tilden, Bobby Riggs, and Jack Kramer. Dick was known for his classic strokes, especially his devastating backhand chop and inside-out forehand. His experience was not limited to just playing and teaching but included designing the Newport Beach Tennis Club after teaching at the Riviera Country Club and Balboa Bay Club. Shortly after I met Dick, he founded and designed Blossom Hill Tennis Club before eventually retiring to Medford, Oregon, and buying the Rogue Valley Tennis Club.

Dick played professional tennis from 1935 to 1946, losing to Fred Perry in the finals of the 1941 US Pro Championships. Skeen reached as high as number seven in the combine amateur-pro rankings for the same year. Ray Bower's rankings had Dick as number two professional tennis player for the same year, reaching the semifinals in four other professional tournaments.

During his eleven-year career, he had wins over Bill Tilden, Don Budge, Ellsworth Vines, Fred Perry, Bobby Riggs, Karel Kozeluh, Vinnie Richards, Frank Kovacs, Welby Van Horn, Bruce Barnes, Wayne Sabin, and Les Stoeffen. Fred Perry told me personally that Dick was an amazingly talented tennis player who gave off an air of being arrogant. He said his arrogance was because he was so sure of his ability to control a tennis ball. This conversation with Fred Perry took place shortly before Perry passed away. Our conversation happened while we were sitting on the steps of Hong Kong's Government House during a special event. He said Dick was definitely one of the greats of his era. After the years I spent with Dick, I realized he wasn't arrogant, just immensely confident and talented, and he always let his racket backup his talking.

In 1972, at sixty-seven years of age, Dick was approached by the National Heart Association. They found Dick an amazing specimen of fitness for his age, so they offered to sponsor Dick to play the grand slam of senior tennis. These were the four US national events—US grass, clay, indoor, and hardcourt championships. Dick told me before he left that he wouldn't lose to any of the "old fogies" in the sixty-five-and-over age category. So he entered the fifty-fives and sixties simultaneously, easily winning every set in the sixty-fives to finish the year ranked number one. Bobby Riggs ended the year number 1 in the fifty-fives and stated he was thankful Dick was playing two other singles events each day. Riggs said he would have been in trouble in his age group if Dick had concentrated only on the fifty-five to fifty-nine category. Dick seemed to defy age and time when on a tennis court.

Skeen also seemed to attract famous people no matter where he went. While teaching and playing in the LA area, he taught many famous Hollywood stars such as Errol Flynn, Bing Crosby, Gary Cooper, Cary Grant, Fred Astaire, Kirk Douglas, Ginger Rogers, Doris Day, Joseph Cotton, Merle Oberon, Johnny Weissmuller, Norma Shearer, Hugh O'Brian, Dolores del Rio, Robert Stack, Efrem Zimbalist Jr., and Cornel Wilde.

I DO IT ALL

I spent many hours practicing and teaching and, generally on down times, sitting around talking and listening to one of the most respected teaching pros of Skeen's era as he related some amazing memories. I gained a respect for the history of tennis, getting the opportunity to spend time with a living legend. Dick seemed braggadocios recounting some wild stories of defeating some of the greats of tennis. Two of the most memorable stories were especially hard for me to believe. When Don Budge was retiring from tournament play, he was asked to play an exhibition in Las Vegas, Nevada. The organizers looked around the West Coast for the perfect player to highlight Budge's amazing skills when Dick Skeen's name was brought to their attention. Dick was eventually invited to journey to Vegas and play the exhibition. This, of course, was to honor Budge as he would be able to display his enormous tennis abilities.

When Dick arrived in Vegas to play, no one expected to witness what eventually transpired. Dick only knew one way to play tennis, and even though this was an exhibition to feature Budge, Skeen played his normal game and embarrassed the organizers by easily beating Budge. Skeen's ability and talent were on display instead of Budge's. Dick did this with only the loss of a few games. I found this story hard to believe until I went through Las Vegas and met the teaching pro at the Desert Sands. When he found out Skeen was my coach, he recounted Dick's exact story as we sat on the veranda by the tennis courts. He said it was a disaster for Budge and the organizers, and they had never really forgiven Skeen.

You would think Dick would have learned his lesson, but a few years later, when he was in his early forties, he was asked to come across San Francisco Bay and play another exhibition. This time it was against Tom Brown. Tom had just finished an amazing run at Wimbledon, winning the doubles and mixed doubles while losing in the finals of the singles at the Championships. The organizers again made a big mistake as they felt Dick's consistent style of play would allow Tom to display his immense ability, which had led to his success at Wimbledon. Again, Dick couldn't help himself and destroyed Tom 6–1, 6–1. This again highlighted Skeen's amazing ability, rather than Tom Brown's game. Members of the club related the same story to me a number of years later and again had not forgiven Dick for spoiling an event they had organized to feature Tom Brown.

Through my own travels across the US and around the world, I was able to confirm many of the seemingly wild stories Dick related to me. He was my tennis mentor, and more importantly, like others who have come across my life, an inspiration to follow as I worked through difficult times. Listening to their stories and watching them never give up helped me not to give in and accept any popular consensus. The popular consensus going around as I was lying in my hospital bed in Hong Kong was that my active lifestyle was over. Most people thought I needed to come to grips with that reality and accept the inevitable life as a paraplegic. I had been blessed with many individuals who influenced me to never give up, and Dick Skeen was just one of many. As important as these individuals were through the years, that still small voice in my head was loud and real. Hearing that voice gave me the true strength and determination to believe I could and would get better, walking and running again.

SCREECHING TO A HALT AND COMPLETE HELPLESSNESS

For five years, I had been doing everything at light speed. Once taking up triathlon, I began traveling to many countries around the world to compete in this new sport, loving every minute of this adventure. I visited many Asian countries, such as China, Philippines, Malaysia, Singapore, Taiwan, Borneo, Macau, Australia, the US, and Europe, enjoying success and winning every triathlon in the Asian races. My rapid improvement surprised me and all the veteran triathletes in my age group. Even with my success, I had bigger dreams and plans. I expected myself to continue improving, eventually to win a world title in my age group. I was just enough of an egomaniac to think I could "do it all." My long hours on the tennis court in the hot humid sun never bothered me. It helped me to be energized for my many off-court activities. I couldn't wait to wake up and start another full day knowing there were more tennis tournaments coming up or triathlon events for more travel and to experience another exotic venue.

1st ITU race in Beijing, China

Great Wall Triathlon

It was an exhilarating feeling to be in total control of my life and my body. I was so full of myself that I thought everyone else must be having a great life too! My family were healthy, with my children were going to one of the best world-class high schools possible. My wife was also busy and involved in the middle school program as a teaching assistant. I was deluded to think they were as happy and fulfilled, just because I was on a super high.

The Bible calls our body a clay pot, which is also referred to as a temple of God's Holy Spirit. I was celebrating my clay pot instead of the true essence that should be filling my clay pot. Everything was coming up roses as far as I was concerned. I was in total control until everything changed in a twinkling of an eye.

Getting used to the complete helplessness I was experiencing every day and night was difficult and almost impossible to accept. All I could do for myself was painfully wash my face and brush my teeth and my hair using my undamaged right hand and arm. Even moving my undamaged right arm caused deep pain in my upper back and neck. Being helpless was difficult mentally, psychologically, as well as physically. It was especially hard to accept the first few times I had to be bathed and washed by the nurses on duty. This made me feel as helpless as a baby. It turned out to be one of those times in my life where I needed to humbly accept the help that was necessary and so willingly provided. As an adult, I was still very shy when it came to being completely exposed. It was almost as if I needed to close my eyes and pretend the nurses also had their eyes closed when bathing me.

The paralysis also affected my ability to perform normal bodily functions, such as relieving myself. Again another problem popping up! A bladder bag had been inserted during the initial operation, and the release of solid waste had stopped for a few days. The nurses were concerned and monitored me closely as to when or if my body will start to function normally again without assistance. If that did not happen, a colostomy would need to be performed to rid my body of this waste. I felt desperate when they informed me of this possible scenario. Thankfully, a colostomy was never needed. The result of this problem turned out to be another one of those unexpected side effects. Controlling myself ended up being a major trial for me during my hospital stay and for years to come.

Things we all take for granted were becoming a daily trial for me in the hospital and for the years ahead. Trying to relieve or control myself until I could find a nearby facility turned into a daily ritual. Some days I could almost make my body function properly, but it always took a concentrated effort. On other days, the nurses would need to manually take care of my body. How humiliating feeling like a baby again, having this done by others, especially the first few times. Later on, it became a private joke between myself and the nursing staff as they would ask if it was "glove time" when I rang the nurses bell. They even gave me an inflated surgical glove, which looked like a balloon when I was finally able to leave the hospital. This was a special remembrance of my stay and part of the nurse's going-away gifts.

There is a special connection which develops between patients and the nursing staff in long stay and care situations. There is no adequate way to say how important the nursing staff is in the care and recovery process. They kept my stay at the hospital positive when the enormity of my condition could have gotten the better of me.

Helplessness reminded me of when I was around eleven years old and we went to visit a family from our church. The mom and dad, Marie and Willis Walker, were my parents' age, and their children were in the same youth group at our church. Willis went to Northwest Nazarene College the same time as my dad. While they were there, Marie was stricken with polio. In spite of the subsequent trials forced on them, Willis maintained a straight-A average, graduating with honors. Marie was wheelchair-bound after polio attacked her body.

One day after church, we went to their home to visit Marie, eat lunch, and spend the afternoon. I was taken aback when we entered their living room to find Marie in an iron-lung machine, allowing her to breathe properly. When she had contracted polio in college, she was able to be in a wheelchair. But not long after, she was relegated to spending most of her life inside this metal-and-glass container. Willis was committed to taking care of his wife and did everything he could to make her as comfortable as possible. The disability facing Marie did not stop her from being in charge of her household. She organized everything to make sure her two daughters were able to have a normal childhood. Her children were also straight-A students and had nothing but the utmost respect, admiration, and love for their mom and dad.

Marie's condition was very difficult for me to view as I couldn't imagine how she was able to be so bright and positive. She was wonderful and had a strong, vital faith in Jesus. She was always happy to share her faith with anyone willing to listen. Willis was a positive, no-nonsense kind of guy who seemed settled into embracing the situation they had unexpectedly found themselves in. I looked on with utter amazement, first thinking of what it must be like to be her. I thought I would not be able to handle something like that. It almost made me sick to my stomach to envision a life that way. Secondly, I tried to put myself in Willis's shoes as he constantly made sure Marie was comfortable and taken care of. He was trapped as much as Marie, yet he seemed to be fine and looked to always maintain a positive outlook. I couldn't imagine myself in his position either. Then looking around and seeing their two bright and successful daughters made me finally realize they were an amazing family going through the unimaginable. They were staying positive about the present and the future, living life to the fullest.

Their deep-abiding faith and hope in God and His Son Jesus allowed them to press on even in the most trying of circumstances. I could hardly imagine this as an eleven-year-old. As desperately as I never wanted to go through a similar event, I intently watched Willis and Marie Walker and their two daughters. Their entire family displayed a grace that transcended their obvious difficult environment. They were an inspiration and wonderful to be around. I may not have wanted their particular situation, but I did see qualities in their lives I desired in mine. It was an experience I would never forget.

Lying paralyzed in Hong Kong reminded me of how fortunate I was not to be in an iron lung. Although I needed almost everything done for me, I realized how fortunate I was to be alive and not in a claustrophobic tube. I had hope of a future, even with the doctors' negative prognosis. God did miracles, and I believed deeply there were more miracles out there for me. It was a miracle I was alive; I was now praying for a miraculous future.

After my last roommate left me with a private room, the nursing staff would often cross the hallway and come in for a chat when they weren't busy. We could laugh and share together without the worry of bothering another patient. They would often arrive during the long slow nighttime hours. The staff were right about my not sleeping much without the pain medication. They were welcomed company to keep my mind off the ever-present pain and discomfort. Together we would check out what was on the late movies. Given it was Hong Kong in 1992, the TV selection was very limited. There were only two English language stations broadcasting, and late-night programming was limited, especially after midnight. The gifts of flowers, chocolate boxes, and fruit baskets were literally filling up my room. When nurses arrived, we would check out the fruit, snacks, and chocolates for a midnight brunch. For me it became party time to break up those long, hard dark hours. I looked forward to them coming in, helping me celebrate my small improvements and getting me through my sleepless nights.

They also helped me with the many flowers arriving. There were some patients on the floor who had very few, if any, visitors. The nurses would always let me know when a patient needed cheering up. They suggested I share some of my many flower displays with these other patients. We would go through the flowers and allow some of the corporate gifts to be passed on to other rooms to brighten up their stay. The nursing staff were always thinking of ways to make everyone's stay as positive as possible.

Activity was constant during the day and sometimes almost hectic on the fourth floor. I was reluctant to use the nurses' bell to ask for anything. The staff were incredibly busy with one urgent task after another, easily viewed from my vantage point. During my first week, two of the nurses came into my room and let me know that I needed to start using the call bell. I always waited for them to come in to check on me. Sometimes it would take longer than I expected for them to arrive, as they were super busy. They asked why I never rang the bell. From my viewpoint, they always looked occupied, rushing around and didn't need to be disturbed any more than necessary. They informed me I was the most seriously injured patient on the floor. I found that hard to believe but took their word for it. By my using the bell, it was the only way for them to know when I needed some help. Otherwise, they were required to come out from behind their desk, physically walk over to my room, and check out what was going on. I was actually causing them more inconvenience. I sheepishly listened to their lecture and started using the bell.

Most of the day, I kept myself occupied by doing what exercises I could think of lying flat on my back. These included trying to make my toes move, open and close my left-hand fingers, and flex my undamaged right arm as much as possible. Too many things to work on to think about ringing a bell. I promised them I would use the bell more often in the future. It is never fun to be lectured like a child when you are an adult. The nurses were right and were always sensitive and caring in their approach. They knew how to be firm and loving at the same time. Sounds like the perfect parent.

When you run into a bus at 50 mph with your head and body, there are a variety of injury problems that suddenly exhibit themselves. Another one of these unexpected conditions, which made life interesting and difficult at times, was hyperesthesia around my upper rib cage. This sensation transmitted an alternating buzz of severe burning and itching. The result of this sensation was to sweat profusely while at the same time wanting to scratch and rub my skin raw, hoping it would go away.

This sensation brought back memories of an earlier time where I needed to deal with a severe itching. This memory was from an injury that happened on an early fall evening when I was quarterback of our Little League football team. We were enjoying another undefeated season with our dad as coach and my brother Ken playing center. Ken would hike the ball to me on every play. We had practiced many times during the summer with the entire backfield in our backyard. For a little league team, we worked together like clockwork, enjoying each other's company.

This particular day was one of those beautiful late-afternoon Indian summer fall practices we regularly experienced in Boise, Idaho. My dad had put us through the usual disciplined practice session, and with only fifteen minutes left, he decided to run some live scrimmage where we would run plays at full impact to replicate gameplay.

Idaho's Little League football during those years was played with full tackle equipment using pads and helmets just like the high school or university teams. When putting on our uniforms, we all felt invincible and loved the look of being so big and strong.

As with most plays, I as quarterback was under the center to receive the ball from Ken. When he hiked the ball, the unusual happened. I mishandled the ball and fumbled it under my feet. I turned quickly, found the ball, and bent over to retrieve it. Just as I picked it up, I was hit on my lower right leg, creating a pain I had never felt before. As I fell on my face, someone fell on the same leg finishing off what was most likely a minor break into a serious spiral fracture or green twig break. The fracture started just below my knee and spiraled downward to just above my ankle.

As I lay on the ground in pain, not knowing what was happening, my dad rushed over to aid me, thinking I had a cramp. He started massaging my leg to work out the apparent cramp. I had never experienced pain like that, and as much as he massaged, it didn't get better. The pain only increased. My dad finally gave up on the massage, carried me to the car, and drove off to the doctor's office. As it turned out, the doctor confirmed my broken leg, and my dad's meaningless phrase popped out, "Your mom is going to kill me." He had to face the music when he took me home with a cast from my upper thigh to my toes. This statement, "Your mom is going to kill me," was familiar and repeated many times when my brother or I were injured with my dad encouraging us to play sports. This was always a "lighthearted" phrase that had no real meaning as our mom was understanding, supportive, and served as a perfect mom to nurse us back to health. She, like every good mom, hated to see her children hurt or in pain but supported our ever-present active lifestyle. She also knew we were going to stay active, and these mishaps would likely continue through the years.

My first broken-bone experience was not good, as the break had also, unknowingly for the doctor, completely severed the tendon connected to my big toe. My broken-bone pain was compounded because of the severed tendon, which kept me awake at night. The muscle that worked my big toe had rolled up to just below my knee, causing a spasm, which could not be alleviated. This extra pain kept me from getting a good-night's sleep for two weeks. My mom was up almost all night with me when I couldn't quietly handle the pain. I slept upstairs near my parents' bedroom, on the living room couch, so they could provide comfort during those long nighttime hours. I was very young but was learning a little about absorbing pain that fall. I also learned how a mom and dad would sacrifice their sleep to take care of their children. I did my best to be as quiet as possible with my discomfort to avoid bothering my parents, especially at night. I knew they needed their sleep for their next day's work and activities.

The spasms finally subsided after a few weeks. About the same time, an almost unbearable itching sensation began. The itching only worsened inside the full-length leg cast. I could barely put up with it. After some creative thinking, I devised a way to relieve some of the discomfort. I took a metal coat hanger and bent it in half so it was rounded and smooth at one end. This way, no sharp edges would touch my skin. I would then gently slide the smooth rounded end into my upper cast and edge it down to where the worst itching was happening. My leg had shrunk or atrophied enough by then to allow room for the coat hanger to slide inside the cast. Awe, wonderful relief as I gently slide the clothes hanger up and down against my itching skin.

When I went back to the doctor's office for a six-week appointment, my doctor was appalled at what I had devised to relieve the itching. It was time to remove the full-leg cast, replacing it with a walking cast from my knee to my toes. He was fearful I may have scratched myself and broken the skin, with my anti-itching contraption, possibly causing an infection. Everything turned out to be fine, but I carried that coat hanger everywhere for another month. The doctor kept the cast on two weeks longer than necessary to make sure I wouldn't try to play the last few weeks of the football season. With my leg shriveled up and atrophied muscles, he had nothing to worry about. I was shocked at how small my leg looked when he removed the final cast. I knew then it would be some time before I would be back to normal and at full strength. After those twelve weeks, and a lot of pain, I was still out of the cast in time for our winter ski season. Skiing allowed me to build my leg back to full strength in no time at all. The fast healing of youth allowed for my quick recovery. I was wishing I had that fast healing ability while lying in a Hong Kong hospital.

This itching from hyperesthesia in Hong Kong was more intense than anything I had endured in Boise as a child. Hyperesthesia caused me to sweat profusely. My sheets and gowns would be soaked clear through within an hour. The staff had to change my bedding and gowns many of times a day. One particular day, they discovered a shortage of fresh hospital gowns. They informed me a fresh gown would be arriving in the next hour or so. In the meantime, I would be in the "buff," lying under the freshly applied sheets. Not being able to do much for myself, modesty was less of a factor, and what choice did I have? The staff were always doing the best they could in a somewhat hectic environment. While I waited for a fresh hospital gown, it became apparent that the hyperesthesia and related sensations had decreased to the point where my sweating had all but disappeared.

Being naked under the sheets and keeping them at waist level, I could manage the discomfort and eliminate the need to have the sheets changed so many times a day. The nurses and I decided to try going buff during the rest of my stay. Dealing with so many injuries, smashed-up hand, knuckle, wrist, left arm, ribs, head, and two dramatically broken vertebrae made my friends wonder why this sweating was such a big deal. Taking care of little irritating items can make your minutes pass much more comfortably. This then made it easier to deal with the obviously more serious problems. Lessening the itching issue was huge for me and made the rest of my stay in the hospital easier to cope with.

I was constantly driving the hospital staff crazy with my requests to make my life seem seminormal, even while using the nurses' bell as little as possible. I was determined to keep myself busy with whatever activities I could think of. I did everything to make sure I was stimulated in a very boring environment. The nursing staff were getting used to saying no to me but still took time to patiently listen to my ideas. Then I came up with a great idea! Maybe the craziest idea I had come up with since arriving.

A DAY OUT

Life before being admitted to the Adventist Hospital had been spent enjoying fresh air, sunshine, and out-of-doors every day of my life. In Hong Kong, I was either playing tennis, teaching tennis, swimming in the pool, cycling, or running along the waterfront of Deep Water Bay and Repulse Bay. Weekends were spent going to the beach, hiking on one of the many country park trails, having a picnic in a local park, or being taken on wild mountain bike adventures with my two sons. This was all happening while living and working in Hong Kong. Our travels also took us to countryside settings, beautiful beaches, or mountains around Asia and the world. We always targeted locations that provided warm outdoor activities, like climbing Mount Kinabalu or rafting down a wild whitewater river. This was the first time in my life I was forced to be trapped inside for a lengthy period of time. Even with serious injuries when younger, I had always found a way to keep active and go outside.

My broken leg incident in fifth grade had left me with crutches to get around, hopping along on my one good leg. After a week, I was up, out of the house, and back to school, even with the pain and lack of sleep. After school, I would still hang around and attend the football practices and games. Another member of our team had also been injured and was on crutches. We devised some competitions where we would race each other up and down the sidelines, balancing only on our crutches, using them like pogo sticks. We got pretty good staying balanced, so we could race for twenty yards or so without letting our one good leg touch the ground. I learned to stay active after watching professional athlete's active lifestyle when the unexpected happened and they were faced with a temporary disability. They would find ways to continue an active lifestyle, sometimes while participating in their chosen sport, even if it was only recreational.

One fall in Boise, we were fortunate to have a former Olympic skier from Switzerland come in town to condition us for our winter ski season. We loved the hard gym workouts as we were all looking forward to another great season on the slopes. Not long after ski season arrived, we heard that our Swiss trainer had been involved in a serious accident while on the slopes of Sun Valley, Idaho. He had been standing near the edge of small cliff looking out over the beautiful scenic view of Sun Valley when an intermediate skier lost control and slammed into him. He was hit so hard it knocked him off the edge, landing on another ledge thirty-five feet below. Him standing there had probably save the life of the other skier, but he had suffered a badly fractured leg.

We were all devastated for him, hearing this disheartening news. Wow, out for the entire ski season. "It must be horrible for him," we thought. Three weeks later, while skiing at Bogus Basin, we saw him up on the mountain. He was not sitting in the lodge sipping a hot drink but out on the slopes again. There he was with a cast on one leg from his thigh to his foot and a ski on his one good leg. He was jetting down the slope, seemingly without a worry in the world. He still looked to be one of the best skiers on the slopes that day, skiing on his one good leg! Nothing was going to keep him from enjoying the outside and having a wonderful ski season, not even a broken leg. We never know how much these chance encounters affect the way we view our life in the future.

Now with my own disability, I was always looking for new ways to keep myself busy in the hospital. These ideas helped time pass more quickly. Keep life interesting and fight off boredom was what I had learned since I was young. Since the new arrangement with the sheets was working well, I was feeling much better. One day while looking outside and seeing a beautiful clear-blue sky, I came up with what I thought was a brilliant plan. I was no longer listed in serious condition, so why not have the nursing staff, which felt like my good friends by then, arrange to have my bed wheeled outside and placed in the beautiful gazebo and garden area? I would be able to enjoy fresh warm air, birds singing, and basically get wheeled out of my room for more than going for another exam. It would literally be a breath of fresh air for me, now that my condition was improving. I desperately needed to feel the outside again. The outside had always been my domain. My life was lived there, not inside. I may not be able to move my legs, but I could hardly wait to be out in the fresh air again.

With my best persuasion, the staff finally relented and wheeled my bed into the lift. Before I knew it, we were down and out the front door of the hospital heading to the gazebo, which was across the driveway entrance. They positioned my bed in the middle of what was to me a beautiful lush, tropical garden. This little gazebo was actually in the middle of the large roundabout that served as the entrance to the hospital. I didn't care; it was paradise to me after being locked up inside for so long. Being there lifted my spirits more than they could imagine. I relished the wondrousness of the outside world again. They left me there alone to enjoy the ambiance of a beautiful, warm Hong Kong afternoon. They let me know they would be back later to return me to the fourth floor and my ever-shrinking room. It is amazing how walls tend to close in when you are just lying in a bed with next to nothing happening and that huge wall clock right in front. I was literally trapped with nowhere to go.

Lying outside, I could still barely do anything for myself other than slightly raise and lower my bed with a battery-powered button. There I was in the buff, lying under a thin sheet, enjoying every single minute. Every now and then, a visitor to the hospital would cut through the gazebo and be surprised to find me lying there in bed. A few conversations ensued, which made my time even more enjoyable. I felt like I was back with the real, vibrating world of Hong Kong again. I was taken outside around 2:00 p.m., and I was entranced by the blue sky and warm sunshine. Time passed swiftly as I hardly noticed the shadows lengthening. It wasn't long before the sun dipped low in the afternoon sky, eventually disappearing behind one of Hong Kong's high-rise buildings. This was so relaxing compared to the busyness of the fourth floor activity. The hectic environment on my floor was probably the reason no one came to check on me. I found this marvelous, as I loved the extra time outside, but amusing at the same time. I suddenly realized the 4:00 p.m., nurses' shift had come and gone while I was enjoying my wonderful outside adventure.

Sunset arrived, and lights came on in the drive as I lay helpless in the garden. Darkness of evening was fast approaching, and still no one had come to take me back inside.

With the darkness came the chill of evening. For me with only a thin sheet to protect me from the elements, coolness of evening was becoming unpleasant for my upper body. The other noticeable item was nobody was coming through the gazebo anymore. The garden was not lit like the rest of the drive or walkways, so visitors arriving to the hospital tended to take the lit walkway around the driveway to avoid the darker path through the garden gazebo. As I lay there, I found it humorous, thinking of the next nursing shift. How long would it take for them to realize I was missing? With no evidence I been taken out for another exam, I was hoping they would start inquiring about me. My legs were still paralyzed, so I could not help myself get back inside. I really started to feel chill in my upper body, where I had feeling. I decided it was time for this adventure to end, but with no bell at my disposal to ring for help, I was clueless as to how I was going to get back inside.

It wasn't long before a gentleman leaving the hospital finally took the shortcut through the garden. He was startled to see me lying there and asked if I needed help. He found it strange to find someone in a hospital bed in the middle of the gazebo, especially at night. I told him I had tried a daring escape, but the steep driveway leaving the hospital was too difficult to negotiate in a hospital bed. After a laugh and our short introduction, he was kind enough to call the nurses station on the fourth floor informing them their missing patient was in the middle of the roundabout with nothing on but a sheet. It was a great adventure for me and provided many red faces and laughs from the staff, who had all but forgotten about their patient during the shift change. I guess I was easier to forget than I thought possible.

I felt a surge of encouragement from my escapade, refreshing my spirit from this short time outside with beautiful green nature surrounding me. For me, it was a sign that I would soon be outside again on my own, believing I would be doing all of my past activities I so loved. I was more determined than ever to do what I could to improve.

MIRACLE BEGINS

My doctor would visit at least once a day, sauntering into the room in his white smock, holding a small tablet and acting like life was wonderful. After asking how I was doing, he would begin his daily tests to determine if any sensation was returning in my lower body. Most often, he would visit in the evening when my family would be keeping me company. These tests would include inserting a long needle from my waist down. Lying there, looking at the ceiling, I was not able to witness the exact nature of these tests or where he was inserting the needle. My doctor would always ask if I could feel anything. I could hear my children in the back of the room whispering, "Come on, Dad."

My usual response was, "I think so. It feels like maybe someone is leaning on me."

To this day, I don't remember if I really felt anything because I desperately wanted to feel again. This was very discouraging for my children, realizing their dad could not feel a needle being stuck in his muscles like I was a piece of dead meat. What the results of these tests might mean for them or for the future of our family was unimaginable.

In spite of my surface sensation not quickly returning, I was able to start moving my toes and feet. It didn't take long before I could force myself to slightly bend my knees. These results didn't happen all by myself. I needed help, more than I even imagined.

On the third day and after the doctor stated, "You will probably never walk again. The chance is one in a million," I contacted the rehab department and requested a therapist to visit my room. I was insistent, as I wanted to get started on my recovery. I was way ahead of myself and a real nag! I was in complete denial regarding my injuries. On day five, the therapist finally arrived, took one look at me, and asked why I had called him out of the rehab department to come up to the fourth floor. I said, "I can't move them"—pointing to my legs—"I want you to do your thing, massage, mobilization, whatever, move them for me!" He politely informed me it had only been five days since arriving with a badly broken back. I was still listed in serious condition. He also knew he was not allowed to work on me without authorization from my doctor.

The next day after much persuasion, I obtained the authorization from my doctor for limited mobilization and massage as long as it caused no movement to my back. Every day after that, he appeared in my doorway, ready to carefully and slowly move my legs more and more, massaging my muscles and manipulating my legs, feet, and ankles. Although I could not feel anything on my skin, I was able to slowly move my lower limbs. I cannot express strong enough how much encouragement this gave me in continuing my best effort to move forward. Even with my efforts, I knew what I was seeing was a miracle. Realizing my daily improvement had nothing to do with some strong mental ability, I was humbled. My doctor, friends, and family tried to give me credit for these small improvements. I would quietly thank God for blessing me and saving my life every single day.

My doctor looked puzzled and a little frightened as he could not understand how this unexplained improvement was beginning to happen or how any movement could be happening so soon after arriving. In his mind, none of this should have happened. All his empirical medical knowledge told him otherwise, and not being a spiritual person, he didn't believe in miracles. For my doctor, everything had to fall into an explainable category, which he had some control of. At the beginning of my third week, with my constant harassment, my doctor decided to go with the flow and let me attempt to stand up. Medical information regarding my injuries will suggest this should not take place before week six or eight.

When the big day arrived, it was like a procession filing into my room. Four fourth floor staff arrived with my doctor. A back brace was very carefully put into place to support my vertebrae and muscles in my back. Three nurses and the doctor slowly positioned my legs over the side of my bed, then lifted me up for the first time in seventeen days. Dizziness and a wave of nausea surprisingly swept over me. I had been flat on my back since the accident took place, other than the bed being slightly raised and lowered. When my doctor first said that I could try standing up, I thought, *What do you mean try? Just give me the okay, I'll stand up on my own. Don't you know what kind of an athlete I am?* I knew my condition was serious but had not until that very moment realized the enormity of the so-called simple task of standing up. It took three nurses and my doctor to gently raise me up while I grasped onto a walker with my one good right hand and arm. With all the help and my right arm holding onto the walker, I was finally on my feet again. In less than ten seconds, my upper back hurt so bad that my head began pounding, and I felt sick to my stomach. With more help and support, they gently lowered me back down in bed, completely exhausted to recover.

How could this possibly be? I thoughtfully asked myself. Just seventeen days ago, I was one of the fittest men my age in the world, competing in two sports and near the top-of-the-world senior level in both. To my astonishment, I was not discouraged with the results of my first effort to regain my abilities. Setting very small and attainable goals, ones which I could measure daily, occupied my mind and efforts. Since I had no other commitments other than just lying in bed, I concentrated on moving my toes, feet, and bent my knees more each day. I never stopped my finger exercises on my left hand or lifting light weights with my right hand.

Contemplation about the past, present, and future were in my thoughts constantly while lying in that hospital bed. I reviewed the number of times unexpected events happened during my life, and I somehow found ways to forge through them. Our parents provided the source of our "never say die" attitude. When things happened, which could be taken as bad, my dad would always say, "Take it as a challenge, and come back stronger." Then even more was the spiritual upbringing, which taught us all things work out for our benefit, if we keep God in His proper place in our life.

After my fourteen-stitch chin incident, the first remembrance of a challenging experience was with my broken leg, then Ken getting his front tooth knocked out playing baseball, smashing my thumb in our car door and getting the nail completely ripped off a few days later during wrestling practice. A broken foot playing baseball and so on and so on kept life interesting in the Bozarth household. There was never a lack of challenges for the active Bozarth boys. Inadvertently, these mishaps taught us a lot about pain and how to best handle these situations.

One of the junior high school wrestling coaches had a brilliant idea when I ripped my thumbnail off. He took me into his office and said he had a sure-fire remedy. He took out a bottle of Absorbing Junior from his cabinet; removed the cap; and stuck my raw, bleeding thumb into the half-empty bottle to block the opening. Then before I knew it, he turned it upside down, drowning my thumb in the liquid, creating a shockwave of pain, which nearly made me pass out. It felt like fire! It's a wonder my thumbnail ever grew back as on the bottle it stated very clearly, "For external use only." He must have thought, even though my thumbnail was completely gone, my raw, bleeding thumb was on the outside. Absorbing Junior was used for massage to create heat and loosen up your muscles. On an open wound, it created more than heat. It felt like a blast furnace. Maybe this was one of those early life experiences preparing me for the future I was experiencing in Hong Kong. What doesn't kill us makes us stronger, right? I think whoever made up that saying had never been seriously injured.

I also contemplated on how life continued to be positive even with the setbacks. Winning the Idaho State singles and doubles tennis titles two years in a row, rafting down the Boise River in the summers, water skiing at Lucky Peak Dam, camping at Payette Lake, snow skiing at Bogus Basin, or just playing on the many sports teams made life great in Idaho. I loved everything about my life in Boise.

Now in Hong Kong, I wasn't about to stop because of a negligent minibus driver. My active life couldn't possibly be over. I had to remind myself of this each and every day when I woke up. I also thought about how our surprising moved to California was almost like having an injury. Everything I knew was suddenly ripped away, and I was forced to take it as a challenge and start over. My quarterback days were over after injuring my elbow during an early fall practice playing football at Drake High School, then after our move to San Jose, California, and my refusal to play football for the first time since second grade. Ken and I grew up playing musical instruments as well as being active in sports, so I kept myself busy with band and tennis, my junior year in San Jose.

I missed playing football my junior year, so I decided to try out for the varsity football team my senior year. I, of course, racked up my knee pretty good one day in practice. Within ten days and a serious taping job applied on my knee before each game and practice, I still played the rest of the season and loved it.

There were those who thought I was accident prone with sprained ankles, broken ankle, injured elbows waterskiing, injured arm high jumping, and a broken collarbone when riding my bike home from the club in Medford.

Cycling and I had an interesting past as I lay there thinking of my many cycling mishaps. Before we left Boise, I had been racing down a steep hill when a car flew past, immediately pulled in front of me, and screeched to a stop. Slamming into the back of the car, I was vaulted upward, sliding over the top of the vehicle to land mostly unhurt in the road. When we are young, we bounce like a rubber ball and get up running. *I am certainly not like a rubber ball now*, I thought as I lay there in Hong Kong. The parts of my body I could feel felt like a thousand brittle pieces of broken crystal.

There was that late evening in Medford when cycling down a hill in a quiet neighborhood, I found myself suddenly lying in a grassy ditch in a semiconscious state with horrible pain and a shattered collarbone.

Injuries kept coming, as one time I tore my soleus muscle, snapping it completely into while working out Jonathan Stark, one of my tennis students. It sounded like a gunshot from a small bb gun when it snapped in two. The small muscle, which lies under the two large gastrocnemii or gastrocnemius muscles of the calf, rolled up close to the back of my knee. It seemed like I couldn't get a break when it came to getting into top shape for competitions, especially for tennis. For some reason, I always got back up and kept trying. My dad had instilled in me the attitude to concentrate on what you can do next and leave the worrying behind. "Leave the past in the past!" This kept me positive even when crazy mishaps took place. I was fortunate having positive, supporting individuals surrounding me.

Even with memories of injuries and setbacks, I thought about how I had always enjoyed an amazing lifestyle, winning a number of team championships and individual events. I loved the atmosphere of team sports where teammates worked together for a common goal but also loved individual sports where you had total say in your performance and the eventual outcome. Now lying there in Hong Kong, I knew it would take a team and individual effort to get me through this latest mishap.

Another memory came to mind when I was in junior high school wrestling for the city championship in Boise. I was so far behind on the judges' scorecard that my coach got frustrated, gave up on me, and walked down to one of the other three wrestling mats. Correctly thinking, he thought I was hopelessly behind with less than thirty seconds to go. When he walked away, I was behind eighteen points to five. In the last few seconds of the match, I reversed my opponent and pinned him, winning the match and the city championship. For some reason, I always relished being the underdog, then doing my best to upset the favorite. Don't get me wrong, it is also nice to be the favorite because of all the hard work you put in to be in that position. Lying there in Hong Kong, I thought I couldn't be more of an underdog than the situation I found myself in. Doctors were saying I would not be able to have an active lifestyle anymore and probably never walk again. Visitors would have that look of resignation, thinking I would not be able to come back from my injuries. I set my mind to do everything I could to prove them wrong and gain my life back.

As much as I enjoyed team sports, I loved individual sports like tennis where there was no coach once you walked on the court for a match. I somehow liked seeing the nervousness in the stands, knowing that only you or your opponent could decide what was going to happen next. Staying positive and doing your best to win always inspired me whether I won or lost. Giving your all to come back and win was instilled in me by my parents. I have always been grateful for their encouraging advice. Life never stops throwing you curveballs or roadblocks. These sudden detours seem to always happen when you least expected it.

*****

So many positive memories after forty-five years of living. I loved and enjoyed replaying every part of my childhood. We were a close-knit family who were very traditional at that time in the States. It seemed everyone went to church in the '50s and '60s. At church, I was fortunate to interact with many of our senior members. While my friends were running around playing outside after the church services, I would often get the opportunity to have life changing conversations with many of the church's elders. They would happily share many of their life experiences while at the same time take a sincere interest in my life and activities. They had so much wisdom to share and were more than willing to pass them on to a sincerely interested youngster. I would stand there transfixed by their life stories. It was amazing as all of them had gone through difficult times. However difficult their past journey had been, they were positive, inspiring people to be around. Each one passed on the same similar encouragements. First was to love God; second, respect everyone; third, live life in the present and to the fullest because life is very short.

Lying there in Hong Kong and thinking about my life experiences, I knew I had made some big mistakes. Some of those mistakes had led me to be in that very hospital. If I could have changed the past, I would have said yes. My life came very close to being very short and over on April 22. Did I quickly learn from my mistakes, or did I still make mistakes after the accident? Absolutely, as I could be a bonehead at times. One thing I did know, every good decision I had made had been based on those three principles, which I learned when

I was very young. I have always had a firm belief in God; I have done my best to respect everyone, believing that every human being has special gifts and qualities. We just need to take the time to intently look and quietly recognize that God created every one of us uniquely special. And finally, I have done my best to stay in the present and grab a hold of the opportunity to live life to the fullest. With these memories constantly in my mind, I couldn't help but realize how fortunate I was to be alive. I was being given another opportunity to recover and enjoy what was still out there in my future.

Only once during my hospital stay could I remember being slightly depressed or discouraged. The nursing staff said I was always upbeat and encouraging when they were working with me. There never seemed to be a moment where I needed to work myself up to stay positive. I was always focused on what little I could do to see genuine results, no matter how minor. In some ways, this was a miracle given the traumatic circumstances I found myself in. I was still staying "active."

I realized later that this attitude happens because of our lifestyle and faith before a traumatic life-altering experience. No one suddenly changes and becomes completely different after an accident. I could have easily spent my time thinking, *Ten seconds, one way or the other, and I would have avoided that bus.* Instead, without much effort, I found myself focused on my new goals. I didn't have time to think about the apparent injustice of being in a perfect, wrong place at the perfect, wrong time. Wrong place at the wrong time? Isn't that the definition of every mishap or accident in life? Dwelling on this apparent injustice will only lead to a bitter, discouraging existence. I wanted nothing to do with that mindset. The constant attitude of what-if, only leads to a long, slow, and bitter recovery. *If* there is ever to be a recovery and a positive life in the future.

One of the many things I learned early on was the myth that communities, businesses, and associations you are closely connected with will come to your aid and support you. There are always very close true friends, who will stay with us in our time of need. The other truth, everyone else tends to get on very quickly without you and leave you hanging out there by yourself. This is understandable as they have their own very busy lives to take care of. The myth promoted in movies is "everyone will rally around you, raise funds for you, and constantly be there for you in your time of need."

That scenario makes for a great movie, but in the real world, you are mostly left on your own to deal with the pain, setbacks, and, of course, the numerous bills which pile up after the cards, flowers, snacks, fruit baskets, and chocolates finish arriving. Nobody is to be blamed. Who wants to spend time in a hospital, being reminded of their mortality and spending time with someone who makes them feel uncomfortable? The hospital staff are the real heroes in these situations. They are the ones who really care about your comfort and recovery. It may be their job, but in my experience, they have a passion for caring and doing their best to help you stay positive. Their positive smiles are greatly needed while you work your way through all the pain and discomfort.

Only sixteen days into my hospital stay, I discovered the Aberdeen Marina Club had changed their executive insurance policy a few months prior to my accident. This reduced my coverage to a maximum thirty days hospital stay. I also found out my excellent USPTA tennis professional association insurance did not cover any accidents overseas. Acquiring this insurance was the main reason I joined the USPTA. I should have read the fine print before I joined and moved overseas. All this latest news was like being hit with one body blow after another. Although this was not good news, this motivated me to do even more exercises to get better. I knew right then I had to be released in thirty days or face a steeper uphill financial battle, which already looked challenging. Bones don't heal in thirty days, but somehow, I didn't think about that then. With no tennis lesson revenue for the month, our savings were quickly drying up, especially in the high-maintenance society of Hong Kong.

This was one of the reasons my doctor relented and helped me stand up as I was determined to leave the hospital by day 31. Why he allowed me to try standing up so soon turned out to be a mystery. Another doctor reviewing my MRIs and X-rays a few years later said he couldn't understand, as every indication was for me to remain in bed with no movement until my vertebrae could completely heal. I nagged my doctor every time he came into my room, even though every indicator looked negative. He probably had to psych himself up every time he came for my daily visit and examination. I could be very persuasive when I wanted something, and my doctor finally said, "For some unknown reason, your body is healing faster than possible." I didn't want all the facts then, just wanted to get better and leave the hospital. With all my nagging, he probably wanted me out of the hospital as badly I wanted to leave. I wanted to leave the hospital as soon as I could, especially with the recent news from Aberdeen Marina Club and the USPTA. But how could I possibly leave the hospital in a month? My doctor had earlier stated, "You need to prepare yourself for a minimum six-month stay," and with the prognosis, "You will never walk again."

After my initial trial of attempting to stand up, I asked the nurses to come into my room many times a day with the therapist to help me to my feet. It always took at least three nurses to safely help me sit and stand up. After that initial dizzying effort getting to my feet, I felt a little better each time I was upright. I was determined to stand longer each time they came, in spite of the deep ache in my upper back. By the third day, I could finally stand, weaving back and forth walker assisted, for about five minutes. I was holding myself up with the walker, more than really standing!

This was all great, but how could I learn to walk again? There was little response in my ability to move my legs. The doctor was emphatic; he would not release me unless I could walk around the entire fourth floor unassisted. He would allow me to hold the walker slightly off the floor to avoid any misstep or a bad fall. The therapist who came to my room daily said, for me to learn how to walk again would require me to throw my hips forward using my upper body and core for balance. With little to no feeling in my core, this proved to be difficult. Nothing was simple with the ever-present deep pain and ache in my upper back. The back of my head hurt continually. Swinging my hips from side to side allowed my legs to swing forward, providing my version of walking. Keeping my balance was more difficult than I thought possible. The walker assured my ability to stay upright as I swayed back and forth. I eventually was able to head down the hallway with walker in hand. The first time trying this, I would have fallen on my face, had it not been for the ever-vigilant therapist and caring nurses by my side. I took every opportunity I could to learn how to walk again and strengthen my muscles. I was suddenly back to a workout schedule, however brief or limited. Whenever the nurses were available to help me sit and stand up, I was working on my newly acquired skill of "standing and walking." Just like learning a new sport, I found I could do a little more each time I tried. But I was shocked at how quickly I became exhausted.

It doesn't take long to find out who your true loyal friends are with a long-term hospital stay. These friends are the ones who continue visiting after the first few days. They always come in with that hopeful smile, encouraging you with any of your improvements, no matter how insignificant. They would catch me up on the latest news at the club or the triathlon and tennis community. I had a few of these wonderful encouraging friends in Hong Kong. They would continue to pop in almost every day with their positive attitude. One daily visitor was a fellow triathlete who always made me feel great, making me laugh and smile in spite of my dismal prognosis and circumstance. His name was Paul Terry.

Chocolate Therapy

Those who provided my biggest encouragements during my stay were my family, friends, and the many unexpected visitors. Hospitals are not the nicest place to spend your free time, especially if you are healthy and not a patient needing to be there yourself. There is always that disinfectant smell in the air to remind you of the ever-present aroma of sickness and broken bodies. That stale disinfectant smell is hovering everywhere in the hallways. Hospitals are always a reminder of where we can end up spending time in our future. Most of us want to avoid thinking about that reality. So we hope our friends stay healthy so we don't have a reason to visit there. I was blessed with a flood of visitors during my first week at the Adventist Hospital. This was because of my TV and newspaper exposure and the notoriety I received in *South China Morning Post*'s coverage of my spectacular accident. People who followed sports in Hong Kong knew who I was and my son's sporting exploits. Even with that notoriety, after that initial week, the numbers declined significantly, except for my true loyal friends. One of my favorite visitors was Paul Terry, a fellow triathlete, twelve years younger than myself. Paul and I traveled to most of the Asian triathlons together and raced very close to each other. He would pass me on the run in many triathlons, and I would finish just ahead of him in a few races.

Paul was a real character like many other triathletes I have met. Paul was an athlete who knew how to enjoy life to the fullest. He was an excellent triathlete, who traveled to most events to enjoy the camaraderie and beautiful venues, as much as to race fast. One time in Borneo, while racing on their steamy hot roads, I witnessed Paul as he spotted a cute young local lady cheering us on by the side of the road. When she waved to cheer him on, he pulled over, stopped his bike, and introduced himself. Without any hesitation, Paul made a date for later that evening. He had a way of being the life of the party without being wild.

It was Paul who inspired me to run faster after the bike portion of a triathlon race one Sunday a year before. We were competing on Lantau Island in Hong Kong when Paul flattened on the bike course, putting him out of the race. He still wanted to get in a good run, so he joined me as I was running by. I was not aware he'd had a flat and was out of the race. I thought we were racing each other when he suddenly appeared beside me. He kept pace with me, yelling for me to stride out more. By the finish, I had run faster than I thought was possible. Only when crossing the finish line without him beside me did I realize Paul was just helping me to run faster and was out of the race. Paul and I had a very close relationship because of the triathlon community. So it was always a joy to see Paul's face peak around the doorway of my hospital room with that infectious smile beaming across his face.

I was convinced Paul came to see me at the hospital to encourage me, but while visiting, he took time to sample the many biscuits and snacks in the fruit baskets. Mostly, Paul wanted to explore and sample the numerous chocolate boxes lying around the room. One box in particular had captured Paul's interest since it arrived. It was the biggest box of chocolates I have ever seen, and it also caught my undivided attention. I had spent the last two and a half years avoiding any sweets or sugar, but then came these chocolate boxes. I couldn't move, and there they were, always right there in front of me, calling out for me to taste their delicious variety. A local billionaire had somehow found this one box of exquisite chocolates and thought I needed them to cheer me up. The chocolates came from Europe and, without a doubt, had the best tasting an exquisite variety of chocolates Paul and I had ever experienced.

Paul was a self-confessed chocoholic and worked his way through this delectable box with the conviction of a connoisseur. I was just as enthusiastic in joining Paul, slowly sampling each mouthwatering piece. These were the kind of chocolates you wanted to savor, taking your time to let each delectable piece melt slowly in your mouth. Taking as long as possible to enjoy its wondrous smoothness and flavor couldn't help but put a smile on our face. After a week of enjoying this chocolate adventure, we both agreed that every sample seemed to be superior to the one before, even though we had been convinced the one we had just savored was the best piece of chocolate we had ever wrapped out mouth around. Paul was there almost every day of my stay, and Paul's story is contained in an article I wrote in a later excerpt. Paul was an inspiration whether he was just relaxing with friends, racing in a triathlon or for me, taking the time to "make my day" by visiting me in the hospital.

Paul can be partly thanked and responsible for my new pear-shaped body when I was eventually discharged from the hospital. However, I wouldn't have traded a trimmer body, if it meant Paul would not have been there to encourage me, laugh at my dumb jokes, and, of course, share in the "World's Best Chocolates."

BIONIC MAN...?

My left arm and head received the full impact when slamming into the right rear corner of the minibus. It was a miracle I had survived the blow to my head, which crushed my T5 vertebrae. My left arm was also a real mess. A number of operating procedures were necessary to reconstruct my arm, wrist, and hand. A titanium plate was inserted to repair the compound fracture of my left radius. My ulna had to be winched back together, and three long pins were inserted into my hand and knuckle to allow more broken bones to set and hopefully heal correctly. My fingers ended up swelling to twice their normal size, turning a very dark brown, almost black. I found relief by opening and closing my blackened fingers while holding my arm as high as I could in the air. Holding my arm up helped reduce the swelling and kept my fingers from getting too stiff. The sight of my fingers shocked my visitors, as they looked more like overcooked burnt hot dogs than resembling fingers. To make matters worse, the outside layer of skin on each finger eventually started to peel off, resembling a thick dragon-type skin. Seeing this happen reminded me of a chapter in C. S. Lewis's Chronicles of Narnia book *Voyage of the Dawn Treader*. A character called Eustace had been turned into a dragon because of his greed. To be reborn into a boy again, the outer thick dragon skin had to be peeled away. Friends and family visiting could see this same difficult peeling process on my fingers. Those who had read Narnia said my fingers reminded them of Eustace. They all agreed that seeing this process happening in person made them a little squeamish. Paul was intrigued by my entire situation, being off painkillers and seeing my attempt to improve and hopefully recover.

Paul was so taken with my effort to regain health and fitness that less than two years later, when Paul had a serious problem of his own, he elected to have a local anesthetic so he could view his own brain operation back in London. He said the reason he elected to witness his operation was because of me. He wanted to be one up on me, saying he didn't think I would even do that. He was right! I would not have done that. The things I did were to guarantee my best chance of recovery and being normal again. There was never a thought in my mind to prove I was braver or stronger. Comparing myself to anyone else was of no use when trying to get better. I was on this journey to hopefully get my fitness back and was fortunate to have help and encouragement from those closest to me. Concentrating on myself and what I needed to do and improve every single day was my clear and a definite focus.

We sometimes spend huge amounts of our time trying to please others or prove we can live up to or down to others' expectations. When this happens, we are constantly looking to others to validate our self-worth or measure our achievements. Our self-worth should always come from "knowing we have done our best in the moment and then leave it in the past, where it belongs." For some reason, it is only human nature to congratulate ourselves on achievement but then to always expect more by comparing yourself to others. This is living life in a pressure cooker! This only compounds when other people make you feel "anything you do or accomplish is never enough." This attitude puts more and more pressure on individuals who are looking to others for validation. This also strips joy out of our everyday life. Contemplating this in the hospital, I knew things were now going to be different. I had been living off the adulation from others as most of what I was doing before the accident came fairly easy and was natural for me. I now needed to find strength from within and trust God more than ever. I needed to remind myself daily He knows what is best for me. I then needed to make sure I got my validation from Him, not others. "In His eyes, we are always enough while doing our best to improve."

Days seem to drag on forever lying in a hospital bed. During my third week, which felt like three months, my arm and hand cast was scheduled to be removed to check on the incisions and redress my wounds. I was looking forward to this day as I had not seen my left arm since before the accident. I had no idea the extent of the injuries. I only had my injured left arm described to me by my doctor. My injuries were completely covered by bandages and a cast. My arm didn't feel that bad as pain was reduced because of the titanium plate and the wenching and pinning to repair the multiple fractures. The doctor had given me some details of my wounds, but as they say, "Seeing is believing." When the cast was finally removed, the side of my forearm facing my body was immediately visible.

It was somewhat of a shock looking at my formally strong fit arm now a shriveled-up mess. I remarked to the doctor when seeing the fresh bright incision, "Wow that's a big ugly scar!"

My doctor looked up and said, "You are looking at the good side."

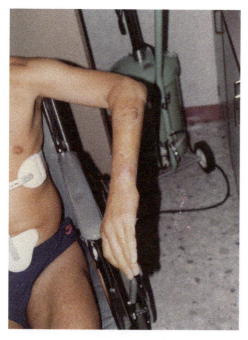

Damaged left arm

The other side of my forearm was where the broken radius had exited twice through muscles and skin, about an inch apart. The outer side of my forearm also showed the operation that opened up my wrist and reattached the end of my ulna, winching it back together. From where I was sitting, my forearm looked pretty messed up. A titanium plate had been inserted to hold my radius together, and I could view the stitches of the six-inch incision looking fresh and ugly. The bent ends of three wire pins were protruding through different places in my hand, holding the base knuckle of my index finger and bones in my left hand in place. Only then did I begin to understand how badly my left arm had been injured and the effort it would take to get my arm back in shape. This was a minor concern compared to my back and the paralysis problems looming in my future.

I watched intently as the doctor took a pair of pliers, then twisted and tugged to eventually release the wires from my hand. Once the two-inch pins were removed, I requested my former cast be replaced by a waterproof version. I was already planning to get back in the water and start "swimming" again back at the Marina Club. From the beginning, I was in constant denial, like so many others with similar injuries. I had big plans, thinking before long I would be back to my preaccident level of fitness and exercise routine. It really felt like my body was beginning to mend. Why not make big plans? Stitches were being removed, and my broken ribs were mending enough for me to start laughing out loud again. The only thing left for me was to walk around the entire fourth floor of the circular Adventist Hospital so I could be released before my insurance ran out. I was being judged by most as an invalid who would be severely handicapped for the rest of my life. My outward appearance would have led anyone to believe that was true. I was determined not be judged or mistaken by my outward cover.

My outward cover did not look promising. It would take a miracle to work my way out of my present situation. The encounter I had with my dad's middle school teacher friend helped me find a way forward. He had shared a secrete passed onto him by an energetic ninety year old when I was at his house. His mentor said it was very simple and my dad's friend took the time to pass it onto to me.

First was to complete or finish three tasks each day. He said completing this one simple item will allow you to fall asleep every night knowing you have had a successful day—stress relief! Most people can go weeks or months without completing or finishing one task, leaving a mountain of unfinished business to face the following day. This pile of unfinished tasks leaves any individual feeling unsuccessful, exhausted, and overwhelmed at the start of each day. He told me to make a list of the smallest, seemingly inconsequential items in my life and complete three of them each day. By finishing these simple seemingly inconsequential goals each day, we start eliminating the nagging clutter in our lives and our minds. Unnecessary clutter takes up our mental and psychological energy, leaving us drained of inspiration. By completing three tasks every day, we experience success, allowing us to fall into a peaceful deep sleep each night. Once this clutter in our lives is removed, small, medium, long-term, or larger life goals start to take shape.

Second, make a list of major life goals—fuels our passion. Third, start breaking these life goals down into lists of smaller items necessary to achieve each goal one by one, energized by life. Before you know it, you will be living a life well lived, achieving more than you would have ever expected. He mesmerized me while sharing what he had been taught. He was willing to share with me or anyone willing to listen intently to what had changed his life. I haven't always followed this to the letter, but I have followed his advice enough to change the course of my life many times. We are all more than the cover of our book. These few secrets are a way to make sure you are feeling successful each day, even if it only means just straightening up your room before falling into a deep restful sleep. "We all deserve living a successful and vibrant life."

Little Goals, Big Goals

The difference between being positive and negative is experiencing some level of success no matter how small. Staying focused on small improvements no matter how incremental will give us motivation to keep working hard and moving forward. These minuscule improvements will keep us inspired, eventually allowing us to reach our small, medium, and eventual major life goals. Looking through the eyes of an athlete, the concept of setting small goals to eventually reach and attain major goals is understood. Even if finding it frustrating at times, it is just part of your everyday journey as an athlete. The amount of sacrifice necessary is usually hidden from the public eye. Only the final results and successes are witnessed by a crowd of spectators and media. When asked if the sacrifice is worth it, World or Olympic champions all say the same thing: "The discipline and supposed sacrifice and time given up with friends and frivolous but fun activities is completely worth it." That moment of success when achieving their goals makes all the early mornings and dedicated effort completely worth the struggle. The euphoric feeling of being extra fit, strong, and healthy cannot be adequately expressed in print. Does it always make it easy to get up each day and stay committed? No, I don't think so. It just becomes a habit pattern of living, which somehow overrides your desire to stay in bed. Energetic living will take precedence over a lazy lifestyle.

For those lying in hospital beds with broken bodies or illness, there is no media praising them for winning a race or becoming the world's best. Their finish line may just be putting one foot in front of another or getting out of a bed by themselves. The same principles still apply in battling through their circumstances. Fighting the pain, discouragements, and setbacks and then to get up and do their best is exactly the same as any athlete preparing for an Olympic event. The big event for a hospital patient is being healthy, out the front door, and on their feet again. No applause, no medals, just the satisfaction and realization you are out enjoying life. Having a body free of constant pain, allowing a semblance of your previous life, is every bit as satisfying as winning an Olympic Gold Medal.

As an athlete, it has always been important for me to visualize an end goal. Then break it down into small and attainable goals so every week I feel a sense of success. If I placed too much emphasis only on reaching major end goals, I miss out on the joy of the daily journey, never feeling like I am quite succeeding. After an injury, everyone wants to quickly be back to where they were originally. Being so far away from your end goal and not too far removed time-wise from your original fitness may make the end goal seem out of reach and impossible to attain again. This approach almost always leads to discouragement, eventually causing people to give up. Discouragement can be so overwhelming we become blinded to the small improvements, even though these small victories will eventually lead to our end goal. No one ever knows how far they will reach when striving toward a goal. You may even surpass your original goal. Even if you do not reach it, you will reach far beyond the normal possibilities by staying the course and attaining one small goal after another. No one can ever take these victories and small successes away from you! You have earned every single one of them!

For those lying in a hospital bed, the achievements they reach may seem almost boring to the average person who has never had to go through a mass trauma accident or experience a major physical setback. When I first started moving my toes, I would get so excited I would show all of my visitors. They couldn't understand what the big deal was. It seemed simple enough to them. For me it was huge! These achievements, what I refer to here as "red-letter improvements," produced huge positive psychological gains. This is how I stayed positive when everything around me could have become depressing and negative. Most of the time, positive thinking is the furthest thing from a person's mind. I stayed focused on the next small goal directly in front of me. I was surprised when different individuals held me up as a positive role model. People right now going through what I was going through know better than anyone else the effort it takes each day to move forward, sometimes with only their lonely thoughts of self-reflection, setbacks, and goals to keep them company. That's how it was for me.

When I had my leg cast removed in the fifth grade, I was amazed at how small my leg was with the atrophied muscles, making it much smaller than my left leg. My doctor was encouraging as he gave me some very simple exercises to complete each day. He did two very important things for me. He gave me exercises to perform, and just as important, he assured me that complete recovery would happen if I would be diligent in completing the daily routine of exercises. Once the end goal was assured, I was willing to do the tedious simple exercises necessary to reach my goal. By the end of winter, I was skiing again with my leg completely recovered. I was able to take part in any activity I chose to join in.

There were at least five red-letter days that really lifted my spirits while still in the hospital. These huge days came about because of achieving small seemingly insignificant gains when left alone in my room. Following a simple program I came up with allowed me to improve in private and avoid the boredom and depression that could have so easily enveloped me. The staff said I was never down except once that they witnessed. That one time was only for a few minutes. Surprisingly, it came at a time when it should have been a great day. These red-letter days helped carry me through what could have been a more difficult time in the hospital.

My red-letter days were simple items we all take for granted when we aren't sick or injured.

Things We Take for Granted

These were my huge red-letter days in the hospital:

1. Day the bladder bag was removed
2. Day they helped me to sit and stand up
3. Day first cast and pins were removed
4. Day I could use the walker by myself
5. Big surprising day—being able to take a shower again

Bladder Bag

This was the day my doctor said indicators were present to remove the bladder bag. They were closely monitoring me because I had no surface feeling from my core downward. This proved to be a serious question regarding normal use of my bladder. I was excited about this news, but as anyone can expect, it carried a sense of foreboding. Would I be able to control myself? The bladder bag had taken care of me without my realizing it for days. Would I wake up with an embarrassing situation? Or embarrass myself and others when out in public with friends? Like everyone else, I had never thought about having this kind of problem. Friends would no longer joke about my iron bladder. That was before. I now had this to worry about.

This was another of many obstacles to overcome. I was still excited as this indicated my doctor felt my body was on a path to recovery. This not-so-simple improvement encouraged me to work even harder to move my toes, feet, and knees. Feeling a surge of energy and excitement, it was like being reborn, and I was excited.

Standing Up

Standing is taken for granted by 99.999 percent of human beings on our planet. Why not, it is what we learn how to do by around two years of age. By age three or four, we drive our parents crazy, hearing them yell out, "Slow down and stop running in the house." One minute they can't wait for us to learn how to walk, the next minute they are telling you, "Go outside if you are going to run around."

For years, I ran everywhere with my friends without a moment's thought. Here I was at forty-five years old, weaving around like a drunk with no equilibrium. Somehow, discouragement wasn't part of the equation, only the excitement of being on my feet again. From wheelchair-bound prognosis for the rest of my life to standing was all the motivation I needed to stay positive.

Day I Used a Walker by Myself

My doctor finally felt I would not fall if left alone with my new friend, the walker. I don't know if he really believed it or just got tired of my persistence. Once he approved, I headed out of my room and went directly down to rehab to start my workouts. Really a joke as my eventual therapist, Nalini Advani, stated. She said I looked like death warmed over when I arrived. My face was etched with pain and concentration as I edged past her desk. It took me some time to shuffle through the reception area before entering the main rehab therapy department.

She watched intently as I struggled to get on the leg extension machine and sat there completely exhausted. Continuing to observe me, I mostly just sat on the machine, doing nothing except a few efforts to raise my legs set at the lowest level of resistance. My memory was completely different as I thought I was doing a normal workout like I used to do at Aberdeen Marina Club. I must have been in a fog of my own imaginary world, as I don't remember any of what she related back to me. I was just excited to be on my own and back to my previous exercise program. All I could think of, *I was on my way to another triathlon by the year's end.* This motivated me again. Crazy maybe, but I was positive about my improvement, and I couldn't care or think about reality then.

I utilized my trusty walker whenever nurses or therapists were available to help me out of bed.

Shower by Myself

Showering was an amazing day for me psychologically, as it not only felt wonderful to feel warm water cascading over my body, but it represented the day I could start taking care of myself again. Reality again may have been something else, but it felt incredible in ways I didn't know were possible. The feelings and emotions I felt were impossible to adequately express in print. Who would guess something so normal could be so stimulating, satisfying, and luxurious. I remember the moment the nurses asked if I would like to try a shower instead of the usual body wash in bed. It was like an early Christmas present.

Plaster casts were not new to me, and the inconvenience they produce was obvious everywhere you turn. Casts make you alter your daily habits and routines whether they were for your hands, fingers, arms, legs, feet, or toes. Taking showers with my other injuries, I always invented ways to keep a cast from getting wet. My parents and I would improvise ways to cover and seal them so simple showers could be taken. A wet plaster cast can start to deteriorate, and any moisture getting inside will make you itch, driving you crazy!

I could hardly believe it when the nurses eventually helped me out of bed with the usual brace-and-walker scenario. They helped me into the shower stall while I held tightly to the walker. After adjusting the shower, I asked if they could leave me to shower by myself. There was a buzzer right there to use if I needed help. They reminded me to hold my left arm up to avoid getting my cast wet. I stood there under what felt like a tropical waterfall. As I closed my eyes, I could picture myself standing in a secluded tropical Borneo pool surrounded by lush vegetation and a perfect waterfall coming out of a rocky escarpment in the jungle. It was the most wonderful luscious feeling I thought I had ever felt. I stood there for the longest time without even washing. With water cascading over my head and body, it awakened sensations I didn't know were possible.

To this day, every shower I take reminds me of how wonderful it feels. I have never taken a shower for granted since then. It wasn't long before I heard the nurse asking, "Are you all right?"

I responded, "Please let me stay a while longer."

However, whenever I stood up, it was painful. It always produced a tremendous deep ache in my upper back. This was made worse by having to hold my left arm up high, out of the shower. I was surprised by how good the water felt cascading over my head and shoulders but just as surprised and alarmed at the total lack of feeling in my lower chest downward. I could not feel the temperature of the water with my lower body. I realized then I would need to be very careful not to test water with my lower extremities, especially hot water. I stayed in the shower for what seemed like thirty minutes or until the ache in my back became too intense. The nursing staff also insisted it was long enough. What a day and how clean I finally felt! A body wash while lying in bed never really leaves you feeling quite the same!

Cast and Pins Removed

I had heard, "You have never really lived until you've almost died." I never completely understood this, as I lived a highly stimulating life before my accident. Maybe a harsh statement but if you extrapolate that a little bit, this statement can relate to any loss and subsequent recovery—*recovery* being the operative word. When the cast was removed from my left arm and the three pins holding my hand and knuckle together were removed, another red-letter day was crossed off. Before this day, I only had my toes, feet, fingers, and legs to work on. Now I had my shriveled-up left arm to work on. The rehab department was now part of my daily schedule, twice a day when possible. Plaster cast was gone, pins and stitches out, and a removable waterproof fiberglass cast was now in place. I felt I could really get to work now. Best of all, I could take a shower without holding my arm high in the air!

We go through life taking so much for granted. I was learning what for many suffering people around our small planet intimately realize, "We need to be thankful for these seemingly small gifts." Once they are removed, they are greatly missed and don't seem so minuscule after all. With these red-letter days popping up more frequently, I knew I was on the mend. I couldn't wait to leave the hospital and start swimming, cycling, running, and maybe even have enough balance to hit a tennis ball again. I was committed to do everything in my power to accomplish that! My willpower alone was not going to be enough as I was to completely realize later on. I was still of the mindset that I could "do it all," if I would just put in enough effort.

HOSPITALS, ROUTINES, AND FIGHTING BOREDOM

What is it like to be confined to a hospital bed day after day or held in a hospital for more than a week? For me in particular, it was definitely an adjustment. One which I had no choice in making. One day, I was as active as anybody could possibly be. The next, I was glued to a hospital bed, unable to even take care of myself. A big room clock was right in front of me, reminding me how slowly minutes and seconds could tick by. When teaching tennis, the minutes, hours, and days seemed to fly by as I remained focused on my students, my personal athletic goals, or the other seemly endless activities in Hong Kong. Lying in the hospital with very little to occupy my mind, the minutes ticked by more slowly. I couldn't read because of my diminished eyesight or even write very well because of my stationary position. I did what simple exercises I could think of when no visitors, nurses, or doctors were around to keep me company and talk with.

TV with only two English language channels and very limited programing was hardly an option. I was pretty good with mental gymnastics, so when left alone, I would occupy much of my time watching the visitors coming and going from the lifts. I would imagine who they were and who they might be visiting. When they would finally leave, I would wonder where they were going and how they might be enjoying their evenings—maybe take in a movie, go out to dinner, or take a walk by one of the many sea walls surrounding Hong Kong. Most of them were probably heading back to work or at the end of a long day, going home to spend time with their family. How I wished I could get up, head out to work, or go home for an evening with my beautiful family.

Hospitals have routines to avoid missing any of their patients' needs. You can basically set your watch to their daily rounds. Okay, time to wake up and have your morning wash, change your gown, and get ready to order your meals for the day. Time to check your pulse, blood pressure, and temperature. Change of bedding would be fit into the morning schedule. Lunchtime and the afternoon checkup would take up some of your time. Dinner would eventually roll around, and thankfully, what I looked forward to most, evening visitors. Then came your doctor's daily visit. He would saunter into the room like life was wonderful and ask how you were doing, like he didn't already know. Then he would poke and jab to see what if any improvement was noticeable. He would do most of the normal tests the nurses had taken earlier in the day.

One item, which had not changed for me, was my ability to enjoy food. Even with this being hospital food, I looked forward to the meals arriving. So after putting in orders for breakfast, lunch, and dinner, you could hardly wait for your breakfast selection to arrive. The smell of meals arriving to other rooms would always make your salivary glands work overtime. I would always take my time eating each meal to make sure it lasted as long as possible. By extending the enjoyment of eating, the clock became tolerable and seemed to move a little quicker.

Sometimes the routine would be irritating and disruptive to the patient and to me in particular. Sleep is a valuable commodity when you are laid up in the hospital with painful injuries, trying to get much needed rest for recovery and escape the ever-present pain. Activity never seems to stop, even during the nighttime hours. Getting a little extra sleep by napping during the day can be a real blessing, especially for me once I stopped the painkillers. Anything to make that irritating clock move faster was a help. The hospital routine can ruin a glorious afternoon nap. Time to change your sheets or take some medicine, change a dressing, or check on your vital signs. Boredom can easily set in without hope of a better future. I often thought about being released and discharged, hoping to take control of my life again. I never stopped dreaming of the day when I could leave and get back to my normal, hectic life of tennis, triathlon, modeling, commentating, and consulting. Hospitals are never anybody's choice for a rest stop during life's journey—a choice nobody voluntarily makes.

Nick Vujicic

No matter how bad it seems things were, there were always those around me or those I had heard of that had things much worse. I somehow continued to stay positive and upbeat. One individual I heard about much later on was Nick Vujicic. Born with basically no arms or legs, Nick is living a vivacious life inspiring everyone he comes in contact with.

My daughter, Crystal, went to a camp one summer and, returning home, shared an event that impacted her life tremendously. Nick Vujicic had come to the camp and shared how God had directed his life even with his almost insurmountable disabilities. Nick was there as a motivational speaker to inspire any teenager willing to listen. Nick was born in Australia with tetra-amelia syndrome. It is a rare disorder characterized by the absence of arms and legs. His story is an inspiration and can be found on his website, lifewithoutlimbs.org. My situation paled when compared to his challenges. The one thing I have learned is that God's grace is sufficient for anything we face or might go through. We just need to have the will to get up, keep moving forward, then reach out and receive His amazing grace so freely given!

Nick speaks with high school and college groups, inspiring young people to live their life loving God while grabbing hold of everything life has to offer. My situation after the accident seemed miniscule compared to others I have met on my journey and read about. I had it pretty good in the hospital with the staff doing everything to make me comfortable and encouraging me to improve each day. Spending my time recovering, I saw some real suffering with no hope of coming out at the end of their dark tunnel. To most people, Nick Vujicic was horribly handicapped with basically no chance to live any kind of a normal or productive life. That is until you go to his website and see that he has embraced life, enjoying many of the activities an able-bodied person enjoys.

It seemed every time I could have felt sorry for myself, something or someone would appear to keep me positive and inspired. Mostly it was the few friends and family who continued to keep me in their busy schedule and visit me, again helping that ever-present clock move a little quicker. I was continually thankful for these continued blessings in my life. The biggest blessing at that time was again the miracle of being alive and my ambitious plan of complete recovery.

Remembering and sharing stories like Nick and others always helped me see the positive. I had been wired to stay positive since I was young, so it wasn't as hard for me as I am sure it can be for others. Just when we think things are really going well, the unexpected can sneak up from behind and throw us for a loop. This is where God always keeps his promises, making a way for us to see the positive.

POSITIVE AND SIMPLE

My only disappointing and difficult day in the hospital came on what should have been an enormously super positive red-letter day. This particular day should have been the best possible red-letter day during my hospital stay. The Adventist Hospital is a round, circular building, easily recognizable when coming up from Happy Valley and downtown Hong Kong. I had been in the hospital for almost a month and been out of bed a number of times this particular day practicing my walking. With back brace securely in place, I was determined to hold the walker a few inches off the floor and see if I could shuffle and swing my legs forward, completing an entire lap around the hospital's circular fourth floor. My doctor insisted I demonstrate this for him before he would sign my release. To this day, I am sure he thought this would delay my release by weeks or a few months. It took all the concentration I had to attempt that simple lap around the hospital's fourth floor, making it feel like a mini marathon. It felt like my first triathlon in Singapore repeating the *Little Engine That Could* "I think I can, I think I can" over and over as I finally finished one full lap. Successfully arriving back to the nurses desk without letting the walker touch the floor was a victory for me. I had wobbled, shuffled, and swayed around but finally achieved my goal.

I was elated that I had crossed my imaginary finish line between my room and the nurses desk in front of the lifts. I knew what this meant! I would soon be leaving the hospital, if I could only repeat this feat for my doctor. I was sure he would still need some convincing.

At that very moment, the lift doors slid open, and two friends, also tennis teaching pros in Hong Kong, stepped out of the lift. *Perfect*, I thought! I was excited and ready to share my latest accomplishment, and there they were! I again thought, *What great timing.* I was so excited I eliminated the usual friendly greetings, asking them to watch what I could do. Picking the walker up a few inches off the floor, I shuffled over to them. One look into their horrified faces told the whole story. They couldn't believe this pear-shaped, stooped-over old guy could possibly be the young-looking fitness icon they had known and admired a month earlier. They actually looked physically sick. For me, it was like the air had suddenly been sucked out of the hallway!

Only a few awkward remarks passed before they hurriedly rushed back into the lift. I was left standing there feeling isolated, alone, and in a sudden cloud of darkness. Just a few minutes earlier, the hallway was brightly lit and had felt full of hope. Now darkness and fog flooded my heart as I slowly edged back toward my room. My fellow tennis pros had left without even going to my room for their usual visit or sampling some of my chocolates. I had always been lying in bed when they arrived, looking fairly normal. This was the first time they had seen me on my feet attempting to be my fit self again. Scarfing down some of my delectable chocolates or fruit was their usual routine. Them leaving so suddenly was completely new for me as friends would usually hang around, sharing what was going on in their lives, giving me a needed glimpse of the outside world and where I desired to be. They had not seen me up and trying to walk before. It was a shock for them to see me on my feet looking frail and every bit the damaged person I was. I hung my head, which was easy with my injured neck and slowly slinked back to my room. Eventually working my way back into bed, I lay there and started thinking for the first time what kind of reception I would receive when leaving the hospital and reentering the fast-paced world of Hong Kong's society and, hopefully, Aberdeen Marina Club? Finally back in bed and for the first time since me accident, I started to feel sorry for myself. Less than ten minutes passed by before one of my favorite nurses, originally from the Bahamas, appeared in my doorway. She took one look at me and said sternly, "Knock it off!"

"What do you mean?" I innocently asked.

"You know exactly what I mean," she said. "You haven't been down or discouraged one moment since arriving here. You have inspired everyone, and now you are going to let a couple guys get you down because they can't handle or deal with the challenging circumstance you are dealing with?"

Wow, it was like she was preaching to the choir. I had instructed so many students and church kids of this very same principle. There will always be critics who will find fault in any endeavor we attempt. If what we are attempting makes them uncomfortable, so be it. Let them walk away; we don't really need that kind of input. As we improve, these same individuals will hopefully understand and appreciate what we were going through. Everyone needs to stay focused and positive, but it is not always easy. "Stay the course and you will surprise everyone, even yourself," I told myself. Now I was being given the same encouragement from a beautiful nurse who understood just how to wake me up and keep me on track. What goes around comes around. There is no way to express how much I appreciated this nurse and what she did for me in a temporary moment of discouragement.

I was also surprised she could clearly see what I was feeling. She immediately brought me back to what was important. She obviously had a ringside seat to witness the entire event with my friends since the incident took place directly in front of the nurses station. I only had a few days left before the miracle of being released from the hospital, and I needed to stay focused on my goals. This was an example of how important positive influences from the nurses play in every patients' recovery.

I had learned early on in life, if you look to others for your inspiration, they will eventually let you down. Your inspiration must come from within, and most of all, "from above." I understood this, and I used to talk the talk, but now was when I would find out if I could really "walk the walk" and eventually learn how to walk and run again. This process was going to be harder than I could have ever imagined. We all know the little simple slogans that say things like, "When the going gets tough, the tough get going," and "Only under severe pressure can coal turn into diamonds," and "Tribulation worketh patience." How tough was I, or how was I under pressure? I like most people didn't like tribulation. Who really likes tribulation? But I definitely was going to need more patience. There was another saying I heard, which was also simple but profound, "Easy to say, hard to do." Would I have the patience to do the hard yards? I was about to find out. I thought it would be up to me and only me. But to completely follow through, I would need to look for strength from above.

Albert Einstein was quoted with the following:

> "Stay away from negative people, they have a problem for every solution. A clever person solves a problem. A wise person avoids it. Any fool can know. The point is to understand. Life is like riding a bike. To keep your balance, you must keep moving. The true sign of intelligence is not knowledge but imagination. If you want to live a happy life, tie it to a goal, not to people or objects. I "CAN" is 100 times more important than IQ. In the middle of every difficulty lies opportunity. You have to learn the rules of the game. And then you have to play better than anyone else. Logic will take you from A to B. Imagination will take you everywhere. The one who follows the crowd will usually go no further than the crowd. Those who walk alone are likely to find themselves in places no one has ever been before. There are two ways to live your life. One is as though nothing is a miracle. The other is as though everything is a miracle.

Einstein's last thought was what has carried me through what could have been my darkest moments.

Definition of Success

Years ago, while still in California, I was asked by an area newspaper to write down my definition of tennis. A number of people thought I taught differently than other teaching pros in the area. This came as a surprise to me. I didn't feel I taught differently than the other excellent tennis teaching professionals in the San Francisco Bay area. After several months of coming up with what seemed like good definitions of tennis, none of them seemed quite right. Then out of seemingly nowhere, a perfect definition came to me in the middle of the night. The clarity with which I woke to this definition was startling. It was like Einstein inferred, "Live like everything is miraculous." My awakening felt miraculous. I have not changed one word in over thirty years. I believe it is still an accurate definition of not only tennis but also success in anything in life. Definition of tennis: "Tennis is the ability to simplify one's movements, then focus one's concentration so you have the freedom to play creatively." After sharing this definition with professionals in a variety of fields, they agreed I could insert any other sport, occupation, skill, or creative art to replace the word *tennis*, and it will define success in all of those fields as well.

Where did this definition come from? It came from that same still, small voice waking me in San Jose, California, that also spoke to me on that dark Clearwater Bay Road in Hong Kong years later. Successful living comes from simplifying one's life and focusing on the important things so we can attain the freedom to live life creatively or, in other words, be inspired by life. How simple this seems until the busyness of life swamps us with seemingly legitimate chores to dominate our time. Recovering from my many injuries, I was faced with the pressing reality of figuring out what I needed to do to keep things simple. This wasn't going to be easy as my life had become warped with success. I found it hard to think clearly with all the pain and awkwardness I was dealing with and then figure out how to simplify. Somehow, I needed to figure out what to focus on in my present situation to allow me to live a creative life again.

Miraculously, with all this happening, I was somehow staying positive. With help from a few key people surrounding me, I was going to keep my life as simple as possible or, in other words, "walk the walk."

I had been blessed with unexpected amazing individuals who shared their real-life inspirational stories with me in the past. This had always helped shape my attitude during difficult periods. These people were often the most unlikely individuals until you really got to know them.

Tennis student

Hong Kong always kept me alerted to the unexpected. Teaching tennis at Aberdeen Marina Club allowed me to meet many interesting, wealthy, and influential individuals. One of these unexpected encounters started as a simple tennis lesson with another Hong Kong businessman. He was respectful and seemed sincerely interested to learn this great game. We never got into his personal life, and I just assumed he was one of the thousands of successful entrepreneurs in Hong Kong's business landscape. Anyone affording a membership at Aberdeen Marina Club needed to be successful. We hit it off from the beginning, and he invited me to join him at the poolside cafe for lunch one day. He inquired how I ended up at the Marina Club and some of my past experiences. He seemed genuinely interested in me, and I was honored to spend my lunch break with him. I made it a policy not to get personal with my students unless they offered to open up to me on their own.

It wasn't long before my teaching schedule included his wife and four children in private lessons. Having six members of the same family taking private lessons with me weekly required a fairly large income. This represented a few thousand US dollars a month in lessons. I began to suspect I was only seeing the outer cover of his life's book. I will call him Chuck to protect his privacy. Over time, Chuck and I became fairly good friends with invitations to join him for many lunches.

One day, he invited me to his office downtown for lunch. Arriving at one of the top floors of a high-rise on edge of Victoria Harbour, I was shocked to realize he owned a number of well-known recognizable companies. It became obvious Chuck was an incredibly rich and successful businessman. His office was huge, with one of the best possible views of Victoria Harbour spreading out through his panoramic huge windows. After a short meeting where his secretary gave me some expensive welcoming gifts, he led us to a private restaurant on the same floor. We then entered an even more private secluded room to savor some exquisite Chinese cuisine.

It was here in this private setting that Chuck opened up and shared a little of who he was. I was only then able to understand his influence and a peek into how much he was worth. He owned multiple large beautiful homes in the US, France, Australia, as well as four homes in Hong Kong, three of them on an outer Island. He had incredible influence in China, helping China develop some of their new first-world developments. He also was contacted to head a huge enterprise in one of the USA's major cities. This he did for nothing as he was quoted, "They couldn't afford me."

It wasn't long before he invited me to visit his home on Lamma Island. This was where he had his own private zoo, a massive home aquarium surrounding a large swimming pool. There were also enclosures for rescued exotic animals, a tennis court, and golf putting green, and driving range. I then realized he was a billionaire and felt honored he included me as his friend. I enjoyed reading the inner pages of his life as he allowed them to slowly opened up for me to leaf through.

He had not always had it easy. Coming out of China during the cultural revolution, he had next to nothing when arriving in Hong Kong. He was a self-made millionaire/billionaire and continued to work hard every day. He was always an inspiration to be around and an honor for me to call him a friend through the years.

I kept reminding myself, don't judge a book by its cover. Chuck was more proof of how surprising and wonderful life has been for me.

HONG KONG MAGIC

What is it that makes Hong Kong so unique? Why has it mesmerized so many visitors and expat businessmen throughout the years? Many visitors and tourists are somehow drawn to this magical place and end up finding a way to permanently move to Hong Kong, eventually calling it home. For me it was a little different. I was not a visitor or tourists on some whirlwind world adventure with Hong Kong one of my many stops. I was surprised with the unexpected opportunity to relocate to the Portuguese territory of Macau, a one-hour Jetfoil ride from Hong Kong. This happened without any idea of the draw Hong Kong and Asia would eventually have on my life.

After only a short time in Hong Kong and Asia, the energy and excitement completely enveloped my life. What was it about this territory that kept Hong Kongers coming back to spend their lives on this relatively small island and peninsula? The land size and population make it prudent to build upward rather than outward. The high-rises and skyscrapers are everywhere stretching high toward the sky like different-shaped monoliths, some at dizzying heights. It is stunning to see the skyline of Hong Kong spreading from the Island side of Victoria Harbour to Kowloon. Hong Kong continues to fill in Victoria Harbour, adding more land to erect new and higher structures. Victoria Harbour is beginning to look more like a river for the longtime residences, as the waters of the Harbour continue to shrink. Today the skyline has spread clear out to the once quiet areas of New Territories.

One of the many surprises about Hong Kong is the numerous grocery stores seen everywhere while walking on the swarming, hot, and humid crowded sidewalks. There seems to be a grocery store on every other corner. This is strange to most newcomers, coming from spread out suburban areas where most of them need to drive some distance to the nearest store or shopping center. How can these businesses possibly survive with so many stores packed closely together? Entering any store, there is never a lack of customers as you squeeze your way down their narrow aisles. There is a simple way to help visitors understand what I soon discovered. Stand on a sidewalk and ask them to "Look up." Everywhere your upward gaze takes you, are twenty-eight-to-forty-story high-rise apartment buildings with at least four apartments per floor. The lower few floors are usually occupied as offices for many of the thousands of businesses located in Hong Kong. Hundreds of families also live in the upper floors of these buildings. When you think of how many people live in each building, the numbers add up very quickly. A forty-story building can easily contain as many as 400 to 500 people, assuming only one family lived in each apartment. The locals have a way of economizing, sometimes packing, several families in one apartment. A number of these buildings can occupy a four-block radius, which represents thousands of people. They all need to eat and shop. Instead of being spread out like a US suburban area, they all live upward and come down to shop and eat. All the stores popping up everywhere make sense and only adds to the allure of Hong Kong.

Hong Kong is a tropical city, which means hot and humid most days of the year. The streets are full of people moving along at breakneck speed and will eventually run you over if you don't get in step. Hong Kong has one of the most efficient mass transit systems in the world, transporting the seven million residences, who call it home. Their MTR (Mass Transit Railway) can take you just about anywhere on both sides of Victoria Harbour. Above ground, you have the double-decker buses and the antiquated tramline, once located on the Harbour's edge, on Hong Kong Island side. Nowadays you need to walk a few blocks to reach the water's edge with the many landfill projects. The airport is now located on Lantau Island and is the only other island serviced by the MTR. The sleepy fishing village of Tung Chung has been turned into a modern, high-tech, and high-rise city of its own. They welcome the many visitors to take the Ngong Ping Cable Car up to the Black Buddha, perched high on the hill above. Many of the airports' employees now live in this once out-of-the-way sleepy fishing village.

Once the airport project was decided, the MTR, along with a huge new bridge, was built to connect it to Kowloon. This easy access inspired Disney Corporation to get approval to build Hong Kong Disneyland on the near side of Lantau Island. Magical Hong Kong now has the Magic Kingdom adding to its allure.

Island ferries are the main transportation moving to and from the many other islands dotting the waters surrounding Hong Kong. You can hire a sampan or other small boats, which bob up and down in the waves and drafts of the larger yachts and container vessels steaming by. These smaller vessels will drop you off at some of the more secluded and scenic hidden beaches and villages. Everywhere you turn, there is something new and wonderful to unexpectedly grab and thrill your imagination. At times you wonder how such a small dot of land on China's southern border can contain so much diversity and wonder.

Central District of Hong Kong is a contradiction of the old and new, packed into the many endless blocks of wonder. You have a choice of walking in the noise and smell of diesel at ground level, or take one of the many elevated walkways, going in and out of the endless modern buildings connecting major shopping centers and business offices. If you live in Mid-Levels, high above Central, you can access the outdoor escalator that operates down in the mornings and upward in the afternoon and evenings. The canopy covered escalator is an easy way to find great eating establishments that line the streets and alleyways on both sides of this moving stairway. In a matter of a block or two, the culture can change dramatically. You can be in upmarket quaint eateries or suddenly in vegetable markets, which seem to have been there for centuries. If you know which alleyway to head down, you will find some great buys on clothes, which are often cheap knockoffs of famous brands.

After leaving a five-star glitzy mall and walking only a few blocks in the heat and humidity, you can find yourself drenched with the overwhelming aroma of incense. Just off many of the walkways, you are surrounded by centuries old buildings with a Buddhist temple tucked into a secluded back corner. Or just as easily, an immense block wall emerges covered with banyan tree roots. The huge banyan trees provide dark shaded areas for the many temples dotting the Hong Kong landscape. It is easy to stop, sit down, take time to cool off and relax, enjoying the wonder of a different era. Just relaxing for a bit in these little hideaways is a great way of getting away from the maddening rush of humanity.

Leaving the temple, you hail a taxi and hold on for dear life, as any taxi driver in Hong Kong will take you on a breakneck race to your next destination. Everyone in Hong Kong moves at a fast pace forward, whether they are driving, riding in a taxi, or just walking around downtown. It is like a never-ending competition. Before you know it, you too are race walking everywhere or getting run over by the locals. Even when heading for a relaxing time in Deep Water or Repulse Bay, it is still a rush to get there. The interesting part of the rush is how you hardly notice it after living there and making Hong Kong home. You get in step and learn to love the speed and energy, which vibrates through every nook and cranny of the city.

With all the rush and speed of Hong Kong, there are also the upscale sports clubs dotted around the Island and Kowloon. These amazing clubs are another way to relax and let yourself be pampered. Each club caters to the super rich. They are also perks for the many international Hong Kong expats who live there. It is interesting as Hong Kong was considered a hardship post for years after it became one of the most modern cities in the World to live. The latest in electronic equipment was available before most people around the world could access them. This happened because many products are manufactured in Hong Kong, Taiwan, and China and find their way into local black market shops before heading overseas.

Hong Kong was the trading capital of the world. This simply means, a huge amount of product move through Hong Kong and "knockoffs" or "back of the truck" items are available everywhere.

Some are found in the Night Market, but often, if you know where to look, you will find them tucked away down some back alleyway. Connections in Hong Kong are amazing and invaluable. It seems everyone has positive ideas and suggestions to keep you motivated. New business ideas are met with encouraging ways to make them even better. This is energizing, and sleep doesn't seem to be so important. At the end of a busy day in Hong Kong, your head hits the pillow and you are immediately in a deep REM sleep. At least that was how it was for me. Before you know it, you have developed a fairly large network of great positive people and businessmen to keep you stimulated.

The British influence created a huge array of country parks and reserve land similar to what you find in London. This is unprecedented for most large metropolitan cities around the world. There is always a place close by to step out of the city and be in the solitude of a country park. Secluded pathways surrounded by lush vegetation awaits anyone wanting to explore some relaxing time alone and recharge. All the tourist pictures of Hong Kong highlight the city landscape of skyscrapers and sparkling lights. For most visitors to Hong Kong, they are caught up in the glitz of Central, the Mongkok Night Market, Nathan Road, the Bird Market, Jade Market, or out in Tai Tam, which eventually takes up most or all of their time.

This is why I chose to live away from the hustle and bustle of the fast-paced life of Central. Our weekends were spent enjoying the other more serene quiet areas, and there are numerous secluded places to explore. Even when living in Macau, we were fortunate to live on the top floor of Baguio Apartment building, high above the only blue waters of the reservoir. We were also backed up to a beautiful hilltop park just a short walk behind. In Hong Kong, we first lived in Baguio Villa on the west side of Hong Kong Island backed up to Victoria Road. Looking eastward, we could view blue waters with container vessels, ferries, or yachts floating by. The view of Hei Ling Chau Island was visible where the famous Bun Festival was held each year. Westward across the road, we surprisingly found stables and an equestrian training center. The unexpected country park trails started beside the stables and led up behind Victory Peak.

This Greenway almost spans the entire length of the island from east to west. You could get completely away from the rushing crowds and relax, while walking or running these many trails. Wild boar and monkeys still roamed some of the park lands when we lived there. This kept you on edge when an unexpected noise in the brush could make you jump. You're never far from the cities' bright lights and energy, but it's still easy to feel totally lost on those jungle-like trails.

Baguio Villa made our transition to Hong Kong comfortable and relaxing. But within a year, we found another place to live, quite a way from Baguio Villa on Kowloon Peninsula. In some people's minds, it was too far from all the action and energy. We moved to Clearwater Bay on the other side of Victoria Harbor. We were fortunate to find a village home beside Clearwater Bay Road. Village homes are designated by the government to be in the country park region and cannot cover more than 700 square feet of land per floor. You are only allowed to build three-stories high, so most village homes are three stories tall and look identical.

We rented the top two floors, which also gave us the flat rooftop to retire and relax. We placed a small inflatable pool on the roof, allowing us to take a dip and cool off during the hot weekends. The location of our flat served us well as we could retreat to Clearwater Bay for swimming. The floating square swim platforms were available to lay on and soak up a few rays fifty meters from shore. If not into swimming, you can enjoy the park at the end of Clearwater Bay Road. Sometimes we would share a picnic down by the water's edge in the middle of the forested area until after dark. We would occasionally be entertained watching a few illegal huge powerboats scream by with Hong Kong police boats chasing close behind. It was a race to stop them before they crossed the border. These large speed boats carried all kinds of contraband including stolen Mercedes vehicles to be sold on the black market in China.

My accident made it difficult to handle vibrations or loud noises, so after some research, we eventually found one of the most unlikely and secluded places in Hong Kong to live. We were doubtful about finding a quiet environment for me to recover, so we were resigned to eventually moving back to the States for my convalescence. Unlikely as it seemed, our Realtor found the perfect place. We packed up and moved to one of the quietest homes on the Kowloon Peninsula. We had a huge swimming pool, one-third acre of property with twenty-three fruit trees dotted around the house. It was secluded, quiet, and at the end of a 1.1 kilometer road through jungle foliage.

This was just what I needed to relax and recover from my accident and my long weeks of work. The jungle growth formed a natural tunnel effect high above our narrow road, reminding me of *Rip Van Winkle*. You could hardly believe you were in Hong Kong when driving or walking down this narrow secluded country lane. Even in the middle of the day, it could be dark and foreboding with the heat and sunlight struggling to find a path through the heavy canopy of branches, huge green leaves, and endless vines. Very few homes were found along this country park road, making it even more isolated and serene. I loved it from the start, even when the real estate agent apologized for the how secluded it was.

View from the property was spectacular. Looking out past the eternity swimming pool and over the heavy jungle growth, you could see the blue waters of Sai Kung and Hebe Haven off in the distance. Dozens and dozens of yachts and fishing boats were moored there. Wild monkeys would sometimes swing through the jungle trees high above the pool, screeching to be noticed. Wild boar and barking deer could be heard and seen moving and rummaging through the undergrowth on the country park trails behind the property. One of our dogs named Blackie and a local farmer's dog was fatally gored by one of these wild boar's huge tusks. Living this far out from Central was wild, secluded, and wonderful, feeling like we were living in the Borneo rainforest while not that many kilometers from fast-paced Hong Kong Island. This move made living in Hong Kong even more magical. We, as a family, loved it! It was just what I needed to convalesce and recover! I spent hours in our own pool.

There were many modes of transportation in Star Ferries and HKKF (Hong Kong and Kowloon Ferry Ltd). The numerous island ferries were constantly leaving from many of the Hong Kong and Kowloon ferry piers. These diesel-smelling ferries would easily take you away from the hustle and bustle of heavily populated Hong

Kong. Every destination seemed to surprise, with unlikely atmospheres and various cultures. Numerous expats congregated in these little out-of-the-way island villages. They would invite friends and family to join them for relaxing weekends of swimming, hiking, and enjoying some of the local food, completely submerging themselves in these secluded and quiet outposts. You never knew what would surprise you at the end of a jungle trail. Sometimes a waterfall with an inviting pool to cool off in awaited your adventure, like we found climbing over and around huge boulders a short distance from our home.

Big Wave Bay at the end of Sai Kung was a perfect example of a great-out-of-the-way place to explore. There were three ways to travel to this unique piece of Hong Kong. You could travel from a secluded pier and hire a local Sampan that would bounce you over the many swells, or you could be invited by a wealthy expat and travel by yacht, anchoring out past the breakwaters. The third way to arrive there was the way we would travel. Our style of travel was inexpensive and adventurous. A double-decker bus was available to drop us off at a trailhead, then we would trek over the mountain, and head back down to Big Wave Bay.

This trail was home to many wild monkeys, and their presence made the excursion all the more adventurous. Big Wave Bay was a sleepy little village, making you wonder how could they survive? There seemed to be no local economy, except for the few scattered gardens growing local vegetables, a small Chinese restaurant, and a snack shop. One surprise was a set of lockers next to the beach, which were specially erected there to lock up surfboards. These were built to accommodate the many expats who would come to surf the local break.

Hong Kong is also famous for its variety of food experiences. Every nationality has been drawn to Hong Kong for the promise of accumulating wealth. Every nation's culinary delight is readily available, no matter where you find yourself. Walking down the many streets and alleyways from Sheung Wan to North Point, you will find one small restaurants after another, tucked secretly away in secluded alleyways and small avenues packed with customers. Each one allowing their customers to enjoy authentic environments and spectacular food. The aroma of these different cultural menus make it difficult to decide which nationalities cuisine to savor next. Every taste and palate will find pleasure in Hong Kong's various eateries.

We once went up to the fourth floor in a tiny elevator in the middle of Lan Kwai Fong to experience a new dining pleasure. The lift was so small you could only squeeze in a few friends at a time. When the lift doors slowly opened, you found yourself entering into an authentic Vietnamese atmosphere. The ambiance felt like we had magically flown to Vietnam through the slow ride up the lift. The decorations, aromas, plants, and music immediately transported you to Nam Pen. The owners, cooks, and waiters were all from Vietnam and made the experience of eating their delicious traditional food truly magical. There are literally hundreds of authentic restaurants tucked away around Hong Kong, so you never get tired of exploring new food experiences, each one tantalizing your taste buds. It is truly a round-the-world trip of culinary delight. We would go out sometimes with no particular restaurant in mind and just walk up a few flights of stairs to visit another country and explore an eatery advertised with a small sign at street level. We were never disappointed with our eating experience in Hong Kong.

Diversity is everywhere, but everyone living there is, first and foremost, proud to be a Hong Kong-ese. We were all "Hong Kongers" and loved it as we embraced the culture, wonder, and opportunity of living there.

Along with the Five-Star Sports Clubs located on Hong Kong Island and Kowloon Peninsula are the many international schools competing for thousands of expat and local Chinese students living in the Territory. There were the American (Hong Kong International School), German/Swiss, English Foundation, or French School to name just a few competing to see who can place the most students at prestigious universities around the world, like Oxford and Harvard. Needless to say, the pressure on these expat children to succeed is tremendous and sometimes not that healthy. However, once graduating, these students never have a problem with acceptance letters from major universities. When not in school, these children flock to the many five-star clubs. Unlike many sports clubs in the States, these clubs offer several five-star restaurants, including at least one of the highest-standard Chinese cuisine. It was amazing to see the many activities at each club—from tennis, fitness centers, swimming pools, bowling alleys, children's play areas and video rooms, with a number of clubs featuring perfectly manicured lawn bowling greens. The most expensive clubs also have marinas with huge yachts on display in the numerous berths. These clubs are surprising considering the limited land space available in Hong Kong.

One day, while teaching tennis to a couple of twin girls aged eleven, I found them complaining when looking down from the Marina Club courts. They were required to go out on their dad's boat for the weekend, again! I asked if their father's "boat" was berthed at the Marina Club? Being on the tenth floor rooftop tennis courts, we had a perfect view down on the many expensive yachts in Aberdeen Harbor. They said, "Sure, his boat is in the first berth." I quickly looked down and found a beautiful eighty-nine-foot Italian yacht floating in the space. It was hard to feel sorry for these eleven-year-old expat twins having to spend the weekend on their dad's boat. Such is the life of expat children in Hong Kong. It is sad in some ways, as many of these expat children are surrounded and taken care of by one or more of the many maids and drivers, often not seeing much of their busy parents. Every club is unique and five star in its own way, continuing to make living the Hong Kong lifestyle stimulating, breathtaking, and again magical.

Taking a boat out to one of the many bays to Jet Ski, skidoo, waterski, swim, or sunbathe on the back deck of a yacht or Hong Kong junk is often a great way for expats to escape and spend a weekend away from their businesses and hectic energy of the work week. No matter how many times you experience these "perks," they never fail to take your breath away. It doesn't take long to understand why expats become addicted to the Hong Kong lifestyle.

Just when Hong Kong has you in its mesmerizing grip, you realize there are numerous exotic holiday or vacation destinations on offer very close by throughout the Southeast Asian region (Thailand, Malaysia, Philippines, Borneo, and Vietnam), or north to Japan,

Korea, or Taiwan to name just a few, lay waiting to excite your imagination. Some of the most beautiful soft white-sand beaches between your toes and temperate oceans in the world await for you to explore.

Grab a snorkeling set or scuba gear and the many colorful coral reefs and fish are available for the adventurous. For the surfers and bodyboarders in your family, there always seems to be a point break to excite those wanting to catch a wave. Many expats like myself hardly ever headed back to their native country for a holiday. These exciting options are conveniently located just a short flight from Hong Kong. Five-star resorts are located on these beautiful inviting beaches with warm water, exotic sunsets, and beautiful sunrises at bargain prices. Delicious spicy food of every nationality is served up daily, so you could eat and relax in the evening's tropical breeze. The warm smiles and sincere greetings from the locals always made each day seemed perfect. Every vacation went by too fast and seemed to be over before you knew it. But knowing these destinations were only a few hours away meant it wouldn't be long before you would be back again for another wondrous holiday adventure.

With all that Hong Kong has to offer, it is no wonder that many expats find a way to return to Asia and Hong Kong after thinking they have left for good. Hong Kong continues to be addictive in a variety of ways. The community and friends developed there will stay with you forever. It is hard to completely sense the complexity and beauty by just visiting for a week or two. However, once you have lived there, it captivates you and never leaves you quite the same. Asia, along with Hong Kong, is certainly a Magical place. The phrase, "I left my heart in San Francisco," may be true for the writer of that song, but for me, part of my heart will always be in Hong Kong and Southeast Asia region. I am a "HongKonger" forever!

This magic also indirectly led me to the Adventist Hospital. Even with that negative impact, I am still in love with Hong Kong and it's never-ending magic.

FORTUNATE GROUNDING

I was fortunate growing up with numerous people who always inspired me, none more so than my father who died a few years before my accident. He passed away from mad cow disease. The only possible way he contacted the virus was from a joke played on him in Hawaii. My dad was tricked into eating some monkey brain by some of fellow soldiers. He was in Hawaii convalescing from his injuries and the horrors of war on Guadalcanal. My mother, who remains young at heart and healthy, still lives in Oregon. I was forever thankful that my father couldn't see me following my accident. My condition would have broken his heart. My parents have always been my biggest fans and inspiration. Both parents were positive about my athletic and business endeavors. They did everything they could to support me, my brothers, and sister on my dad's teaching salary. My father knew how much I loved being active, competing in one sport after another. He would have struggled to see me so crippled up and looking helpless. We were extremely close as he was my coach and mentor in almost every sporting accomplishment I undertook through junior high school. He would push me beyond what I thought were my limitations while always making it fun. As I grew older, I realized more and more how much I appreciated him. He instilled in me the feeling I could do anything, given proper training and effort.

My mom called me from the States as I lay helpless in Hong Kong. I assured her, with my most lively and positive voice, that I was all right and would soon be up and around and back to normal. I could not allow her or any of my extended family to worry and stress out, with me being so far away. I didn't want family members to spend money on international airfare, when there was really nothing they could do to help, by flying into Hong Kong.

My mom always provided a sense of security on the home front, which our family felt and relied on. She never stopped praying for us children, and we could feel her love no matter how far away we were. We always knew we were supported, regardless of what was happening. This combination my mom and dad provided gave us children a perfect childhood.

Many of my friends said I grew up with a silver spoon in my mouth. This seemed strange as my dad was a schoolteacher and coach, and my mom was a stay-at-home mom. We never had extra money lying around, but everyone wanted to come over to our house to spend time and play. Years later, I realized that having money was not the most important thing in life.

My dad and I would go out to ski swaps with my brother Ken and buy old wooden skis, take them home, and over a month or so, take off the edges, sand them down, resurface the base and put on a new finish. They weren't the fancy new skis of all our rich friends, but we were on the slopes skiing at breakneck speeds with them. That's all that mattered to us. My dad was also there when I decided to take up tennis. That was after my older brother, Ken, had talked (almost forced) me to start hitting a tennis ball. I would make my dad get up before school and drive me to the park courts to feed me more tennis balls.

I woke him up early one morning when it was pouring down rain. I knew it was raining, but I was so inspired by tennis I still wanted to go out and practice. He was so tired he didn't notice the rain until we opened the front door. I pretended to be as surprised as he. He relented when he saw how much I wanted to go to the courts. He couldn't help but smile, as we drove down to Ann Morrison Park in Boise. To everyone's amazement driving by, we tried to hit tennis balls on a completely soaked court. Those witnessing us having fun in the rain must have thought we'd lost our minds. We were soaking wet from head to toe. Laughing ourselves silly, we made jokes about the padded wagon showing up any minute to take us off to the "funny farm." Maybe not politically correct but we were laughing too hard to care.

Coming out of the Great Depression and World War II, my dad could be very serious about important issues, but somehow, through it all, he never lost his sense of humor. He always seemed to find ways to enjoy himself and make it fun for others. It was this grounding that taught me how to laugh at myself, never taking things too seriously or giving up. Some of my closest friends think I don't take life seriously enough.

On a serious note, we should never stop being a dreamer when everything seems to be against us. What a great gift my parents gave me. Now after being so terribly injured was the time I needed all the humor I could muster up. I needed this humor, faith, and determination if I was going to manage my surroundings and get on with this wonderful gift we call life.

Roadblocks and detours are part of everyone's life if they have lived very long. We all face unexpected happenings, which seem to throw everything into a turmoil. When these unavoidable happenings take place, we have a choice in how we look at them and then how we handle them. The Bible says, "Plans are in men's mind, but God directs our steps." Embracing this philosophy will allow us to live life vivaciously, with joy emanating from us. Or better said: Living life with great and wonderful expectations. No matter what turn of events, we will be looking for the serendipity factor to bring about a bright and wonderful future. This is sometimes difficult for recent university graduates to grapple with as many find themselves back home, living with their parents. Jobs are not always easy to find, and many times, low-paying opportunities, not related to their major studies, are all that are available. Learning to embrace life with joy is not nearly as easy as they were led to believe without firm belief in God directing their path. Hope and joy, which every young adult should be filled with, seems to be woefully lacking in recent times.

This is where Christians have a huge advantage, if we really believe our God is big enough and faithful to His promises. We can make plans while realizing and sincerely believing God is in charge and will lovingly direct our path. Most of us don't like this because we desire to set our own path and we want what we have planned for. We become so rigid in what we have prepared for we can't see God's path, even when it is smack-dab in front of us. We desire stability in our lives, and we don't like surprises or unexpected "roadblocks" redirecting our lives. The excitement and adventure of living God's way is always filled with energy and will leave each individual filled with wonder at life's journey.

What is a "roadblock"? It is simply a way to point us to a different route to reach our original destination. Roadblocks often avoid dangerous conditions on our original planned route. This new route may be unexpected, but it will lead us to meet new interesting individuals and encounter new and exciting experiences, which we would have never known possible. I have met individuals in my life who had their lives so perfectly planned out they were boring to be around. Worse yet, their children were molded into this same insane mentality. Their lives are so rigid, they will resist disruption to their life's plan at any cost.

I have met friends like this in my travels. Before long, you find you are distancing yourself from these individuals because they are boring and not much fun to spend time with. Nothing interesting seems to be taking place in their life. Their self-made rut becomes deeper and deeper without them even noticing. They are so stuck in their way of living, you need to step down into their ever-deepening rut just to interact with them. You can almost anticipate what they will be saying before they open their mouths. Nothing is new or exciting for them, just the same mundane schedule: Get up at 6:30 a.m., take a shower, fix the same breakfast, drive to work in rush-hour commute, start work at 8:00, take lunch at 12:00 noon, get off work at 5:00, drive home in rush hour, arrive home at 6:00 in another rush hour commute, then dinner by 6:30 unless an accident on the freeway makes dinner at 7:00. Then maybe a little time for their children and wife before dropping into their favorite chair to doze off for an hour or so. Take a shower and to bed by 10:00 p.m., day after day after day after day after day, year after year after year until retirement at age sixty-six. Any kind of imagination or excitement has long since left the room and their life. Is this what all this pressure, which starts in middle school, is really all about? Our very life is miraculous and should be lived as a miracle.

Life is meant to be lived, not endured. Life should be exciting, energizing, and positive for ourselves and those who are in our lives, whether they are family, friends, or just acquaintances. This is where the inevitable roadblocks come in. Instead of focusing on the stop signs indicating "Roadblock, Detour Ahead" and getting upset, we need to get excited, expectantly start looking around for what this new adventurous route might bring. This is not an irresponsible outlook on life but a practical, truthful way to embrace God's promises for us. This is where we need to decide if we are going to live the temporal or the eternal perspective.

Imagine a planned trip where you have detailed your route and started out following your plan exactly. Both you and a close friend planned to travel the same route in different vehicles and meet up at the final destination. Not far along the road, you find construction, which tells you an alternate route is available. You decide to stubbornly wait until the roadblock is cleared, no matter how long it takes. Your friend looks at the roadblock and decides to explore the alternate detour route, which opens up for them. Arriving at your final destination, you wait a month for your friend to arrive. "Where have you been? What took you so long?" you ask, feeling proud that you beat them to the destination by waiting for the roadblock to clear and following your exact planned route, almost like it was a competition.

That is until your friend starts to share the wild and wonderful adventures they experienced by electing to follow a different route. They met some wonderful people along the way, who will end up being lifelong friends. They excitedly tell you about the canyons, mountains, beautiful sunrises and sunsets they witnessed as they traveled their unexpected path. They also let you know how much you missed by stubbornly staying to your planned route. God has plans for us that we have no idea about. The one thing we know for sure, God has wonderful adventures for us, if we just let go and let

God direct our path. Maybe I was on the perfect path for me and my family. People and experiences I encountered while waiting for him might be just the encounters, which will brighten and excite my future. It is important not to judge one another because we took a different route. God has different and wonderful paths for each of us to experience our life to the fullest.

As your life goes on, you could sit around wondering why you friends seems to be having so many exciting experiences dynamically affecting others' lives while your life seems to be passing you by. You find yourself becoming somewhat boring, trudging up and down your ever-deepening rut. Or you can let go and follow His paths for you. God has a wonderful plan for you, which is exciting and adventurous. You will see unexpected and wonderful sights, sounds, and smells to heighten your senses and your life in general.

Do we want a life that is boring or one which is thrilling and makes us a positive person to be around? A life which will bless and also energize those around us is really what we all want to leave behind. Don't we want to be energized regardless of the environment we find ourselves in? It is so easy to write down these ideas, but to live this kind of life takes a commitment to God's principles and daily walking and talking with Him.

Has this always been easy for me? Not in the least! I have invested huge amounts of time and money in different projects and goals along my life's journey. If one would look only at the many roadblocks in my life, things would look pretty bleak. But when looking at the broader landscape of my life, I have had an adventure many would give anything to have experienced. I have traveled and lived in many exciting and exotic countries around the world and worked in a variety of jobs and fields leading me to meet a mixture of individuals from every walk of life. I have had plenty and have had next to nothing. I have washed windows and cleaned toilets, while at other times run worldwide companies, only months apart. I have slept in the finest five-star accommodations and on concrete and dirt floors. I have slept soundly on both but found the hospitality of those who opened up their concrete floors have become lifelong friends and made memories, which I would not trade for all the five-star hotels or resorts I have visited.

A simple life with no debt and wonderful friends is much greater than all the allure and trappings a rich life can bring. Stress is the great killer of our modern society. Everyone seems to be traveling through life so fast we miss out on many wonderful sights, sounds, and people pouring past us each and every day. When apparent roadblocks suddenly appear down our life's road, we need to start looking around for the bright detour lights leading us in a new direction. Hold on because life is meant to be lived, exciting your senses, as you inspire those you come in contact with.

Does this mean a steady job is not God's path for you? No. If it is, God will make that job fulfilling and exciting for you. If that is His will, He will also lead many interesting, exciting, and wonderful people to cross your path and bless you while in that position. This type of life will eventually bless you and also bless the many associates you work with. These associates will undoubtedly lead you to new and unexpected experiences, even while staying in the same position or job.

Maybe someday you plan to be home by 6:00 p.m., but a chance encounter keeps out late having a cup of tea or coffee, sharing in a way that might change your life or someone else's life for the better, or a planned family holiday changes unexpectedly, momentarily throwing everything into turmoil. Things change and you think your holiday is ruined. When looking back at those times, you find they end up being the most memorable. Those experiences are fondly shared and talked about most often by your family when sitting around a winter's fireplace.

Mexico Trip

One of my students, a good friend, and a member of our club in Medford, Oregon, approached me one day with an opportunity to help some children in Mexico. Bill spent part of the year living in Mexico and developed a heart for the Mexican children. Many times, he shared how they had very little but were wonderful to be around.

It didn't take him long to convince me to gather up a number of rackets, tennis balls, and clothing to make available for some children in central Mexico. I shared with my family the idea of going to Mexico, and it didn't take long for us to agree on a planned visit. I decided to donate a month of my teaching time to help these disadvantaged children of San Miguel de Allende discover the joy of playing tennis.

We packed up our Ford station wagon with everything we thought we would need and headed south from Medford, Oregon. The drive from Oregon to the US and Mexico border turned out to be an adventure as we hit a storm in Northern California, which almost ended our planned trip. A huge rainstorm dumped so much water in the area, a five-mile section of Interstate 5 was beginning to look more like a river than a freeway. Smaller cars were already unable to drive through the quickly rising waters. Our Ford was so loaded down with weight that we and a few other heavy vehicles kept moving forward with the flood waters reaching higher and higher. We became worried the water would begin seeping in through our doors. We couldn't believe we had traveled less than two hundred miles and our trip might be over. Our car kept going and eventually took us beyond the flooding so we could continue our trip. The news of the flooding came over our radio informing travel on Interstate 5 was closed shortly after we made our way through. Some smaller cars trying to follow us through had been swept off the side of the freeway and had to be rescued. Had we arrived fifteen minutes later to the flooded section our trip would have ended before it began. In spite of this adventure, we eventually found ourselves parked at the Tijuana airport.

We were all tired but excited to finally get on a plane and head into central Mexico. We went to the desk for our check in and were quickly directed to another desk clerk. After our long tiring trip, we were suddenly informed, Shannon's ticket was somehow invalid. Here we were, a family of five getting ready to fly out in two hours after driving more than sixteen hours, and there was another apparent roadblock. We felt like God had lead us on this trip, and now we were told we had to leave our daughter behind if the rest of us wanted to continue on this flight? Well, that was not going to happen! Was our trip over before it began after driving 1,200 miles? I didn't know what to do, and the airline officials were adamant; there just weren't enough seats on the plane.

Standing there not knowing what to do when things were looking hopeless, another airport official appeared and said he would do what he could to sort out our situation. I was suspicious as they had already said there were not enough seats. I was not in the best mood and was sure my family could see the frustration on my face and body language. What were they going to do, have one of us sit on the wing? He retrieved our tickets and disappeared into a back room for quite a while as our departure time loomed ever closer. After waiting for thirty minutes, he came back to the desk and gave us our full refund.

"Wow, we had our money back, but how would that help?" we were asking ourselves. Were we supposed to turn around and drive another 1,200 miles back home? I had Bill waiting for me to arrive at the airport in central Mexico, and all the equipment and lessons for the children of San Miguel de Allende were with me. The airport official asked me to be patient as he disappeared again into a back room. I was not always that patient, and my stomach was churning on the inside as I did my best to trust that God was in charge. After waiting longer and the departure time getting ever closer, I wondered how this could possibly work out. Just then, he returned with reissued tickets so we could be on our way. This was a mystery as we were originally told there were not enough seats available for all five of us. My patience was wearing thin knowing these new tickets would most likely be more expensive than our original tickets, probably placing them out of our price range. I was surprised when he handed me the new tickets but more surprised when he presented me with the bill. The cost of the reissued tickets was one hundred and fifty dollars less than the refund he had just given me earlier for our original five tickets.

Wow, we had just made $150 US dollars by patiently (or me not so patiently) standing in their airport office. We were continuing to learn how God works, if we stay relaxed and let Him lead. Was I relaxed while all this was going on? I am sure my heart rate and blood pressure had gone up while standing there listening to what seemed like absurd explanations. I wish I could say I had stayed calm, but like all of us, I was not as patient as I wished to be. Life is a learning curve, and through these encounters, I was slowly learning how to be more patient and trust God, remembering the verse, "Tribulation worketh patience!"

Finally arriving in San Miguel de Allende, we spent a wonderful month in central Mexico with a great group of young Mexican juniors. They were eager to learn and never stopped smiling as we hit tennis balls back and forth. We enjoyed eating wonderful food at their evening market enjoying the authentic Mexican music. We watched many families stroll around their central park on warm weekend evenings, making the experience extra special. Our Mexico trip was one we never forgot and always treasured.

Like all wonderful trips, our exhilarating month in central Mexico ended all too soon. More surprises continued as we had a similar experience like the one we encountered in Tijuana on our return journey. Our new good friend, John Durante, from San Miguel de Allende, offered to drive us to the Guanajuato airport. We arrived early hoping for an uneventful encounter when checking in. But it was not to be. When we presented our confirmed tickets and seats, we were again told, "Sorry, we have no seats!" I couldn't believe we were hearing this again. Not having learned enough about patience, I could feel my blood pressure again start to rise.

"That is impossible," I explained. "We confirmed our flight two days ago as required, and here are our tickets!"

Again, "Sorry, we have no seats!"

John Durante, a real-life Indiana Jones character, pulled me aside and patiently explained the situation. An important airline official was looking at our tickets and said there was nothing we could do. Someone more important and better connected than us had taken our seats. That's the way it was in Mexico back then. We slowly walked back to John's vehicle, climbed in, and headed back down the highway for the long return ride back to San Miguel de Allende. After being gone a month, we were tired and looking forward to heading home. Our new confirmed flight was arranged for the following day, we hoped!

By this time, the sun was setting on the High Plains desert, and we were all tired and hungry, especially our three very patient children, Donnie, Brian, and Shannon. Driving down the darkening Mexican highway, John said he knew of a great roadside diner where we could stop for some delicious authentic Mexican food. We had just spent one month in Central Mexico, so I didn't how it could be any more authentic. When John pulled off the highway into a dirt parking area, we were more than a little skeptical. It didn't look like much. We were hot, irritable, and more than a little hungry. There was an open area to sit down, and all the cooking was done on an open-hearth oven, which looked to be a few hundred years old. We noticed the oppressive daytime heat was cooling off, becoming one of those wonderful balmy evenings to relax and enjoy after the airport stress. John said we were in for a treat as he took the initiative to order for us. It was a warm, beautiful cloudless night. Sitting under the star-covered sky, the aroma of delicious food started to waft in our direction, tantalizing our salivary glands.

When dinner was served, it turned out to be the most delicious meal we had experience in Mexico. Our flight cancellation and unexpected stop at this out-of-the-way, deserted roadside eatery allowed us to share a meal together and recount our wonderful month with John in San Miguel de Allende. We have enjoyed sharing our experiences with John Durante many times through the years. We relaxed, talked, and laughed as John recounted some of his wild archaeological adventures traveling through Central America and the world. We will never forget the amazing time we had with John and teaching tennis to the children of San Miguel de Allende. It wasn't our plan to miss our flight and be at that roadside diner, but God's path proved again to be delightful and wonderful as we relaxed under a star-filled sky following another apparent "roadblock."

Many will think you are crazy, not knowing where you are going next or where your next paycheck is coming from or how much it will be. Secretly, I think they are envious and jealous of your relaxed adventurous spirit of trusting God and knowing "He will direct your path." This doesn't mean you don't make plans and be irresponsible, like a chicken with its head cut off. It means that we are flexible to His path for our lives and do our best not to stress out about the apparent roadblocks and changes of direction.

Getting to the end of your life knowing you have really lived without any regrets is what we all want. I don't believe there is anything worse than looking back and saying, "Oh, I only wish I had done this or that, gone here or there," knowing you took the safe and boring route. How can we bless anyone if we are not relaxed and we seemed stressed out about every little change of direction? It is never too late to live with God in control, blessing those we come into contact with. Roadblocks? No such thing, only new and wonderful opportunities to get blessed and to bless others! Live the adventure God has in store for you! Because God's way is miraculous and fulfilling.

Reliving the roadblocks in my past while still in the hospital made me come to the realization, I was in the middle of the biggest roadblock of my life in Hong Kong! I was desperately looking to see where this detour was heading, as I was hoping and planning to leave the hospital behind.

Uncle Thompson was an individual who had sacrificed much and reminded me that I was not alone with life's many setbacks.

Years ago, while living in Tooting Bec located on the outskirts of London, we had an opportunity to meet a unique gentleman from Barbados named Uncle Thompson. He was the uncle of the lady who had just lost her husband. We were housesitting her flat in Tooting Bec when Uncle Thompson came by to check on us one Sunday. He was making sure we were all right, as she had asked him to do.

One look at Uncle Thompson and you would recognize he was a hard, muscular construction worker. He was of African descent, heavily muscled, and had skin as dark I had ever seen. Uncle Thompson was a character with an infectious personality and a bright huge smile to light up any foggy London day. On this day, while dropping by to say hi, he asked if it would be okay to make one of his favorite dishes from Barbados. He went right to work in the kitchen cutting up cucumbers and mixing in his special spices and ingredients.

My wife and I sat in the kitchen sharing stories with Uncle Thompson while he prepared his specialty. When his bowl of cucumbers was finally finished, he said we probably wouldn't like what he had created as it was a spicy dish. He was correct as one bite felt like fire on our tongues. Uncle Thompson had huge muscles with gnarly hands and broad fingers from daily hard construction work. When talking, his bright-red tongue, no doubt from his spicy cucumber concoction, and bright white teeth contrasted against his charcoal skin. He was a delight, and we immediately became friends!

My wife picked up her guitar and started playing while we sat together in the kitchen and sang a few Christian songs. It was then the book of Uncle Thompson's life really opened up to reveal the special inside pages of his remarkable life.

Uncle Thompson casually mentioned that the same song played in a different key would have a much richer tone. *How could this beat-up looking construction worker know anything about music?* we secretly asked ourselves. He then asked if it would be all right to hold the guitar. Once he gently handled the guitar, you could see a deep love for the instrument come across his face as he lovingly caressed it with his heavily calloused and beat-up hands. He immediately began playing the tune my wife and I had just been singing. We sat stunned and mesmerized listening to his ability. The pages of his incredible life slowly started to leaf open. He began sharing his earlier life with us as he continued to play the guitar. At first, the stories seemed unbelievable. But we were almost mesmerized by his musical talent.

Uncle Thompson said he had formerly been one of the premier classical guitarists in the world. He claimed to have played before dignitaries and heads of state of many countries around the world. This included an audience before the Queen of England. As outrageous as this sounded, Uncle Thompson continued to share and effortlessly played beautiful tunes on the guitar. He said he had previously been able to pick the "Hallelujah Chorus" on his own classical guitar. His stories sounded pretty unbelievable until he actually started to fingerpick the "Hallelujah Chorus." With his beat-up broad huge fingers from construction work, he still impressed.

He hadn't touched or played the guitar in twenty-five years to keep a promise he had made with his wife. She had been jealous of his celebrity status, watching him travel around the world. His wife had forced him to choose between the guitar and life with her. Choosing his wife, he left his beloved guitar untouched for twenty-five years. That was until that day in that Tooting Bec kitchen, privately performing for us. We were blessed to share that Sunday afternoon with Uncle Thompson.

His book cover looked torn and beat up, but the inside was filled with wonder and color to brighten any rainbow. My life seemed simple and easy compared to the complicated hard life he had so willingly chosen. I continued to remind myself to never judge a book by its cover.

Uncle Thompson taught me a valuable lesson in graceful living, "Leave the complaining to others."

Miracle Continues

I had hundreds of hours to mull over my surprising journey while feeling almost helpless after the accident. Even with all my wonderful and incredible memories, I still desired a bright and exciting future. With this in my mind, I stayed focused and consistent in doing what little I could to get better.

My doctor was almost as stubborn as I could be. After daily visits and watching me achieve one goal after another, he relented and agreed to release me from the hospital on the thirty-first day of my stay at the Adventist. He reluctantly signed my release papers after watching my celebration lap around the fourth floor hallway, unaided. He advised me to be extremely careful once I arrived back home in Clearwater Bay. He also said I would most likely not be able to handle the homestay very long. With the inconvenience of no nurses, no bed to raise and lower remotely, homestay would be difficult and he thought impossible for me to deal with. He was sure I would be back in the hospital within a day or two. He should have known by then how determined I was to be on my own and back to my previous lifestyle. In my doctor's mind, I was a real nutcase, with no grasp on reality.

Surprisingly, my discharge from the hospital was considered newsworthy and was somehow covered by the Hong Kong press. There was a great celebration with the press, my family, and friends, as I "walked" out the front entrance of the hospital. There was my favorite gazebo from my "day out," only this time I was heading home. My family were surrounding me, making sure I made it safely to the car. They were supporting me in more ways than one. My wife, Sally, and daughter, Shannon, carried many of the gifts from my room. Donnie and Brian aided me, almost carrying me as they held me up on each side. Suddenly shorter and fatter than them, I couldn't have made it to the car without their assistance. I did my best to act and look normal in front of so many well-wishers and the press. I was the only person I was fooling. I gratefully edged into our vehicle finally able to go home. Had it really been only thirty-one days since I was super healthy, fit, and vibrant? This was the longest month I had ever lived, with each minute slowly ticking by on that huge room clock always in front of me.

I had changed since I arrived thirty-one days before and would only realize the scope of that change in the months and years to come. The very first thing I noticed was the uncomfortable car ride home. It was difficult to edge into our car with my ever-present brace in place. It seemed there were many more cracks and potholes in the roads on both sides of Victoria Harbor. My upper back was jarred to the bone with every minor bump. I kept asking why we had to hit every bump in the road. What was a huge vibration-filled ride for me was a smooth ride for my family. The parts of my body I could feel were so sensitive, it felt like shards of shattered glass rubbing together in my muscles and upper spine. Where I had feeling, I felt every minor vibration, and it was painful!

Where was my soft hospital bed now? Was my doctor going to be right? Even with the pain, I loved being out of the hospital. It seemed like I had been glued in that hospital bed forever, dreaming of this very day. Now it was actually happening, but for some reason, it still felt like a dream. Gazing out the car window was like seeing Hong Kong for the first time. High-rises were stretching up everywhere against a beautiful blue sky spreading out above Victoria Harbor. There were still the busy, crowded roads to contend with as everyone was racing from one destination to another. The only thing that had changed was me. I was uncomfortable but at the same time excited and embraced the entire ride home. First we headed through the Eastern Harbor Tunnel, which was completed shortly after we arrived in Hong Kong, then up through the new Tseung Kwan O Tunnel, where we eventually viewed the bright multigreen foliage of Clearwater Bay area in the distance. *Almost home,* I thought. I could feel my excitement building. I couldn't wait to finally arrive at our country park abode.

Our Hong Kong village home was identical to almost every other house in the area. It was three-stories tall with only 700 sq ft per floor. We were renting the second and third floors, so I knew what awaited me. It was not going to be easy as I had the narrow second and third floor stairwell to negotiate, with of course, no lift (elevator). The narrow stairway awaited us after the difficult process of helping me out of our Toyota Corolla. The process of going upstairs turned out to be like watching the Three Stooges carrying a piano up a flight of stairs.

We went agonizingly slow, one step at a time, with me weaving back and forth in pain and I not able to balance myself. Thank goodness for the back brace to keep my back stable. My sons did their best to keep me upright and not fall. The effort was not much different than helping a totally inebriated person up a flight of stairs. I would not have made it up to our flat without Donnie and Brian practically carrying me. Laughing and struggling between the pain, they were finally able to haul me up stairs to the third floor. Putting me in our own bed was glorious, finding myself totally exhausted from the journey. Just to see our home again with all the familiar trappings felt wonderful. Another red-letter day! Our home felt strange and familiar at the same time. Had I actually been gone just a month? Why did everything feel so different? Or was it just me? It felt like a lifetime ago I was here. I was hoping to find my previous self waiting for me once I entered the front door, but the new me was evident everywhere I turned.

It was great being home but the realization I was in a bed that I could not easily adjust, or with a call button to summon nurses to come to my aid, quickly sobered me up. Even though I could move around with a walker, I still didn't have the ability to easily get out of bed by myself or go to the bathroom without help. Everyone had to go to school or work early in the morning, and I was left on my own, except for a daytime maid who came in each day to clean and cook. I was so out of it, I still have no recollection of who she was or what she even looked like.

I would just stay in bed, with no TV to watch, and I was still unable to read the few books that were available. I would lay there doing what simple mental and physical exercises I could dream up before I got bored and fell back to sleep again for short naps. It was not much different than the hospital bed except no nurses to help me or staff to bring me my meals. Other than a few agonizing trip to the bathroom, I was stuck in bed. Before the accident, there was very little time spent at our Hong Kong village home. It was just a place to go after a long day to eat dinner, have a little family time, fall to sleep, then eat breakfast in the morning after our early-morning cycle. All of our living was spent out and about in Hong Kong, either working, schooling, or exploring the wonders of that region on weekends.

Now that I was back home, I couldn't wait for everyone to come home and walk through our door after they finished school. I could then have some company and help getting in and out of bed. Although we had a large bed, I had to sleep alone most of the time. A side effect of my condition made my legs shake and flail around during the night.

This condition is called clonus, and clonus provided many unexpected and humorous moments for those around me during the years to follow. "Nice to know I could provide come comic relief." Everyone has seen this similar condition, only it is usually related to babies. Babies will jerk, sometimes almost violently as their nervous system wakes up and develops. It is caused by the newly activated nerves becoming exhausted, making their muscles jerk and shake involuntarily. This may be cute in a child, but for an adult sleeping in a bed with a spouse, it is quite a different scenario. The spouse ends up being kicked or scratched by toenails, resulting in a very poor night's sleep for both. Sheets and blankets were all over the place in the morning, as if someone had intentional torn the bed up during the night.

After school, my sons would make a beeline into our bedroom and insist it was time for our daily walk. *Wow*, I thought, *who raised these kids?* I had big plans for the future, but I believe my sons and daughter had even bigger plans for me. They wouldn't settle for me being anything less than what I had been before my accident. I loved their positive attitude, but this wasn't always easy for me. When you are feeling broken, awkward, and almost helpless, it is easy to just vegetate by staying in bed or glued to a comfortable chair rather than face reality. I needed my children's help more than they even knew. They would pull me out of bed and help dress me. They hauled me down two flights of stairs, then out into the fresh air. This was always an immense struggle, but it was worth it to finally be outside, feeling alive and smelling the moist jungle like air. There was no level place to walk where we lived. So choice number 1, go uphill, or choice number 2, go downhill. The sidewalk was a little wider and straighter downhill, so that is the direction we chose to take our walks.

I'm sure to this day, the motorist watching us thought we were an odd threesome. I would do my best to imitate a walk, throwing my legs forward in an awkward, almost animated motion while being held up by two teenage sons. I was always worried about my sons holding me tight enough so I wouldn't fall into the road and be hit by another minibus racing by. Minibuses were constantly flying up and down that narrow Clearwater Bay Road. My sons would laugh and joke, telling me not to worry. They securely held me up, but I was not my previous confident self. Not even with them holding me! Fear of having another mishap began to find a way into my consciousness. I was feeling vulnerable.

As parents, we always know in the back of our minds, the things we teach and put our children through will someday come back to haunt us but also make us proud. While on one of these walks, this happened earlier in life than I had thought possible. As a tennis teaching pro, I would train my children, as well as my other top junior tennis players. One of the things I would often ask them was, "Have you had enough?" toward the end of an exhausting drill?

They would invariably respond with an emphatic yes. I would then respond, "Okay, then we'll do, just a little more." One day while on our walk, my sons seemed concerned for me and asked, "Have you had enough? Are you too tired to go on and still be able to walk back up the hill?"

The first time they asked, I was exhausted and responded with my own emphatic, "Yes, let's go back to the house!" I should have anticipated their response, but it still took me by surprise. I was expecting them to feel a little sorry for me with my condition.

"Okay," they said, "then we'll do just a little more downhill before we go back!"

I couldn't believe it! Had they really said that? By then I'd really had enough, but they just looked at me with that quizzical little smile which said, *We know, and now it's your turn.* So after another chuckle, which thank goodness was always present, we went a little further before allowing me to head back home. I learned that day that they had been listening all those years and now had no intention of letting me just lie in bed and vegetate. They were there pushing and encouraging me when I didn't feel like it, just as I had been there for them in the past.

REJOINING FAST PACED HONG KONG

Every day was proving to be painful, exhausting, and consistently awkward while doing the simplest of tasks like getting out of bed, putting on shoes, going up and down stairs, or just walking. Even with these daily trials, I knew I needed to get back to work and as soon as possible. During my lifetime, I had witnessed how quickly people could be replaced, no matter how indispensable they or anyone else may have thought they were. Once I arrived home and eventually learning how to get out of bed and move around on my own, I started a limited exercise program. Our third floor roof was ideal for a retreat and my alone time for private exercises. My exercise routine was limited, but I felt I was at least doing something. Just getting up the stairs was a workout. I did some arm strengthening, simple leg movements, and limited abdominal crunches; and I do mean limited. I was only able to raise my knees and feet a few inches off the ground before my back would ache too much to do more. I was at least doing something.

These were the extent of my exercises. Anyone witnessing this workout would have wondered what I was doing. My exercises were so simple; it would have seemed useless for a fully fit individual. I was able to begin some therapy back at the hospital with Nalini Advani. After a dedicated month back home, and the daily walks with my sons, the decision was made to head back to work. It had only been two months, and somehow, I was able to head back to the club. Miraculously, this was with Aberdeen Marina Club's blessing. Most clubs would have arranged for a replacement and I would have been out of a job. They were very good to me, and I never forgot that blessing. The blessing I somehow put in the back of my mind was the miracle right in front of me. Being on my feet with bones healing faster than they are supposed to heal should have woken me up. My ego still believed I could "do it all," if I could just put in enough effort.

Trying to look alive on our rooftop

Returning to my position as tennis director and head tennis pro was difficult as my body said, "Stay in bed!" Every movement was painful and awkward. It was far too painful for me to hit a tennis ball as I could barely maintain my balance when moving around without help. I knew having a walker or crutches on the tennis court would not be a consideration, if I was to keep my teaching status as head pro. It was strange putting on my tennis clothes when preparing to teach again. The clothes looked the same, but everything else felt strange and looked different. My shirts fit tight around my waist, and my legs had shrunk, not quite filling out my shorts.

My son Donnie turned out to be a lifesaver for me. He would come to work with me, then feed and hit tennis balls with my students. I would stand by the net post and casually use it as my support. I would do all my teaching from there. A photo of me hitting a tennis ball had been taken a few days before the accident for the Clearwater Tennis Tournament. It was hard for me to believe I looked so controlled, relaxed, and vibrant but now feeling off balance, out of control, and holding the net post for stability.

Photo for Tournament—3 days before accident

At the end of the lessons, I would leave the court for five minutes and lay down behind my desk. This was the only way I could relieve some of the pain and deep ache in my upper back. Pain became almost intolerable when standing for any length of time. Lying down was the only way I could get some relief. After lying down, the arduous process of rolling over, pushing myself to my knees, then using my desk to haul myself to my chair took all the strength I could muster up. I kept convincing myself that it was still a whole lot better than lying paralyzed in a hospital bed. I looked so awkward when standing back up; it made my staff uneasy. They said they tried not to watch but couldn't help themselves. I tried to make sure no one else was around when taking my breaks. Members witnessing this would only then realize the extent of my pain and disability as I continued to do what I could to fake being well. I desperately wanted to keep my job. Smile, then fake it till you make it, right? I kept reminding myself daily to look as normal as possible. The only person I was fooling was myself!

One of the most difficult times after arriving back to the Marina Club came because of the response I received from two of my assistants. They had visited me at the hospital a few times and assumed I would never return to my previous level of teaching or director of tennis responsibilities. With this in mind, they had been jockeying between the two of them for my position as Head Tennis Pro and Director of Tennis. When first hospitalized, I asked them to fill in for me and be responsible for teaching all of my students until I could return to the Marina Club. Seeing my condition and hearing the prognosis, they conveniently convinced most of my students I would not be able to teach again. Even if I did return, I would not be able to teach at the level I taught previously. You can imagine their surprise and disappointment when I returned to teach a limited number of students and take over my director of tennis responsibilities. This limited teaching schedule turned out to be a blessing for me. I would not have been able to handle any more lessons with the way I was feeling.

Before the minibus altered my life, my junior program had flourished with as many as 160 juniors registered for lessons. All of my junior students were now being taught by my assistant coaches. This looked like another roadblock. I began to look for a detour sign, allowing me to take a new direction. Why fight the roadblock? So I started a new program for the very young four-to-six-year-olds. Initially only one parent was brave enough to sign their child up for the class. Word was being spread around the club that I was too disabled to still teach quality lessons. Several parents with young children came to watch me teach my only student. After viewing the lesson, these two parents were willing to add their children to the program. They were skeptical but were willing to test my class. Four more parents signed their children up by the fourth lesson, and so on, until I had to ask my third assistant Mei Lei to teach with me.

Mei Lei was an amazing help. She had been a top Asian player when younger, living in China and Indonesia before settling in Hong Kong and winning the Women's Open Tennis Championship. She was always positive and encouraging for me personally and wonderful with the children. By the end of two months, we had two classes twice a week involving thirty children. These children were some of my best encouragement and inspirations, especially at the beginning of my recovery back on the tennis courts.

Young children are wonderful because there is no beating around the bush or PC (political correctness). If they wanted to know about my back brace, which was easily visible, they would just walk up and ask. Satisfied, they would immediately go back to learning tennis. No preconceived notions or ulterior motive in their questions. With these young children, I was also able to witness the chronological age of my legs and my recovery process. I watched these amazing little ones also try to control their movements and balance around the court. I began to understand that my damaged central nervous system was relearning and remapping the simple mechanism of automatic movement, without my consciously thinking about each step. It was a conscious effort for me to just stay upright. I had to tell my legs and feet to do the simplest tasks such as take one step in front of another when I wanted get a drink of water or go to the other side of the net. These little ones had to think and tell their legs to do the correct footwork, which was foreign for them when playing tennis. They were doing their best to stay balanced and hit a tennis ball with the correct stroke. "They were awkward, just like me!" I felt right at home on a tennis court with them. I looked forward to their lessons more than any other during the rest of my time at the Marina Club.

DON BOZARTH

Inviting Clear Blue Water

Swimming was the one sporting activity I looked forward to more than any other and could hardly wait to "jump" in the pool. Mentally, I was ready to return to triathlon training and racing. Physically it was another story. Swimming would turn out to be my favorite physical activity when I attempted to train again. There is something special about diving into a refreshing body of water on a hot day. Feeling the coolness and buoyancy allowing you to float and move smoothly forward is invigorating. There is no way to adequately share in print how much I missed swimming when I was laid up in the hospital. This is the reason I insisted on a removable plastic cast after my original plaster cast was removed. I needed to convince my doctor I would only take it off while taking a shower. He wasn't convinced, but again, he was tired of arguing with me, so he went along with this and my many other requests. A removable waterproof plastic cast was necessary if I was to get in the pool and start swimming again. Finally, out of the hospital and back to work, I was looking forward to my first swim in the Marina Club's third floor rooftop pool.

I was always trying to push the envelope, so the second day back to work I made the decision to attempt swimming. I was excited, but still a sense of foreboding hung in the air. Every endeavor I undertook proved to be difficult and took all the mental strength I had to move forward. Getting ready to swim took some thought and preparation as I continued to move around like a drunk. With back brace securely in place, I headed down to the pool. This brace would be part of my attire while swimming for weeks ahead. I also had the issue of my frozen neck to deal with, not allowing me to turn my head from side to side. Looking from side to side required me to rotate my entire body. To accommodate this disability, Donnie arranged a snorkel set before heading to the pool. My children continued to play a big role when I began swimming. Someone needed to be nearby in case my enthusiasm got the better of me and I found myself in trouble.

Understandably, my fitness level was worse than I wanted anyone to recognize. My family knew the truth, especially my boys, after hauling me out of bed, getting me in and out of the car, or taking me for our daily walks up and down Clearwater Bay Road. I looked a sight with my pear-shaped body in a Speedo swimsuit. Body (back) brace was firmly secure and with snorkel and mask set in place. I was a sight to behold! We've all heard or seen the jokes about old men in Speedos. Wow, now it was me, the big fat joke in the Speedo! Had I really gone from looking twenty years younger to now looking twenty years or more older? I was excited but couldn't help being self-conscious. However, nothing was going to take this moment of triumph away from me. I had been looking forward to this moment since the first few days lying in the hospital. My ego needed to take a back seat for now, maybe forever. Who knew what the future had in store for me?

As I approached the edge of the pool, excitement, along with deep foreboding, gave me chills as I negotiated my first entrance into the deep-blue water. The pool was empty of other swimmers, and the cool glassy waters looked so inviting, I wanted to run and dive in. Not possible in my condition; I couldn't run, much less dive. Not with the condition of my back! It took a concentrated effort just to turn around and edge my way backward down the ladder. Donnie was there guiding me so I wouldn't lose my balance and take a nasty spill. My worrying seemed almost crazy when I thought about it later. I would have only fallen in the water, but that's how fragile I felt! Finally slipping into the pool, there was that glorious feeling as the water slowly enveloped every inch of my body. I could finally feel that wonderful coolness when the water reached chest high, where I had complete feeling. Before the accident, I would sprint one length of this twenty-five-meter pool in around eighteen seconds. Now my goal was just to complete one lap, down and back of only fifty meters.

Shooting pain-seared white hot through my upper back as I attempted a simple breaststroke motion. The pain was unrelenting and terrific as I set out on my fifty-meter journey. I was not prepared for what I was experiencing, even with the wonderful weightlessness the water provided. The hundreds of nerve endings surrounding my spinal cord seemed to fire off pain at the same time. I could only attempt a very limited breaststroke motion. Even with the pain, I was excited. I was thrilled to finally be in a swimming pool beginning my journey back to full fitness. With limited ability to kick, I moved my arms and hands about six to twelve inches to propel myself forward with a simple sculling motion. The pain in my upper back made it impossible to try anymore movement. I don't know how long it took to complete my marathon fifty meters. I held onto the edge of the pool for a rest after only finishing the first twenty-five meters. I was thankful for the five-minute rest, breathing heavily from the exertion and pain. Recovering enough energy and courage I swam back. Finally reaching the pool's edge again, I was excited but totally exhausted. I asked myself, *Tired after only a fifty-meter journey?* When I finished, more help was needed from Donnie to exit the pool. I HAD GONE FOR MY FIRST SWIM AGAIN! WHAT A MIRACLE! I headed down to the pool every day I was at the Marina Club. Within two weeks, I could carefully get in and out of the pool by myself. No diving, but that would come. I was sure that would come in the future!

Fake It till You Make It

For years I had encouraged my tennis students to "fake it till you make it." Very simply put, you don't need to act like you are intimidated when competing against someone who is seeded higher or has more experience than yourself. You are always in control of how you project yourself. In other words, act like you are in control and that everything is going just as you planned. This doesn't mean having a big ego or thinking that you are superior to someone else. Since nobody but you knows your plan, why let them know your plans aren't working out exactly as you have envisioned. At the very least, those watching and your opponent will wonder if you know something they don't know and have something up your sleeve.

Heading to the club each day, I needed to display this very character trait while recovering. "Go to work as if everything is fine" was my plan, then be ready to take on a normal day's workload. Putting a smile on my face, while hiding all the pain and awkwardness was not easy. Everything in my body was screaming otherwise. More than once I wanted to head back home and hide away in my bedroom. I wanted to fall into a deep sleep until I felt better and the nightmare I was living would magically disappear.

Another serious test of my character happened when Andrew Sams of TVB phoned shortly after I arrived back home and asked if I was able or willing to do the commentary for the Barcelona Olympics. This was a huge inspiration and honor for me just for him to ask and knowing my condition. Andrew had been one of my consistent visitors in the hospital. He had witnessed how badly I had been injured. As a close friend, Andrew was one of the few who really understood how badly I felt in my new body. Inviting me to join him for the commentary was a great challenge and one I was willing to attempt. The amount of discomfort and pain I was experiencing made me wonder if I could pull this off and do a proper job for Andrew and TVB. I was still wearing my body brace, so we needed to figure a way to deal with the brace so it didn't show. It didn't take much encouraging for me to agree to Andrew's invitation. This was what I wanted—to be normal—and I was open to the challenge and immediately started preparing myself. Viewers want to see confident and self-assured presenters when they watch the Olympics. I would get in front of a mirror to practice looking relaxed and smiling with no pain etched across my face. *Could I pull this off with such an uncomfortable and awkward body?* I asked myself.

Andrew had arranged a panel of four other commentators, and I needed to look upbeat, especially when on-air. If I was careful, I could remove the brace just before going live and put it back on when off camera. In other words, "fake it till I could make it."

"Smile, look healthy, and get excited about the Olympics," I reminded myself every time we went live. It definitely worked because a number of people thought I had made a complete recovery after watching TVB's Olympic presentation. The reality was, it took all the energy I could muster to smile and look excited. I was excited but mainly because my good friend Andrew had enough faith in me to include me for another Olympic telecast. The Olympic program ran for seventeen days straight, with much of the telecast aired live in the middle of the night, Hong Kong time. We would have short breaks between events when live commentary feed was sent through from Barcelona. With my brace securely back in place, I would find a quiet place to lie down on an empty set for a few minutes to relieve the ache in my back. This would allow me to recover just long enough to be ready for the next on-camera session.

Andrew will never know how grateful I was that he had confidence in me and asked me to be part of his panel. This did wonders for my self-confidence, with me only a few months out of the hospital. I had wondered many times, if my life could ever be the same. A very small part of my previous life was being pieced back together with the successful Olympic commentary. I may have been faking my wellness, but I was beginning to learn just how important that little phrase was: "Fake it till you make it!"

The Tennis Court Beckons

Following the seventeen days of Olympic commentary, I continued to toss and hit a few tennis balls to my little future tennis pros. If I was careful, I could gently hit without losing my balance or falling down. My doctor had reminded me many times, "Don't push your recovery until I give you my approval, so do not attempt jogging, only slow walks!" He knew by then I could be a stubborn patient. He really didn't need to worry too much. As much as I wanted to be out running again, there was that huge fear factor residing in the back of my head. Would I stumble, take a bad fall, and end up worse off than ever? With these negative thoughts in my mind, I was still anxiously looking forward to that day when I could try jogging and running again. This was for two reasons: One, the thought of running again was glorious, just like swimming had been. Two, it would mean eventually not having to wear my brace twenty-four hours a day, seven days a week. Wow, to walk around the house or be in my office without the brace supporting my back would be a dream come true. "Would my back ever be that strong again?" I asked myself. I wouldn't accept negative thoughts, like having to wear that brace the rest of my life. I knew the brace would be with me for some time in the future, especially when starting to run again or playing tennis. That was okay with me, as long as I continued to see improvement.

August 2, 1992, was my mom's birthday. After calling my mom to wish her a happy birthday, I went directly to my doctor's office for my usual checkup. It suddenly felt like it was my birthday! My doctor finally gave his approval for me to begin "running" again. My three-days-a-week therapy sessions were paying off. I spent hours with Nalini Advani during these sessions, and those painful massages were obviously paying dividends. Just 101 days had passed, but it seemed like an eternity to me. Certainly another lifetime ago when I was super fit and training hard to finish on the podium at the World Championships in Muskoka, Canada.

One of my last runs before qualifying for the Worlds was at the Hong Kong Track Association's mile race. I had never run an official mile event for time, so I wasn't sure what to expect. I surprised myself and everyone else when I ran an official time of five minutes and thirty-two seconds. A great memory but another lifetime ago. I was excited when my doctor gave his approval for me to begin running. Instantly, a negative thought came roaring back, "What would happen if I tripped and fell?" The fear of breaking my back again was terrible and frightening and never far from my mind. Even with those thoughts, I was still determined to start running. I was not about to let fear control my life. My balance still caused me to sway around when walking, and I was forever struggling to stand up without losing my equilibrium. I had to completely concentrate on every movement of my legs and feet to walk from one place to another without stumbling.

As soon as I left the doctor's office, I went straight back to the Marina Club. Heading to the gym, I dressed down into my running shorts, shoes, and, of course, my ever-present back brace. Walking past a mirror, I still looked fat with skinny legs. Not what I enjoyed seeing, but I was still headed out for my first run, and I was sure my shape would eventually change. I took the lift down from the fifth floor gym and walked out onto a brightly sunlit road in front of Aberdeen Marina Club. It was another one of those hot, humid, steamy, sunny summer days in Hong Kong, but I hardly noticed it.

All I could see was the wonderful road stretching out in the distance beckoning me to run again. What a wonderful feeling to be out on the road again after three and half long months. This had special meaning after being told I would never walk again, much less run. I could feel the goosebumps start to raise up on my arms as I crossed the road to start my first of many more runs.

Standing there on the sidewalk, looking down the road toward the boatyards, I was immediately taken back to the comments I had casually made over the last number of years when I was healthy and fit. Numerous people had asked me, "How can you run twenty kilometers without too much trouble, and ten kilometers in less than thirty-seven minutes on your best days, at forty-five years old?" In other words, they were asking, "Where do you start?" Without much thought, I had always blurted out, "One light pole at a time!"

Well, there I was, standing in front of the Aberdeen Marina Club. I was trying to figure out how I was going to make it from this light pole I was leaning on, to the next light pole? I know I had a look of determination as I fixed my gaze on that next light pole and took off for my first run. "What a shock." I couldn't even get my feet off the ground. My movement was more like a waddling shuffle. I don't know what I was expecting. But it was far from what I was hoping to experience! I was doing my best to run but also hoped not to trip and fall over at the same time. First one step then another, it seemed like the light pole was stretching out there getting farther away. The shock of the impact while trying to run was like stepping off a step when you think there are no more steps. *Thud*, a shock wave, and reverberation went from my toes right up through the top of my head. It felt like my whole body had been fused together and was trying to break apart while at the same time loosen up. I urged myself forward, forcing myself to continue moving, finally reaching my goal, finishing my first light-pole run."

Totally out of breath, I was thankful for reaching that light pole as I grab onto it for support, needing a place to rest and recover. I was exhausted and excited at the same time, just as I felt after my first swim in the pool. As little as this run seem to be, I was able to complete it. After a much needed rest, I turned to run back. How ridiculous it must have looked for any bystander or visitor arriving at the Marina Club witnessing this stranger's attempt to run no more than twenty-five meters in front of the main entrance. I was so totally focused on my goal, I didn't care! To me it was a great victory! Shuffling back to the lift with goosebumps on my arms again, I knew I was on a new and great adventure. ANOTHER MIRACLE! I had big plans and hardly noticed some of the small miracles unfolding right in front of my face. Was I about ready to "do it all" again. My ego was again trying to take control!

    I continued to follow the advice I had given for years of improving "one light pole at a time." After only a week, I was able to "run" two light poles without stopping. My waddling shuffle turned into an awkward jog as I was able to slightly lift my feet off the ground. I tried to double my distance each week for the first month. But like everything else, I found it hard to contain myself, and enthusiasm got the better of me. I increased more than I originally planned. Thirty days later, I was able to run, jog, waddle, or shuffle about 1.2 kilometers before I had to stop and "run" back. I was beginning to take too much credit for these accomplishments, still not realizing the extent of miracles swirling around me. How can we be so blind to what is right in front of us? We tend to get caught up in our own little world of plans and endeavors so much so that tunnel vision of self-importance takes over. My big ego and temporal goals kept taking precedence over the eternal and what is truly lasting. God wasn't finished with me quite yet.

COST OF IMPATIENCE

One month since I began running again brought me to September 1. I was getting more excited by the day because of my improvements. Four months and a week had passed, and I was feeling like I might actually end up doing it all again. I was looking forward to waking up to the hopeful days of my past. I seemed to be filled with more and more energy. My legs felt awkward, like they belonged to someone else, but small improvements kept me hopeful, positive, and moving forward. My big ego convinced me I was some kind of miracle man as I repeatedly harassed my doctor about taking the metal plate out of my left arm. He kept saying, "It's too early." The lumps from the screws pressing against the inside of my skin were irritating and painful when hitting or bumping my left arm.

The plate continued to bother me, and I was insistent, questioning about when I could have it removed. I found out later this plate was actually designed for a tibia, not for a radius. A mistake was made in the rush to put the broken bones of my arm back together. The wrong plate was hurriedly screwed into the radius of my left arm. The screws holding the plate in place were bigger and longer than they should have been. The end of each screw extended through the bone so much they could be seen slightly pressing against the underside of my skin. Uncomfortable and painful at times, I pressured my doctor relentlessly to have the plate removed. Like many of my other requests, it wasn't long before he gave in to my petitions.

He only agreed by stating, "Your improvement continues to surprise me." By the middle of September, he reluctantly agreed to remove the plate and the irritating screws. Excitement is an understatement to describe how I felt. It was like I had won the lottery. Once that irritating plate was removed, I would be on my way to a full and complete recovery. No more operations and reduced doctor visits!

Friday morning saw me up early and excited, heading to the Adventist to have this oversized plate removed. I checked in early for what would be my last operation. Another red-letter day in my road to recovery. The caring hospital staff provided a hospital gown, then wheeled me into the operating room before inserting the usual IV. It wasn't long before the chill of the cold, sterile operating room began seeping into my body. My mind wandered thinking how wonderful life was starting to feel again. I didn't even mind waiting for the doctor to arrive. This would be my last operation. Every day was like a miracle with all the improvements I was experiencing. I was looking forward to these hospital visits being behind me. Waking up early was beginning to be part of my routine, as it had been for years before my April 22 roadblock and detour. I was hoping my grandmother's statement in the past would be true for me now. "And this, too, shall pass!"

At 6:00 a.m. on another beautiful late summer day and the staff whom I knew all too well by then were cheerful and bright. They also knew this operation would likely be the last they would see of me. There was the usual activity, rustling around getting equipment ready for the operation. But it wasn't long before the activity stopped and everyone disappeared. Quietly lying there, the chill of the room started to seep into my body. Then I began wondering why the activity had stopped. I was left completely alone with no more staff rustling around. Where was my doctor, and why had he not appeared? An hour slowly passed before a nurse came in with the news I did not want to hear. My doctor could not be located. They assured me they were trying their best to reach him. *Is this another opportunity for me to learn more patience?* I questioned myself. I struggled to wait patiently, wishing this could go quickly and smoothly.

Noticing I was shivering, one of the nurses offered to bring me a blanket to help stay warm. I was grateful to finally warm up but also wondered what kind of doctor would schedule an operation and leave their patient of five months shivering in this cold operating room? Jokingly, I suggested to the nurses he might be at Aberdeen Marina Club playing tennis. I had previously given him tennis lessons there on Friday mornings. I dozed in and out of sleep as time passed slowly by.

Finally showing up two hours late, my doctor had been found playing tennis. My operation had somehow slipped his mind. I floated into unconsciousness again as they injected me for the operation. I couldn't wait to drift off, then wake up, and have this ordeal over with. However, it started: I was thankful to finally wake up and have that metal plate removed. I felt all the operations were now behind me. The only warning the doctor provided was, "Take it easy, and no extreme pressure should be placed on your arm for a month. The holes from the removed screws need to fill in before the bone will obtain full strength."

Leaving the hospital, everything felt perfect. With improvements way ahead of schedule, this final operation behind me, I couldn't have felt better. I was scheduled to fly out for Japan to watch my two sons compete in the first Asian Triathlon Championships in just two weeks. The timing of my operation was perfect. Donnie and Brian had trained by themselves for two months during the summer in the States. They had stayed with their grandparents in Beaverton, Oregon. I had given them a simple training program to follow, and they had copied Dave Scott's swim workout. I had no idea how they would race during the event. I hadn't seen them race since their first and only Olympic-distance event in Thailand the previous December. Donnie and Brian were seventeen and sixteen years of age, so I was looking forward to watching them compete. This would be doubly wonderful now that I finally had that irritating plate out of my arm.

Life somehow doesn't always work out as we plan with one detour after another popping up. God still needed to whittle away at my huge ego. The unexpected happened on Saturday night, shortly after falling asleep. Only forty hours since I had left the hospital, and I was awakened by a loud scream of pain. I found my wife at the end of our bed, on the floor, screaming. Turning on the light, I found the source of her pain. Our cat was biting her calf and hanging onto her leg by digging its claws in as deep as possible. Stepping out of bed in the dark, she had accidentally stepped on our cat sleeping there.

Reacting instinctively, I reached down with both hands and twisted the cat's claws off her leg. I instantly felt a sharp snap of pain in my left forearm. As soon I released my wife from the grip of the cat, I stared at my forearm. It was bent upward like an inverted "V." I couldn't believe what I was seeing. I had rebroken my arm just forty hours after having the plate taken out. My doctor was right; it was too soon! My family tried to console me saying, "It might just be a muscle spasm." With my past experiences, I knew it was broken. Also knowing our financial position, we couldn't afford another emergency room visit and treatment. I elected to wait until Monday morning to head back to the hospital and have another X-ray and face my doctor.

Sunday was not much fun walking around with an untreated broken arm. Monday couldn't arrive soon enough as I again arrived at the hospital early to avoid my doctor. He was probably out playing tennis anyway, remembering the operating room fiasco. Knowing the staff in the X-ray department from my many visits there, I went straight in and requested them to take an x-ray of my arm. They couldn't believe it when they saw me walk in, especially holding my broken arm. After a quick x-ray, they confirmed what I already knew; it was snapped at the original break site, bent at a 15 degree angle. No muscle cramp, as my family had so hoped—more like a comedy of errors! I could have done without this life lesson of not rushing things.

My therapist was first to see me as I took the X-rays down to my doctor's office. His office was located right outside Nalini Advani's therapy department. Nalini was standing behind the reception desk when I walked in. She took one look at me and my arm and had the look of, *What next?* Nalini had invested a number of hours working on this same arm getting it back to normal strength, so she was as disappointed as I was. She said I could go in and put the X-rays on his screen. My X-ray would be the first thing my doctor would see when he arrived.

He eventually arrived without noticing me. Sheepishly, I edged in behind him. He immediately saw the X-rays hanging on the darkened screen. Looking up, he exclaimed out loud, "What's this?" Turning on the lamp, he viewed the broken bone, then finally reading the name on the X-ray, he sounded angry when he said, "I don't believe it!" He had been so careful to warn me. I then let him know I was there by saying, "I didn't do it on purpose!"

The absurdity of the event was not over as he silently led me down to the familiar emergency room to set the bone. Arriving at that all-too-familiar room, he sat me down on one side of the X-ray table and gave me a tablet while gathering up materials for another waterproof caste. He walked up and casually asked, "Are you ready?" Looking at him guardedly, I hesitantly said yes. He wasn't looking happy as he grabbed my left forearm above and below the break. I could tell by the look on his face he was upset. The look was like I had borrowed his favorite car and totaled it. With my arm directly between us, I looked straight in his eyes with disbelief, as he attempted to mobilize or move and set the bone straight by twisting and bending my forearm. This went on for what felt like fifteen to twenty seconds before he stopped and asked, "Doesn't this hurt?"

"What do you think?" I asked as we were both looking upset by then.

"Well, you're just sitting there without any emotion."

My angered response was simple, "What do you want me to do? Let's just get this over with!" My blood pressure was certainly rising. Neither one of us was in a good mood by then!

The anger and absurdity of the moment seemed to block out most of the pain because I was furious. I was angry with myself for what had happened on Saturday night but just as upset with a doctor who seemed to have no compassion! This did not make for a pleasant experience. He adjusted my forearm a little more, finally stopping just when I thought I couldn't handle any more pain. Here I was, another waterproof cast and what I knew was at least six more weeks of recovery. I did my best to laugh at myself thinking of the last few days. Laughter had always been a great release for me and a way to relax in stressful situations. This was one of those times when it was harder to find even a thread of humor. At least I will be out of the cast in six to eight weeks, and this time, no plate to deal with and no more operations.

How little we know about the future and where these roadblocks and detours will eventually take us. God is always working with us, and I could still swim, ride, and run with the new waterproof cast, so my training could continue without a "break," no pun intended. When I was very young, my parents used to say, "We don't know what the future holds, but we know 'who' holds our hand." Right then, I needed a little handholding…with my right hand.

Each day of the following week, the pain in my arm increased by the hour rather than getting better. This was odd after experiencing more than my share of broken bones. With the pain increasing daily, I was finally fed up with my current doctor. I reached out to seek a second opinion from the foremost orthopedic specialist who was back in Hong Kong. Dr. Chow had moved back to Hong Kong after working with top professional athletes in the US. His wife happened to work with my therapist, Nalini. After her recommendation and introduction, I took my X-rays to Queen Elizabeth Hospital where his office was located. This was where I discovered the truth about my first plate. It was actually for a tibia, not a forearm. Next, he gave me bad news I did not want to hear. The way my arm had been reset from the recent break, it would not heal properly. The bone had not been aligned straight and would not heal to full strength without opening up my arm and inserting a new plate. *Oh brother,* I thought, *not another operation!* I didn't know if I should laugh or cry. I knew I wanted the increasing pain to stop and go away. I was scheduled to fly out the next day for Japan to watch my two sons race that coming weekend. I asked if I could schedule the operation for Monday morning upon my return. He said, "If you can take the discomfort and pain, it's up to you." I wasn't looking forward to the next six days, but I was anticipating the enjoyment of watching my sons race in Japan.

Traditional Japan

How good can it be when you go to Japan with a broken arm that for some reason, your pain increases each day. I had to accept this pain and inconvenience if I was to watch my sons compete alongside seasoned professional triathletes. This was, however, the first Asian Olympic-Distance Triathlon Championships, and I was determined not to miss out. When arriving in Tokyo, we were driven several hours to the race site and shown our accommodations. Of course, God was still working on my patience. No beds, as they had arranged for us to stay in a traditional Japanese-style hotel. I was still finding it difficult to get on my feet when on the ground. With only one good arm to help me stand up, I viewed the thin mats rolled out on the floor. Futons (a thin padded mat you open out on the wooden floor for a bed) were the sleeping arrangements. This was accessorized with a small "hard" pillow, which felt and looked more like a cement brick. It was even worse for me with my still frozen neck. Trying to sleep under these conditions, with my aching arm and a "brick" supporting my head, was not easy. This detour was not turning out to be enjoyable. I started to wonder if I was living in some kind of reality sitcom where I was the source of all the laughs. Since the entire Hong Kong men's triathlon team were sleeping in the same large room, I had to quietly lie there, pretending I was okay while hardly getting any sleep. They all fell asleep quickly, and I didn't want to disturb anyone, days before their big race. I forced myself to just quietly lay there for a few more long mostly sleepless nights.

From a Spectator's View

Parents all over the world have supported and watched their children train in a variety of activities and sports, hoping they would excel and achieve their dreams. The level of commitment and sacrifice necessary is witnessed everyday by their parents who often commit time and energy of their own, supporting their children. For children with heavy school schedules, the organization of their time becomes critical to their success. There are only so many hours in a day to attend school, study, do projects, and train for their chosen activity. To excel at anything, sacrifices need to be made. For a teenager, it means foregoing parties, hanging out after school or weekends with schoolmates or church friends.

Triathlon training can take up even more time than most sporting endeavors. Because triathlon contains three sports, triathletes spend an average of four hours a day training six days a week. Fitting that in with a heavy school load and evening studies is a logistical nightmare. The intense school load at Hong Kong International School made this even more taxing. My sons had adopted my bike schedule of waking early, 3:45 a.m. to get in their two-hour cycle by 6:00 a.m. Brian would swim during his school lunch and run immediately after school. Donnie was no longer in school but still had a busy schedule assisting me on the tennis court. Both Donnie and Brian assisted me on Saturday mornings with my junior program.

When parents witness this kind of commitment, they are as emotionally involved when their children line up on race day. After spending five months in intense recovery of my own and doing my best to follow my son's progress remotely, I was emotionally invested in how they would race at the first Asian Olympic-Distance Triathlon Championships. This was also their first serious Olympic-distance race. In spite of my broken-arm problems and lack of sleep on a futon the few nights before, I was excited for my sons as well as myself. Watching them race was also like being in the race myself. But for the first time, I was just one of the huge number of spectators on race morning. There was a deep ache inside me as I wondered how long or if ever it would be before I would be able to line up and race a triathlon again.

When race day finally arrived, I wasn't sure what to expect. I had not personally viewed my sons race or train since my accident in April. The accident had stopped all three of us from lining up and racing together, as we had originally planned. At the beginning of April, a few weeks before my accident, I had qualified for the elite team. This race had been one of my primary goals for 1992. As I stood there looking out at the swim course in Japan, there was a moment of melancholy as I thought of what could have been. It seemed like a faraway dream from my past and, at the same time, like yesterday since my "fit" days. My past was beginning to feel like another person's life or an alternate reality.

As my boys lined up for the swim start, I was hoping they would have a top ten finish in the Asian junior category. They were racing against the top junior triathletes from the best Asian countries. Many had trained for years before qualifying for this event. My boys would be facing serious competition, with only a year of training and limited racing under their belt.

The elite pros and juniors were set to start their race together. I was thrilled to see my sons dive in with the elite professionals when the starter's gun sounded. I felt slight tears well up in my eyes and chills on my arms as I watched the race begin. As with every triathlon, it is impossible to follow individual triathletes on a swim course. The thrash and splash of a few hundred triathletes obscures the actual bodies in the water. All you can see are arms flying everywhere and water splashing like crashing waves at the beach. After the start of the 1,500-meter swim, some fellow spectators asked who I knew in the race. "My two sons," I proudly exclaimed. They asked how I thought they would do, and I told them, "I didn't have a clue, hadn't seen them train for five months." They were obviously taken aback that I knew so little about my own children. They, of course, had no clue of our circumstances.

A 1,500-meter swim takes under twenty minutes for the better elite swimmers, so it was quite a wait before we saw them stroking toward the exit of this one-lap course. Even with the field being spread out, it is still impossible to identify individual swimmers by their swim technique. Only when finally standing up and running up the exit ramp can you recognize who they are.

The fastest pros whom I knew personally came out of the water first. Then to my surprise, my youngest son, Brian, came out of water on their heels in seventh place. I was shocked. My reaction also surprised the spectators I had just met. They then inquired how my other son would come in? Donnie always appeared to have a more laid-back approach to training and racing, so again I wasn't sure. Brian had said many times that Donnie was immensely talented, quite possibly more than him but was more of a "surfer dude." I expected Donnie to be in the middle of the main pack, still more than four minutes from the finish. There were, however, five more triathletes in a small pack, at least two minutes ahead of the main field of swimmers, only a minute and a half back from Brian's group. To my surprise again, there was Donnie in twelfth place overall. *Maybe he wasn't so laid back after all,* I thought. I was stunned by both Donnie and Brian's swim results. I knew they had been together training hard in Oregon, following a great swim program, but had no idea how much their swim times had improved! Their dedicated swim workouts definitely paid dividends in the swim portion of this triathlon. I was swelled with pride as I watched them run into transition and head out on the bike course. I completely forgot about the pain in my arm as I watch them cycle away.

A number of spectators followed me to view what we could of the bike portion of the race. These spectators followed me as they were now very curious about how I would predict Don and Brian's cycling skills. They weren't shy to ask my assessment. My sons had been cycling the steep hills around Hillsboro and Beaverton, Oregon, to get ready for the race. They had obviously built up their strength since I had last seen them cycle. "I'm not sure how much they have improved," I replied. "They would probably fall back from the pro field because of their young age. They've only had eleven months of training as triathletes and much of it on their own."

The bike route was two laps of twenty kilometers each, so we could only see them three times during the forty-kilometer bike course. I, along with my new friends, waited to see how they would be fairing at the twenty-kilometer turn around. The course officials had the triathletes come by the transition area located right in front of us. When the pros started coming to the roundabout, we all started counting together. One, two, and so on until we saw Brian appear, still in seventh place overall! We continued to count, and to my disbelief my laid-back son, Donnie, had also held his position staying in twelfth place. Both of them were way ahead of the top juniors in Asia. They were first and second in the junior category! I was surprised and also very proud. I assured all those around me that to ride twenty kilometers hard was one thing, but to ride the next twenty kilometers the same would be very difficult given their ages of seventeen and sixteen and limited experience.

How wrong I turned out to be, as both my sons came off the bike to start the run, still in seventh and twelfth place respectively among Asia's top professionals. Their cycle training in the hills of Oregon had paid huge dividends. They had gone even further ahead in the junior category, as the next junior to finish the bike course was more than twelve minutes behind. The spectators surrounding me were sure I must be the worst absentee father of all time, as I never shared with them my situation. They must have wondered how could I know so little about my own sons' racing ability.

Don and Brian did slow a little and lose some time on the ten-kilometer run, finishing twelfth and seventeenth overall among the pros. What a day they had when they finished first and second at the first Asian Junior Championships clearly in front of the other top juniors.

It was a great day all around, celebrating their victory with the Hong Kong Triathlon Association officials. I was thrilled to have been able to witness them race, even with the pain continuing to grow in my arm. I wouldn't have traded that day or experience for anything. I was proud of Donnie and Brian as they had done training on their own and came through as champions. I was excited for them and their future as triathletes. After watching them, I was more determined than ever to get back to where I had been before my accident. They were now my inspiration!

Back to Reality

My sons had done their part. I couldn't wait to arrive back in Hong Kong and have a new metal plate screwed in place. I was anxious to start training hard again, after watching Donnie and Brian race so well. My new doctor was very professional and made arrangements for a private room at Queen Elizabeth Hospital. Since "tribulation worketh patience," I was learning more about patience than I wanted to know and thus the tribulation that inevitably goes with it. I had grown up admiring adults who had great patience. I didn't realize at that time the tribulations they must have endured to attain that positive character trait.

As can be expected in life, there was a mix up at the hospital because of an overload of patients from a busier than normal weekend of accidents in Hong Kong. Dr. Chow notified me my previously arranged private room was unavailable. My operation was still scheduled so arrangements were made so I could have a bed space in a large room, which looked more like a hospital ward from the TV war series *M*A*S*H*. They directed me to the only remaining bed available. Some of the thirty or so patients in the ward looked to be directly out of that *M*A*S*H* TV series. The gentleman in the bed just across from me had some kind of infection which had eaten away his flesh and muscle to the point you could see part of his upper tibia and hip bone, when his sheet unexpectedly slipped away from his body when being treated. I had to look away to avoid feeling queasy. After viewing this ward I was placed in, I was feeling very fortunate to have my procedure of a new plate, and know I would be leaving within twenty-four hours. Minus the pain in my arm, life would be blissful again in the near future. Maybe being in that ward was a way for God to show me how really blessed I was.

I had heard many hospital horror stories by the time I arrived at Queen Elizabeth Hospital. Because of this, I had become a little paranoid. So paranoid, I kept reminding the nurses who were wheeling me to the operating theater, that it was my left arm and not my right arm which was to be operated on. Like there could be any mistake with the cast removed, and fresh scarring everywhere on my left forearm. My forearm was beginning to look more like a road map.

I had reason to be paranoid after hearing of an incident that took place when I was at the Adventist Hospital. A young boy had accidentally stepped on a needle while spending time with his family at Deep Water Bay Beach. The end of the needle had broken off inside his foot. When he was x-rayed in the emergency room, the X-ray had inadvertently been placed on the screen back to front. Viewed by the rushing operating doctor, he mistook it for the opposite foot. The boy was taken into surgery, and after some time searching for the needle in the wrong foot, the mistake was discovered. The youngster now had both feet operated on and left the hospital in a wheelchair, as he was not able to stand on either foot. Paranoid maybe but I felt I would rather be safe than sorry.

The operation went well, and a new correct-sized plate was screwed in place. This time with six small screws. A waterproof bandage was put on, and I was able to start swimming and running the very next day. I requested to be released later that day, and my doctor agreed. I was thankful to get out of the ward as my family were appalled at the condition of the other patients there. We were all happy to be heading home together.

God had not finished working on my patience, as the comedy of errors continued. It wasn't long before we discovered another problem when my therapy resumed. When closing up my arm after inserting the latest plate, one of the internal stitches had inadvertently trapped a nerve. This in simple terms is tying off a nerve with one of the knots. The pain from this minor mishap was worse than any I had experienced to that date, and that was saying a lot.

When a spot on my upper wrist was touched or bumped, it was like getting a serious electric shock. It felt like a bolt of lightning going straight to the end of my thumb. It felt like the end of my thumb had blown off the first time I experienced this severe shock. I had to make a choice of either having another operation to correct it or using massage therapy to release the nerve. I decided on therapy as another operation was unthinkable at that point in time. The therapy proved to be very painful, but I decided to put up with it. Eventually, the nerve did release, and it all came good, thankfully without another operation.

WAKE-UP CALL

October thankfully arrived with all the operations behind me. My sons were triathlon enthusiasts by then and entered a triathlon in Macau (the Portuguese enclave where I had first come to work in Asia). We always enjoyed the one-hour Jetfoil ride from Hong Kong on the southern coast of China. Macau brought back fond memories as the transition area from bike to run was surprisingly located at Taipa Island Resort, where I had been the resort manager. I had another great time watching my sons excel but also had that longing to be racing again. Brian had a faster swim and bike time than a member of the British elite triathlon team.

Standing around following the race, many photos of my sons had been taken. Unknown to me, I had been captured in some of those same photos. Later on in October, I was appalled when I had a chance to view these photos. I was shocked as I looked like a bent-over ninety-year-old that suffered from osteoporosis. My head was so far forward on my shoulders, it looked impossible and grotesque. I asked my sons if I always looked like that? Their answer, "Yea, didn't you know?" They had always been upbeat and positive with me and assumed I knew what I looked like.

Wow, I thought, *how many more surprises were still coming my direction?* I knew I couldn't move my neck very much, as it was always stiff and sore. I had become used to having to turn my body to look from side to side. I had no idea how far forward my head was now sitting on my shoulders. I knew my previous long neck was now squashed down, but I could only view myself straight on in a mirror and thought I still looked fine. I went back to my therapist and asked what I needed to do to get my neck straightened out. She took a long, slow pause and finally said she didn't know if it could be done. The pain would be horrific with all the nerve endings in that area, and it could take months of painful therapy to break up the scar tissue.

I was already going to therapy three to four times a week, but now this? I had asked her at the start of my therapy what she would do if I begged her to stop because of pain? She had given me a straightforward and correct answer I needed. She indicated she would go on with the treatment if she knew it was best for me. With my neck, I almost regretted that promise, as the pain was everything she said it would be. During those sessions, tears would well up in my eyes, and many times, I thought I would pass out with my eyes rolling back in my head. But she was faithful to her promise, and through many months of massage and manipulation, my head now looks fairly straight, although still slightly bent forward. I now have 95 percent movement from side to side. She was a blessing and provided many hours of smiles and laughs, becoming a personal friend through the years.

She would call me up sometimes and ask me to come in and give a few words of encouragement to patients going through painful therapy. Mostly, I just had to encourage them, but there were some who were more difficult and stubborn to talk with. One in particular was a businessman who had been involved in a serious car accident. He had been very lucky to come out alive from a head-on crash in one of Hong Kong's tunnels. He had fortunately survived with only a seriously broken leg and ankle. He was giving my therapist all kinds of grief during treatment and would not cooperate because of her painful massage therapy.

When I arrived in the therapy department, he was in the middle of a session. Nalini introduced us, and he asked why I was there. I told him I had been in an accident myself a few years before and knew a little of what he was going through. He had arrived in Hong Kong after all the publicity of my accident had died down and was not aware of its seriousness or me personally. Sarcastically he asked

I DO IT ALL

what I had wrong with me. I looked fit, healthy, and tanned to him. He couldn't imagine me going through what he was experiencing. I explained to him the details of my left arm. He was not impressed. My therapist said, "Tell him the rest." I explained the extent of my paralysis, serious injuries, and the ongoing painful back and neck therapy. Talking with him was the only time I ever spoke sternly to a patient in the therapy department. He needed to hear someone say, "Stop feeling sorry for yourself and let Nalini give you the needed treatment so six months from now, your leg will be 100 percent, and this will be a long, distant memory." He was shocked I had been so blunt, but he needed to hear it from someone who had gone through similar treatment.

I had to remind myself of this same thing all the time as I strived for improvement and regain my previous fitness. October was a busy month as I had a full-time job again and was sponsoring, promoting, and directing an international triathlon in Hong Kong. I didn't know how to stop, rest, and just take it easy. I flew in the top Japanese triathletes to compete at my Silvereign International Triathlon. I had previously met these Japanese triathletes while racing through Asia and competing at two World Championships together. They had known me when I was fully healthy, racing fast and winning. We arranged to house them at our home in Clearwater Bay. Being around them for a week was a real boost for me, as they were continually positive and encouraging. Rubbing shoulders with them daily made me want to do even better and try harder.

On an early Saturday morning, while setting up for the Silvereign Triathlon, my sons caught me by surprise, saying, "It is time for you to get back on a bike!" They were standing with the top four Japanese professionals when the entire group agreed it was time for me to start cycling again. Talking about pressure, I still felt off balanced just standing up and walking around. Here they were, a group of my triathlete friends all looking on and expecting me to jump on the bike like it was no problem. Like all dads, I was still a hero to my kids, and they still thought I could do anything. How could I deny that look in their eyes? They brought over a bike and helped me get on. Understandably, I was very unsteady and apprehensive, as some of that unwanted fear crept in. Just getting on the bike was difficult, even with their help. I wobbled and weaved around as I started down the road until I found my balance. It was not as hard as I had thought it would be. Only a few blocks on the road and I was enjoying the thrill of being on a bike again. My children again had faith in me and pushed me forward. Without them, I would not have gone cycling so soon. I didn't know it then, but that was the beginning of keeping my promise to them competing in a triathlon by year's end.

There were other private goals that I kept to myself to avoid more criticism about my triathlon training and the obvious self-induced pressure that would bring. Many of my friends and acquaintances said I should have learned from my accident. They felt I was too old to do this kind of physical activity even before my accident. I was tired of listening to all their well-meaning advice, so I began keeping my personal goals private.

Reaching for the Stars and Goals in My Notebook

Some of my private goals were the following:

1. Become Hong Kong's number 1 veteran triathlete again (over the age of forty)
2. Become the Asian Champion again in my age group
3. Compete at the World Championships again and finish in the top 20
4. Compete at the World Masters games and finish in the top 10
5. Be able to train with my sons and enjoy the freedom to know my body would not break if I took a fall
6. Return to my former level of coaching and business activities

These were huge goals, but I always reach for the stars when making goals. The only ones who knew the extent of these goals were my immediate family members. I was blessed as they supported me in my efforts to achieve these. There were other minor goals, but these specific goals were the primary ones I was focusing on in private. I know I was reaching for the stars, but I also felt I would not be denied. I would do what was needed, no matter what it would require.

I learned very quickly that a certain amount of selfishness was necessary if I was to return to the level I was striving for. I realized early on that I needed more rest now than I had previously required. Training the same distances took much longer, making my days seem much shorter. These decisions were not easy as other important areas in my life were regrettably sacrificed. With the necessary treatments and changes in my life, my mind was clouded, and I was unaware of the temporal nature of my goals. These goals continued to dominate my time and thinking. I was almost obsessed with my goals, even more than before my accident. Waking up every day with an uncomfortable body always talking to me made it very hard not to think about my situation, making me more and more self-centered. My work combined with my training goals to allow a complete recovery left little time for anything else. The eternal or real important goals somehow faded in a fog, even after that huge early-morning wake-up call out in Clearwater Bay. I was again completely consumed with my own selfish desires. I was consumed with trying to "do it all" again by myself.

Some of the items I set aside were made for me. I was physically unable to participate in many of the activities I had been fortunate to enjoy before. Modeling, commercials, and magazine photoshoots were out of the question, as my looks did not meet their required standards after the beating my body had taken. The strain of constant pain had taken a toll on my face as well. I didn't have extra energy for consulting or organizing major events other than the Silvereign Triathlon. It took a huge amount of energy and effort to complete my daily work schedule as tennis director and head tennis pro at Aberdeen Marina Club six days a week. I was just too exhausted by the time I got home to consider doing the evening work and consulting I had done previously. Arriving home, I would eat dinner with my family and pass out on a couch or immediately drop in bed.

Other decisions were a lot harder to make. I had always spent quite a bit of my free time with my family before the accident. Now

I didn't have the energy to hit tennis balls with my sons and daughter during open times in my schedule. This may have been hard on me, but I know it was even more difficult for my family. They had spent an amazing amount of time visiting me in the hospital and tending to my every need once I arrived home. I am sure there were questions like, "We spent so much time for you, and now you don't seem to have extra time for us?"

Weekends now were spent staying at home lying around trying to rest up so I would have enough energy for the coming week. My daughter, Shannon, received the full brunt of this less than active and attentive father. Shannon was in middle school at the time of my accident, and her high school years were spent with a mostly absentee Father. Coming to terms with a very uncomfortable body left Shannon without the father she needed and desired. Pain and discomfort were my constant companions. I did my best to keep it to myself so those around me would not be left feeling uncomfortable themselves. I would pretend to be fine at work so I could keep my job. I kept saying to myself, "Fake it till you can make it." My family were the only ones I felt I could share my discomforts. Even then, I did my best to hide the full extent of my discomfort. This was not good for them as they had a hard time understanding how I could seem so bright, happy, and okay at work, then climb in the car and collapse in pain. Their once positive father seemed to drop into a moody, negative state of mind compared to what they had experienced and grown up with.

Going through life-altering experiences cannot only change your physical ability but also your emotional and psychological responses. I became a little short with people and less diplomatic than what had been typical for me. The pressure and weight of my daily situation was heaped on my family's shoulders, especially Shannon, who was unintentionally isolated from a father who had always been close. To this day, I regret not making the sacrifice of working a little less and spending more time with her. It's so easy to see clearly looking backward. With the ever-present numbness, pain, and awkwardness, it was difficult to stay focused on anything other than myself and keep a clear head.

Don and Brian were encouraging me to keep training so I could eventually do another triathlon. They reminded me to work out every day and checked on how my running was coming along. The only cycling I was doing that fall was the same as when I first got into triathlons. I was on a LifeCycle stationary bike in the gym during my lunch break after a swim. Don, being out of school, spent his time with me at the club, helping with my tennis lessons.

Shannon became more interested in art projects at school rather than sporting endeavors. I was vaguely aware of her newfound interest and only understood how talented she was when I attended a parent's school night and saw a couple of her projects on display. She was very talented, and I could see she had developed a great relationship with her Art Department's teacher. He was wonderful, and she used this teacher to fill some of the void left because of her absentee dad. I was very grateful for this positive input in her life, but this saddened me at the same time as a distance had begun to develop between us. Because of the continued positive influence of her mom and brothers during this time, she has developed into a wonderful person and a terrific teacher. After years of teaching in Shanghai and Hong Kong, she is continuing to pursue her love of art in London.

Tau Luu

Many people end up in Hong Kong for a variety of reasons. Some are looking for a change. Others are looking for an opportunity, but others ended up in Hong Kong trying to escape the horrors of war. With the Vietnam and Cambodia conflicts and tragedies taking place nearby, it is understandable that Hong Kong became a desired destination for escape and find a new life from those war-torn regions.

One of my friends who continued to encourage me after the accident turned out to be one of these stories. Playing tennis in Hong Kong's premier league allowed me to meet some amazing tennis players from around the world. They came from the US, Europe, Africa, New Zealand, Australia, and other Asian countries. Most of them were making a living instructing tennis at one of the many five-star clubs spread throughout Hong Kong.

With so many accomplished players, some being former Davis Cup participants, made for a very competitive premier league. All league matches were well attended and exciting to be involved in. One of the league's real characters was Tau Luu. Tau Luu played for the Chinese Recreation Club. Tau Luu was definitely different from the many expats playing on other teams. Everyone looked fit and ready to represent their clubs honorably. Tau Luu looked different when confidently sauntering onto a tennis court, appearing to look more like Buddha's twin brother. To say he was overweight when I met him would be an understatement. Tau Luu, with a well-manicured bowling-ball-shaped belly, gave the appearance he was unable to move quickly around a tennis court, much less have the ability to hit and control his shots. Tau Luu was famous on the local tennis scene and seemed to know everyone when I first encountered him on the other side of the net. Crowds of spectators would gather around any court he was assigned to watch his amazing skills on display. Seeing his popularity, I knew from the beginning to expect something special. I instantly learned to respect his ability to control a tennis ball and the entire court when opposing him in doubles.

Tau Luu and I became good friends through the premier league matches, and I discovered him to be a kaleidoscope of personalities. He never seemed ruffled on the court, and for that matter, in any area of his life. I always wondered where he had come from and what was hidden inside the pages of his life? He seemed to be good friends with Hong Kong's most famous billionaires, celebrities, and tennis enthusiasts. So many tennis players are one dimensional, where tennis is all they care about and really even know. Tau Luu was different.

One day, Tau Luu invited me up to his apartment after a practice session at the Chinese Recreation Club. Walking inside his apartment, I found his living room filled up with knockoff tennis rackets he had just brought in from Taiwan. These were the actual frames of a major racket manufacturer. Taiwan had done an overrun and sold the extra frames to Tau Luu, with his own logo and insignia applied on the rackets. Once Tau Luu had his own insignias applied, he sold them out the "back door" around Asia for much less than the original manufactures rackets were being sold.

Over lunch, Tau Luu shared a little of his life's story. He had grown up and played Davis Cup for Vietnam and was so good, he received the opportunity to workout with the Australian Davis Cup team. This included the likes of Laver, Rosewall, and John Newcombe. He had the opportunity to workout with some of the greats of tennis at the famous Kooyong Grass Court Club. Kooyong was the home of the Australian Open for years. He had a reputation of being one of the best doubles players in the world when he played out of Australia. As outrageous as this sounded, I was able to confirm this while playing doubles with him at the same Kooyong Club a few years later. He was treated as a celebrity the moment he entered that famous clubhouse. Many of the older members crowded around to warmly greet him.

He was so famous among Vietnamese tennis players, he received a celebrity-like status when he and partner Randahl King played a national Asian tournament on the Rose Garden Tennis courts in Portland, Oregon, one summer. He never failed to surprise anyone who was around him for very long.

When Tau Luu and I played doubles against the Hungarian team, they totally misjudged him after seeing his Buddha-like belly. I had just won my singles against their number one player, so they thought it best to avoid hitting in my direction. They were not aware of Tau Luu's abilities and reputation, so they continued to hit most of their shots to his side of the court. It was only after losing nine straight games did they wake up and realize his amazing ability. He was almost single-handedly destroying them. We ended up winning easily with only the loss of one game. The Hungarian top doubles team had totally underestimated Tau Luu. I had an enjoyable time watching him outclass and out play them almost by himself.

The outer cover of Tau Luu's life book looked a little disheveled, nothing like the scintillating pages you discovered leafing through his inside pages. I was honored to play doubles with him at the Italia

Cup in 1990 as he continued to play world-class doubles even with his Buddha-like belly leading the way. Thinking of Tau Luu always reminded me how others had not always had it easy and my journey was nothing special, just my journey.

MY PROMISE

Promises are one of the most important, positive character traits in our lives but only if they are kept. Those we love need to know that we keep our promises no matter what it will take to fulfill them. During my life, I have failed in some of the most important promises I have made. But with God's help, I have also tried to get up and make sure I keep every future promise. We need to sacrifice other "seemingly important" items in our lives to make sure even minor promises are fulfilled. Stretched out in the hospital, I made some outrageous statements to my doctors and my family. These statements regarded crazy improvement predictions. I had no idea at that time how serious my spinal cord injury was or how it would affect me for the rest of my life. With this ignorance, I could be forgiven for thinking life would quickly return back to normal. I thought, with enough effort, I could actually do it all again. After all, hadn't I always been able to overcome other serious injuries and recover to live a vibrant, successful lifestyle? But what was my new "normal?" Would I really be able to do it all again?

By November of 1992, after seven months of working hard to recover, I was finally getting to grips with the difficult realization of the arduous slow road ahead. The amount of effort and dedication needed to keep improving was enormous. When the last day of November finally arrived, Don and Brian bounded into our living room with a huge smile on their faces and a big surprise. Behind them, I found a great-looking carbon graphite fiber Trek triathlon racing bike. They had purchased this wonderful bike with their own money. They were giving it to me with one intention in mind.

One look at this bicycle took me back to some wonderful memories yet with some trepidation, and again, that "fear factor." I was still unable to completely relax, thinking of riding a bike. The small glimpse of my last almost fatal ride down that fateful hill was always there in my mind. This Trek bike was a used bike but looked and felt brand-new. One of the best professional triathletes in Asia and a good friend of ours had been racing on this Trek bike for a few years. He had kept it in perfect condition. My sons said, "Now is the time to start training on a bike, if you are going to keep your promise and complete a triathlon by year's end!" I knew about my promise and secretly hoped they had forgotten. What was I thinking? Children never forget anything!

I had privately done my homework and knew of a triathlon in Thailand. It was scheduled for the twenty-seventh of December 1992. Professional triathlete, Ian Rayson, who's Trek bike I now owned, along with other Hong Kong triathletes, were heading to Hua Hin for this race. I decided to check out the details and see if I was still able to enter the event. With a lump in my throat, I sent in my registration. Having ridden on the LifeCycle stationary bike in the gym at the Marina Club for five months, it wasn't long before I felt some confidence and power again on the bike. Unlike running, which had become something like my own little torture chamber and where my body felt like a heavy concrete block, which would hardly move no matter how hard I tried, there was no impact with cycling. Bike riding felt great, except for the uneasy feeling when training on Clearwater Bay Road again.

My swimming had indeed come around, although not quite as fast as before. My feet would almost always cramp when pointing my toes to kick. When the cramping became too unbearable to point my toes, I would use very little kicking to relieve the cramping. This slowed down my swim, having to drag my legs behind me, but I could still move through the water fairly fast. Long-distance swimming was a slow beat kick, so it didn't cost me too much time during the swim. I was just happy to jump in any body of water and swim again. The weightlessness that water provided always made me feel normal. When I want to feel completely normal again, all I need to do is dive into a pool, lake, or ocean and my spinal cord problems disappear into the past.

Once boarding the plane to Thailand and settling into my seat, I started thinking, *Am I crazy, trying to complete a triathlon so soon after my horrific accident, especially after being told I would never walk again?* I was still stumbling around at times, even falling down when I wasn't completely conscious of my movements. It would only be eight months and eight days since that horrible day. *But if not now, when?* I asked myself. I had to keep the promise I made to my sons and family. They had put so much faith, strength, and time into me, encouraging my every step. They had never given up on me! I couldn't think of giving up on myself!

So there I was looking out of the plane's window on my way to Hua Hin, Thailand, to race an Olympic-distance triathlon again! I had been able to visit Hua Hin and nearby Cha Am in the past to witness this beautiful part of Southern Thailand. This amazingly idyllic region was known as the summer vacation destination or Holiday Palace of the king of Thailand. The beaches are stunningly beautiful up against a pristine blue ocean. The jungle mountain area is enchanting, bordering the sliver of Cambodia coming down the western border. The food and hospitality is what you come to expect from Thailand: exquisite. I was really looking forward to being back in Hua Hin, seeing the vintage train station that brought Thai citizens and holiday revelers from around the world to experience this wonderful region and, of course, the Thai hospitality.

The only difference this time was I was getting ready to compete in a triathlon. "I was getting ready to race and keep a promise!" The first time I came to Hua Hin was to recover after a successful Phuket International Triathlon. That had been an idyllic, relaxing time of lying around, running down the beach, or taking a day to motorcycle out west, into the jungle. When we arrived in Hua Hin this time, it was not the weather report I was hoping for. There had been a typhoon in the Gulf of Thailand and the South China Sea. Remnants of this storm might bring in heavy waves and surf on race morning. Everyone was hoping this would not eventuate, none more so than me. My body "body" was still feeling fragile. I was praying for calm seas to get me back into the swing of competing in a triathlon again. The washing machine churn of typhoon supported waters and a few hundred triathletes all trying to find their place amongst flailing arms, kicking legs, and big waves can be very intimidating even when you are strong and healthy. This can even be more intimidating when you feel like a fragile piece of crystal. I didn't need the addition of huge waves and wild surf to add to my anxiety and nervousness.

Trying to get a good night's sleep was difficult as I couldn't shake the worry and foreboding of the following day's race. "What would happen? Would I be able to finish the race? Would I be able to relax and enjoy it? Was I competing too soon? Maybe I would surprise myself and have a respectable finish. Or would I fail miserably and be unable to complete the race in a horrible fashion?" Both outcomes were considerable, but I had done my best to prepare for my first race back. Most importantly, I was keeping my promise to my family. Most of the triathletes in Asia knew my story and were surprised to see me back attempting to race eight months after my injuries. Anything I accomplished on race day would be respectable in their eyes, but I had a hard time seeing it that way. I always wanted to do my best and look in control. My ego again. I had no idea how this race would play out. I kept reminding myself I was only there to keep a promise to my family and myself. Everything felt different from the last time I had raced. I had always come to races expecting a great race and usually ended up winning. Now I was here just to finish, hoping with all I had in me, to do just that—finish! It was almost like being back in Singapore doing my first triathlon.

The day of a triathlon always starts early and before dawn for the competitors and officials. It takes quite a while to check in, get numbered, and set up the transition area before the race starts. You need to warm up in your room by stretching and doing simple exercises like pushups, sit-ups and stretch cords to wake up your body and get your blood flowing. I always made time for a short run and cycle to make sure I was properly warmed up and my equipment was carefully checked out before every race. Then onto the transition area where you check in, get numbered, and find your bike-rack placement. You then carefully set up and lay out your gear. Time it right and you can have a practice run through transition so you have a clean, quick entry and exit from swim to bike and then bike to run portion of the race.

There is always a large crowd of triathletes greeting each other, wishing each other to have a great race. This hub of activity can look a little disorganized to many of the spectators who also arrive early to view the start. Spectators are always milling around to encourage and cheer on their family and friends. Many of them are thinking triathlon to be a crazy sport. They also know the discipline and commitment their loved ones have completed to line up at the start of one of these events. Once your transition is set up, the nerves really start to kick in as you head out to the ocean, where the race will begin.

When we stepped outside our accommodation at 5:00 a.m., the temperature was warm and thick with humidity as it always seems to be in Thailand, night or day. There was an eerie calm in the air that race morning. Everyone hoped to see calm seas as well as we headed through the transition and down to the beach. What awaited us was a very angry-looking gray ocean as the sun had started to rise in the distance. Where was the clear-blue calm waters of Hua Hin I had enjoyed on my holiday a few years before? There wasn't even a consistent swell where you could bodysurf on a wave when coming back into the beach later, just huge, angry waves and surf going wildly everywhere at once. It was choppy, gray, and foreboding. My heart sank as I viewed the swim course. You could barely see the two huge buoys going up and down in the wild swells some 500 meters from shore and spread 500 meters apart. There was some talk among the officials about the safety of sending us out in these conditions. A previous Asian Triathlon in Hualien, Taiwan, had seen some inexperienced triathletes drown in typhoon-fed seas off their coast in the Philippine Sea from similar typhoon conditions.

After some heated discussions and delay, they decided to continue with the race. Many of us had flown in from other countries, so with this in mind, they decided to go ahead with the event. When the starter's gun finally sounded, I slowly shuffled forward as I watched everyone else run full speed into the surf. I was left behind, finding it impossible to run in the soft sand. I could only jog slowly then walk till I reached deep enough water to start swimming.

This is great! I thought. *I am starting in last place!* The seas were like swimming in a washing machine; but swimming the length to the first buoy, 500 meters away, was not the only problem. We all soon realized we had difficulty sighting the buoys swimming in these huge waves. In all practicality, we were swimming blind in the currents being tossed about in this washing machine. We just hoped we were swimming in a straight line, as we were subjected to wild conditions. I would periodically slow down, then ride a swell to the top, thrusting myself as high as possible to see the buoy. There were a number of other triathletes near me who depended on me to guide them when I would begin to swim past. This really wasn't possible for long, as I was still a fairly good swimmer, definitely faster than the slowest swimmers. I had caught them after they had charged into the waters ahead of me. It wasn't long before I caught them and swam passed. I would be on my own again, catching up to many of those still out front. My fears before the race were abating as I was completely focused on my swim in these typhoon-fed waters. With every swimmer I reached and passed, I would get a surge of energy and grew in confidence.

I swam and bounced around in the ocean for what seemed like forever before rounding the second five-hundred-meter buoy and heading back to shore. By then I was getting excited knowing I only had five hundred meters left in the swirling typhoon-affected waters. I had passed a number of triathletes but still felt like I was near the back of the field. It was impossible to tell where I was, with swimmers spread out over a large area instead of the usual long, organized group like most triathlons. Finally standing up on the beach, I saw one of the elite Hong Kong triathletes running into the transition area thirty meters away. I felt relieved seeing him that close. I knew then I had done better than I thought in the ocean. This fellow Hong Kong triathlete was the slowest elite swimmer, but still a sense of relief and encouragement flooded me to see him that close. Heading into transition, I looked like I was jogging. No one but me knew I

I DO IT ALL

was running as fast as I could run. It wasn't my fastest transition, but I was able to mount my bike without falling off. Victory! I was then on my own to start my favorite leg of a triathlon, the forty-kilometer bike course. This used to be my favorite discipline! What would it be now?

Seven or eight kilometers passed before I got over the fear factor of being around other cyclists while racing down those hot Thai roads. Finally picking up speed, I began passing a few more triathletes. My cycling felt smooth and fairly powerful, allowing me to enjoy the bike portion of the race. No impact allowed me to feel pretty much back to my normal self again. I was relieved and surprised as I gained more confidence. I even passed some of the other Hong Kong seasoned triathletes. Hope surged as I began to feel I could not only finish the race but finish in a respectable fashion. Even with the sun rising higher in the sky and the typical Thai tropical heat warming the roads, I felt great. I finished the forty-kilometer bike course in a much better position than I expected. Transition 2 was much like the first as I took it slow and easy so as not to stumble and fall down while dismounting my bike and putting on my running shoes.

Now for the part I was dreading the most, the 10k run. Even when you are fit and healthy, ten kilometers is a substantial distance to run in the steamy heat of Thailand. It is even more challenging after swimming in the ocean and coming off a long bike ride. Ten kilometers had never looked longer than that day when I stood up in transition. As I headed out on the run, I, again, wasn't confident I could finish the race. The rising temperatures weren't making any of us feel any better. No matter how my run was feeling, I was there to do my best and keep moving forward. I reminded myself over and over of my "promise," as I looked down those steamy roads. Having completed a number of triathlons around Asia in the past, I had seen runners on out and back courses running so slow, I would think to myself, *How can anyone run that slow?* On this day, I was about to find out. I was more than six kilometers into the run when a few runners started to edge by me that I recognized from previous races. To my shock and surprise, they were the very same runners whom I used to think were "so slow." What amazed me was the fact they didn't appear to be running much faster than I remembered them to run in those previous races. This time, they were somehow passing me. I was running as hard and fast as I could and they were still passing me. Maybe they weren't running as slow as I had thought. I was fortunate that my swim and bike were still fairly fast. This gave me a substantial lead off the bike over most of the triathletes and, surprisingly, all of those in my age group.

I started to laugh to myself when some of these slow runners edged past. I realized, "I didn't care!" I encouraged them to keep going, as they had done for me in the past when I flew past them. I was racing this triathlon as I had promised. Nothing could take away my personal victory, "If I could somehow finish!" It was almost unbearably hot, humid, and sticky; and it only kept getting hotter the longer I was on the road. Forcing myself to keep moving, I again saw the beach road beckoning in the distance. A quick right turn started me down the long finishing beach road. I could see the balloons, colorful banners, and festivities of the finish area some 600 meters in the distance.

I could hardly believe it! I was going to finish the Hua Hin Triathlon and keep my promise. Instantly, I felt a wave of emotion come over me, which I had never felt, at least in any athletic endeavor. I started to cry and weep, as tears splashed down my face. I slowed for a few meters to gather myself so I could stop crying. I then ran with renewed energy for the finish line 500 meters away. Somehow, I was able to maintain my composure without bursting into tears as I crossed the finish line. Well-wishers who knew what I had gone through rushed up to congratulate me. I politely asked them to please give me a few moments. I quickly went through the transition area, back to the beach, and away from the crowd of spectators and well-wishers.

Arriving on the beach, all the emotional buildup of the last eight months came pouring out as I wept with joy, feeling like I was back in the "human race." I'd experienced very little emotion about my accident until that very moment. The only ones to witness my moment of release were a group of young Thai children happily playing and splashing in the surf. They stood transfixed as they watch this grown man exalt in feeling alive on their beautiful beach, with tears washing down my face. This was the greatest victory I had ever experienced.

I did happen to win my age group, as most of the better triathletes my age in Asia had elected not to come due it being the holiday season and wanting to stay home with their families. I would normally have been with my family, but I had made a promise to them and myself, which I miraculously ended up keeping. I had not come to win the race, only to finish. I had achieved my goal and kept my promise. It felt great, wonderful, exciting, energizing, and many more feelings so deep it is impossible to express in print.

I learned a few things from my first race back.

1. I was able to finish.
2. Humor is important.
3. Those who appear to go slow are still giving it their best and not going so slow after all.
4. Doing a triathlon slow was harder than racing fast. Time spent on a hot humid course is much more difficult to deal with, as the middle of the day only gets hotter, especially in Thailand.
5. Most important, winning or placing high is not where it counts. Doing your very best and enjoying the moment are where it's at. I had realized this when finishing my first triathlon in Singapore but had lost sight of this after winning so many races. It also reminded me of God's perspective of finishing the course.

Beautiful Land Down Under

Don and Brian were training and racing overseas most of the time, so my training and efforts did not affect them as much as it did their sister, Shannon. In fact, I was able to spend more time with Don and Brian after leaving Aberdeen Marina Club. The three of us would travel to Australia, and I would have the privilege to train near them or with them during part of each year. Being in Australia, away from the hectic work schedule of Hong Kong, made it possible for me to finally relax, rest, and get some extra and needed treatment. Because of this, I was able to see even more improvement physically. Being around super-fit world-class and elite triathletes who accepted me really encouraged me. It was amazing that they let me join their group and train with them. It did wonders for me psychologically. I felt I was really getting back to my preaccident lifestyle.

After a normal day of triathlon training, I had time for a number of recovery treatments. I went for deep-tissue massage, rolfing, acupuncture, moxibustion, and finger pressure massage. Then there was the amazing warm waters of Pacific Ocean on the east coast of Australia inviting me to completely relax in the surf every single day. I will probably never know how much living near a warm Australian beach did for me physically and emotionally. It was truly a blessing. However, being away from my family in Hong Kong was a sacrifice, which eventually cost me my marriage.

I had forgotten my commitment as a husband in my effort to recover. Becoming fit again consumed my life and swept me away with the temporary joy of the moment, attempting to feel young and fit. There is never an excuse for not being the husband I was called to be. The Bible states clearly that husbands need to "love their wives like Christ loved the Church and gave Himself for it." I had totally lost focus in what was ultimately important. Sacrifices need to be made when coming back from mass trauma experiences, but looking back, I would have been more careful with some of these decisions. Again, I had been looking at the temporal instead of the eternal. I know this is easy to say looking in the rearview mirror, but when in that much pain, discomfort, and lack of energy, it is not as clear as you would like. I always felt alone during this period, removed from individuals or mentors, who would have helped me see clearly what I was doing. In the final analysis, we can only do as we determine at that time and not keep looking back asking, "What if?" "What if" is a mental state that drains energy from the present and is never productive. Learn from the past; don't live in the past.

I DO IT ALL

Living Life in a New Body

So what is it like to live with residual spinal cord damage?

For years, I found it difficult getting out of bed because of the stiffness in my legs and pain in my back. Many times, people would ask me how I had cut my leg without my being aware there was anything wrong until I saw the rivulet of blood on my skin. Usually nothing serious, just scratches from slightly rubbing up against a bush or something sharp. Hundreds of times I have had people ask me if I had sprained my ankle or twisted my knee because I was limping again. I have tripped while walking, running, playing tennis, hiking, or just found my legs jerking and collapsing while standing still. Many times, I would suddenly be on the ground with scraped-up arms, knees, and, a few times, cracked ribs. One time, I tripped playing tennis in Australia, landing on my left arm and breaking it again. This fall took another titanium plate to repair my arm, which is still in place today. I had gone from an accomplished athlete, who felt quick, agile, and coordinated on his feet to this new lifestyle of awkwardness. This was not an easy transition to handle. What I was really experiencing was grief. I was experiencing a certain amount of loss that couldn't be regained, certainly not as before. Dealing with loss isn't easy for anyone, even if you have the determination to do your best.

Some days, my legs will feel relatively normal, fooling me into thinking nothing's wrong and I am completely recovered. Other days, focus is still needed to feel comfortable, even when walking. When I get too tired from exercise or just a long day of teaching tennis, my legs start to shake or jerk awkwardly while standing still or lying down. This shaking can make it difficult to sleep. Driving a car becomes interesting when my legs refuse to stay relaxed and jerk unexpectedly.

Over the years, I have gotten used to the sudden realization that a restroom is necessary. A nearby bathroom is needed within a few minutes to avoid another embarrassing moment when I am riding a bike, teaching a lesson, in a meeting, out on a run, or even just shopping. One time while working out with my advanced junior tennis players, my leg gave out while moving forward for a short ball. My leg suddenly jerked, throwing me upward and forward, landing on my back and rolling to a stop. Thankfully without any noticeable injury. It scared one student so much, she yelled out, "Don't do that again!" This student thought I had really hurt myself with such an awkward fall. My two youngest children, Daniel and Crystal, were present. They just looked at me like, *Really, Dad, again?*

To say I ever get used to these different sensations would be lying, but every day when I wake up and walk by myself, I count it a blessing. I will never forget the many miracles that happened these past number of years. My lower back was so bad for a long time, it was painful for me to get out of bed in the morning or even stand up out of a chair. Even with this problem, I was fortunate to be invited to play tennis on an advanced tennis league team in Australia. I had wonderful teammates who understood my problems, allowing me to play competitive tennis again. I never knew how my body would feel or respond each time I arrived for a match. Sometimes I could move okay and hit the ball without any serious restriction. At other times, I could barely serve or turn sideways to hit my groundstrokes, always yelling, "Yours," when there was a lob over my head.

We twice made the finals of the league championships, mostly because my teammates were excellent and encouraging, regardless of how I was playing. They said they enjoyed having me on the team. I appreciated this as I could be the weak link when not feeling well. Playing on their team was one of the many miracles that happened to me on my new journey. I played every match each season and enjoyed the opportunity of being on a tennis court again with excellent tennis players. They will never know how much they encouraged me to keep doing my best and steadily improve.

Good days, bad days, they are all good days when you survive a situation where you are supposed to be dead or in a wheelchair for the rest of your life. Instead, you find yourself racing in triathlons at exciting venues around the world, playing tennis with your children almost every day and getting the chance to see more beautiful and exquisite sunrises and sunsets. My life was amazing before the accident and, in some ways, more amazing since. I couldn't completely appreciate how lucky and gifted I was before, but I now wake up every day deeply appreciating what I have been given.

I have had more mishaps while training for triathlons and tennis. Some people say, "You are crazy. Haven't you learned your lesson?" I have come to the conclusion that I can either sit around, moan about my spinal cord inconveniences and vegetate, or get up and keep moving. I choose the latter even if it isn't easy at times. Life is an amazing gift, and we shouldn't waste a minute of this precious time we have on this beautiful planet. We all make mistakes during our life that seem horrible and stupid at times. We can sit and wallow in these mistakes, thinking of the past or get up and try not to make the same mistake again. We need to do our best to live a better, more fruitful life. God forgives us, but sometimes it is harder to forgive ourselves.

Hot, burning sensations still suddenly appear in very specific locations in my legs, mostly my left leg. Most of the time, it happens on the outside side of my left knee. The feeling is very intense, like accidently touching the edge of a red-hot iron. I also get feelings like a fly or a bug is crawling up and down on my skin, anywhere from my waist downward. The continuing sensation of hyperesthesia is always with me. This feels like I am wearing a two-inch-wide metal belt just below my chest, which carries a small electric current. Sometimes it will become much more intense. This is something I never think about or notice, if I am fully concentrated on other tasks at hand. I have found that being actively focused on important goals keeps me from noticing these apparent debilitating sensations. My doctor said I would need to be on medication the rest of my life to handle this constant nerve pain. I refused medication then, and I am thankful to have avoided being on any recommended pills. I never notice hyperesthesia unless I am reminded about it with friends in a conversation or like now when I writing about it.

We all have times in our lives where outside disturbances try to pull us away from concentrating on a particular task we are trying to accomplish. When we totally focus on an important task, apparent disturbances seem to fade into the distance, almost disappearing.

This ability can be a learned trait, which is vital in achieving our best in life.

I have a completely different life now than I experienced in the past, but I wouldn't change anything. My body is an adventure in discovery every day. I have married again and have two beautiful children who are a blessing to me. My three older children are all doing well, and I am still able to participate in physical activity. I was the oldest father at the US Public Parks National Father-Daughter Championships, where Crystal and I were able to reach the semi-finals, losing by only two points to the eventual winners. Sure it is hard at times not to be disappointed at my movement and the awkwardness I feel. It was a wonderful tournament competing with my daughter Crystal. To make it even better, my son Daniel and I also competed, losing to the eventual winners in the quarterfinals. Being able to compete in tennis again, even with my spinal cord problems, made this event that much more special.

Spasms sometimes rack my lower body while just standing still and talking with people. My body will jerk from my waist downward, throwing one of my legs forward like I am kicking a ball. I have narrowly missed kicking people at times. At the end of a long day of teaching tennis, riding my bike, or a long run, my feet might severely cramp, causing my toes and arch to curl up in pain. While swimming in a triathlon, severe cramping have forced me to swim, keeping my feet at a ninety-degree angle, unable to point my toes. Life has become an interesting journey where I never know what body I am entering when the sun comes up. My life resembles a wilderness adventure with no clear map of each day's route.

With a third titanium plate in my left arm from my most recent break, my arm aches with pain at times but usually lasting only fifteen or thirty seconds. I still have some numbness on the back of my head, which aches and causes cramps downward through my neck and shoulders at times for no apparent reason.

I only mention these side effects to let people know I am not belittling spinal cord damage when I talk about the lighter side of paralysis.

I DO IT ALL

Spinal Cord Racing

The World Masters Games in Brisbane, Australia, were held a few years after my accident. Every triathlete loved swimming in the Brisbane River. A strong tide was flowing with us, assisting our efforts, giving us amazingly fast swim times. So much so that a number of us were almost swept past the exit dock. Race tabs held on by Velcro were used by the organizers to record our swim, bike, and run times. Triathletes were required to hand-in the appropriate tab at the conclusion of each discipline. My tabs dislodged and started to fall off when I tripped on the dock exiting the water. Frantically looking around, I couldn't find my swim exit tab. Finally, an official noticed my swim tab had come loose but fortunately saw it was still stuck to my tri suit. Losing only a small amount of time, I was thankful to be heading out onto the bike course.

Donnie had loaned me his sponsored time-trial Zipp bike, and it felt great. I enjoyed the bike course and was happy with my bike time. My adrenalin was pumping so much I wasn't thinking when I came into the bike/run transition. When I stepped off my bike and started to run, I was focused on staying upright while not tripping. Running as fast as possible through transition, I made a mental mistake. Having competed more than a hundred triathlons, I knew the rules. I had never made the mistake I made then as I raced through transition to rack my bike.

Automatic disqualification is usually assessed if you unbuckle your helmet before you rack your bike. Trying to stay on my feet without falling, I subconsciously unbuckled my helmet before securing my bike. An official stepped in front of me, stopping me as I headed out of transition for the final run. He informed me of my infraction and that he could disqualify me, ending my race right then. *Wow*, I thought, *I had traveled all the way to Brisbane, Australia, to race, and now I would be disqualified because of my stupid error?* I made the best plea possible, actually begging, so I could continue and finish. Unashamedly, I used my accident to persuade him. He turned out to have a heart and held me for a two-minute penalty. Thankfully, he sent me on my way to finish the race.

I was so excited to be allowed back in the race, adrenaline got the better of me. I exited the transition almost sprinting for the first hundred meters, faster than I imagined I could run. The beginning of the run could be viewed by the race announcer and hundreds of spectators. As I disappeared around the first corner from the crowds, I heard the commentator over the PA system yell out, "Whoa, what did he eat? He is really moving. Wonder if he can keep that pace up?" Brian Chapman, the announcer, happened to be a very good friend of mine and was surprised to see me running so well. He also knew me well enough to know I couldn't keep running like that for long.

Brian Chapman also made a huge announcement when I was finishing. As I headed down the long Brisbane Riverside Promenade to the finish line, he announced I had been paralyzed a few years before in a bike accident. For some reason, I was always a little embarrassed when commentators would announce I had been paralyzed, as he did then. Although, it didn't seem to bother me to bring it up with the official earlier as I begged to continue the race. Triathlon is an interesting sport where many spectators wonder how triathletes keep going and press forward on a hard run. But it is always amazing how much energy you gain when the finish line suddenly appears off in the distance.

The only time this wasn't true was when I turned the last corner and could see all the colors of the finish area, ten kilometers away at the 70.3 half-ironman event in Rayong, Thailand. This race happened before my accident, when my run felt fine. That final ten kilometers was on a beach road, where the gentle curve of the shoreline allowed an unobstructed view across the water to the many colorful flags of the finish area. For the longest time, you feel like you are never getting any closer to those flags. No matter how hard or long you keep running, the finishing area seems to stretch out there, always calling for you but appears to never get any closer.

This is when the long-distance training really pays dividends. Somehow your mind takes over and tells your body to keep running. One stride after another, one hundred meters after another, until it finally becomes one kilometer to go and the finish line is actually right there in front of you. You then know you have beat back the demons, which keep telling you to take a break, walk a little, or just sit down for a moment under the alluring shade of the many swaying palm trees lining the bay.

Seeing that finish line and the crowd of spectators gives you that final burst of energy knowing you have not only won the race but won the inner battle to keep going, arms raised in exaltation. Once you start a triathlon, it is all about finishing, not necessarily to be first across the line. That is what I keep in focus when I race nowadays. I have won dozens of races since my accident but always feel I have succeeded, as long as I finish. Life is the same. If we get up and do the best we can with what is right in front of us, we are a winner. If we listen to the crowd of critics, we will hear them saying things like, "You are too old," "You are too banged up," or "With your disability, you should take it easy and relax." These well-meaning friends or acquaintances are only asking you to do what they are doing, thinking your efforts are fruitless, too difficult, and you may not succeed at reaching your goals.

You wake to rain pounding on your roof, and you debate whether to stay in a warm bed or get up and face a cold, dreary outside. If life was idyllic like it was day after day on the Gold Coast in Australia, there would be very few days you would not want to roll out of bed and get going. I always try to think about what I will feel like in an hour or two if I haul myself out of bed, start running, cycling, or swimming versus the difference of not getting up and get moving. On the worst of days, this thought usually gives me enough energy to crawl out of bed, eventually relishing the early-morning excitement an awakening world brings. It is then the voices of the naysayers fade away and I feel alive, looking forward to whatever God has in store for me.

Getting to the Lighter Side

Is it possible? Can there ever be a lighter side of paralysis? Paralysis always has a serious side. Looking only from the serious side of anything can be very disheartening and depressing. It's been said, if you lose your sense of humor, you may as well be dead. Maybe an extreme statement, but it certainly leaves you not very fun to be around. In every situation, you come to a point where you either find the lighter, more humorous side or be a miserable person to be with. You will find just being around yourself will be hard. I, like everyone, had to make my choice after my first year of rehabilitation. Without realizing it, I had become so focused on getting better, doing the exercises, going to therapy, and following my necessary workouts that I was becoming a sour and ultraserious person to be around. I had lost my smile and was losing my sense of humor while developing a furrowed brow and leaving me much less fun to associate with.

Before going on with my personal adventure, this should be mentioned: to say there is a lighter side to paralysis, is not meant to insult anyone or make light of individuals who are paralyzed. It is horrible to suddenly find yourself paralyzed and unimaginable not being able to control one's body. Even more so when it happens at an age where you have been in total control as an elite athlete. There are so many people in the world who have had life-changing accidents like mine, and for one reason or another, they have not experienced a miracle like I experienced. I have friends and met a number of people who are, to this day, still paralyzed and inspire me every time I think of them.

Many of these amazing people have gone on to achieve mind-boggling successes, which make my journey pale by comparison. For those still struggling to come to grips with their own battles, I am in no way making light of anyone else's experience. Jesus said, "My grace is sufficient for you, for My strength is made perfect in weakness" (2 Corinthians 12:9). The hard part is reaching out and accepting that wonderful gift of grace so freely offered. We all have our battles to fight in the best way we can. I have found that a little humor helped me get a better perspective on living a full and rich life again, even with my continuing problems.

Hua Hin Thailand was wonderful and successful, but I still had my original goals firmly in my mind and clearly in focus. I organized a plan to race a few more triathlons in the coming months and see if I could realistically improve my finishing times. I decided to race in Taiwan with my two sons in April, also an Olympic-distance race, and continued training to see if I could swim, cycle, and run faster. With Taiwan, my race goal was more than just to finish. I was now setting specific times in my training so higher levels of training techniques and effort were necessary. This required more intense workouts. With this higher intensity, I suddenly had to deal with another surprising and not very fun serious problem that my spinal cord damage brought on.

First, my clonus would pop up unexpectedly and violently spasming a leg muscle, throwing me off balance, where I could take a bad fall. Secondly, I discovered a serious problem with incontinence. I had made a decision in the hospital not to rely on a bladder bag and such. I instead would somehow make myself control my bodily functions on my own again. You know, be back to normal! Sounds easy? Think again! I desperately wanted to be in complete control of my body. This worked out pretty well, as long as I was in close vicinity or easy reach of toilet facilities. Thirty seconds or so were required when the inevitable message arrived. In other words, not much time was given for the need to relieve. "Congratulations, you now have what is known as a spastic bladder," I was told. In simple terms, the bladder does not completely empty itself like it should or did for years. This left me with the opportunity to visit toilets many times a day. I could make a map of Hong Kong's downtown available toilets because of my need to relieve. I had the opportunity to visit toilets twenty times a day, particularly at the beginning of my rehabilitation. The other thing, which happened, was brought on by my loss of sensation. I found it almost impossible to control myself until I could reach a facility, leaving me with many embarrassing situations. This happened a number of times, and although not pleasant, I knew I had to keep trying if I was to finally gain control. It was either this or face the possibility of having a bladder bag reinserted or worse.

Lastly, I found training longer distances at higher intensity resulted in another unexpected problem. I will share this as politely as possible. I would suddenly get the notice I had a problem brought on by the extreme effort of trying to run long and hard. I suddenly knew I would become incontinent if I couldn't find a toilet within a matter of seconds, and I do mean seconds!

How cool is this? I am running along a very busy Deep Water Bay Road in Hong Kong in the middle of a beautiful day, with multitudes of people milling around at the beach, on the sidewalk, and driving by. I suddenly realized I am going to lose it. I was caught completely by surprise the first time this sensation appeared. I stopped running and did everything within my power to keep from having a complete "blowout!" This pleading I was having with myself happened while tightly crossing my legs. This was happening with everyone walking and driving by. I was so surprised, I completely lost it, literally filling my running shorts. I was only wearing a pair of tiny Nike running shorts and shoes and no shirt, and I was a mess. I had to walk to the nearest toilet and clean up, which was about fifty meters away. How humiliating to have no more control than a baby in the middle of the busy public beach area of Deep Water Bay. Babies at least have diapers. Was that going to be my future, diapers?

I did some real soul-searching following that event. I decided right then, I was not going to let this stop me from achieving my goals, no matter how humiliating it could and most likely would be in my future. Later on, my children would say I was like a wolf that would mark his territory wherever I trained or raced. I had to find places at a moment's notice to take care of myself—behind bushes and trees or building, places that were out of sight. It was something I had to live with, or stop training and racing. In the middle of the day, I tried to do my running on secluded trails or where I knew there were public toilets frequently along my route. Early-morning runs became my favorite. To this day, darkness allows me to take care of myself as very few people are up at 3:30 or 4:00 a.m. I had gotten used to dealing with this while training and was looking forward to racing with my sons at the April triathlon in Taiwan.

The Taiwan Triathlon and Messy, Messy Encounters

Our journey to Taiwan was amazing as we were treated like royalty, once arriving at the Taipei Airport. The Hualien Triathlon was Taiwan's first international and Asian triathlon event, and the Taiwan Triathlon Association wanted to impress. The organizers provided transportation to the East Coast and food on the longer-than-expected eight-hour trip. Hotel and pocket money (for what, I don't know, as everything had already been taken care of) was handed out to each of us international triathletes. Travel to the race site could have been much shorter had they not taken us on the scenic drive. The organizers thought we would enjoy the scenic route by driving north, following the coast road. Driving the beautiful coast road northward eventually took us east then south down the beautiful eastern coastline to Hualien. Part of this coast road was carved out of the steep mountainside cliffs dropping down to the blue Pacific Ocean. Heading in and out of a number of tunnels cut into the same mountainside made for a beautiful and unforgettable drive. The Taiwanese were wonderful hosts, so nobody dared complain about the length of the trip. Hualien was a relatively small seaside Pacific Ocean city. We were tired and grateful when finally arriving to our destination. They checked us into the prepaid hotel to rest up and get ready for the race in a few days' time.

The race site was set up at the beautiful, calm blue Liyu Lake. Liyu Lake was inland about 35k from our hotel in an idyllic country setting. It was a perfect location, and on race morning, the sun rose on a stunning clear, blue day, unlike the tumult we experienced in Thailand. I had trained properly for this triathlon and was ready to "race," not just to finish. My training had exceeded more than I had expected—better than my wildest dreams or my doctor's prediction would ever be possible. Not as fast as before but I was feeling fit and excited to be in Hualien. Brian had also traveled there to race, so it made the event an even more enjoyable experience.

When the starter's gun sounded on race morning, my 1,500-meter swim felt great, and I came out of the water with an excellent swim time, first in my age category. My cycling did not disappoint as racing along their beautiful, smooth forest-lined roads gave me an exceptionally fast forty-kilometer bike time. My bike race was momentarily thrown off when my Cateye (speed monitor) snapped off in my spokes, spinning off like a Frisbee into the woods beside the road. I didn't stop or even go back later to look for it in the dense, forested area. I was glad my wheel was not damaged and concentrated on heading to the bike/run transition. Then came the part I had dreaded most in Thailand, the 10k run. This time was different, as I knew I could finish the ten kilometers. My run had improved enough in training to avoid the dread of not finishing I had felt in Thailand. I was excited to be running when I headed out of transition near Liyu Lake.

As I took out north from transition, I was surprisingly happy with how good my run felt. Never as fast as before but I was pleased with how I was moving and enjoyed the vistas along the run course. The route headed north on the two-lane wide road number 9 before crossing a large bridge over the river and heading back west toward Hualien and the eventual turn around. The five-kilometer turnaround came up before I knew it, and I couldn't wait to head back to the finish line. I couldn't believe how great I felt! It was wonderful, and I was enjoying the run. Then suddenly, at 5.5 kilometers, I had the "urge." This was the first time this desperate sensation had happened in a race, and I was in deep trouble.

The setting may have been scenic and great for racing but not ideal for finding a private place to relieve oneself. I was running on a smooth two-lane paved mountain road, which dropped off one hundred feet to the wide, flowing river on my left. I was not fortunate as there was a fifty-feet-high vertical cliff to the right side of the road into an overgrown forested area. There was no way to negotiate the cliff on either side. "So there I was, stranded!" No place to hide and the urgent need to relieve.

Two-lane wide road, with no place to leave the road or hide for privacy—what was I to do? I literally stopped in my tracks and tried to make the urge go away by tightly crossing my legs. How could this be happening? I was supposed to be running, not just standing still. Wow, it suddenly seemed to work, so after thirty seconds, I started to run again. But like a bolt of lightning, it came back again, even stronger. *Why now?* I asked. *I am having such a great race!* I stopped and started again! The third time it came back, I felt like I was going to burst! I knew I couldn't control it and let loose like Mount St. Helens. Try to visualize this picture! I am racing in a small vest top and Speedo swimsuit. My Speedo completely fills up so much so that it feels like it is going to pull off. I am still trying to run but realize I need to get as much of this added weight out and quickly. After all, "I am still in a race." I have only one tool in which to dig for "gold," and that is my right hand. I did the best I could by throwing it on the cliff to the right as I continued running. In the process, I got it all over my lower back. I was a mess, smelt like a sewer, and still had 4k to the finish line. Amazingly, my run still felt pretty good, maybe even better now, without the extra weight. The views continued to be wonderful looking up the valley to the mountains, seeing the bridge beckoning slightly downhill in the distance.

I became more determined now than ever to finish this race as strong as possible. Another 500 hundred meters down the road, the top Taiwanese elite triathlete came up beside me. Seeing I had slowed down significantly, like most triathletes, he decided to give me some encouragement. He slapped me on the lower back and said, "Come on, try to pick it up again!" He had no idea why I had slowed down; he just wanted to encourage me. After the "splat," I knew immediately his right hand must be covered, but he headed on down the road totally unaware of his new predicament. He didn't have a clue what had just transpired as we were all perspiring heavily in the heat and humidity. When we heard the splat, he had assumed it was just sweat. How wrong he was as about three minutes later, I could still view him just ahead of me. He slowed slightly and started looking around. Suddenly, in dismay, he looked at his right hand. What a shock as he tried to figure out where this stuff had come from, then how to shake it off. I started to laugh so hard I could barely keep running. I laughed and smiled my way across the bridge and through the last two kilometers, finally arriving to the finish chute.

Coming to the 200m finishing chute with hundreds of spectators cheering us on, the inside and back of my legs were brown, as well as my shoes. I ended up having a great race, and a number of people came up to congratulate me. I was making an effort to get away and cleanup in Liyu Lake, when my son Brian and Hong Kong professional triathlete Ian Rayson came up to congratulate me. Not knowing my predicament, Ian started to sniff the air and remarked, "Wow, they must keep cattle around here!"

Brian, knowing me, immediately looked down at my brown legs and shoes and, in shock, blurted out, "DAD!" I again burst out laughing as I rushed away, down to Liyu Lake to clean up. This was my first in many mishaps and humorous racing adventures around the world. I won my race plus money for fastest swim and bike times in my age category. I had a hard time containing my smile when thinking of the Taiwanese triathlete and my great results.

THE LIGHTER SIDE

I was fortunate to experience many wonderful encounters that brought a smile to my face over the years. A young Chinese was one of those.

Young Chinese

Art Ching (not his real name) was in his late twenties when I first met him in the Aberdeen Marina Club gym. Art was a fit, strong, and confident young Chinese. Every time I saw him in the gym, he was disciplined in his routine of lifting weights. He and I met following my accident and return to the club. Art had read my story in the *South China Morning Post* and found it hard to believe I had made such a remarkable recovery.

He never failed to say hi and start a positive conversation while we both went through our exercise routine. Art seemed to be the typical young Chinese, who had available access to an up-market expensive club like the Marina Club. When we first met, I thought he was the son of a wealthy businessman, probably spoiled with all the trappings that money can buy.

One day, Art and I retired to the coffee shop on the main floor, where he shared a little of his life with me. It turned out I was only partly right about who Art was. He came from a rich family whose dad had started a successful company, years before. The part I didn't know was his dad had passed away unexpectedly when Art was still in his late teens or early twenties. Although his dad made a good start to the company, Art took over the reigns and had turned it into a much larger and very profitable enterprise. I was impressed as his attire in the gym was always an old gray pair of gym shorts and a T-shirt with holes and rips in it. He didn't look anything like a successful young businessman.

One day, Art invited me to join him and some other friends on his boat out at Middle Bay for a relaxing afternoon in the warm sun. Art also invited my sons to join in the fun. I had to finish a couple of afternoon lessons and said I would be there as soon as I could. I asked him to describe his boat for me so I could swim out and join them. I was thinking most likely he owned one of the many refurbished huge Hong Kong fishing junks. He said his boat would be easy to spot. It would be the only eighty-nine-foot Italian yacht anchored offshore. It was right then I realize I had totally misjudged Art. Even getting to know who Art really was still made me feel he enjoyed being the Art I found in the gym each day. He owned a fleet of the finest sport cars and classics and lived in an amazing home in an upscale secluded area. I believe the pages of his successful life was more easily defined by watching how comfortable he was in the gym working out with me.

There was a serious side to Art, but the lighter side I experienced in Marina Club gym and on his yacht was where Art really looked relaxed and alive. I witnessed a number of members misjudge Art in their casual encounters with him, seeing only the cover of his amazing life book.

ATTEMPTING NORMAL

Once back to work and able to train again, those around me said I was becoming ill tempered and short with myself, but worse, I was becoming impatient with everyone else. This was something they had not seen before. In my effort to recover, I was taking myself way too seriously, leaving me less enjoyable to be with. How could I change this while trying to cope with my new uncomfortable body? Most of the time, I was able to hold these feelings in and fake it with my students at the club, but even this became more difficult as the days and months passed by. I was impatient with my improvement.

Before my broken body I never seemed to worry about anything. I encouraged everyone including my assistant tennis instructors. Knowing I would always have a full teaching schedule, I promoted my assistants heavily. Now I wasn't sure about anything, including having enough students to cover my expenses. All my new medical bills and pressing court case was constantly on my mind. I was becoming a little jealous of their full schedule. I was impatient with my rehabilitation and started to wonder if I would ever return to my 100 percent healthy athletic body. This may be understandable with clonus, hyperesthesia, and multiple trips to toilets as constant companions to use as excuses but not a great way to live a full, happy, and vivacious life. After many months of heading down this track, I finally stepped back and took a good look at myself. I realized I had to make a choice. I could either be upset at the way life was now;

get angry and miserable every time I felt awkward, clumsy, or lost control of my bodily functions; or I could see my life as some kind of comedy sitcom. I began to realize that most of these new circumstances and situations viewed in the later context of a sitcom were actually very funny. Maybe I should have sold this idea to Hollywood and made some money.

When my dad was dying of mad cow disease, the hospital psychiatrist was called in to examine him. He was smiling and laughing for no apparent reason. They didn't know at the time what his problem was, and they were determined it must be a psychological abnormality or breakdown because of the smiling and laughing. I was in Hong Kong at that time and was only able to talk with him on the phone. I asked him why he was laughing so much? Not knowing what his problem was, his response was simple and classic, "I can either laugh or cry, I choose to laugh." There were red faces all around the hospital when he was transferred to Stanford University Hospital and diagnosed with mad cow disease. I decided to take my father's advice and see the comic relief in my various situations. With that heavy load off my back, I was finally able to let go and again enjoy my life's wonderful journey. I can't say I was always perfect after that "aha" moment, as new situations continually caught me by surprise.

One afternoon, while coaching a number of young children with their mother's looking on, I tried to run for a ball, when one of my students rolled another ball in my direction. As you can expect, I step right on the ball and sprained my ankle. What I remember was a shooting pain going through to my bone marrow, then finding myself on the ground, with my ankle swelling. All of my young students had burst out laughing. I couldn't figure out why they would all be laughing when I was lying there in obvious pain. One of the mothers, also trying to contain her laughter, helped me from the court. She then explained why they found it funny. When I had stepped on the ball, my reaction was not normal. Clonus had reared its ugly head again and had caused my leg muscles to violently spasm, shooting me straight up in the air. The mothers said the sight was hilarious as I resembled an animated cartoon character. Trying to picture myself shooting straight up in the air, again reminded me to take a lighter approach to my problems and hopefully be able to laugh at myself even with the obvious pain. Thinking about it later, it was hilarious; an animated cartoon character flying through the air?

Children have such a simple way of responding to life's issues. They don't know to be embarrassed about the awkwardness of learning a new task or skill. They will get on with learning new things with little or no awareness of what others might think of them. This becomes increasingly more difficult as we get older. We all want to appear in control of our surroundings and impress others. As a fairly accomplished person physically before my accident, I had become accustomed to being in control of my body, especially when it came to sports. It always feels good to have people say things like, "You make it look so simple and effortless." Now I was faced with not only looking awkward and out-of-control physically but was faced with embarrassing situations, making myself and others nearby uncomfortable.

Living a Messy Life

Life for me had always been very pristine and controlled. Looking sharp and together were part of my persona in my "pre-accident" endeavors. Even though many of my plans may not have succeeded, I was waking up each day positive and excited about life. Now I could suddenly be caught off guard in a moment's notice, at times feeling like I needed to be living in an assisted living facility with full-time help to keep me together. Things seemed to be falling apart wherever I looked. Staying positive took a conscious effort every day, after arriving back to work.

Whether it was meeting with the senior sports ministers and business partners in Beijing, sitting in church, going to concerts, or just riding in a car or plane, I would be faced with the sudden urgent "call of nature." Sometimes I would find a facility quickly; other times, I would be left with the feeling of helplessness, losing control, and facing one embarrassing moment after another.

Cleaning up in public facilities was becoming an all-too-common occurrence as I struggled to gain control. Even with these occurrences, I was thankful every day for the ability to be on my feet and able to walk and run again. I was busy again, so I didn't have time to feel sorry for myself. I discovered ways to adjust to each situation, clean myself up, and keep moving forward. Every time a mishap took place, I became more determined to get through that day and improve.

Meetings in Beijing was difficult after a mishap, but with overnight dry-cleaning available, I was able to be presentable for the rest of the week. Living a messy life is never easy to accept. I was one of the lucky ones and did my best to recognize this and stay positive even with this inevitable messy lifestyle.

Once you get to really know an individual, you realize there is always more to their story than what you see on the outside. My messy inside pages were there, but I tried to hide them as much as possible as I moved forward.

Crystal, Daniel, and Dad in our
Hong Kong serene pool setting

Lady in the Black Mercedes

Our country park home provided a unique opportunity for me to run on secluded trails and remote, mostly empty roads located a short distance below our home. Our country park setting was serene and mostly empty of traffic except for a few local residences. The overgrown jungle everywhere allowed me to find secluded places when necessary. It was only a short run down a jungle trail to reach the end of a mountain road. I loved being alone on these almost empty roads, learning how to run again without worrying how I looked to any prying eyes. One day while training in the country park, I was running down the narrow road toward Hebe Haven. Hearing a car approach from behind, I moved over to the right edge of the road, causing my right foot to catch an uneven portion of the pavement. Slightly turning my ankle set off a severe clonus reaction. This spasm in my right leg threw me off the road and down a soft steep embankment covered with eighteen-to-twenty-four-inch-high wet wild grass and weeds. It had been raining for a few days, and the soil was muddy. As I fell, I did a good job of collecting weeds and mud all over my body, miraculously not hurting myself.

Driving a Mercedes by at that time was a nice-looking middle-age Asian lady. She immediately stopped, rolled down her window, being concerned at what she had just witnessed. Since Hong Kong is right-hand drive, it was easy for her to view my predicament. As I lay in a heap halfway down the slope, I looked up just in time to see the horrified look of concern on her face. She obviously thought I had suffered a heart attack or something very serious for me to collapse when I suddenly flew off the road. I took one look at myself, then her facial expression, and burst out laughing as she asked, "Are you all right and do you need assistance?" Between bursts of laughter, I let her know I was all right. Her expression suddenly changed from concern and dismay and then to fear. She must have thought I was deranged or crazy lying in the weeds, laughing out-of-control. She definitely had that look of horror on her face when she hastily put up her window and sped off toward Sai Kung.

I continued laughing as I kept replaying the look on her face as she sped away. I would have loved to hear her relate this experience to her friends and family later that day. I eventually climbed back up the slope and continued the remainder of my run, smiling and laughing as I strode along, feeling very fortunate to still be outside running with no new injury.

DON BOZARTH

Over the Bars in Hong Kong

One early spring morning of 1993, the weather was as usual, unpredictable in Hong Kong. Donnie and I decided to go for a fifty-to-sixty-kilometer bike ride out to New Territories and back on what was another sunny and humid day. The roads in Hong Kong are not what you would call bike friendly with double-decker buses, minibuses, and taxis streaking by at breakneck speeds. None of these public transportation vehicles give way to cyclists. Some of Hong Kong's elite cyclists have been run over and killed by these public vehicles. I was very nearly another one of these casualties! It wasn't unusual for my sons to come back with road grime ground into one side of their cycling gear from a double-decker bus rubbing up against them.

It is always safer to cycle with other cyclists when possible in Hong Kong. There are almost no flat roads in Hong Kong—either you go uphill or downhill and usually on a fairly steep grade. Twenty-five kilometers into our ride, we noticed some serious clouds developing on the horizon and decided to time-trial our way back home to beat the fast-approaching storm. Clearwater Bay and New Territory hills make it challenging to maintain high speed. As we headed home, we could see it was going to be impossible to stay in front of the fast-moving storm clouds. We were five kilometers from home when the deluge began. Only those who have lived in Asia and tropical regions can understand the intensity with which the rain can be forced out of the clouds. It is literally like standing under a waterfall, with the rain drops sounding like pellets on your helmet. This was the type of rain that came down then. Even when it is pouring rain, the cool rain is still refreshing with warm temperatures in that region.

We had been living in Hong Kong for six years by then and didn't mind the deluge. Both of us took it as a challenge to reach home as fast as possible. The roads were flooding in a matter of minutes. The water was reaching four inches deep on one of the few level roads. By then, we couldn't even see the road surface. Donnie had charged to the front with a shout, "See you at home." Not to be out done, I tried to keep up. This, of course, was fruitless, but I was determined to arrive as soon as I could, hopefully surprising him. I saw him pulling away across an intersection just as I was vaulted over my handlebars, landing on my back and sliding my way to a stop in the middle of the same intersection. As I was sliding, I did my best to lean from side to side to lessen the inevitable road rash. The knowledge to do this comes from previous mishaps. Only from having other accidents or roadblocks can we really have the wisdom to instantly react properly to lessen the deep road rash sliding down an asphalt road can cause. Finally coming to a stop, I immediately assessed my body for any major damage. No broken collar bones (whew!), no broken arm, and my legs felt fine as I stood up. My back, neck, and head also felt okay. I could hardly believe it; I had taken a massive spill and had suffered no serious damage.

Now to my bike, as it was still lying in the middle of the road. The handlebars were turned sideways, which was easy to adjust, and to my amazement, the front wheel could still be ridden. It was out of balance and would only need to be trued up at the bike shop later. Straightening the handlebars, I got ready to take off toward home again. This is when I noticed a number of people running in my direction and flashing red lights from a police vehicle, which was stopped and blocking the intersection.

Those running in my direction were five policemen. Their police van with lights flashing was blocking the intersection. What they had seen amazed and shocked them. They had been waiting at the red light on the opposite side of the intersection. They had a ringside seat of me vaulting over my handlebars. The police quickly blocked the road with lights flashing and jumped out to assist what they assumed would be a seriously injured cyclist. They arrived by my side just as I stood up and reached my bike. They kept yelling at me to lay down and be still while they ordered an ambulance. I ignored them while straightening my handlebars. I then yelled out in excitement, "No ambulance is necessary. I am okay!" I was excited about not having any broken bones or worse. I just wanted to get home and tell Donnie what had happened. I was acting like I just won the lottery. The police kept insisting that I needed to let them take care of me, looking at my shredded-up cycling jersey and shorts!

As soon as my handlebars were straightened, I jumped on my bike and took off toward home. I left the police stunned and standing in the middle of the intersection, still in a tropical downpour. I am sure they stood there perplexed as I cycled away down the road. It was still pouring, but I didn't care. For the first time in about a year, I didn't feel like my body was made out of fine crystal that would break into a thousand pieces with the slightest bump.

I'm sure the officers left standing in the road thought there was something wrong with me mentally, or I hit my head too hard in the fall. I must have looked a sight wearing shredded bike clothes cycling away down the hill. They never tried to follow me, that I know of. I reached home safely, with no more problems. Donnie was shocked to see my shredded bike clothes and resulting road rash. He could hardly believe what had taken place behind him, as I recounted my adventure.

I immediately called my physio Nalini and told her of my mishap. She said, "Maybe you are excited now, but wait until tomorrow morning when the bruising comes out!" She asked me to come into her office the next morning to assess the damage. By the time I arrived the following day, I was sore and stiff. I almost didn't care, as I felt I could now take a hard knock and survive without serious damage to my body. I may not be a rubber ball, but I could now bounce back. Another red-letter day in my road to recovery and feeling normal again.

Donnie and I went back to the intersection the next day to see why I had gone over my handlebars. There it was, a piece of asphalt had gone missing in the road, leaving a two-inch-deep hole. With the road flooded, it was not visible for us to see, and I had hit it perfectly with my front wheel to be vaulted upward. I was thankful Donnie had avoided the same pothole.

Fear

After more mishaps and taking the inevitable spills; sprained ankles; pulled, torn, or strained muscles, at times I wondered, *How can I keep moving forward?* Doubt of never being able to truly achieve our previous best can creep in, leading to the most debilitating emotion—fear! Fear can stop us from moving forward, if it is not accompanied by passionate ideas and goals. Improper fear can rip away the ability to have a vision or ever dream again.

Fear is one of the most incapacitating factors we can face in life. What exactly is fear? Fear is that overwhelming sensation or emotion that unexpectedly grabs us when our inner self feels out of control or threatened. These threats can appear in a variety of ways. Fear is usually easily explained. Fear of heights, fear of snakes, dangerous animals, or swimming in deep shark-infested water where you can't see the bottom, or a strong current pulling us away from safety is understandable. Fear of going too fast in an out-of-control vehicle or walking alone down dark or dangerous alleyways in foreign cities makes sense. For most of us, there is always the hidden fear of not being able to take care of ourselves or family members who depend on us for daily necessities like shelter, clothing, and food. These threats make sense because they involve being wise and keeping us safe from injury, sickness, or even death.

What about the psychological aspect of fear where it involves the unknown or out-of-control situations in life? These life fears usually revolve around losing a job, becoming ill, or contracting a disease or injury like mine, which incapacitates us, leaving us feeling helpless. Fear of death makes sense to many who don't have an eternal perspective and assurance about the eternal or afterlife.

Then there is the fear of not living life to the fullest. This fear can leave us with the inability to make decisions. What if I make the wrong decision? Maybe another opportunity will appear if I just stop and do nothing. Fear can not only protect us but also can be the most debilitating factor in our life, leaving us frozen, unable to move forward, and take calculated chances. With this happening, indecision begins to take over our everyday life.

There are special courses available for executives who have lost their edge and are no longer as productive later on in their careers. Older executives can become fearful of taking chances and following what they perceive to be a safe route. Realizing they might be losing their edge and thus the ability to benefit their company, they avoid any risk-taking. They start playing it safer and safer, fearing they might make a mistake. Holding onto their position becomes paramount in their mind. When they were younger and trying to make a name for themselves, they would come to work with creative ideas they would be willing to take action on. Then, without hesitation, fearlessly present them to their superiors. They were fearless in their attempt to make their mark on the world. They were young and bold, feeling they could always find something else if their original ideas or job didn't work out. Now much older with many more responsibilities, they are facing a new generation of young upstarts. This latest generation are fearless and have an eye on replacing them, if they aren't as productive or creative as they once were.

As the years slid by, somehow, things changed; and it became easier to be complacent. Fear creeps in as they hope to keep their job by not causing any unnecessary waves or mistakes. They desperately hope not be noticed for their complacency, with our ever-evolving world and new technologies. A person can easily feel left behind and redundant, especially in the high-tech industry. The new young university graduates are eager to get a foothold in the workforce. They have been studying and learning the newest creative ideas and discoveries. Recent graduates have just spent the last five or six years studying all the latest developments in their chosen industry. They are up to speed and ready to hit the road running. The forty- or fifty-year-old manager realizes he may be edged out of his job if he doesn't stay up with all the new information in our fast-paced world. This is not an easy proposition as he still needs to fulfill his work responsibilities before spending his free time studying the latest developments. The stress this job situation produces puts extra strain on him and his family. This, combined with his responsibilities at home, can cause extreme pressure and stress. Fear can slowly and almost imperceptibly creep in, paralyzing an executive from being as productive as he once was or could be. Creases start etching across his once smiling and carefree face as life seems to become more and more serious. Creative living is slowly being sucked out of him. This is not living. This is a fearful existence.

I was hoping this would not happen to me as I also held tightly onto my employment at the Marina Club. I had never felt a desperate fear like this in my life. Fear seemed to be ever present from the moment I woke until I fell into a fitful sleep each night. I continued to force myself to get up and do my best to defeat this demon called fear. It was a daily battle I kept to myself. I felt like I was desperately hanging onto to a cliff with my fingertips.

Fear is debilitating. This can easily be seen when a snake is put in an enclosed space with a mouse. The mouse instantly freezes with fear and cowers in a far corner. The mouse makes no attempt to escape, as the snake slithers back and forth, slowly moving in for a meal. Mice are very quick and could at least try to avoid the snake, but fear totally immobilizes the mouse, leading to his eventual doom. The same can happen to the executive who freezes in his cubicle or office, hoping no one notices him while he desperately hangs onto to his ever-boring job and his family income.

To be honest, I was desperately trying to hold onto my job by avoiding the top executives I had been close to earlier. If I hid away on the tenth floor tennis courts, maybe they wouldn't notice or question my disabilities and leave me alone. By hiding on the roof, I could still make an income for my family and hopefully earn enough for the club.

There are certain types of fear which help us lead a healthy and safe life, like not sitting on the edge of Half Dome in Yosemite Valley, two thousand feet above the valley floor. God gave us this type of fear to keep us safe. Where is the line between good fear and debilitating fear?

Good fear can drive us forward to excel at a task so we succeed and reach seemingly impossible goals. The Bible talks about, "Fear of the Lord." This is a good fear. This fear can inspire us to live an honorable life that is pleasing to the Lord. Good fear helps us stay up late studying to do well on a test or practice the piano an extra hour so we perform well in a recital. For an athlete, it means finding a smarter way to improve or spending extra time in the gym, on the field, or on the court to perfect their desired skills. This hopefully will lead to a successful outcome. My fear led me to be more creative with the tennis program on my return to the Marina Club. Adding different events for adults and juniors allowed the program to grow and be better than it was previously. I was motivated by fear, but that doesn't make fear any healthier. I was driven, and in the process, I became much too serious, allowing worry lines to etch across my face. Where had that nonstop smile gone?

Bad fear can lead us to give up and not try as hard as we should because we feel we might be incapable of being good enough, no matter how hard we work, practice, or train. This can end up being a built-in excuse. An athlete can always say, "If I had practiced more, I would have won." I can't tell you how many times I have heard that from athletes. There is no excuse not to find out your true potential in any endeavor. Not doing your best because you didn't try hard enough is not what anyone wants to experience. Many are afraid to find out their true potential. With that pressing fear, "they might find out they don't have the necessary attributes to be the best in their chosen field." In our "you have to be the winner" society, many have given up on finding the true limits of their given potential. Everyone is gifted with unique skills and attributes. Finding one's uniqueness or passions usually takes a number of trials and errors, bringing us to the unavoidable dead ends. When one views this correctly, apparent dead ends will lead to other avenues to explore and succeed in. Life is an adventure to be embraced but only for the brave. I don't know if I am brave, but I didn't want to become a couch potato.

If we are not careful, we become helpless and frozen in our own little corner of life, waiting for the snakes of defeat to devour us. We need to make sure fear moves us forward and not box us into a corner. Moving forward in life with a purpose and challenging goals allows us to look forward to each and every day. I always encourage myself and others to do all that we know to do in any endeavor before deciding to move in another direction. You never want to be left with the "what ifs" in life! God has a wonderful plan for everyone's life if we will move fearlessly forward.

With all of my knowledge and life experiences, this does not become easier as I get older. There will always be naysayers in our society. Many have settled for the easy life of eat, drink, and be merry.

We are continually surrounded by the temptation of taking the easy road. This can involve a number of mind-numbing activities, if they can be called activities? Anything which encourages us to live a sedentary life. Watching TV, spending hours on social media, playing video games, or going to bars and drinking with friends for hours on end after a day's work are just a few of the mind-numbing so-called activities.

Am I guilty of some of these? Of course, I am! Sometimes it is out of fear. I am getting older, and it is easier to just plop onto that couch and let that mind-numbing TV transport me to another false reality. Fear to stretch, exercise, or use my stretch cords because I might find out I am not able to achieve what I did previously is always in the back of my mind. It is so much easier to remain laid out on that couch and dream about still being super fit. I have lots of photos to look at which show me as fit, as I dream about. I can either look at them and dream about past exploits or get up and live a passionate life now.

Fear, that silent thief, steals years from our lives. Before we know it, another day, week, month, or even a year has been ripped away, making us even more fearful to get up and change our sedentary lifestyle. Now that I had another accident, was I going to let fear of more accidents stop me from getting back on my bike and reach for my goals? That was a decision I had to make every single day. Sometimes it is not easy to make myself get out of bed and move forward.

For me personally, every decision I made after my accident was weighed with how I would do. There was also the thought about what others might think. Then the big question was, am I willing to excel at a lower level than before and be satisfied with my effort and results? I was fortunate, as I was still passionate about what I was doing. The fear of looking bad or awkward played on my mind as I went through one therapy session after another. It felt like my improvement was taking forever. Fear of failing miserably while trying so hard to excel has always been a factor, even when I was fully fit and healthy. Now I was coming to grips with the reality that my legs might never let me run as well or as fast as before. What was I going to do? Give up and forget competing in more triathlons? Or become creative and find another way to succeed? I chose to be creative and improved my swim and bike times to allow me to be competitive again.

All these new fears were so deeply ingrained after my injury. It was hard to make myself get up some mornings feeling I might just be hitting my head against that proverbial brick wall. My stature had changed, being three inches shorter, and my stomach seemed to defy the effort I put in to reduce it. I found getting fit very easy before my accident. My fear was all wrapped up in one phrase: "fear of failure." Like many had said to me, "Why are you doing this? You had years of athletic success, why not just sit back and relax now that your body is not what it used to be?" This just added one more fear—fear that the naysayers might be right!

The real truth is simple: doing nothing is the ultimate failure. Fear has won the battle in your mind when you give in and give up. Doing something while fighting off fear is always the better choice. No one claims this is easy, just a better way. In the end, defeating fear is much more rewarding. Let the naysayers say what they want. There will always be the spectators in the grandstands cheering you on like crazy while trying to figure out how you are doing what seems impossible to them.

With most people, they just don't know how to start or get out of that easy chair and begin moving forward. The goals seem too far away and out of reach. My son Brian suggested we put together a triathlon training site, which would allow triathlete wanna-be's get started and keep a simple training schedule. You know, my advice from years ago, "one light pole at a time." By following a simple, detailed schedule of activities, they would begin to see their efforts pay off and avoid injury. The eventual triathlon training site, altabrio.com means: "Live life with gusto." Isn't that what we all want while we are on this big blue ball called Earth?

Son Does a Double-Take, 1994

Doing my best to put fear aside, I headed Down Under. I was looking forward to Australia and continued training on the Gold

Coast. I was also anxious to receive more treatment from my osteopath and acupuncturist. Within a few days of my arrival, my son Donnie encouraged me to enter a short triathlon at the Robina Sports Field located in a beautiful residential area. I had been conscientious with my daily training in Hong Kong, so I was still race fit. Although this was a short-distance triathlon, the contestants for the elite field contained many of the world's best ITU triathletes and one Olympic-distance world champion. They had all come to the Australian summer to train for the upcoming-year ITU events. As is customary, the professionals started first. I always enjoyed seeing the intensity of their racing. This time was extra special as I watched my son Donnie come out of the water right alongside the world's best. Later during my race, I was to experience an intensity of my own that would rival anything they experienced.

I always enjoyed the Australian triathlon scene as everyone was friendly and the competitions were closely contested in every age category. For a small event, they could have as many as six hundred competitors. This event was not quite that big but still contained a large field of triathletes. Once my event started, I had an excellent swim and, as usual, a pretty fast bike for my age group. When I came off my bike to run, I was surprised when they announced I was in first place, but even better was how good I felt. I had been doing my run training in the hills of Hong Kong. Because of that, my legs didn't feel so heavy and tight. I actually felt like I could run. This was always a mystery for me. Feeling fairly normal some days while other days I struggle to walk around without losing my balance. However, this was one of those exceptional days I relished. Times like this made all my hard training worthwhile.

During the first lap of the five-kilometer run, I took in the scenery as we ran through the park trails located behind the many homes and across a few streams over their wooden bridges. It was a wonderful shaded setting and made my run feel even better after the heat of Hong Kong. At halfway and coming by the transition area, they announced I was still leading my category. This spurred me on to keep running fast. But as I neared the last kilometer of the race, I suddenly knew I had another recognizable problem. I was still leading my age group but also knew my main competitors, who were all fast runners, could not be far behind. I started to slow down a couple of times looking for a place to quickly take care of my ever-present problem. Each time I slowed down, I also thought of losing the race because of stopping. When I had less than 200 meters to go and still leading, it became desperate. I had to make a choice, either run off the course, take care of myself, and lose the race, or run the last 200 meters while filling my Speedo again!

This was all happening with crowds of spectators and triathletes visible just ahead, cheering me on to win the race. I chose the latter and ran through another finishing chute in an embarrassing fashion. To make matters worse, Donnie was waiting for me just beyond the finishing line with two young ladies he was trying to impress. As I ran past the finish line, he approached me, wanting to introduce me. He did a double-take when he noticed my condition of brown legs and shoes and quickly turned them away. Not knowing the extent of the damage, I went into the sports house toilet to clean up. It was hopeless, as I was really a mess and "stuff" starting flying everywhere. It seemed the more I tried to clean up, the more it spread. It was like a horror movie for me watching the area resembled an explosion. I realized I needed a larger place to wash up and headed for the swim course of Robina Lake.

All in all, it was a successful event as I won my age group and two lucky draws with only a few athletes knowing what had happened. I felt sorry for the cleaner who walked into that men's room but not without a slight wrinkle of humor on my face. I was again experiencing passion about my training and triathlon racing instead of fear moving me forward.

Chinese Boulevard

My first opportunity to race the Asian Championship was eighteen months following my accident and was set in China. Tianjin, China, was the site chosen for the second Asian Triathlon Championships. Tianjin is located southeast of Beijing and directly west across the Bohai Sea from North Korea. Tianjin, an industrial

I DO IT ALL

city, was not known for its cleanliness. Why Tianjin was chosen, nobody was sure, but nevertheless, we found ourselves there. Tianjin was one of the most polluted industrial cities in China at that time, with toxic colors of the rainbow coming out of the many smokestacks dotting the skyline. This is what welcomed us when we arrived a few days before the race. None of this was important to me, as this time, I would be lining up to race, not just watching from the sidelines. We were greeted warmly by the Chinese delegation in Tianjin. Pollution was evident everywhere, hanging heavily over the city. Besides the air pollution, which made breathing labored through the colored haze, the roads were covered with debris, causing many flat tires during our training rides. There was much talk about how we were going to avoid the garbage and debris so we wouldn't get a flat tire during the race.

However, stepping out of our hotel on race morning, a glorious clear blue sky was spread out before us. With great assistance from the local citizens, the Chinese Triathlon Association had done the seemingly impossible. Firstly, by closing all the factories the previous day, they gave us beautiful clear blue skies and clean air to breathe. Secondly, we also awakened to pristine clean roads everywhere we looked down the 40k bike and 10k race route. We were shocked, thrilled, and puzzled how this had happened like magic while we slept. During our night's rest, they had transformed the race course into beautiful, clean boulevards and pure air to breathe. When you have millions of people willing to help, we realized anything was possible. The evidence was right in front of us, and we all looked forward to a great race.

The swim was held at a lake nestled in the middle of Tianjin's central park. Donnie and Brian were the favorites to win the junior competition again as they continued to train with professionals overseas and were improving their race times. I was just trying to get through the triathlon and enjoy racing again instead of watching from the sidelines this time around. When they were organizing the race, they inadvertently entered me in the junior category because Donnie and I had the same name. This was another one of those apparent detours you learn to flow with.

We didn't realize this mistake until the race heats were being called and I was ordered to line up for the start. I tried to explain to the officials, who spoke very little if any English, that I was in the forty-five to forty-nine category; but they insisted, in broken English, that they had to follow my race number, and according to the information on their race sheets, I was a junior. The professionals and elite juniors were starting at the same time. I couldn't believe I had to line up with my sons and start alongside Asia's best elite professional and junior triathletes. Everywhere I gazed up and down the start line were super fit and cut bodies. Here I was with my somewhat pear-shaped body, still trying to even finish a race respectably. Two years before, I had been training to race the elite pro category and now I was given the opportunity. I somehow couldn't find the humorous side when lining up to race!

The warm lake swim made the water feel heavy, and as expected Donnie and Brian were out in front with the top professionals. I was lost back in the thrashing field of slower junior swimmers trying to find some clear water to swim in. I had come to compete in the triathlon, so I wasn't about to be deterred! I was happy to be there, even if I had to start with the elite athletes. My swim was okay, still finishing ahead of a number of juniors. Once out of the lake, I was looking forward to the forty-kilometer bike course, always my favorite discipline. I felt comfortable once I was cycling and was able to pass a number of the juniors. Just past the halfway turn, I came over a rise in the expressway and noticed a large group of officials and medical staff at the bottom of the hill where the road leveled out. As I picked up speed, I saw Brian's red Zipp bike lying on the road. I slowed and saw his front wheel totally collapsed. Slowing down even more, I saw Brian and asked if he was okay? Thankfully, he said he was fine. I asked if he wanted to use my front wheel so he could continue and again win the junior title. My race wasn't nearly as important as his. He was not injured but insisted I continue with my race knowing how much it meant to me.

Brian was in third place among the professional triathletes at the time of the accident, way out in front of the junior field when he hit a large brick. The race organizers had placed some bricks

I DO IT ALL

instead of cones, in the middle of the road to guide the cyclist over to another lane. Brian had his head down and didn't see the brick until it was too late. His mishap was caught on video by a Japanese camera crew, which showed him hitting the brick, then doing the splits, as he vaulted over the handlebars at full speed. He then miraculously landed on his feet, skidding and sliding down the road on his cycling shoes without falling. The spectators and officials, said they had never seen anything like it. It was a miracle he wasn't badly injured.

I felt horrible for Brian as he would have easily won another Asian junior title he had trained so hard for. Since he wouldn't use my wheel, I soberly continued on with my race, reaching the bike/run transition without any mishap. I started the ten-kilometer run, having no idea how I was doing in my age category. The forty-five to forty-nine age group triathletes started five minutes after the elite pros and juniors. So far, none of my age group had passed me by. I always found racing in China a wonderful experience. Previously, I had raced the first ITU triathlon in China called the Great Wall Triathlon. This had been before my accident, when I was super fit and healthy. I had easily won my age group race then and loved how we were treated by the organizers. The awards ceremony for that ITU race was held in The Great Hall of the People, which made the event truly memorable. We all agreed that the government officials must make it a public holiday in the area, as thousands upon thousands of spectators lined the entire final ten-kilometer run, waving small flags, screaming and cheering us on to the finish line located in a stadium full of spectators.

It was pretty much the same in Tianjin as we headed out for the ten-kilometer run. At 5k or halfway point of the run, there was a massive large 4.5 feet-high orange cone in the middle of their largest boulevard. The boulevard was ten lanes wide with thousands of spectators lining both sides of the avenue. It was here, that it happened. Suddenly, I was in distress with literally nowhere to go or hide again! Why did this have to happen again with thousands of spectators and no way out? I immediately stopped, leaned on that huge cone, crossed my legs, and tried my best to concentrate and stop the inevitable. As I was doing my best to stop the flow, one of my good triathlete friends came running up to the turn around and yelled out, "Come on, Don, GO."

I yelled back as I burst out laughing, "That's what I'm trying not to do!" You can imagine what that did for my self-control. I burst a gasket again, right there in front of thousands of Chinese spectators. My Speedo was full again, and this time, I didn't have the limited privacy of a lonely Taiwanese country road to try and clean myself up. I had no choice but to start running and finish the last five kilometers, totally embarrassed and soiled.

One final disaster was still to unfold for our family. Donnie had taken over the lead in the Junior category once Brian vaulted over his handlebars. At two kilometers in the run and with a huge lead a (water) aid station handed him a drink, which he gulped down before he knew it wasn't water. It was saltwater, and within one hundred meters, it reacted in his system, and he started throwing up. He continued to throw up until dry heaves took over, causing him to dehydrate. I came up on Don at the 8k mark with him walking. He looked terrible; his face was white and washed out. I could tell he was totally drained of his energy but still trying to find a way to finish his race. I couldn't believe it. I thought he had already finished his race, winning the junior category this time instead of Brian.

What a day we were having as I was running with my Speedo full, Brian had crashed out because an official had put a large brick in the middle of the road, and Donnie looked like a ghost as I encouraged him to keep going. Sometimes things work out perfectly, and other times, life throws you a curve or a brick or saltwater or a full Speedo to check out if we still have a sense of humor. Can we step back see the bricks in our way and still laugh at ourselves? This was one of those times when, as a family, we sat back with a big smile and enjoyed the moment, still able to celebrate everyone else's success. After all, how many families get the chance to travel around the world to beautiful, interesting, and exotic places while racing beside each other in triathlons?

Comic Relief

A unique and beautiful setting awaited a few thousand finely tuned triathletes when we arrived in Manchester, England. I had prepared as much as my body would allow and could hardly believe I was able to race the ITU World Championships again. A challenging one-way bike course from the bogs to the center of Manchester awaited triathletes from around the world. The swim was located up in the bogs, high in the hills, twenty miles outside of downtown Manchester. The upper hills outside of Bolton turned out to be a typical cold and dreary English day when we arrived to view the swim-to-bike transition on our first day to view the course. The water temperature was freezing cold at thirteen degrees Celsius. This required us to wear two swim caps, one of thermal quality, plus our wetsuits to keep us from going into hypothermia. The outer cap was the official swim colored-and-numbered race cap.

The bike course was technical as it rose steeply upward out of transition for 500 meters before heading steeply down a narrow, winding English country road. Dirt and pebbles were everywhere, making some of the turns downright dangerous. This dangerous and technical descent eventually fed into beautiful, smooth country roads lined with huge dark-green hedges hiding beautiful old English country homes. A long, steep uphill section awaited everyone at fifteen kilometers and wilted a number of triathletes before reaching the summit. Once reaching the top, a fast descent thankfully awaited everyone, carrying us down to the M1 Motorway, which was closed for the Championships. This fast, smooth section led us into the middle of Manchester's business district. The bike-to-run transition was laid out in the center of Manchester near the final finishing straight. The run was a two-lap course winding around the many blocks of Manchester's downtown business district and a central park. The run was hardly ever in a straight line for more than a block or two. We wound around downtown, unable to see other triathletes, normally seen on out-and-back race courses.

There is no way to express how excited I was to be racing the World Championships again. I had diligently trained to qualify and have a respectable finish. My two sons were again representing Hong Kong in the elite junior category. Brian had been training in San Diego with some top professionals, including Michellie Jones and Peter Coulson. Brian was being recognized as a top world junior competitor by then and was anticipating a great race. He had excellent preparation, winning a couple small professional events in Colorado before heading to England. Donnie was doing well but had taken a more relaxed attitude to his training and wasn't expecting the same results as his brother, but he would still race well. Donnie trained harder than most gave him credit for. When he wanted to race fast, he had it in him to hang with the best. They were both doing well as they had been in triathlon for two years when Manchester World Championships rolled around. I was just excited to be racing again at the World's, not expecting too much as far as my placing was concerned. Given everything, it felt wonderful to be there with my sons and hanging out with some of the fittest people on the planet.

Manchester was very cold compared to the hot and humid weather of Asia and San Diego, where we had been training. Brian immediately made contact with Michellie Jones and Peter Coulson, who also flew in from San Diego. The Hong Kong team was staying at Bolton College outside of Manchester, halfway to the Bogs. Michellie and Peter were staying at a five-star hotel in downtown Manchester, provided by the organizers, as Michellie was one of the professional-race favorites. After we made contact with them, they gave us a ride back to our accommodations following a race briefing in Manchester. Seeing the calm atmosphere of Bolton, they inquired about staying with us. Amazing that they would trade five-star accommodations to stay with us in Bolton.

After making the necessary arrangements, they transferred to Bolton that same day. This was incredible for us, riding and swimming the course for a few days with the potential women's World Triathlon champion and Peter Coulson who was a former professional cyclist. They had their own vehicle and I became their official driver. We couldn't have had a better lead up to the race. The water temperature at the lake was so cold at thirteen degrees Celsius, it was enough to make your face go numb. It felt like your head would literally explode when entering the water. The pain in our sinus was so intense for the first three or four minutes of the 1,500-meter swim, you wondered if it was worth doing the race.

Peter constantly made fun of my weight but always in a light-hearted manner. Both Peter and Michellie encouraged me to continue training and get back into great shape. When I headed out for an easy run the night before the race, Michellie asked if she could join me. I couldn't believe she was asking, but I felt honored she would consider to run with me. Michellie has always been a class act, and it was great fun to run with her. She watched my run and commented that it was looking fine. She will never know how much this encouraged me. She is what a great champion is all about, as she inspired my sons and me before a big race of her own.

Race day arrived early, and we all viewed a cold, wet, and dreary morning, not that unusual for England. My sons had raced the year before in Canada, and it was the same type of weather in Muskoka. There was lots of complaining in transition while getting our gear ready for the race. Triathletes were saying, "With all the warm areas around the world, why two years in a row is freezing weather greeting us?" I didn't care because of my journey to be there. I was just glad to qualify and race the World Championships again. I also had an advantage. I couldn't really feel the cold water from my chest down. I still had very little surface feeling on my skin. We all had to wear wetsuits or possibly suffer hypothermia. When the gun finally sounded for my race, my face and sinus, like everyone else, felt like they were going to explode for the first four minutes in that freezing lake. After the initial effects of the freezing water, the painful sinus effects wore off, and I settled into my swim stroke. With the aid of my wetsuit, I ended up having a surprisingly good swim.

Michellie, Peter, and the Bozarths had spent quite a bit of time scouting out the cycle course, which allowed us to gain time on the technical sections. This was especially true on the descent down the narrow, winding country road. Don, Brian, and I had gone over this section a number of times to find the perfect line, avoiding the rocks and gravel strewn on the road. I personally had an amazing race when

I found myself unexpectedly passing many other competitors in my age group during the forty-kilometer bike portion.

Excited at how good it felt, I flew through the bike to run transition and started out fine on the run leg. Michelle had so encouraged me, I found myself moving better than expected. I stayed relaxed as I ran around the many blocks of downtown Manchester. Then at six kilometers, I felt that sickening message notifying me an immediate toilet break was again necessary. This was a serious problem here as the run was located in the center of Manchester's downtown business district. I frantically looked for a place to relieve myself as I continued to run. Just when I knew I would lose control, I noticed a car park on my left. Making a quick left turn off the course, I dashed to the back of a large high-rise parking lot. I looked around and dropped down behind the last car. It was just in time! After some minutes, I was finally able to make myself decent. I exited the parking lot and rejoined the race, losing more than five minutes. At least this time, I wasn't totally soiled and could finish the race with some dignity. The smell of cattle was still evident in the air at the finish line until I was able to shower off in the recovery area.

One of the interesting things that happened later at the awards ceremony took place when the top veteran triathlete from Great Britain whom I knew from Hong Kong approached me. He related what went through his mind when he spotted me ahead of him on the run. At the 5k mark, they gave us a wristband to put on, so near the finish, we would be directed correctly to the finish line. When he and I passed each other going in different directions, he saw I was wearing the wristband and panicked, saying to himself, *Oh my goodness, I'm losing to a cripple!* I was about a kilometer ahead of him at that time. Maybe not politically correct thought or comment, but that's how he felt. He was a great runner, having made the podium at the World Duathlon Championship and put in a big effort to make sure he passed me before the finish line. He never saw me on the course and thought I had finished ahead of him. He had no idea that between the time he saw me, when I was a number of blocks in front, that I had lost more than five minutes in a parking lot. He had passed the parking lot I was hiding in, just a minute before I exited and rejoined the race. I never related this to him, as racing was now a matter of enjoyment, regardless of where I finished.

Don and Brian had mixed results, and Michellie Jones had a great race winning the elite women's pro ITU World Championship in a sprint finish with American Karen Smyers. Brian had the most disappointing day. He had a great swim. Leaving the swim to bike transition, he felt even better after all the cycle training he had done with Peter Coulson. He immediately passed a few junior cyclists, who had finished just before him out of the water. When Brian arrived on the M1 motorway, he could see the race favorite in the junior category, Ben Bright, not too far down the road. Ben was leading the junior race at the time.

Brian kept passing one cyclist after another, moving forward to reach and pass the next. Just when he thought he might be able to catch Ben, an event monitor on a motorcycle came up beside him and ordered him to pull over to the side of the road and stop. The monitor had come over a rise in the motorway just as Brian had come up behind another cyclist and thought Brian had been drafting. Drafting is sitting so close behind another cyclist, it allows you to relax and use less effort or rest for a bit. Drafting on another cyclist was still an infraction of the rules at that time. Brian had not been drafting but was just starting to pass when the monitor saw him. No amount of convincing by Brian could make an impression on the official. Brian was made to stand there for two minutes before he was allowed to continue his race. Donnie again enjoyed racing another World Championship and was happy with his race. Brian will never know how he would have finished in Manchester, had it not been for that official. Brian has always had a good attitude about what transpired that day, better than I think I would have had. It was, however, an all-around memorable day for me in Manchester, England. I was racing at the ITU World Championships again with my sons, so how could my life get any better?

With all the tall buildings in Manchester's business district towering above that parking lot, I still wonder if there were any spectators viewing my predicament from the upper floors. For their sake, I hope not.

Digging Deep

My life before April 22, 1992, was filled with confidence, feeling like I could do pretty much anything, as long as I had the desire and the will to put in the necessary effort to succeed. Did I achieve all my hopes, dreams, and aspirations? No, but in the process of pursuing my dreams, hopes, and aspirations, I had traveled around the world and lived a wonderfully positive and fulfilled life. I started every goal with a positive approach and a plan to succeed. I began every endeavor with the thought I would reach my end goal. I would research any available material to guarantee I was approaching my goal intelligently.

Water Skiing—Few years before accident

As a tennis teaching professional, I was fortunate to be able to pass on this hopeful, positive, and focused attitude to my students. I had the privilege of watching a good number of them succeed and achieve their dreams. Family, close friends, and mentors surrounding me provided more than enough support and belief to carry me through many of the setbacks life threw at me. Quite frankly, all of us experience unexpected curve balls hurled at us through the years. I always loved challenges, especially those that required physical effort, along with the mental side to figure out the best and simplest way to accomplish a goal. I also liked it when people would say that a particular task was impossible to achieve, especially when it dealt with age. I would go off by myself, research, and experiment with ideas on how to prove them wrong; then conscientiously work out a way to achieve the task before me.

I felt completely in control of my body and relied on my God-given coordination and quickness to enjoy the physical side of life to the fullest. It is no wonder I took every opportunity to join sporting activities such as softball and basketball church leagues, white-water rafting with friends, snow skiing, waterskiing, swimming, bodysurfing, golfing, backpacking, along with running and cycling to keep myself busy and fit. This all took place outside of the forty hours a week on a tennis court, teaching and playing tennis. To say I was an active person would be an understatement. We all love to participate in activities where we excel and get compliments. I was no different. So when learning new activities, I would often spend extra time alone, practicing new techniques to make sure I would excel and look proficient when finally competing in the public eye.

When picking up the sport of triathlon, I found myself in unfamiliar territory. I was learning to go from a quick twitch, short sprint sport of tennis, squash, racquetball, or sprinting to first base, to the long distance sport of triathlon. I had confidence my physical abilities would allow me to excel, even though the effort was totally foreign to what I had ever experienced. In the beginning, I couldn't run more than a few kilometers before my muscles, lungs, and heart would complain and burn. The effort made me want to stop and take what seemed like a necessary and much needed rest. Did I really need to stop, take a rest, or was I just giving into my bodies complaint, regarding this new discipline?

If I did give in and stop to rest, this new activity would never feel good or improve to the level I was desiring. I would see other triathletes running, cycling, and swimming faster and longer without taking a rest and then even go some more. How did they do it? What did I need to do to be able to make my body respond the way I was desiring?

I went through the necessary process before my accident, and somehow, confidence pulled me through. I eventually learned how to build up my muscles and cardio (heart/lung) health and strength so I could go long and hard without stopping. I saw my times drop dramatically in less than a year, and as usual, my body did not let me down. Before long, I was finishing in front of seasoned age-group triathletes. I began setting very high goals for myself in my second year of competing. I was never satisfied with just being able to compete. I was so excited I started to share some of my new goals. Immediately, there were comments like, "That goal is not possible," or "You are starting triathlon too late," or "You are too old," or "You know how much time that would take," and finally, "You know how much money it takes to be a triathlete?" Ignoring these negative comments, I was able to improve and eventually prove most of them wrong.

With every athletic endeavor, there are setbacks of strained or torn muscles, sprains, or just overtraining while learning how to balance your effort to maximize improvement. I was learning this with triathlon as the excitement of my improvement would often lead me to overtrain. I would then strain my legs, shoulders, hip flexors, my back, or one time, plantar fasciitis flared-up in my feet. I learned much more about my body when I added triathlon to my tennis regimen. I found triathlon training and racing stimulating and exciting. I loved being on this new adventure. I wished, a number of times, I had discovered all this information when I was trying to make it as a tennis pro. My transforming body made me feel like I could accomplish anything. With my new intelligent training, I was able to drop my swim times to twenty-one minutes for 1,500 meters. My cycle was under an hour for forty kilometers, and my 10k run had dropped to an amazing 36:45 a few months before my accident. These were done as separate times, not back-to-back like in a triathlon. With proper training and discipline, my body continued to respond to any effort I required. This didn't really surprise me, as I anticipated my body would respond, and that my times would drop.

Was it easy to keep up the consistent training when I couldn't seem to run under forty-three minutes for ten kilometers or barely cycle up some of the steepest hills in Hong Kong early on in my training? No, it is never easy to be patient when acquiring new skills and proper techniques to propel you past those discouragements and seemingly impossible barriers. But when I started to reach small goals in one of the triathlon disciplines, it propelled me forward to believe I could achieve goals in the other two disciplines. When one sport is not going well in triathlon, you could take encouragement from the one that is going well.

This concept in triathlon was similar to what I discovered with tennis. In tennis, it would be one stroke going well while another one was lagging behind. It seemed with triathlon, there was always something positive to keep me motivated. I loved the positive challenge triathlon training presented. After a race, you could hear triathletes who'd had a bad race, still talk about the one discipline that had gone really well. Not getting lost in a large transition was something to be positive about. This was part of my instant love for the sport. Everyone seemed to relish one another's accomplishments and improvements.

I was so positive about triathlon that I drove a number of experienced triathletes crazy with my endless questions and seemingly impossible goals. One such goal was to be the first forty-to-forty-five age-group triathlete to go under two hours in an Olympic-distance event. They all said I was crazy as that was impossible for anyone that age to produce that kind of time. I never achieved this because of my accident, but nowadays, when you look at Olympic-distance triathlon times for the forty to forty-five age groups, there are times as low as one hour and fifty-three minutes, proving that I was not just dreaming. It was a possibility!

But what happens after your body is smashed up and paralyzed and your confidence has been crushed to a pulp? Those around you have the look of discouragement in their eyes when they view your condition. This doesn't make it any easier when you are doing your best to work yourself out of this deep dark hole. These same people used to be the ones believing you could do anything. Now you could see a new look in their eyes of despair. They no longer believed. They had lost any hope you could ever come back. You try to run and find your time for a ten-kilometer run twenty-five minutes slower than your personal best, no matter how hard you try to improve. Maybe the naysayers were right? The injuries while training are more frequent and more serious than before, and it seems like there is one setback after another to depress and discourage you from even wanting to believe things will get better. Before all this happened, I thought I could "do it all."

Cycling ended up being most comfortable for me, although I still had to walk my bike up many steep hills I used to ride up with confidence. I was lucky to ride 40k in ninety minutes rather than my previous hour time when I first started cycling again. There was no way to express my swimming experience. My arms rotating forward would send shooting pain through my spine, and my upper back muscles felt stiff as a board and full of glass shards.

The one thing that kept me going was the miracle of even being able to stand and walk. I would wake up every morning thanking God for allowing me to be on my feet. That very thought was enough to get me out of bed, in the pool, or on the road looking forward to what each new day would bring. The smallest improvement would encourage me to keep going. Everybody faces challenges and we all decide what each day's efforts will produce. Spinal cord damage definitely brings changes, and I had to accept that fact. My body would now handle the stress of training differently. The tightness in my leg muscles that spinal injuries bring on required more patience in the length and intensity of training. A tendon in my left calf muscle feels like a steel rod, making it impossible to use my feet the way I would like. I have had to adjust my run style to accommodate this. My body wasn't the same, but I was still blessed with teaching tennis again along with swimming, cycling, and running.

My swimming had become fairly fast before the accident. My kick had been extremely strong and one of the reasons for my improved swim times. Now I couldn't depend on a strong kick as my feet would cramp up, along with my calf muscles when swimming. It was almost impossible to point my toes without the cramping. There was no suppleness with my leg muscles, even though they didn't look much different.

To make up for my reduced kick, I still needed to find a way to improve my swim times. On my next trip to Australia, I researched and found an excellent swim coach. Another difficult learning experience awaited! Mark Fraser-Bell was the perfect coach to start me with a new stroke technique. He was a Christian who also believed God could do anything and knew miracles were possible. I wasn't sure what to think when he said I needed to start from the beginning, after accessing my swim. It sounded eerily familiar to when Dick Skeen, my tennis coach, had said the same thing. He said I wasn't even swimming in a straight line but snaking through the water.

How was that possible? I thought I was a pretty good swimmer before I came to him. I was hoping he would just tweak my swim stroke a little. I knew without my previous strong kick, I needed to improve my stroke, but snaking through the water? I was willing to follow Mark's instruction, but that didn't make it any easier. Humbling myself and starting over again like a beginner was not easy. Retraining my muscles to swim correctly was very difficult. Mark wouldn't let me get away with improper drills. Four thousand or more meters a day in the pool eventually showed some stroke improvement. After months of dedication and a new stroke, I saw my swim times improve. Swimming correctly allowed me to swim as fast as I did before the accident without much of a kick. I finished fourth and seventh out of the water for my age group at two of the following ITU World Championships. Even with tight leg muscles I had found a way to swim fast again. All made possible because of Mark's dedicated instruction and his absolute belief in me.

Cycling improved quickly since it was a no-impact sport. When I first started triathlon, I research to learn how to cycle correctly. I knew my run would take weeks, months, and maybe years to redevelop, so I concentrated on my bike skills. This ended up giving me one of the fastest times in my age-group races. This, along with my swim, would hopefully give me a substantial lead heading into the final run leg.

I was fortunate to spend time training on the Gold Coast in Australia with my sons and other professional triathletes. The Gold Coast also turned out to be a favorite place for former professional cyclists to retire. We would enjoy riding these outer hinterland roads together in the early mornings. This region provided wonderful and challenging rides. Once leaving the coast and heading west, there were some difficult steep hills. All of us lived near the beach, so most of our rides would take us from the beach, then up the various valleys where the serious hills were located and over the various mountain ranges. The roads were mostly empty with beautiful scenery and farmland stretching out toward the hinterland. Some of the farmers would set out their local fruits on tables beside the road. It was an honor pay system so we could stop and get some refreshment near the halfway point of our rides. We only needed to drop a few two-dollar Aussie coins in their paybox.

The shortest bike rides were 60ks with the longest ones stretching 100 to 120 kilometers to the west. This was the main reason my cycling improved to the level it did, while living and training in Australia. Local and former professional cyclists were friendly, and I enjoyed meeting up with them and their groups out on the valley roads. They were willing to share many of their cycling techniques, which improved my cycling even more. Trying to keep up with them was a stretch for me, almost impossible. At times, they would begin racing each other back to the coast, and I would do my best to keep them in sight. Every time I started to feel great about my cycling, some former Tour de France rider in his early to late seventies would fly by spinning his wheels effortlessly in an easy gear. There was always someone to chase down on the Gold Coast to keep me humble and improving. I loved every minute there and couldn't wait to get up each morning! If I had my choice, I would still be living on the Gold Coast. Like their promotional advertisements stated, "Beautiful one Day, Perfect the Next!" After more than seven years living there, it felt like the truth, not just a promotional ad.

Now came my run training. I continued to improve my swim and cycle skills, with the strategy to have a decent lead after the bike in a race. This always gave me hope to finish well and start winning a few races again. While racing in Kota Kinabalu on the island of Borneo in Malaysia, I ran into a top middle-distance runner from Australia who was there to compete. After striking up a conversation and swimming together, he said he would help me learn to run a little faster. He indicated my stride was too long, and I should try increasing my cadence. Cadence, being the number of times your feet hit the ground in one minute. My stride was too long and was therefore wearing out my large muscles too soon on a long run. He said I should time my cadence to get it up to at least 186 steps per minute. This seemed impossible at first with my tight leg muscles, but I watched him run effortlessly with a fast cadence and listened closely to everything he was willing to share.

I spent the next six months increasing my cadence and found my run improving. I was researching everything possible to improve. A number of world-class runners helped me look at my body position, relaxation, staying on my toes more when I pushed off, along with faster cadence and special breathing techniques. My run would never be like before, but I was doing my best to improve. No one can ask more of themselves than that.

Is triathlon easy? No! But is it rewarding? Yes! The triathlon community is amazing and encouraging. Everyone is fit and willing to help everyone else who is committed to show up, do their best, and be part of their love of the sport. Friends from this community tend to stay connected through the years, and I have found this to be true for me. Triathlon was the one community who encouraged me the most when I left the hospital. Everyone was positive and wanted to see me back racing well again. They never gave up on me, and I was inspired to continue training hard and improve every time I entered a race.

Maybe I was just fortunate to connect with the right people. Even Gold Coast Triathlete bike shop in Australia, was a wonderful contact! Every time I dropped by the shop, they made me feel welcomed to just hang around and visit. Noel, who owned the shop, never failed to ask how my training was going and take a genuine interest in my results. He would sometimes mention he had seen me running down the Gold Coast Highway and say how good I was starting to look. These little comments of encouragement inspired me to make sure I always ran my best. I always tried a little harder to run correctly after these positive compliments.

Does it make it any easier knowing how to reach a goal? I have learned along the way that it always takes the same gut-wrenching effort and consistency, regardless of your knowledge or conditioning. Months or a few years is required to build up the necessary balance of anaerobic (muscle) strength and aerobic cardio (heart/lung) strength before the mental side can be employed during a race. Mental strength eventually makes the difference between winning or losing an event or, for that matter, even finishing anything difficult in our life. No matter how strong you are with your anaerobic or cardio, without the necessary mental skills, you will never reach your potential. This is never easy as it takes consistency, discipline, and concentration to reach any goal. If you try too hard, you tend to tighten up, actually causing you to slow you down. When you relax too much and take it easy, your times will also slow down. It is a matter of balance, and this is where the mental side makes the difference in average or great results.

Unless you are a professional athlete who gets paid to train, there will always be distractions and disruptions to take us away from our planned schedules. Being able to adjust to the disruptions will eventually determine success or failure. I learned very early on that when things come up to disrupt my plans, instead of doing nothing, do something! If you only have time for a ten-minute swim, go swim. Many people I have come across will say, "What's the point, it is only ten minutes," and kill their swim training altogether for that day. I have found doing a little exercise helps you stay on track to reach your end goal. Go do something; it will revitalize your body, but more importantly, it will revitalize your mental state and outlook. With this view on training, you will never give up on yourself or your goals.

Disruptions and disturbances were ever more frequent during my recovery. Returning to work and maintaining a regular training schedule was difficult. Every involvement seemed to be fraught with tension or controversy. Life seemed so smooth in the past, even with the setbacks thrown my way.

I was forced to release one of my assistant tennis instructors, and then Marina Club management said continuing to be both director of tennis and head tennis pro was too much for me to handle, with my apparent disability. Personally, I think they were just trying to save some money and use my accident as an excuse. My director of tennis salary was suddenly gone, and without my knowing it, the Marina Club held out on my sizable bonus until it was too late for me to legally appeal. Sleep was difficult with my legs shaking so much, so I was never completely rested at the start of each new day. I now had to fit my rehabilitation into my already tight schedule. This made everything seem like a mad rush. Tension and stress became part of my daily routine.

This was a crazy time of adjusting to my new life. Getting better and solving the inevitable daily problems, which arose, was almost too much to handle. After a year of recovery and finally feeling my tennis lessons and programs were revitalized, another roadblock appeared on the horizon. It took fourteen months to reorganize the tennis program, and when I felt everything was very much back on track, Aberdeen Marina Club hired a new general manager. He was an American, and I thought that would be positive for me. I also believed there would be a natural connection between us. I couldn't have been more mistaken, as it wasn't long before he called me into his office. He said a club as prestigious as Aberdeen Marina Club could not have a disabled head tennis pro. He gave me one month to pack up and leave.

I had two immediate emotions well up inside. First emotion was to get on my knees and beg for him to change his mind and let me keep my position. I felt I needed to keep my job to provide for my family. The second emotion was to jump across his huge desk and beat the living daylights out of him for calling me disabled. I was spending my free time in rehab and training so I could be 100 percent fit again, and he had the nerve to call me disabled? I was glad to have held both emotions in check and just sat there, stunned. This was a huge roadblock for me, especially after I had worked so hard to rebuild the tennis program. The Marina Club eventually asked me to stay on for the rest of the year. This was unexpectedly extended because it took this new general manager four months to find a high-level replacement. Hong Kong has a unique way to reward those who treat others poorly. After the way the new general manager had treated me and a few others, he found himself without work six months after I left. Maybe my close connection with the owner's families and still teaching some of their children had something to do with his release.

How many more disruptions did I need to go through before life would get back on an even keel? This was all happening between the Manchester and Wellington World Championships. Each day was a struggle to find time for my physical training and rehabilitation while making a living for my family. When people tell me they don't have time to take care of themselves, I know that is just not true. It just feels like the truth. We are just too worn out, discouraged, or tired to get up the gumption to do anything.

That is what I felt like before heading to New Zealand for the 1994 ITU World Championships. I was still trying to do it all by myself. This was just like before God's miracle of saving my life and hopefully waking me up. Would I ever learn?

Wellington, New Zealand, 1994

How easy it was for me to drop back into my hectic lifestyle where I began feeling more and more in charge of my life. In the process of adopting this busy schedule again, I also felt like I could "do it all,' just by sheer willpower. Even with this weight of spinal cord damage dragging my body down, I was amazed at how well I started doing activities again. I knew I didn't stand as tall (three inches shorter), and I didn't quite meet up to the standards required for photoshoots and commercial endorsements like I did before. But I was alive, seeing improvements every month. These improvements could be measured accurately in my triathlon training and racing. My tennis lessons were still providing income for our family expenses. My damaged body never stopped talking to me, but I was on a roll. Even though my ego had taken a big hit, I was feeling pretty good about myself. When will I ever learn to trust in God more than myself?

I was committed now more than ever after Manchester to improve. I kept to my regimented schedule of being up by 3:45 a.m.

to cycle, maybe get in a "fast" mile run, then off to the Marina Club. My teaching schedule was increasing in the morning; then running, swimming, and the gym at noon before finishing with a few lessons in the afternoon. My running was still struggling, but I added a run toward the top of the hill behind Hong Kong Country Club toward Ocean Park and down the far side, back to the Marina Club.

This new run route involved the staircase under the tram line, heading over the top of the steep hill toward Ocean Park. This staircase run completed three times a week did more for my run strength than anything else I did. The stairs began just a short distance from Deep Water Bay Road behind the Hong Kong Country Club. It headed straight upward for a considerable distance. The stairs were directly under the tram, and people riding the gondola to Ocean Park would often yell down their encouragements as I ran the stairs. Once the stairs ended, the concrete path would undulate for 400 meters before going upward through a small valley connected to the back side of the hill and back entrance to Ocean Park. Once on the other side, it was all downhill toward the Marina Club. I was able to work on my uphill and downhill strength at the same time. It took months before I was able to run the entire staircase without stopping. More than once, I had strangers stop me in downtown Hong Kong and ask me if I was that crazy guy running the stairs under the tramline. They recognized me because of my ever-present mustache.

Because of this committed training schedule, I was able to become the Hong Kong and Asian Veteran Triathlon Champion again. Two more of my goals were achieved. Now I was looking for even greater goals. I wanted to have some specific times for the Olympic-Distance Triathlon of around two hours and ten minutes. My ego was so big, I really thought I could do it. At the same time, I was coming to the realization that my residual spinal cord damage might just hold me back from achieving this difficult goal. I was doing everything I could to improve, as I looked forward to Wellington, New Zealand, the site of the 1994 ITU World Championship.

Nineteen ninety-four was turning out to be a good year for me triathlon-wise and with my improvement. I came to realize that tennis competition was probably not in my future, at least not nearly to the level I had played before. I was, however, able to play some doubles and found a small group of local tennis pros who put up with my awkward and slow speed around the court. This allowed me to play tennis once or twice a week. I still had my racket skills, and with only half the court to cover and understanding partners, tennis still provided a level of "frustrated" enjoyment. Triathlon was a way for me to measure my improvements and gave me inspiration to keep moving forward. Knowing my run would probably never completely return to my former level, I continued to improve my swim and bike techniques and times.

Fortunately, one of the swim coaches at the Marina Club would often do his personal workouts during the noon break. This was the same time I would come to the pool for my daily swim. We became friends, and it wasn't long before he took an interest in my swimming. He spent a significant amount of time giving me tips on improving my swim technique. With him and Mark/Fraser Bell in Australia, 1994 saw my times improve more than I thought were possible. I can't thank them enough for their willingness to share their expertise.

Me, Brian, and Donnie at HK International Triathlon 1994

While I was improving my swim times, my 3:45 a.m. bike training was paying huge dividends. My sons would still get up with me and cycle on the roads through Clearwater and Junk Bay, when I was training in Hong Kong. Most of the time, we went the other direction from our house remembering my accident. This new direction took us back toward downtown Hong Kong. We headed mostly downhill from our house toward Junk Bay. Junk Bay used to be a large bay where there was a ferry terminal. Since we had arrived in Hong Kong, they had filled in most of the bay connecting one of the small islands. Developments for more housing, large factories, businesses, and shopping centers were built on this added land. The new TVB studios and film lots were built on the former island portion and became the site where I did all my future work as a commentator. We were fortunate to train in that area because it was mostly beautiful smooth new empty roads. Garbage trucks often passed us going to and from a huge garbage dump and landfill site on the far side of the island.

This route still provided challenging hills to work on our strength, but also some long flat areas to work on our time trial skills. By this time, both Don and Brian had become excellent cyclists, and it was impossible for me to keep up. If they really took off and wanted to drop me, I was left behind. They were not only strong but also had developed cycling skills to handle the technical sections of the road. One morning, while heading down the steep hill to Junk Bay, it started to slightly mist. Brian had already gone through the roundabout at the bottom of the hill, and Donnie was just in view flying away from me. Being fearful of another fall, I had slowed significantly with the damp roads. I didn't want to slide off my bike again with the drizzle making the roads slick. I watched with dismay as Donnie went into the large roundabout at full speed, literally sliding around the corner with no apparent concern. I was surprised at his ability to handle his bike and not hit the deck.

Both sons inspired me to improve, pushing me to regain my former confidence on the bike. I knew my base strength may not come back the same, but I was convinced that improved cycling techniques would allow me to still lower my cycle times. Now with both my cycle and swim times improving, my run would not be as much of a handicap during a triathlon. I had a simple plan. Get a lead on the swim, increase that lead on the bike, then hold off the faster runners. This was the only way I was able to win the Hong Kong and Asian Triathlon age-group titles again.

The summer of 1994 was again spent in different places around the world for Donnie, Brian, and myself. We were all signed up to race the World's in Wellington, New Zealand. I was excited to show my son's how much I had improved my fitness and racing ability. They had both been improving their triathlons, and we were looking forward to meeting up "Down Under."

Before I knew it, I was Down Under in New Zealand for the next World Championship. Donnie and Brian were also flying in from different points around the globe, and both arrived in great shape. Wellington, New Zealand, known as the windy city and Sister City to San Francisco, was the site chosen for the fifth Triathlon World Championships. Wellington is located on the southern end of the North Island, nestled up against hills on one side and Lambton Harbor and beautiful Oriental Bay on the other side. We arrived one week before Race Day to acclimatize ourselves to weather conditions and the race course.

After training in different places around the world, we all arrived safely in spite of the extreme wind conditions. The wind was Chicago windy and cold. When landing at the airport, the person sitting beside me remarked he was looking out the side window almost straight down the runway on our approach. The plane was really bumping up and down. The side wind was so severe the pilot had to crab or bring the plane in at what seemed like a forty-five-degree angle to offset the wind. Just before touchdown, he straightened the plane up for a perfect landing, to everyone's relief. This was just a prelude to the extreme wind conditions everyone faced in the coming few days. Triathletes were everywhere, going through their last-minute training programs. Two triathletes were knocked off their bikes by the severe wind in separate incidents—one breaking an arm and the other, an elite pro breaking his collarbone. It is difficult to express the disappointment one feels after a year of training hard for a huge event. Sad to say, neither was able to participate in the Championships after making that long trip to New Zealand.

One section of the bike course was so windy while I was on a training run, I had to help a cyclist push his bike back around the corner of Evans Bay Road to get out of the crazy wind and back to Oriental Parade so he could continue his ride. It was one of those, "Walk at a forty-five-degree angle" type of winds.

Everyone worried about race day and how these wild winds would affect the race. For the third year in a row, there was again grumbling in the transition area about the temperature of the water for the swim. The jokes were going around about the iceberg that must be just under the surface. The water temperature was "again" around thirteen degrees Celsius.

I went down to the harbor with my sons for a trial swim the day before the race to check out the swim course. A number of professional triathletes we had trained with in Australia were standing on the seawall, including Miles Stuart, former world champion from the Gold Coast. I stepped down in the water almost to my waist when Miles looked down and asked, "How is it?"

Without thinking, I said, "It's not too bad." Five elite triathletes immediately jumped off the sea wall into Lambton Harbor. Well, you have never seen five triathletes come up so fast, exiting the water shivering. The look they gave me was not the best as I remarked, "Sorry about that, I forgot that I don't have much feeling from my waist down."

While spending the week training there, we fell in love with the citizens of Wellington. They were remarkably friendly and willing to help every visiting triathlete at a moment's notice. Donnie was caught in a minor accident which wasn't his fault and slightly damaged his bike, but thankfully not his body. Some of the locals who witnessed his accident helped him get his bike repaired in a couple of hours at a local bike shop. The citizens of Wellington were wonderful and made our stay there even more special. Over 1,500 triathletes had invaded their city. This did not include the numerous officials, coaches, and accompanying family members bringing the total number of visitors to over 10,000. For any city to host a World Championship is a major undertaking. A World Triathlon Championship literally shuts down major sections of city roads on race day.

Being in Wellington reminded me of how all the dedicated training not only allowed me to race at another world championship but also the opportunity to visit another famous city and meet up with many of my friends in the triathlon community. You always made new friends and ended up making lifetime memories, which never fails to bring a smile to your face. I wouldn't have traded one early morning workout to sleep-in and miss this adventure.

The ITU World Championships are always unique in their own cultural way, especially at the opening ceremonies. New Zealand did not disappoint as the local aboriginals arrived to perform their traditional dance. Before the finish, they came into the crowd and invited a number of triathletes on stage for their final Maori Haka Dance. For those who have never seen the Haka, it is a depiction of their frightful war dance done to intimidate their enemies. With their face tattoos and face paint, it can be terrifying. Brian was selected with a number of other triathletes to face off with one of the dancers. They performed directly in front of the triathletes, coming forward so close with their scowling faces, it would frighten their enemies into submission. Brian was fortunate to experience this, up close and personal, and he was presented with a spear. Another wonderful experience being able to compete at a World Championship. Coming away with that ceremonial spear for his experience made the buildup to race day even more stimulating and memorable.

Race day arrived again at 4:00 a.m. for the 1,500 triathletes. We were greeted by a glorious clear blue day with no wind in sight. We couldn't believe how fortunate we were to be looking at the best day we had seen since arriving in Wellington. Nothing could change the water in the harbor as it was still freezing cold. We were all resigned to what awaited us in the Harbor, whether we liked it or not. A few elite triathletes went into hypothermia shortly before finishing the 1,500-meter swim. Their body fat was so low, they barely made it out of the Bay on their own. Their severe shivering made them unable to start the bike portion of the race. I was happy with my swim, even though the first few minutes were spent dealing with agonizing pain shooting through my sinus. There was some solace as you knew every other triathlete was facing the same discomfort. Still a few pounds overweight and the ever-present lack of sensitivity, I did not feel the effects of the water temperature in my lower extremities like the other triathletes were feeling. Wow, the sensation of your face, feeling like it will explode is hard to describe. Again, the only solace came from knowing everyone else was experiencing the same pain. We were all glad to finally exit the water after swimming for twenty to thirty minutes in that freezing bay.

The bike course included a serious climb up through Charles Plimmer Park and Mount Victoria. With no wind in sight to knock you off, there were no complaints. This was like heaven after the earlier training rides in strong gusting winds, pushing hard against our bikes. My bike ride felt strong, and my result was very similar to Manchester, giving me an excellent bike time. I came into the bike-run transition in a much better position than I thought would be possible.

I was having an excellent race and looked forward to see how my run training would work out this time in Wellington. There were a few competitors I hoped to finish ahead of this time around at the Worlds. I took off on the ten-kilometer run feeling great, definitely the best I had felt since my recovery. I was hoping and praying I wouldn't have the same urges, which took me off the course in Manchester and regularly seemed to happen at my other races.

The run was laid out as a two-lap course—two five-kilometer loops where you could see the other competitors going out or coming back three times during the run. I was pleased when I saw I had a big lead on the few competitors I wanted to finish ahead of. When I went around the five-kilometer cone I anxiously looked to see if they had gained any time on me. When we eventually passed going in opposite directions, I was close to the 6k marker, which meant I had a two-kilometer or nine-minute lead. I was thrilled as I knew it would be impossible for them to bridge that gap before the finish line.

More adrenaline poured into my system with the large crowds lining the road, screaming their encouragements. My run felt great.

For a while, I thought I was going to get through this race, without another problem. Then suddenly, two minutes further down the road, "It hit again." It couldn't have been a worse place on the route for this to happen. I thought, *Is there ever a good place in a major event?* On my left was an eight-feet-high solid white wall; and on my right, were a few thousand spectators lining the road, cheering us on. Nowhere to even leave the course and hide. I was trapped! Just then, I noticed a door in the white wall just ahead. As I ran up to the door, I was praying it would be unlocked. I needed some place to hide and have some privacy. I was desperate! I wanted to do well in the race but also wanted to find a way to finish without another embarrassing moment. I had made the decision to race knowing this possibility could arise. Now I had to deal with it.

Luck was on my side as I could see the door was not only unlocked but also slightly ajar. Surely people living or working there had been peering out at the race moments before. I stopped running, looked at all the spectators, peered inside the wall, and saw it was a nursery with plants everywhere. They were mostly low shrubbery plants, but as I stepped inside, I found some taller plants along the wall to the right. I had no other option. So I found my way behind the taller plants and just in time. While hiding down low, I could hear voices coming in my direction. I couldn't think of a more embarrassing position to be found in and again prayed I wouldn't be noticed. Rushing to get my gear back on, I didn't even look to see if anyone saw me. I rushed out the door weighing less and feeling more energized. Thankful to be returning to the course, I continued my race.

As you can expect, my run actually felt better now that I was a few pounds lighter. I took off with renewed energy, going around the 7.5 kilometer cone, heading for the finish line still 2.5 kilometers in the distance. I lost a little more than four minutes during my nursery escapade. I was now anxious to see how much time I had lost to those few triathletes I was trying to finish ahead of. Two minutes after rounding the turning cone, I saw them heading toward me going the other way. I had lost four and a half minutes but still had over a four-minute lead. I smiled to myself as I saw them glance at their watches. They knew running could be my Achilles heel. Like me, they were looking to see how much time they had gained on me since the 5k marker. They must have thought I was struggling with my run because they had cut the gap from nine minutes to four minutes in 2.7k. I am sure they believed they would catch me just before the finish line. But I knew the truth; they could not catch me. I was feeling better now and picked up my pace, finishing four minutes in front of them. As usual, I tried to keep my excursions off the course discreet. This was another episode for Donnie, Brian, and me to laugh about later while lying around at the hotel.

I jumped into the cold Lambton Harbor when I finished, for my initial clean up. Then to the outside showers to finish my wash. I couldn't have cared less and couldn't stop smiling about my results while thinking of that wonderful open door. It made me think of that riddle, "When is a door not a door? When it is 'a jar!'" I was so thankful that day it was ajar. I had made the decision to train and race, even if I could expect many more embarrassing situations. I had finished in the top 20 percent after losing that four minutes. I ended up about the same as I had finished at the Walt Disney World's race before my accident. I was thrilled with my improvement and was determined to do what I could to keep my triathlons moving in that direction.

Before the awards ceremony that evening, I was walking down a wide sweeping carpeted spiral staircase when clonus reared its ugly head again, causing one of my exhausted legs to jerk out in front of me like a military "goose step." I did the splits, tumbled, and slid down the stairs before coming to a halt, startling many of the participants standing around. Brian was there with that quizzically little smile, viewing another one of his dad's laughable situations. He then helped me up from another memorable moment.

As long as I could keep the humor in these unexpected but inevitable happenings, I could keep racing and moving forward with an active lifestyle. I was still placing too much importance on my own efforts, forgetting the many life lessons my parents and spiritual mentors had tried to instill in me. One extra pushup, one extra situp, run an extra mile, or cycle up one more hill was in my DNA. I still didn't understand where true victory came from as I pressed forward, trying to accomplish everything from my own brute strength and mental effort to "do it all."

Pineapple Respite

Phuket, Thailand, is one of the most idyllic places in the world to spend a holiday and relax away from the worries of this fast-paced life we find ourselves in. I had been fortunate to enjoy this tropical paradise on a few holidays and also race a few triathlons there when I was completely healthy. Phuket is also one of the greatest places to hold a triathlon, except for the incredible heat and humidity wilting plants and athletes in the middle of the day. The atmosphere is idyllic with warm late-afternoon breezes blowing through the palm trees and rubber plantations at the Laguna Phuket Resort. The resort is a beautiful complex of five hotels all on the shores of a very large common lagoon. Four of the resorts also have ocean frontage, looking out over the Andaman Sea. Three of the hotels—the Laguna Beach Club, Dusit Thani, and the Sheraton are five-star, while the Banyan Tree is six-star. The Alamanda located on the inland lagoon is rated as a four-star, although it feels more like many of the five-star hotels around the world.

With tropical pools at every hotel and the freedom to enjoy each hotel's amenities during your stay, Phuket certainly made for an exotic experience for every competitor and their accompanying family and friends. Thai hospitality is internationally known as they never disappoint. Smiles never stopped, no matter where you went. The many restaurants offered stunningly prepared spicy and exotic cuisine, which would stimulate your palate and bring a smile to your face.

The organization was everything you would expect from a Hawaiian Ironman qualifying race. The swim was 1,500-meter ocean swim in the Andaman Sea. Then exiting to run across the beach, over a small sand hill, you entered the lagoon for a final 300m swim to the other side. This is where the bike transition area was setup. The bike course was fifty-five kilometers, up over some very steep testing

I DO IT ALL

hills. Once past the ten-kilometer marker, it was mostly undulating secluded roads through rubber plantations, past small villages with numerous children and adults lining the road, cheering us on.

Make no mistake about it, this was Thailand, and by the halfway point of the 55k bike course, you start feeling the heat. Even the professional triathletes talked about the foreboding anticipation of running their final twelve kilometers nearing the midday heat of Phuket. After finishing the 55k bike, the run awaited. Beginning at the Laguna Beach Club, you would pass by all the other resorts during the finishing twelve kilometers. First on paved roads, then down sandy country roads, through farmland before turning left down a deserted dirt trail, you would pass beside banana and pineapple fields, then across a running stream and on and on, with more sand roads and trails until finally coming to the Banyan Tree Hotel entrance and, with relief, the finish line. In spite of the difficulty of the race and the exhaustion that everyone felt at the finish, every competitor had a smile on their face as they feasted on tropical fruit and snacks provided in the recovery area. Ice packs to cool off overheated, exhausted muscles and complimentary massage made for a day every triathlete would fondly remember and look forward to repeating again, in coming years.

As for my race, all went really well as I was trying to qualify for the Hawaiian Ironman. I felt I had a real chance to qualify, after some excellent training and preparation. I enjoyed an excellent swim, allowing me to come into the bike transition in first place in my category. The bike course was as difficult as it promised to be, but I felt I had a strong enough ride to maintain and maybe increase my lead. I ended up finishing with one of the fastest bike splits among all age groupers. I was feeling good while still holding onto first place. When it came to the run, I figured I had enough of a lead from the swim and bike to go out steady at the start and hopefully build my speed little by little, winning the race and qualifying for Hawaii.

I couldn't have asked for more as I felt pretty good running past the four resorts, then onto the sandy roads splitting the golf courses. At the 5k marker, I started looking around for a place with a little privacy again. I was trying to qualify for Hawaii, and now this? I could have been discouraged, but I was here in marvelous Thailand on my feet doing what I loved. I started to walk while doing my best to maintain control. There were some Thai village homes up against the road to my right, and what turned out to be a large young pineapple field on the left. If you were to squat down in the middle of the pineapple field your shoulders and head would still be visible to everyone. Not ideal for hiding!

I walked on the road for a minute or so before I realized I had no other option but to head left into the pineapple field. As I looked to find a suitable place in the field, other triathletes began yelling, "You are going the wrong way." Waving them off, I headed out to hide in the middle of the young pineapple plants. This took me quite a-ways into the pineapple crops before I could take care of myself. This was another weird experience, as I could see the farmers on the far side of this large field to my left looking in my direction, along with the triathletes on the other side running down the road who had asked me where I was going. I started laughing, looking at my predicament, fruitlessly (no pun intended), trying to hide in a pineapple field. I took care of business but, in the process, lost huge amounts of time in the race. Laughing and grateful for the opportunity to continue racing, I got up and exited the field to finish the race, with some dignity. I still thought, *How could life get any better,* even though these moments could be expected.

Once I finished and the results were posted, I saw I failed to qualify for Hawaii by one place. The time I lost in the Pineapple field cost me the race and my spot in Hawaii. Did it bother me? Maybe for a moment, but nothing can ever take away the joy I have, every time I am fit enough to line up for another race. Especially in an exotic place like Phuket, pineapple field and all! I felt like the luckiest person in the race.

Mango Shakes, Eating Pavement and Beautiful Subic Bay

The Asian Championships were scheduled to be held in Subic Bay, Philippines. We had raced here a few times before, and we all loved the amazing hospitality of the Filipino people. I felt I was going to have a good race as my training was going exceptionally well. I had found a way to avoid the usual toilet escapades by not eating for a few days before race day. Maybe not the most advisable way to prepare, using energy gels and proper hydration, like energy drinks and water, I was able to race well in short distance triathlons. With that problem mostly solved, there always seemed to be plenty of surprises to contend with.

I should not have been surprised when I had to deal with another unexpected situation. During the cycle portion of the race, I had another "over the bars" incident. To this day, I have no explanation. I was again racing for another Asian age-group title and had developed a substantial lead following a great swim. Leaving the transition, my cycling felt extra good, passing a number of younger age-group competitors. For some reason, my cycling was on fire. With only ten kilometers to go, I was able to pick up even more speed and drop the few much younger triathletes, who had stayed near me. I had moved up to seventh place among all age groups with only four kilometers left to the bike-run transition.

I felt like I was flying when I came around a sweeping right-hand corner. I stood on my pedals to pick up even more speed, when my pedals suddenly spun with no resistance. This threw me forward over my handlebars. For a moment, I thought, *Lucky me*, as I found myself still on my bike but looking straight down at my front wheel. My hips were lying on the handlebars as I desperately held on. For a split second, I thought I might be able to save it and not crash. Unfortunately, just as quickly, my front wheel slightly turned sideways, bringing my bike to an abrupt halt.

It was like hitting that hole in the road back in Hong Kong. I was instantly vaulted over my handlebars, landing on the road with an almighty whack. As I rolled and slid, I was thinking, *Not again.* Once I slid to a stop, I checked myself out for anything broken, and luck was on my side, I felt okay. I couldn't help but think, *How can this be happening again?* Other than the skin taken off my hands, arm, shoulder, back, and knees, I was okay to continue racing. There were Subic officials and police monitoring that very corner, and they all witnessed the crash. They came running up, insisting I be still, as they were calling for medical help. I waved them off, yelling, "Not now." I wanted to finish the race as I only had a few kilometers to the bike-run transition, and I knew I had a substantial lead in my age group. Nothing was going to stop me from finishing this race! I rushed back to my bike and found the chain was off the chain rings. I wrestled for a few moments to get my chain back on. By the time I finished with the chain, I was covered with black grease mixed with blood. It was spread over my arms and hands. As hard as I tried, I couldn't get my handlebars to move and decided to ride the last few kilometers, with handlebars twisted at a thirty-degree angle. This made me a strange sight when I finally arrived at the transition area. I was a sight to behold, covered in blood and grease, and handlebars skewed at an angle.

Some of the spectators joked later that being American, they would expect red, white, and blue; but red, white and black was a surprise. A triathlete who saw me racing from behind said I looked a mess with road rash, tore up tri-clothes with blood on my upper back, shoulder and arm and black grease on my hands and forearms.

During the run, I came up to a Hong Kong junior triathlete and saw it was Christine Bailey, the daughter of a fellow veteran tri-athlete and good friend. Christine was a great runner but was struggling a little on her run because this was her first Olympic-distance race ending with a hot humid ten-kilometer run. I encouraged her to pick it up and run with me. To my amazement, she immediately picked up her pace and ran her last 4ks looking fresh. She started her race in an earlier wave, so she took off for the finish line when I still had my final 2.5k loop to run. She was a beautiful runner, and as I watched her glide away from me, I wished down deep inside I could run like that again.

I finished the race, won my age group, Asian Title and had a fairly high overall finish. Cleaning out my wounds later in medical tent was not fun, but I was still pleased with my race. It remains a mystery why my pedals spun out, throwing me over the handlebars. I have finished every triathlon I have started and was pleased to have been able to finish this one in Subic Bay.

I DO IT ALL

Noosa Triathlon over Again

Noosa Multisports Festival is one of the largest triathlons in the world. Besides being a huge triathlon, it is staged on the beautiful Sunshine Coast of Australia. A complete week of racing is organized featuring ocean swims, aquathlons, road runs, kids triathlons, and finally culminating in an ITU Olympic-Distance Triathlon. The professional race is an ITU sanctioned race bringing together the world's best triathletes. The age group triathlon race brings together triathletes nineteen years of age and up to seventy-five up in five-year blocks such as thirty-five to thirty-nine and so on. Noosa's transition area is so large that you must rehearse your swim-to-bike and bike-to-run transition a few times, or you could easily get lost trying to find your bike among the many rows of bike racks. I have seen age groupers spend as much as four minutes trying to find their bike while running up and down the forty-meter-long rows, searching for their equipment, screaming out in frustration.

Noosa is a great race, very well-organized and one of my favorites. The swim is usually wetsuit approved for age groupers so your swim is pretty fast. The bike is basically an out and back course with a long, challenging hill on the outer portion. The run is flat and fast for the runners who can run but very hot by the time us age groupers finally hit Noosa's hot humid roads. Very little shade accompanied us on the run but the crowds made up for it. Houses and holiday apartments lined the run course. Many of the residences use their hoses to cool down the triathletes as they ran by. The atmosphere is electric, as spectators cheer on the slowest of triathletes just as much as the professionals. The commentators makes a point to announce every triathlete by name as they came in and out of transition and ten kilometers later finally crossing the finish line.

This was a race where I was fortunate on the run. When my usual urge arrived, I saw a portable toilet a short way off the course and was able to take care of myself in a modest fashion. No tall buildings, walls, or wide boulevards to contend with in Noosa. I could run with dignity while finishing the Noosa race. But earlier in the race, I did have a problem.

With the huge crowd of spectators screaming and yelling, it was easy to get overly excited while racing and forget yourself. I had the best swim ever for me following my accident at 22:30 for 1,500 meters and came through with a very fast bike split. Training on serious hills on the Gold Coast had paid huge dividends, allowing me to pull away from dozens of competitors on the long steep uphill portion before the twenty-kilometer turn. I reached over eighty kilometers per hour on the downhill but got a little nervous toward the bottom when I saw another competitor had come off his bike. Still excited at how good my cycling had felt, my adrenaline was pumping. Cycling toward the transition area and the massive screaming crowds, easily numbering a few thousand, got the better of me as I rode up to the dismount line.

Our mind is a strange thing. Your mind always remembers your best and, given enough leeway, can convince you of things, which are no longer true. This is what happened to me when I dismounted my bike. I had already taken my feet out of my shoes and had swung my right leg over the saddle, ready to hit the road running. With hundreds of people screaming and yelling their encouragements, I forgot that I couldn't run as fast as I could before my accident. I was going too fast for my present condition. So when my feet hit the ground, I couldn't catch up to the speed my bike was traveling. My legs just wouldn't go that fast. I lost my balance, caught my right foot in the spokes of my back wheel, and the rest was history. I somehow was propelled forward over my bike, catching my left foot in the spokes of my front wheel. I went sprawling and tumbling forward right in front of hundreds of spectators and the announcing podium. My bike shoes flew off my bike pedals in different directions. I was separated by a few meters from my bike when I finally came to a stop and a crumpled heap. I could hear the announcer say, "Wow there, fellow, are you all right? Take it easy," just to spotlight my situation.

Trying to be as cool as you can be in front of that many spectators is hard while gathering up your scattered gear, with skin scraped off and toes on both feet bleeding. I was trying to look as cool as I could in front of so many spectators. I tried to look like I was tough and would be okay. Finally arriving to my transition bike rack, I had to make a decision. Would I continue to race or retire with bloody toes and skinned-up body? The Noosa officials in the transition area were encouraging me to continue. Carefully putting on my shoes, I headed out for the run. Up to that dismount disaster, I was having a fast race. The crowd remembered who I was when I exited transition to begin the final 10k run. The roar of encouragement from the crowd really lifted my spirits, and I couldn't help but smile as I headed down the road. I hardly noticed my sliced-up toes to finish the day with my fastest Olympic-distance time since December 1991 of two hours eighteen minutes. I didn't have a podium finish for my age group but what a wonderful memory, knowing I had again broken through the two-hour twenty- minute barrier. Would I have had a podium finish without the exciting dismount? I don't know and didn't really care as I have always loved being around so many fit, encouraging friends and fellow athletes in wonderful Noosa.

Australian National Championships, Mooloolaba

The Land Down Under is one of the best places on planet Earth for triathlon training and racing. Soft white-sand beaches with a warm ocean always inviting you to stay forever. I arrived at the Mooloolaba Triathlon excited to race, and with great expectations. I had continued my hill running in Hong Kong before coming back to Australia for more acupuncture, osteo, and massage. Considering everything, I felt great and thought I might be able to challenge the best Australian age-groupers, secretly hoping for a third-place finish in my age category. First and second place were virtually impossible for me as the ITU World Champion in my age group and his close rival were in the race. Mooloolaba is on the sunshine coast north of Brisbane and Noosa. Beauty of the east coast of Australia never fails to draw you in and make you feel at peace with the world. Race organizers in Australia are professional and make everyone feel welcomed and important when they arrive at the check-in desk. The race was Olympic distance comprising a 1.5 kilometer ocean swim, a 40 kilometer cycle on their local motorway. Then a two-lap ten-kilometer run, four times navigating a difficult hill with views of the ocean, separated by lush-green grass parkland.

My swim wasn't what I had hoped it would be, as I had been pool swimming in Hong Kong instead of ocean swimming that I enjoyed when staying on the Gold Coast. Once exiting the water, I immediately got into a good rhythm on my bike. When I turned onto the motorway, I was thrilled to find myself passing a number of age-group competitors. There was a significant tailwind going out, and I found myself traveling at or near 50 kph. I was passing one cyclists after another, which always makes you feel energized. Nearing the 20k turnaround, I saw the world champion in my age group, Brian Barr, already heading back in the other direction. Brian was still a world-class swimmer at fifty-three years old, and I couldn't believe I was so close to him. Just as we were passing, he yelled out, "Nice train, Bozarth." I glanced behind to find a number of triathletes I had passed, illegally drafting behind me. There were now at least thirty competitors forming a line, enjoying my draft.

I was shocked to realize I had gained no time on these cyclists I had passed. I was actually helping them conserve energy. A little discouraged, I decided to let them pass as we rounded the twenty-kilometer turning pilon and dropped in behind to see how it felt to draft on them. I couldn't believe it; my effort dropped significantly as I flew along the road in their draft. Now with a headwind, it felt even better to ride in their slipstream. As good as it felt, not having to face that headwind, I knew I couldn't stay there as the Australian National Championships for age groupers was a nondrafting race.

I still didn't finish too far behind the pack when arriving into transition. I then started what was for me an excellent and fun 10k run. Having done my run training on long, steep hills in Hong Kong, I felt good. I kept passing a number on the uphill and had a strong downhill pace as well. Wow, this was something new for me, actually passing other runners. As I neared the top of the hill for the third time I got that all too frequent message, "Find a relief area and soon." Why now, 'Again.' I was having a great run and a possible podium finish, but my new life was what it was. Knowing this might happen, I had scouted out the course ahead of time and knew there

I DO IT ALL

were toilets in the beach-side park at the bottom of the hill. It was only about forty meters off the course across manicured grass, so not too much time would be lost. Around five minutes were lost at the 7k mark, but I was still happy with how I was running.

Australian National Triathlon Championships
1994—Post accident

My son, Brian, wasn't racing that day, but was there watching from an apartment balcony with a group of his friends, as I raced the last 500 meters to the finish line. One of his friends yelled out, "Hey, isn't that your dad?" Brian said he didn't even recognize me because it really looked like I was running. That made my day as I still had a great race, finishing fifth in my age group at the Australian National Championships! I always felt very fortunate to be traveling around the world, often with my sons, being able to race and train as if I was completely healthy. Spinal cord issues lingered, but I was still able to be out enjoying this wonderful company of athletes. With the plus of being able to enter and race myself, I always felt I was the most fortunate triathlete in every race I finished.

Which Way to the Nearest Restroom?

Before my spinal cord damage, I could train anytime, anywhere and long hard sessions. Now it took more thought, as I needed to plan ahead for the unexpected and recurring urges, or suffer the consequences of more embarrassing situations. These incidents were more likely to happen in training than in races. Races only happened once or twice a month and I did special preparation to hopefully avoid a mishap. I trained hard six days a week with no special preparation. My training took place whenever I could fit it into a very busy schedule. I would just take off running without thinking about a possible mishap. I was learning to understand, that as much as I wanted things to be as they were before, I needed to make some allowances or forever be disappointed, then become angry and upset again. My mind told me I could still do the things as I did before, but the reality was quite different.

I tried playing tennis like before, but found I was too awkward to move quickly and singles was completely out of the picture. My previous asset of balance and quickness were gone, and I had to learn to hit a tennis ball while often being completely off balance. Accepting this apparent disability in a sport I loved participating in was hard, as complete control was now out of the question. It was and remains the most difficult issue for me to deal with mentally. I cannot change directions quickly no matter how hard I try. I have done specific drills to develop these abilities again, but nothing seems to completely work. Doubles remained the only option, but only if I found a partner who didn't mind doing most of the running, especially when our opponents lob over my head. I actually had some fun again playing doubles, although not on the same serious elite level.

I ran into Peter McNamara when he was in Hong Kong coaching Mark Philippoussis at the ATP event. I was doing the play-by-play commentary. He was surprised to see me and asked why I wasn't at some of the International Senior Tournaments. I mentioned my accident and let him know there no possibility of my playing at an elite level anymore. It had been a few years since we played each other at Kooyong, but it brought back a sadness I was trying to put behind me. Most of the International Senior Tournaments he was talking about like Wimbledon would never have invited me anyway. The organizers only invite famous players from the past. It was great to catch up with him and nice to be remembered for our Italia Cup encounter.

I always tried to remind myself that everyone goes through a similar decline with age, although usually on a much more gradual timetable. With time, reflexes, muscle memory, and strength aren't what they used to be. I had always hoped to put this off for many more years. With the introduction of triathlon training and racing, I had been able to turn back the clock and slow the aging process. Now, with serious movement limitations, I was having to deal with age-related problems I would have put off for many years. I felt I had gone from a midtwenty-year-old-type body to one now feeling more like an eighty to ninety year old, proving to be difficult and different every day. These daily ups and downs were something new for me. I had been used to knowing how my body would feel from day to day. I used to get up feeling rested and raring to go each and every day. Trying to accept the way I felt now and how my body reacted each day was not easy. I couldn't put demands on my body like before and just expect it to obey or bounce back. My training and workouts in the past had been more mental than physical. Now it was the opposite, although much of the mental part was learning to stay positive. This new learning curve was huge and difficult to accept at times.

Triathlon continued to be my outlet to see improvement in my spinal cord damage. It was a way to measure my progress and see how close I could come to my preaccident level. I could quantitatively compare my improvement to past results and times. With triathlon, I now had to scope out my planned training route to include the anticipated toilet stops. In quite a few cases, I did my run training in the dark early mornings or after sunset in the evenings. This way, I had dark secluded places I could take care of myself, if no facilities were readily available. The early-morning runs suited me best when I was traveling, and I didn't have time to check out relief sites on my run routes. Well-meaning friends continued to advise me to take it easy and not train or race anymore. When they witnessed the obvious effort etched on my face when training and heard how I would need to find a place quickly to take care of myself, they thought I should just back off and slow down. To them, it seemed like more of a trial than it was worth. I made my choice to continue training and consequently left my mark in the woods, parks, and shrubbery around the world. I have hidden in the landscape of freeway roundabouts watching cars and trucks streak past, not knowing I was there. My decision to keep training has always been worth it, as I was still able to line up at the start of dozens and dozens of events around the world.

I chose to live and not quit. The results of our lives are the choices we make each and every day along our journey. I, like most, have not always made the right choices; but I have tried to learn from the past and improve as I went along. I, like everyone else, find it hard at times to drag myself out of bed and start running, swimming, or biking. But I can honestly state, "I have never come back from one of these workouts wishing I had not gone. I am always energized, feeling like I am alive and living life to the fullest," with that one exception on Clearwater Bay Road on April 22, 1992. The ability to get back up and keep trying is one of the most important attributes we can learn. With these positive encouragements in my recovery, I was still missing something! I couldn't quite put my finger on it but knew there was something I needed to discover, if I was ever to completely relax in my new body.

Borneo Challenge

Before my April 22 date with destiny, I was training for the Triathlon World Championship, the Asian Championships, and also the Borneo Challenge. The Borneo Challenge was a new event on the triathlon calendar in 1992 and was offering a substantial amount of prize money. Prize money was not only for the professionals but for the age-group events as well. I was introduced to this event while winning a unique event in Hong Kong. The Hong Kong event was a few months before my accident. The race in Hong Kong was a swim, bike, run, swim, run, swim, finally culminating with a run. They called it the Hong Kong Endurathon. My main rival in Hong Kong had heard about the Borneo Challenge, and I overheard him talking about it at the lunch following the Endurathon. I had just won the Endurathon by a sizable margin, and the Borneo Triathlon sounded like another great way to visit a new and interesting destination and make some money at the same time. My Hong Kong triathlon buddy was a little disappointed to hear I had signed up, as he had not been able to finish ahead of me in many of our previous races. He was looking forward to taking out first prize without me there.

The Borneo Triathlon was scheduled for May, so needless to say, I was still in hospital when the inaugural event was held. My good friend from Hong Kong took out top honors and the $2,000 prize money as the winner. A few years later, when I was finally able to enter, the *Borneo Press* somehow got hold of my story and decided to write a human interest piece on my accident and return to triathlon racing. The article turned out to be one of the featured press releases promoting the race.

Borneo Triathlon with Donnie and Brian

One of the reasons they called it The Borneo Challenge was because the water is hot, the road is hotter, and the run is blistering. To make matters more challenging, they started the race at 12:00 noon, right in the heat of the day. Equatorial heat is something you need to experience to understand its intensity. We couldn't understand why they started at 12:00 noon until they explained why. In Borneo, noon was the time of day the water was the cleanest due to the daily sewage flush the evening before. The water is so hot it felt like bathwater because it was shallow, only about four to six feet deep the entire swim. The weather doesn't get any cooler as the day wears on. This is one of those races where everyone suffers. There was a picture of Jimmy Riccitello, one of USA's top professionals sitting in a big bucket of ice following the elite race he had just won. One professional triathlete actually passed out while riding his bike in the heat. He was seen fainting and veered off course, collapsing into a grassy ditch, thankfully unhurt.

This particular year, I was excited to be racing in Borneo and find out how I would hold up in the challenging heat. My son Brian was entered to race as well and was there cheering me on after finishing his race. I was having another good race holding down third place against some of the world's best in my category. Feeling all right even though it was extremely hot, after the forty-kilometer bike, I was running well and fairly fast for me. Suddenly 800 meters from the finish line, something seemed strange. This time it wasn't the call of nature. The skyline suddenly seemed crooked, and I couldn't make sense of it. I, like most athletes, had seen videos and news stories where runners at the LA Olympics and triathletes in Hawaii had run out of fuel and dehydrated, losing control of their ability to run or even walk properly. These athletes were viewed by millions, pathetically staggering or crawling across the finishing line.

Well, here I was trying to figure out why things didn't look right when suddenly, realization hit me. I, like those news clips, was an athlete in trouble. I was listing to my right side and couldn't seem to get my body to straighten back up. Somehow I forced myself to keep moving forward, feeling if I stopped, I might not be able to get started again and finish the race. Balance problems with my spinal cord damage always made running a challenge. Now I had to concentrate even more as I could just make out the finish area further down the road. Somehow I forced myself to keep moving, but the finish seemed to get further away. The finish area in Borneo was unique in that you were running on the road, separating you from the finish line by a drainage ditch. You had to run forty more meters before taking a ninety-degree right hand turn over a ten-meter wooden bridge. Then take another ninety-degree right turn. Once completing that last turn, it was just thirty or forty meters to the finish line. It normally didn't seem that far after racing for more than fifty-one kilometers. Still on the road, I kept leaning off balance to the right while doing my best to run. As I got closer to the bridge, I was trying to figure out how I was going to negotiate that first right-hand turn without falling down. I couldn't believe how hard it was to simply turn right and cross the bridge. It was like solving a math equation.

The usual large number of spectators lining the course and finish area were there and became aware of the trouble I was in. They said I looked pathetic, like the international athletes facing the same scenario. By then, my body was really shutting down, and I could barely make out the many encouragements from the spectators. For me, it became eerily quiet, almost like a dream. I wasn't sure I could make it around the first turn much less the second one, that is if I could make it across the wooden bridge. *So this was how those athletes felt*, I thought, having witnessed them stagger and crawl their way through their last few meters. At this point, I realized you just don't care what you look like! All you want to do is finish after the effort put in to go more than fifty-one kilometers in that blistering heat.

Here came the first turn! As I started to turn right, I felt myself list even more to the right and thought, *I am going down!* But somehow, I stayed on my feet. Many of my friends said they didn't know how I did it, as I was listing over so much. I staggered across the bridge, finally approaching the last right turn. Confident that I'd made the first turn to get across the bridge, I felt like I could turn and make it to the finish line. However, without realizing it, I listed even more to the right while trying to negotiate the second turn. My feet went straight out to the left, leaving me airborne and landing on my right side. As I lay there in a daze, I thought, *Oh no! I don't know if I can get up.* I then noticed a pole right beside me planted in the ground to mark the turning point. I grabbed hold and literally pulled myself to my feet. Slowly turning myself around to face the finish line some forty meters away, I took off on what I thought was my very best run to admirably complete the race.

What happened next, I don't remember clearly. Obviously overcompensating, I immediately staggered to my left, then overcompensating again, I veered to the right, heading at forty-five-degree angle across the wide dirt finish area. Eventually, my clonus kicked in, throwing me in the air in a semiconscious state. All I remember was a loud *thunk*, lying there on the ground again with the thought, *I think I hit my head.* Pictures in the newspaper the next day confirmed I had landed on my head. I looked like as arrow with my hands by my side, feet slightly higher than my head going straight into the dirt. Even as I looked at the photo, I thought it looked impossible.

I was now some twenty meters from the finish line and even more dazed. A concerned spectator started running up to help me. Before he could touch me, an official from Singapore stopped him, saying, "Don't touch him or he will be disqualified. I know this guy and he wants to finish." I was thankful for Bagwan, a friend of mine from Malaysia, stepping in to keep me from being disqualified after racing for that long in the Borneo heat. Hearing his encouragement gave me just enough energy to push myself up and stagger to my feet. With a halting, listing awkward shuffle I took more than a minute to cover the last twenty meters, crossing the finish line to fall into the arms of my son Brian. I only then completely understood why they called it the Borneo Challenge!

The good news was, I not only finished but placed third, collecting the $800 prize money. With an intravenous drip, I felt good enough to cycle back to the hotel an hour later. Another exotic destination checked off, on my to-do list, and a story to share with my kids and grandkids. I may have spinal cord damage, but I was still out there having more journeys to fondly remember.

Handicap Time Trial

Moving back to the Philippines to sort out my children's US citizenship, I started managing Clearwater Country Club inside the old US Clark Air Base. I had extra time to do some long cycles and work on my cycling time-trial speed. The roads inside the previous US Clark Air Base were mostly empty and free of traffic. This turned out to be wonderful for me as the roads were in excellent condition, unlike the congested Jeepney-occupied roads outside the base. There was virtually no smog or traffic to contend with. Clark was like my own private training track.

Not only did I have Clark to train in, but I met some hard core cyclist in Angeles who invited me to ride with them on the congested roads around Angeles City, Mabalacat, and Magalang, and up around Mt. Arayat. They were a crazy group who whipped in and out of heavy traffic at breakneck speed. They would then take off to time-trial a few sections where the roads were clear. My cycling improved even more because of staying with them and not get lost.

I met another cyclists who encouraged me to enter a cycling time-trial event in the upscale housing development of Alabang in Manila. I thought why not? I didn't have anything better to do. This friend was also willing to drive me to this event on an early Sunday morning. We headed out very early as it was some distance from Angeles City where we lived. The trip took longer than we expected, as it often does in the Philippines. When we arrived, the time-trial was well underway. We inquired if it was still possible to enter late, and to my surprise, they said, "No problem." That was if I could be ready to race in less than ten minutes. I quickly paid my entry, ran to the car, hurriedly got my bike out, assembled the wheels, checked things out and went for a two block warm up. I rode over to the assembly area just in time to hear my name being announced as the last competitor. The cyclist in front of me had just been sent off down the course.

What a rush, but I was actually looking forward to doing this time-trial of twenty-four kilometers. I had no idea the terrain of the course, but it was a beautiful, cool clear blue morning, and I felt really good. Sometimes it is better not to know what is ahead and just do your best as you get into your rhythm. This was one of those times. They were sending us off one minute apart, and after just twelve kilometers, I had passed two of the previous competitors. As this always does, I felt extra energy as I passed one more cyclists at 17k. I could see the next cyclist not too far down the road as we headed back up the only major hill on the route. This cyclist had started two minutes before me and was looking stronger as the race went on. There were no really steep hills on this course, but this one was still fairly long and testing. We had been going flat out for eighteen kilometers when we reached the hill. I decided to burn my remaining energy on this final climb to pass this cyclist. I hoped I could then hold my pace the rest of the way to the finish line. After all, I thought, *This is a cycling time trial, not a triathlon where I needed to save some energy for the run.*

I was as surprised as he was when I passed him just before the top of the hill. He was looking pretty strong himself. The only question then, did I have enough energy left in the tank to stay in front of him for the final few kilometers. Every time I glanced back, he was still there, fifteen meters behind. I couldn't seem to shake him, but he wasn't closing on me either. I could finally see what I thought was the finish line down the road. Well, it was what I thought was the finish, but actually, it was the line where we had started. Two hundred fifty meters further on was the finish banner. Just as I started to slow down, many of the spectators yelled out to keep going hard, "You are almost there." Only then did I see the finish line still two hundred meters down the road.

When I finished, everyone was pointing in my direction, excitedly talking in Tagalog among themselves. They all seemed to be overly excited while asking my age. I let them know I was fifty-seven, almost fifty-eight. They didn't seem to believe I was fifty-seven. I turned out to be the oldest competitor in the time trial, and they said I had posted an excellent time. I had no idea of the time I had posted. When I went to the timers' desk, they insisted me to produce an official identification to confirm my age. They had to be sure because this event turned out to be a handicap series based on your age. Your age would determine the handicap category you qualified for. The winner of the series was to be awarded a titanium bike frame, forks, and bars, so everyone was insisting my age be verified. I quickly went to the car and produced my passport.

As it turned out, I had finished with the seventh fastest overall time of the day, out of 120 competitors. My time had also qualified me for category 1. This category rating gave me over 300 points, just for the initial event. The closest competitor to me had under

100 points. The titanium bike was virtually mine if I continued to race the series. It was great to be in that position but even better to average forty kilometers per hour for a twenty-four-kilometer time trial. It was times like this which continued to motivate me to keep training and improving, and felt I could still "do it all." I would feel completely normal at times like this, when the effects of spinal cord damage seemed to momentarily abate. Cycling was still a nonimpact sport and continued to be the best of my three triathlon disciplines.

Wax on Wax Off; Not So Easy with Weight

The effort of getting better after an accident is often accompanied by other unexpected necessities. One item that became very evident was the responsibility and liability issue with the minibus company. Policemen had shown up in my hospital room a few days following my hospital admission to take my statement and account of the accident. I could only remember snapshot images of the accident, so I was not much help. Unknown to me at that time, the minibus driver had made false claims to the authorities. That was until I was informed I was being charged with reckless cycling. If found guilty, I would need to pay damages to the minibus company. I couldn't believe this was happening as I already had enough in my life to deal with, and now this? I was forced to hire a solicitor. Through a close friend, I was fortunate to hire an Englishman who reminded me of *Columbo* from the TV series. He was also every bit as good as the TV character. He proved to be everything I could have wanted to represent me. He was slow and methodical when making his presentation to the judge, but it didn't take long for the judge to find me, not guilty of reckless cycling. He also found the minibus driver's ever-changing account unbelievable.

Because of this ruling in a lower court, five years later, I found myself going through a serious court battle in Hong Kong's High Court. I was being represented by my Columbo solicitor and fortunately one of the best barristers in Hong Kong. The financial, physical, and psychological stress was compounded when my solicitor felt it would be better for me to not showed up at court looking so fit.

He felt the judge might not feel my spinal cord damage was that serious. I couldn't really understand this, as my MRIs and X-rays were definitive proof of the serious and permanent nature of my injuries. I had also undergone a serious internal exam with a urologist, which showed undeniable proof I still suffered serious and permanent damage from the accident.

Even though I understood my solicitor's request, this was difficult for me to stop training. I had never wanted anyone to feel sorry for me. In fact, I had done everything since the accident to look as normal and fit as possible. The old "fake it till you make it" routine. I finally relented to my solicitor and barrister's requests and stopped training for two months. I then went on an eating binge, basically eating everything in sight. I found gaining weight was not that difficult to accomplish, as it coincided with the Christmas season. All the rich and fattening foods were available to consume everywhere I looked. And the most fattening Christmas item was eggnog. I drank more than a few gallons in December alone.

I ended up being successful beyond my wildest imagination. I gained over thirty pounds in two months and could not fit into my clothes properly. I had some very old Levi's, which had that great smooth feel only well-worn Levi's have. I loved the feel of them. I forced myself into this favorite pair on one chilly day around New Year's before heading outside to shoot some hoops on our back patio. I bent over to pick up the ball, heard a rip, completely ripping them out, destroying my favorite pair of Levi's. They had always fit me a little loose, so there had been no chance of this ever happening before I gained weight. I eventually went through most of my Levi's the same way. Wow, now I was fat, had spinal cord damage, felt bad, and looked even worse! If it felt bad before, it felt worse now. Being overweight made everything worse. I hated the way I was feeling—weak, fat, and off-balance.

Then just after New Year's, I received the news that the court case had been indefinitely delayed. Being disgusted with myself, I decided court case or no court case, I couldn't live my life being fat and out-of-shape. I told my solicitors I was going back to Australia to get back into shape. I was off on the earliest flight I could arrange to the Gold Coast again to train with my sons and Col Stewart's elite training group. My legal team could contact me there with any new updates on my court case.

Col Stewart was training a number of the world's best Olympic-distance triathletes, including my sons, Donnie and Brian. When I arrived, nobody could believe how big I had become. The first training day with Col's group was at Bel Air Park, for an open-water swim in Lake Hugh Muntz. To my surprise and embarrassment, Col took out a pair of calipers to measure the body fat content of his elite triathletes. They were of course super fit, and their body fat readings were in the range of 6 percent to 9 percent. Trying to hide in the back, I was the last one to be measured. When I stepped forward, Col took one look at me without my shirt on and said, "I don't think there is any point for you to be measured, and besides, I don't think these calipers will open wide enough to measure that," pointing at my rather large spare tire. Col wasn't one to talk as his endearing nickname with the triathletes was Fat Man. But there was a big difference: he was coaching, and I was training. Because of this, I became more determined than ever to work off this unwanted weight.

Taking longer than I expected, the unwanted fat finally melted away. I personally learned a valuable lesson, which I had been teaching others for years. When you first try to lose weight, your body gets the message you are in a life-threatening situation, like being lost in a desert without enough food. To save your life, your body slows down your metabolism to give you your best chance of survival. What a bummer when you are intentionally trying to lose the weight. This makes it almost impossible to see results in your first few weeks. If you stay determined and stick to the new routine, your body's metabolic rate will finally go back to normal. Slowly, the weight does start melting away. I was surprised at how hard it was emotionally to stay with my program when after three weeks of proper eating and hard workouts, I saw very little results. Even with this, I forced myself to stay with my daily and weekly regimen. Being on the Gold Coast and around super-fit elite triathletes every day made this transition much easier than it would have been doing it alone. After three and a half months, I finally saw my desired results and returned back to my ideal weight. Lesson learned, "Easy to say, hard to do!" Or easy to gain weight, hard to lose weight!

World Championships in Perth, Australia

Later in the year was the next ITU World Championship. I had lost the weight, so it was great to be racing at another World Championship, especially in Perth, Australia. Perth is a beautiful city located on the west coast. You realize how big Australia is when flying from the Gold Coast to the opposite side of the country. The citizens of Perth seemed to enjoy having us triathletes inundate their city for the week. As always, I loved the atmosphere at the World Championships. Everyone is fit and healthy, and positive attitudes are contagious. The weather was perfect all week with blue skies and balmy weather. By race morning, everyone was excited to race while setting up their gear in the transition area. Plenty of "Good luck" and "Have a great race" gestures going around, as people bantered back and forth. Dozens of wave starts began early, much before my race would be called. I took the time to wander down to the river's edge to warm up and watch the early starters get ready for their swim.

What I encountered totally took me by surprise. A contingent of handicapped (challenged) triathletes were getting ready to contest their ITU World Championship. This had even greater significance for me as I had just witnessed an ordeal one of the "challenged" athletes had encountered in the transition area. After arranging his gear and setting it out to get ready for the race, he looked ready to head off for the river's edge. He suddenly had a Grand Mal seizure. It was devastating to watch as his father was there to assist with his immediate needs and keep his airway cleared. He was a super-fit-looking young man from the waist up, around twenty-five years old. He definitely had problems with his legs and thus his challenged status. He had trained as hard, if not harder than any of us to qualify and be there in Perth. As I watched his ordeal from a distance, I agonized with him, as his race in Perth would obviously never begin. I also realized again how close I had come to racing as a challenged triathlete.

Now standing at the river's edge, witnessing the rest of the challenged triathletes entering the water, I watched intently as their race began. Some of them needed help getting to the water's edge; others hopped on their one good leg or walked confidently down with little or no use of their arms without prosthetics. Even one was led down to the river by what I assumed was his father. He was blind and had to follow his ever-vigilant Father, who guided him through the entire race.

I had tears in my eyes as they took off swimming. But that was nothing as I stayed there until one by one, they began exiting the swim. I then burst into tears as I witnessed the amazing amount of determination they exhibited heading to the transition area. They were a huge inspiration for me as I watched them eventually make their way onto the bike course, disappearing up the road. As I stood there bawling my eyes out, I realized again how fortunate I was to be able to race the able-bodied age group World Championship. I was now totally psyched up and ready to start my race. I continued to reflect on the inspirational effort the challenged triathletes had displayed. They were my heroes!

I couldn't get the image of the challenged athletes out of my mind when my race began. I charged forward in the swim and felt good with my time when finally exciting the 1,500-meter course. The forty-kilometer bike course was wonderfully laid out and challenging with a few steep hills and plenty of greenery in Kings Park. I enjoyed another good race but again faced the challenge of almost losing control of my bodily functions. This time I was more fortunate than in many of my previous races, where I had been isolated on a country road, straining in the middle of huge boulevard or stuck with seemingly nowhere to hide in New Zealand. This time, it happened when I entered the bike-run transition area. Slowing a little kept me in control as I headed down the final steep hill from King's Park toward transition. I knew if I could just make it into the dismount area, I might be able to avoid the usual scenario and mess.

I dismounted my bike and ran to the end of the transition chute where they had organized a group of portable toilets. Quickly dropping my bike, I ran into the first toilet available and just in time. I lost a few minutes or so but couldn't have cared less as my perspective was unusually clear after being inspired by the challenged triathletes. I worked hard on the run to finish twenty-fourth in my age group. This was the closest I ever came to my top 20 finish goal at an ITU World Championship but still ahead of one hundred others in my age group. I always found solace, knowing my goal would have been reached but for the necessary toilet stops at ITU World Championships.

Before the day was over, I experienced another inspirational sight. The women's professional elite event included our good friend Michellie Jones who was a favorite to win again in her home country. When she came off the bike with the leaders, one of the other elite triathletes lifted her bike's front wheel as she ran into transition, causing her back wheel to swing under Michellie's feet. Her toes and feet were sliced up by the sharp spokes. These were not minor cuts, but Michellie still put on her running shoes to begin her 10k run. Very few who witness this gave her much of a chance to even finish the race, with her toes and feet badly bleeding. To everyone's amazement, she ran the entire 10k with the other two leaders only to relinquish her effort in the last 500 meters. She still placed third, running past the finish line with bright-red bloody shoes. Viewing her amazing race continued my inspirational day.

I went to the massage tent after watching her race, needing to take care of the severe tightness always evident in my left calf. The masseuse gave me his condolences as he worked on leg. He thought I was not able to finish the race with this condition. My calf was always like that, and I only smiled thinking how lucky I really was. After the massage, I was approached by one of our Hong Kong triathletes, Roy Bailey, expressing how unlucky I had been. I had just been thinking how lucky I was when he came up. My name had been drawn in a lucky draw for a free flight to the Phuket International Triathlon in Thailand later that fall, which I had entered. Since I wasn't present for the draw, the flight was awarded to another triathlete. The highs I had experience through the day were worth much more than a free flight to Phuket. What a day I had experienced, being able to participate in the World's again as an able-bodied triathlete. "Unlucky?" not in the least, I knew I was the lucky one!

Thank You

On my journey, many people had inspired me, and to be honest, there had been quite a few. The most obvious have been my father and mother. They made me feel I could accomplish anything. They not only encouraged me but also were always there to patch me up and get me through some difficult sleepless nights.

My family and children were always there standing beside me, encouraging me and making me get up and get going when I thought I was too tired, sore, or stiff to move. Don, Brian, and Shannon who had faith that I would walk again even when all the odds were against me.

Nalini Advani was my therapist and ended up being a good friend. She put up with me for over three years, never giving up on me. She helped me reach many seemingly impossible goals, regardless of how ridiculous they seemed to her at the time.

Paul Terry, a fellow triathlete, inspired me before my accident and visited me almost every day at the hospital, only to lose his ultimate fight two years later.

Michellie Jones and Peter Coulson were a huge boost for me in Manchester. The challenged triathletes in Perth are indelibly imprinted on my mind. Of course, there was the inspiration of watching my sons race in many of the same triathlons. There are many, many more I could thank. There were those who seemed to say the perfect encouraging words at the right time to keep me inspired and going when I could have given up or stopped trying so hard to move forward.

Col Stewart and his elite triathlon training squad, who allowed me to train with them. They encouraged me to keep up with them on their long rides and runs. Some of the pros, who took extra time to encourage me, were Miles Stewart, Matt Reed, Shane Reed, Chris MacCormac, and Craig Walton. They always made me feel like I belonged and was one of them, an elite triathlete.

I was also encouraged by all the Challenged athletes I was privileged to watch and encounter around the world. There was a single-leg amputee in Boulder, Colorado, who could run faster than me with his specially designed running prosthetic. We swam together a number of times at the pool and sometimes ran together at the lake. He always had an encouraging word and an infectious positive attitude. His never-ending smile was contagious.

My Tribe 8 triathlon squad in the Philippines who showed up for almost all my training sessions with a smile. Starting from scratch, they have become accomplished triathletes with a number of them now Ironman finishers.

My wife Nerrisa who continues to put up with my early-morning training and my youngest children, Daniel and Crystal, who are my greatest fans. They have continued to encourage me throughout my many setbacks and follow me on crazy journeys around the world.

Boulder Summer Training and World Master Games

Brian and Donnie had previously trained in Boulder, Colorado, and encouraged me to join Brian there before the 1999 World Master Games in Portland, Oregon. Boulder is a beautiful community backed up to the Rocky Mountain range and the famous Flat Irons. The setting is breathtaking, sitting at a mile high where the air is thin and crisp. I was warned about trying to run at that higher altitude. But I was so excited when arriving in Boulder, I decided to go for a 10k run the same day I flew in. I quickly changed and started my run much too fast. I was sucking for air after only 500 meters, in spite of my excellent fitness. I didn't last more than two kilometers before I gave in to the altitude and turned back to the apartment. I thought, *I was in great shape but obviously not for high altitude.*

My first training ride was the following day, at Brian's suggestion. He directed me to cycle six kilometers out-of-town on Old Stage Road, then turn left on Lefthand Canyon Drive, which would be well-marked. This would take me up to Ward and the Peak to Peak Highway. He said I might want to stop for a break at Millsite Inn before heading further out on the Peak to Peak Highway to Saint Vrain Drive, then back down to Lyon. What he failed to tell me was how long the ride was up to Ward or the terrain on the climb. Lefthand Canyon Drive was one of those climbs that starts out as a gentle, enjoyable climb through some scenic farmland, then gradually gets steeper and steeper. Left Hand Canyon Drive did get steeper, but the different sights kept it interesting. Taking the sign to Jamestown was an option, but I was warned it was an extremely difficult climb. I chose to follow Brian's suggestion, eventually going through Ward, making the journey worth the effort. Seeing these remote towns around the world always had me wondering what their lifestyle contained and how they earned a living? It was an idyllic country lifestyle, but the remoteness made it feel isolated and removed from the rest of the energetic life most people lived. Having lived in Little Applegate, Oregon, I had an understanding of what they were feeling.

My bike ride from Stage Coach Road continued for thirty kilometers where it turned from joy to a serious effort to keep going. The steepest section is reserved for the last couple of kilometers up through Ward. This ride is a real tester, as every time I thought I had arrived, there was another hairpin turn with the road appearing to go straight up. I was hardly moving those last 2k but finally made it up to the Peak to Peak Highway and the Millsite Inn. I dropped down for a much needed and longer rest than planned. I couldn't help enjoying the scenery while taking this much-needed rest. The vistas looking out in the direction toward Estes Park were breathtaking.

Getting back on my bike, the Peak to Peak Highway took me along smooth, undulating roads with open green fields and pine trees in every direction with snowcapped mountains in the distance. The ridge ride eventually ended at a T-junction. Turning left would have taken me higher into the Rockies, but by then, I was ready to head back home. Turning right took me down Saint Vrain Drive to Lyon. This would finally have me headed back to Boulder through Longmont. The entire ride back was breathtaking, with Estes Park stretching off toward the snowcapped mountains in the distance to the left. The elevation of Ward, Colorado, is 9,150 feet and the Peak to Peak Highway is close to two miles high. This was a difficult ride through this Rocky Mountain region. Even with the extreme effort, it was always enjoyable, definitely the most scenic ride I have ever

I DO IT ALL

been on. I did this 120-kilometer ride every other day. I knew this would help with the upcoming World Masters Games.

High-altitude training helped immensely once I arrived in Portland, Oregon, even though my visit to Boulder was limited to six weeks. While there, I ran into many international athletes I knew from around the world, including the entire Japanese Triathlon Team. They were also using Colorado's high altitude to train. Boulder is one of the unique towns in the US where it feels like a throwback to the hippie era. There are many small boutique shops, restaurants, and coffee shops located down the uniquely designed main street. My time there was one of the many great memorable times that triathlon training and racing have allowed me to experience. It seemed that everyone knew each other and the coffee shops and restaurants were warm, welcoming, and of the highest quality. It was not easy thinking about leaving for the airport when my visit was coming to an end. I was in Boulder training for the World Masters Games in Portland, Oregon. I enjoyed everything about Boulder, but summer was coming to an end and the Peak to Peak ride was becoming decidedly colder. My last ride on the Peak to Peak Highway and down to Lyon was so cold, I was shaking uncontrollably when I entered their coffee shop. It took me an hour to warm up holding onto cups of hot chocolate.

I left Boulder with some great memories and flew out to Portland for the World Masters Games. I was looking forward to some positive results after my high-altitude experience. When I arrived at the World Master Games registration desk, I noticed a cycling time-trial event to be held one week before the triathlon. I enquired about the event, and they allowed me to enter the time-trial as well. I was also registered to participate in the tennis tournament, which gave me a busy week of three events. There was a mix-up when they had entered me in the novice-level tennis event instead of the open event. This ended up being okay with me as I withdrew my entry. This opened up my schedule, allowing me to focus on the triathlon and cycling time-trial.

Showing up early for the cycling time-trial near the Columbia River, I was surprised at the huge number of entries and how professionally prepared everyone was. These were hard-core cyclist, not triathletes. Almost everyone was kitted out in the latest time-trial gear. They had specially designed time-trial bikes, along with single-piece cycling suits, covered bike shoes, and swept-back time-trial helmets. Unaware of the serious cyclist preparing for this event, I looked totally unprepared to race. I arrived in my well-worn training clothes and regular road bike. My lack of time-trial gear made me look and feel out-of-place. I felt like shrinking away into the shadows, as if there were any place to hide on this brightly lit blue sunny day. I hadn't taken the time to even tune up my bike or replace my well-worn cleats on my cycling shoes. It was still a glorious, bright, clear sunny day, and I wanted to see how I would match up against these hardcore cyclists. I was happy with my training in Boulder and wondered how it would pay off in this twenty-five-kilometer time-trial event. I didn't look prepared to race a time-trial, but I wasn't about to hide and slink away. My bike was out, and I was still checked in to race, so I made the choice to psyche myself up and do my best. Triathletes were notorious among cyclists for their lack of cycling skills, especially among the older-age categories. I hoped I could help improve that image.

Tucking in my cycling jersey so it would give the impression of a one-piece time-trial suit, I convinced myself into thinking I looked a little more presentable. By comparison, I was a joke to look at, standing among the other cyclists. I kept thinking, "Oh well, I'm here now, may as well give it a go." The officials were sending everyone off in alphabetical order, so it wasn't long before I was called up to the starting ramp.

What I didn't know, the person starting right behind me was the time-trial world champion for my age group and a legend. It was only the second time I had been in a proper cycling time-trial event, and this was also the first time there was a professionally raised time-trial starting ramp sending us off, like you see in the Tour de France. Looking down at the huge crowd of spectators gathered at the start made me a little nervous when the ten-second countdown began. Sitting on my bike with officials holding my bike upright and my shoes in the clips, I was as ready as I could be. I was determined to start fast and do my best to hold it together for the entire twenty-five-kilometer course. I wanted to make myself and the triathlon community proud, proving we could also cycle with the best time-trial experts.

Vaulting down the ramp when the gun went off, I pushed down on one pedals as hard as I could and pulled up just as hard on the opposite pedal. Just as I hit the pavement, my cleat snapped loose, releasing my shoe from the pedal. This threw me suddenly to one side and forward, almost over the handlebars. Weaving all over the road, I was sure I was going to come off in front of that huge crowd assembled there. Memory of my spectacular fall over my handlebars in the Philippines flooded my mind.

To everyone's amazement, including my own, I stayed upright, got my cleat back in the pedal, and took off down the road. This was not the way I wanted to begin my race! This was also not the way to prove that triathletes were excellent cyclists. The amount of time I lost weaving around and getting my shoe back in my pedal cost me a slightly higher finish when the time trial was over. However it started, it wasn't long before I began passing a few cyclists who had started ahead of me. I was feeling great by the time I reached ten kilometers, so I knew the high-altitude training in Boulder had paid off. Suddenly, out of seemingly nowhere at twelve kilometers, I was slowly passed by the cyclist who started behind me. For a few seconds, this really took the wind out of my sails. Until then I thought I was going fast. I had been thinking, *I must be doing great after already passing several other cyclists*. Passing someone may give you energy, but likewise, being passed makes it difficult to maintain your focus and effort.

This cyclist eased by me and slowly pulled away from me off down the road to the halfway point, just ahead. I did my best not be discouraged and increased my speed, determined to hang close to him. This became impossible as he seemed to be increasing his speed, even while facing a slight headwind once past the 12.5k turn. I needed to stay with my race pace or risk completely blowing up my legs. I was able to keep him in sight without hitting the wall, passing a couple more cyclists. I knew I was strong on the bike, but the world time-trial champion was amazing. He won our age group, and he turned out to have the second fastest time of the day even though he was twenty years older than the youngest competitors. We were in the fifty-to-fifty-four year age group of cyclists. The youngest age group was the thirty-to-thirty-five category. When I finished, I was totally spent but happy with my results. I ended up finishing seventh for the fifty-to-fifty-four category, averaging 40 kph. Boulder paid off with huge dividends, and I was thrilled with my time and results. I had originally hoped for a top 50 finish, so this was a call for celebration. With over one hundred serious cyclists in my age group, I left the time-trial hoping for a similar result in the triathlon event the following week.

The World Masters Triathlon event was scheduled one week later. I had good reason for high hopes for another great swim and bike, planning for a top 10 finish. Sunrise broke on another beautiful clear sunny day when we arrived at the triathlon course. I was accompanied to the race by some good friends, who had flown in from around the country just to see me race. I wanted to have a solid race in front of friends and family. Once the gun fired off, I dove forward and felt extremely good with my stroke. I found myself alongside the two leaders in the swim and came out of the lake with them.

After my time-trial result the previous week, I was expecting a great bike before the final run leg. The bike course was located in the hills surrounding the lake, and for some reason I couldn't find any rhythm on the bike. After all the mountain cycling I had done around Boulder, Colorado, it was a mystery why I was struggling, watching other cyclists who had finished behind me in previous triathlons slowly pass me by. I felt weak and listless during the entire cycling leg, but I was still giving my all. I lost time on the bike where I usually gained time on my main rivals.

Triathlons are interesting as you never know for sure how the different disciplines will work out or which segment will feel best on any given day. I was not looking forward to the run in the same very hilly area after my poor cycling. You were either running uphill or downhill on this course. Since I did not handle the hills very well on the bike, the run was not promising as I headed out of transition for the run. I surprised myself again. I suddenly felt refreshed and picked up my pace to finish with a strong run. I ended my World Masters Games on a high with a fifth place finish in the triathlon.

All the difficult high-altitude training had been worthwhile, resulting in excellent times and finishes in Portland. I am forever thankful I have been given the opportunity to compete and train around the world with a great community of athletes, as we always inspire each other to do our best. Very few people have had opportunities like I have experience, and I will be forever grateful. This small community of fit age-group athletes inspire many with their dedication, attitude, results, and most of all their willingness to share freely with others. We all gleaned ideas and information from one another's experiences, which helped us excel in our own personal endeavors. I personally felt accepted and inspired by the elite triathletes as well as the age groupers.

Those just watching triathlons or endurance events can't really understand the camaraderie developed between these athletes. We are all able to share in one another's achievements regardless of our final placing. This is because we all have a profound respect for the effort required in training away from the spotlight. Everyday life should be lived with the same amount of support and encouragement. Being fit definitely changes your view of the world around you. You tend to bounce out of bed, looking forward to another beautiful sunrise as another amazing day unfolds.

Many wonderful experiences happened following the World Master Games which influenced my life in positive ways. Probably the most significant was the marriage of my present wife, Nerrisa, and the birth of our two children. I really felt like I was "doing it all" again. I continued with my rehabilitation, striving to regain all my past fitness and skills. Moving to Australia was a dream come true. The ability to drop into the warm Pacific Ocean every day and feel alive was everything I could have asked for. I was up early everyday enjoying Australian sunrises, cycling back into the hinterland, or running along the beaches; and Burleigh Headland filled my life with energy. Our family embraced the Australian lifestyle, and we immersed ourselves into every aspect of their wonderful and available culture.

Nerrisa, My Faithful Supporter

Crystal, Nerrisa, and Daniel

Still Clowning Around with Crystal at 63

Crystal and Dad, semi-finalists—National Parks Tennis Championships

Shannon and Brian in Rome

Shannon, Dad, and Brian in Paris

Shannon with Dad in Paris

Our children loved Australia and couldn't have wanted anything more out of life. They went to a private Christian school and swam in a program at Bond University. Most weekends were spent at the beach or within a stone's throw of the beach, riding their bikes on the beach side bike paths. After long days of being sun-drenched, we would often pick up fish and chips and stop at Burleigh Heads to lay out a blanket on their grassy parkland. Lying back on the blanket and sitting on their manicured lawns, we would watch late-afternoon surfers while eating our dinner. Daniel and Crystal would head down to the water's edge among the large rocks to hunt for shells. Coming back to share their find with us, we would relax in the warmth of the late-afternoon's setting sun. Sitting there enjoying what seemed like the very best life had to offer, I again felt I was "doing it all."

It was around this time, during one of my early-morning runs, I had my greatest "aha" moment. All along I had felt something was missing but couldn't quite put my finger on it. I was so caught up staying dedicated to my daily schedule, I was getting lost again. I was thinking I could accomplish whatever I put my mind to. I was doing everything I knew to keep improving and also be the very best dad and husband I could be. What could possibly be missing from my life when living on the Gold Coast in Australia?

I Do It All

How many of us feel this way at times? "Doing it all." In the busyness of modern life, it seems like we are doing everything, rushing around, while trying to "do it all." We make a plan, work the plan, and let nothing get in the way of achieving our goals. In fact, we start adding so much in our schedule, we wish we didn't feel like we needed to always "do it all." However, it can become addictive and exciting, adding more and more items and goals to our ever busier day, especially when successfully accomplishing more and more. After a while, we feel we would almost sacrifice anything, just to keep busy. Getting into this kind of a routine, we feel like we really can "do it all." We begin thinking, if we put our full effort into something, we can accomplish it. It is easy to get so wrapped up and confident in this process, we start feeling empowered, getting a larger-than-life ego. We begin thinking we can do anything on our own, certainly without help from a higher power. We can feel completely in control.

I know this is the way I felt before my accident in Hong Kong. It seemed like I couldn't set a foot wrong. I was living my dream. I was director of tennis and head professional at Hong Kong's most prestigious club while playing on the Hong Kong country club's league team in the exclusive Hong Kong open division. I was part-owner of a fitness center in Singapore and was a partner in an Asian Fitness Company. I was modeling and doing commercials for international companies, appearing on international magazines while doing commentary for many different sports, including the Olympics for Hong Kong's TVB. I was even given the opportunity to write and direct a TV sport series introducing Hong Kong Chinese to American football. I was also circuit director for Prince Asian Tennis Circuit for Asia's top juniors. I was also representing Hong Kong at international triathlons and the Italia Cup in Australia for tennis. I owned a consulting company in Hong Kong, which put on events and built tennis courts, synthetic putting greens, and supplied tennis equipment to some of the facilities. Being a resort manager and being able to participate in local cultural events like dragon boat racing, I was too busy to realize how lucky I was. I really thought I could "do it all." Even after my accident, I was given the opportunity to be the worldwide general manager for a company. Commentary for seven different Olympics continued as well as my tennis teaching and winning a number Asian Championships in triathlon seemed to encourage my "I can do it all" attitude. This is a dangerous place to find yourself, as a momentary blip on the horizon can leave you feeling disoriented, helpless, alone, and pleading for anyone to help you out of your self-inflicted mess.

We are all vulnerable to life's unexpected happenings. In an instant, you can feel out-of-control in a dark tunnel with no light at the end to guide you. You suddenly find it hard to accomplish or finish anything, much less "doing it all."

With my accident, I went from living on a super high to literally being helpless. You would think this would wake me up to reality. But for some reason, I was still thinking I could "do it all." I became more determined than ever to make things happen all by myself again, with sheer grit and intestinal fortitude. There were certain things I temporarily could not do on my own. They were obvious, and even though I knew it, I was stubborn and refused to accept my situation. I even refused to ring the nurses' bell for my much needed help. I made ridiculous statements to professionals who knew better, and sometimes I even proved them wrong. I couldn't imagine my life being different. After a few days of being helpless, there was no choice but to find needed help to regain any sense of normalcy in my life. This is where the doctors, nurses, and hospital staff came into the picture and were invaluable.

Once out of the hospital, I needed therapists to manipulate and massage my body for any chance to recover. They would give me a number of simple exercises I could do on my own to further expedite my journey back. I was still stubborn and pushed myself to do more and more, believing I could still do everything if I just forced it. I felt I just needed to try harder, do more, and not quit. I would pretend I was okay, even though I needed help getting in and out of vehicles, going up stairs, or walking on uneven sidewalks. I even needed my son to hit tennis balls with my students so I could hold onto the net post for support and still teach my students.

Even with these obvious restrictions right in front of me, I was still determined to "do it all" by myself again! This was frustrating at times, but I had my goal: I was going to work it and achieve it because I still thought I could "do it all" by myself. It may be great to be positive and push ourselves to be better and improve, but in the end, reliance on ourselves only can lead to a lonely; sad; and unfulfilled, disappointed life.

I often found out-of-the-way places to train so nobody could see my struggle to improve and view how awkward I was. My huge ego was still intact, so I avoided the prying public eyes as much as possible when trying to train and be normal again. Not far from the Marina Club, I found a concrete drainage ditch above Aberdeen in the hills of Hong Kong. This ditch had a nice dirt walkway beside the canal, for workers inspecting the ditch and clearing debris for proper drainage. I would head up to the catchment and do my running out of sight. As I ran along the secluded area, I would be thinking, *I will surprise everyone with my improvement when they eventually see me running again.* Without completely realizing it, I was still on a massive ego trip, trying to prove to myself and everyone else I was some kind of superman and could "do it all."

After being on this journey of recovery for a few years, a surprising and unexpected event happened on an early Australian morning. I had been working hard to improve my health and my triathlon results. I was doing well in triathlon events winning the Asian Championships again and most of the Australian races I was entering. This just furthered the illusion that I could "do it all." I continued to research every possible treatment to revitalize my bodily systems, hopefully including spinal cord repair.

Being able to relocate back to Australia and live on the beautiful Gold Coast was a blessing. I was fortunate to surround myself with some of the best professional athletes on the planet. They inspired me to work even harder to improve myself and stay positive. In spite of the dedicated effort I put into my training, my running still struggled. This was difficult for me to accept. My run had become a source of enjoyment and fairly fast before my accident. Hadn't I run a 36:45-minute ten-kilometer before my accident and a 5:30 mile? I couldn't seem to find a way to resemble that relaxed running form after my return to training. My tight leg muscles from spinal cord damage made intense training difficult. Running too fast or too long was almost impossible without tearing or pulling a muscle. This happened time and again, setting me back and making me feel like I was continually starting over. It was like I was hitting my head against the proverbial brick wall again and again.

I had occasional days and moments where, for some reason, my leg muscles would relax and I could take off on an enjoyable, easy, and fairly fast run. This was wonderful but short-lived unless I was careful. Lactic acid would build up, causing me to again slightly tear another muscle in my legs, mostly my calf muscles. Frustration was always present even though I was grateful every morning when I woke up and could stand on my feet, get dressed by myself, and head out for another run, swim, or bike ride.

I was consistent with my training schedule of rising at 3:45 a.m. to run at least ten kilometers before jumping on my bike and heading out for a sixty-kilometer bike ride through the hinterland. Glad to be back in warm Australia, my schedule stayed the same, hoping to somehow finally beat this spinal cord injury and prove every naysayer wrong.

Then one early Gold Coast morning, after waking early, I did my fifteen-minute stretch routine and headed out for a long run for me of twelve kilometers. My goal was to finish my run in as close to an hour as possible before jumping on my bike to view another inspiring sunrise over the Pacific Ocean. I then planned to head down the Gold Coast beach road on my bike.

My run was feeling extra good. Running in the dark that morning, I had already put in a few one-block sprints when I started my morning conversation with the Lord. I had a habit of pouring out my deepest feelings with God on my long runs or bike rides. This was one of the reasons I enjoyed the solitude of training alone. I guess you could say it was my prayer and meditation time.

After my third sprint session of the morning, I casually asked God, "Help me learn to run again like I did before my bike accident."

Almost instantly, I heard a loud reply in my head, *Help you?* I was stunned. Had I heard correctly? Would God actually say something that sounded sarcastic? Maybe I was just making this up.

I was puzzled as I continued to run along and asked again, "Lord, help me to run like I used to run."

Again, an instant reply, in my head, *Help you?*

It definitely sounded sarcastic and was unmistakable. I knew I heard this crystal-clear response in my head.

I was so stunned I stopped running in that early-morning dark neighborhood with orange streetlights glowing overhead. To this day, I could take you to the very street and place where I stopped. I was determined to understand what I had heard. What was the meaning of this "help you?"

I DO IT ALL

As I stood still there in the street, I implore God again to help me. I made my request detailed this time, with tears in my eyes, saying, "Lord, you know and can see how hard I am working to learn how to run fast again. I need your help for me to achieve this goal!" There was no quick reply this time. I stood there in that dark-orange glow in that silent neighborhood for a long quiet wait before I heard God's response.

He said clearly, *Don't you understand? I never help anyone do anything!* I was stunned as I stood there silently in the dark for another long, puzzling pause. Then the most revealing statement I had ever heard. God said to me clearly, "I DO IT ALL!"

"I never help anyone do anything, I DO IT ALL?" Could I have heard correctly? I know it wasn't audible but it was so loud in my head that it may as well have been audible.

It was there, as I stood still in a deserted Gold Coast neighborhood on that quiet dark morning that I heard from God. This simple statement finally freed me up from the heavy weight of having to "do it all" by myself. As I thought, contemplated, and perceived what he had just revealed to me, I started to tear up again and eventually cried with relief. How could I have been so arrogant thinking I could "do it all?" I had been trying to carry this huge heavy load all by myself. Who was I? Who did I think I was? I had evidently watched too many *Superman* movies when I was younger.

As I stood there bawling like a baby, I finally understood. God really does "do it all" in everything in our lives. Our hearts beat, our lungs work, muscles twitch, eyes see, ears hear, tongues taste, the ability to feel with our skin, the synapses fire off in our brain, allowing us to think and create. This all happens without our conscious effort. We are not in control of any of these amazing gifts that God bestows upon us at the miracle of birth. God was DOING IT ALL from our very beginning without us thinking about it or us graciously even giving Him any credit. Human beings are so arrogant, thinking we are so self-sufficient and in control, especially when everything is going perfectly in our lives.

Finally able to wipe the tears from my eyes, I took off on the remainder of my run with a newfound understanding of my position and relationship with God. It gave me a sense of freedom, allowing me to relax and enjoy the journey I was on. He had me covered, and everything was right where it was supposed to be, if I would only trust Him. I felt like I had arrived in paradise. That early-morning run somehow looked completely different. The stress I had daily put myself under to improve began to melt away. I could now look forward to my morning runs, as I realized for the first time, God was really in control. I could now begin to relax while still doing my very best.

We are taught many ways or techniques of how to be strong enough to handle any situation. So what do we do? We tend to look to every source the world has to offer to answer our never-ending questions. Our Western world is increasingly looking for some mystical or Eastern wise men for the answer to our deepest questions. More and more people are turning to yoga, Eastern meditation, or some so-called wise man or guru to blindly follow. In this process, we naturally concentrate on ourselves, doing everything we know how to do to be stronger. In other words, following man's ways to earn our way to Nirvana, heaven, or some celestial paradise. Christianity is the only following that does not rely on man's efforts. Jesus says He has already paid the price for us so we can relax and have peace, which passes all understanding.

Remembering my definition of success for tennis turns out to be exactly what Jesus asked us to do. He says to set those things aside which weigh us down or simplify. Then he says to focus our concentration on Him, like in tennis, focus on the ball. Jesus says we will then have the freedom to live our lives creatively. Jesus said He came to set us free! Freedom from what? Freedom from stressing, worrying, striving, and needing to have all the answers. He said His ways are not our ways, and our ways are not His ways. His way is a gift freely given, stress-free, allowing us to not only love ourselves but also to freely love everyone else. We can only then see and understand that every individual we come in contact with is special, with special talents and gifts to bless those around them. God didn't make our lives to be complicated. By getting rid of all those things around us that weigh us down or distract us from what God has given us a passion for will allow us to focus more on Him. We can then freely be able to love and bless and interact with those He brings into our lives. Focusing on ourselves is the surest way to be dissatisfied and remain in an unhappy state. This happens because we know ourselves too well and quickly realize all of our glaring weaknesses. This lifestyle ends up being a bottomless pit of never being good enough and always falling short of what we think should be strong enough. This again leads us to constantly compare ourselves with others. Comparing ourselves with others leads us to be either arrogant or bitter.

By listening to what God enlightened me with on my early-morning run in Australia, and applying it to my life, left me free to do the best I knew to do in the moment and let him do the rest or "do it all." After all, "He is God, not me." Now I could start to relax, enjoy the moment, and be able to take in the wonderful scenery surrounding me. Some will think this means not doing your best and just sitting around depending on God to somehow miraculously make us fit, healthy, or successful, leaving us with no responsibility. This idea is far from the truth. We still need to do all we know to do. The difference being, trusting that God is ultimately in control of the outcome and knows what is best for us. Then regardless of the outcome, we can celebrate and enjoy the journey before us. It is not all about us! It is about something much bigger and grander than we can even comprehend. How can we share God or Jesus with those around us, only when they see us? When we follow His way, friends and acquaintances will see something in us they desire. Being surprised they see that quality in us, we will recognize they are seeing Jesus in us. We can then share Him instead of our own big ego. Isn't that what we all really desire? People seeing God in us?

God had shared many principles with me through the years that seemed to gain more clarity after this encounter. God had given me that perfect definition for tennis years before. "Tennis is the ability to simplify your movements, and focus your concentration, so you have the freedom to play creatively." Now in my broken and beat-up body with spinal cord damage, I was learning the same lesson he had taught me in the past. God wanted me to "simplify my life, focus on Him, instead of on myself, so I had the freedom to live my life creatively again." I have not always been successful living this philosophy, but I was finally free to let go and start letting Him "do it all."

There wasn't just light at the end of the tunnel now, but light was filling the tunnel.

Miracles

Why is the word *miracle* so difficult for so many to understand, believe in, or even deal with? *Miracle* is just a word, but the reality of miracles is too difficult for most because everyone wants to be in control. Also, for many people, miracles conjure up visions of witch doctors, voodoo, and hocus-pocus. For me, watching my first child being born was a miracle. Miracles exist everywhere around us. Miracles are the unexplainable happenings that occur in front of us every day. Numerous miracles are taking place, but we are blinded because we have taken most of them for granted, and they seem so commonplace. When we realize that the world we live in is made up of things we cannot see and the unoccupied space between these so-called solid particles is vast, we start to understand the very nature of the miracle called our existence. When I was lying in the hospital, unable to feel anything from my chest downward, I couldn't believe how easy it was for everyone who came onto our fourth floor to stand, much less walk around, with no apparent thought or effort.

How could our very existence happen after two cells came together in a chance meeting? Our very body contains thousands of miracles going on at the same time. Some of the more obvious ones are sight, feel, touch, taste, hearing, laughing, and the ability to love. Our most advanced computers are primitive compared to the human brain. How about our inner ear giving us the ability for balance even while sitting, not to mention standing, walking, running, or performing the seemingly impossible gymnastic routines we see at the Olympics.

These are all miracles when you really take the time to think about them. We can't explain how we acquired these automatic abilities, except to note that we are genetic replicas of the DNA strand from our father and mother. Our DNA strand is so complex and long that it is impossible to call it anything but a miracle. Plants are reproduced by producing seeds that literally die in the soil and then reproduce exactly the same variety of plant it came from. How is it possible for a seed to contain all the information to reproduce the exact variety of plant it came from? This is another type of miracle we take for granted. Many say it is just a fortunate accident, allowing us to enjoy the very food we need to exist and stay healthy.

Now we come to the heart of the situation. What about miracles that defy the very science we rely so heavily on in our modern society called medical science. We depend heavily on our medical experts to keep us healthy and take care of any physical problems that frequently seem to come up. Doctors spend years studying and researching to learn everything mankind has discovered about the human body and ways to repair our bodies when they break down. Doctors are the experts, and we, as a society, demand medical experts to have all the answers for any physical abnormalities.

Doctors are the first to admit unexplainable occurrences when seemingly impossible healings occur. Instead of calling these occurrences miracles, they tend to call them unexplainable anomalies. When the complete blowout of my T5 vertebrae and fractures of my T12 healed enough in thirty-one days to release me from the hospital, my doctor said maybe I just healed faster than everyone else he'd heard about, even though I was forty-five years old.

Then there was the doctor who tried to testify against me in court saying I must be faking my injuries, even though he was astounded when looking at my numerous MRIs and X-rays. Standing beside him in his office, he whistled out loud, then said I shouldn't even be standing up, much less beginning to do triathlons or playing tennis again. He was in complete denial as were other doctors checking me out. The head urologist, his assistants, and lab staff at the hospital were amazed that I could be in the shape I was in after three and a half hours of tests checking me inside and out. He said tests of my internal organs and systems showed I should not be able to do the physical activities I was engaging in every day. He stated, "You are a walking miracle." There it was again, that word, *miracle*.

Why do miracles scare so many people? Are they afraid of miracles because they can't quantify or explain them? Or are they afraid of admitting there could be a God, who cares for us and watches out for us. I firmly believe God just does miracles because He can, to bless us. This doesn't mean I sat back and did nothing. I probably had just about every alternative treatment you can imagine and could find to stimulate my nervous system. Every person treating me said the same thing, "You are a walking miracle," then asked me, "How are you doing it?" It is amazing how they all somehow tried to come to the same conclusion. "You must be super strong physically and mentally and blessed with some unexplainable ability to survive, heal, and keep going." I am not unique, just a walking, living miracle, thanks to God, like everyone else. I never stop recognizing this miracle every time I wake up to enjoy another wonderful day on our big beautiful blue ball floating in this vast, dark universe.

According to the Bible, God spoke everything into existence. Every plant and animal life form is unique unto itself. Scientists have proof that many plants and animals have gone extinct over time. If evolution, they so proudly exclaim were true, we would have evidence of new animals and plants being evolved today. But they cannot because it is not happening. Therefore, there is great effort by animal and plant activists to make sure no more animals or plants go extinct in the future.

*****

In many ways, I have had to invest more effort since my accident. The greatest amount of effort after my accident turned out to be the mental side of questioning my own abilities physically. After being told by many so-called experts that my everyday activities were now going to be impossible for me, I had to fight to stay positive, believe in miracles, and keep investing my energies properly. Each day provided enough excuses to stop moving forward and just sit around, watch TV, or vegetate into a worthless blob. The strained muscles and aches or pains from getting out and exercising were enough to make me want to stop striving to move forward. This is where I am thankful for—the peace I received on that orange-lit road in Australia, remembering what God promised me. He "does it all" gets me through my most difficult days of body aches and pains.

Why haven't I been completely healed so I don't have any leftover feelings of a broken body? My lower back will ache so badly at times, I can hardly stand up out of a chair. The sudden sharp pains that unexpectedly appear anywhere in my legs, like getting the crazy bone in your elbow hit can cause me to take a fall or just stumble around when I am active. I believe these are gentle reminders of my need to rely on God for His daily miracles. He loves me too much to ever let me go back to my huge ego days of thinking I can "do it all" again by myself. Not everyone is as hard headed as I had been or needs to encounter a minibus at 50 mph to wake them up. Even with all the miracles I had witnessed growing up, I still didn't understand that God was the One to rely on for everything worthwhile in life. As fulfilling as my life looked before that minibus, my life since has been more amazing as I have been learning how to rely on God for everything in life. I remind myself every day, "He does it all!"

Miri

Following that early morning wake up, I enjoyed my triathlon and tennis even more. I was winning almost every triathlon I entered and my tennis was even more enjoyable. Playing on our successful league team, I relaxed, allowing me to play even better. Letting God take the place of my huge ego was a huge relief. I wasn't always perfect, but enjoyment of my life was definitely improving.

With all that was going on, we never seemed to settle down in one place. We again found ourselves in another unexpected move back to the Philippines. I didn't mind because I always found it great living in the Philippines. Connecting with old friends and former students, I had coached and raced with or in triathlon training groups, always made living there special. I was again enjoying my training venue in Clark. It wasn't long before I ran into a few Filipino American triathletes and was invited to travel with them to Miri, Malaysia, just south of Brunei for a triathlon. Miri turned out to be a new venue for a Malaysian Olympic-distance triathlon. This small almost isolated area of Malaysia is in Sarawak, part of a small island directly east of mainland Malaysia. This was the first triathlon for this isolated, newly developed region. Kota Kinabalu, where we had raced a number of times in the past, is on the northern end of the same island. The rest of the island is shared by Brunei and south, central, and eastern Borneo. After arriving back to the Philippines, I was struggling with my fitness as my training had been disrupted but was talked into traveling to Miri because of the opportunity to explore a new tropical race site for the Southeast Asian triathlon scene. I knew I would enjoy the triathletes I would be traveling with, so off I went, even with my lack of race fitness.

Kota Kinabalu was our connecting city, and it brought back wonderful memories to see familiar coastline coming into view on our approach to the airport. After a short wait for our connection, we boarded a small local airline to fly south, over Brunei before landing in Miri. Our flight took us along the coast, and we could see every jungle river outlet flowing into the ocean. Our afternoon flight coincided with their synchronized sewage release. We could clearly see the brown water, forming a brown bloom in the ocean at the end of each river mouth. Miri is located right at the end of one of these jungle rivers. When landing, the brown sewage bloom could be clearly seen close to where our swim would take place in a few days. Viewing this I was thinking, *Another Pattaya, Thailand, triathlon polluted swim was awaiting us?* By now I had seen enough of that scenario around Asia to know the sewage would dissipate and the ocean would be crystal clear come race morning. Whether it would meet World Health Organization standards was doubtful.

Accommodations were arranged for us to stay at the new Marriott Hotel right on the water's edge. A beautiful tropical swimming pool was inviting and there for us to relax and swim a few laps. The Marriott was brand-new like the entire city of Miri. Miri a newly developed city, originally targeted as commercial and industrial and was making an effort to become a tourist destination as well. Familiarizing foreigners to this newly developed region was the main reason for holding the Miri triathlon. As with every Asian triathlon, we were treated to wonderful hospitality before, during, and following the race.

My race was memorable for a number of reasons but also included the usual desperate sensation on the run. I was not having one of my best races with my lack of fitness but was still happy to be in Miri and able to compete. I found it difficult to find my rhythm and swim stroke when the race started resulting in a slower-than-usual swim. Used to being one of the better swimmers in most triathlons, it was not easy to feel like a slug in the water. After a disappointing swim, I was not looking forward to the steep hills on the bike and run course, which looked to be challenging. I was still eager to put in my best effort, hopefully having a reasonable finish. I wanted to finish well and as usual pushed hard on the bike. There was a fair amount of drafting on the bike, as I watched a few groups ease by me. I still smiled and ended the forty-kilometer bike leg leading my age division.

Once out of transition, the run headed straight up a long steep hill for a kilometer before leveling off for 1.5 kilometers to the turnaround. I was relieved to be heading back downhill, still with the knowledge I would be required to repeat that challenging uphill one more time. Just before the five-kilometer turnaround nearing the bottom of the hill, I again needed to locate a secluded area to hide from the public's view.

This area of Miri had been defoliated to allow for beautiful new landscaping by the Marriot, between the road we were running on, and the beach. Jungle was everywhere in this part of Sarawak except here, beside the race course. I continued running, looking for somewhere to relieve myself. Finally, close to the turnaround, I spotted a newly landscaped area that had used the original tropical plants and palm trees near the beach. Veering left I made a detour off the course to hide in this small, secluded area. Weary of snakes, this still allowed me to make do with some large leaves. I was now presentable and got back on the road to finish the race. I knew God had healed me and blessed me and was still "doing it all" but couldn't help thinking, *How many times does this need to happen when I race?* Knowing I had lost a huge chunk of time, I took it easy and cruised for the last five kilometers, enjoyably finishing the 10k run. At the award presentations, I knew I had no chance of an award but didn't really care as I was happy to have been given the opportunity to be with friends and experience this newly developed area of Miri. The trip was a wonderful and worthwhile experience.

To my surprise, at the award presentations, they announce I had finished second. Some of the ones I thought I was racing against turned out to be in younger age groups. I was almost embarrassed to receive the award having given up racing, then just jogging along after my escapade in the tropical landscaping. I had still tried my best during most of the race. I loved the atmosphere of being around fit, positive athletes from all over Asia and some from the US. Catching up with old friends and making new friends never gets boring. The encouragement I received at each event always lifted my spirit. These memories are priceless and enduring. Miri, Sarawak, was another new and memorable adventure on my incredible life's journey.

God was still allowing me to live a vivacious life. How much luckier could I be. I was learning to enjoy every moment now knowing He was "doing it all" in my life. Sharing with others that God was in charge of my life never gets boring. The joy of being part of someone receiving Jesus and watching Him be in charge of their lives is the greatest experience I have ever encountered.

Camsur: Going the Distance

Camsur 70.3 Cobra Ironman 2010 first came as an idea when a fellow triathlete said it would be a fun event for me. I had just finished second for those over fifty although I was sixty-four years old at the Alabang Animo Tri in June. I didn't give the suggestion much of a thought at first. I decided if I could get some proper training, I would do what I could to be fit and enter the event in Camsur.

To my surprise, after entering late and with great trepidation, I received confirmation of my entry acceptance less than eight weeks before Camsur. Since I barely finished the Animo Tri, I knew it was going to be a real challenge to finish a 70.3 half Ironman event without crawling to the finish line.

Most of the triathletes in Clark just assumed I would cruise through the race and win my age category. Being a veteran triathlete and finishing over 200 triathlons the last twenty-four or so years, I knew I was up against the wall to just finish this half-ironman event.

For the last five years, I had found it hard to train consistently because of my latest accident. My back and hip just wouldn't cooperate after being taken out on a roundabout by that Ute in Australia. With only two races completed in the last eighteen months I decided to get up before 3:00 a.m. Monday through Saturday for a bike and run so I would arrive back home in time for my children's homeschooling. I was also sponsoring and organizing a triathlon series while getting in a swim three or four times a week. Those around Clark thought I was crazy, as they would often see me going home by 6:30 a.m. when they were just heading into Clark for their training session.

With seventeen days left and counting, I was getting excited about the race. I was able to do a 90k ride hard and then do my run of 13k off the bike in one hour and fourteen minutes. I hadn't run that well in quite a while. The next day, I tried to back it up with a 50k medium ride and see what a 6 to 7k run would feel like. To my surprise, I felt great for an old guy. My feet started to feel light and as I started to stride out, my hamstring tighten up right down through my calf. I could tell it wasn't torn, but I took it easy, getting back on my bike to cycle the 20k back home.

That was the end of my serious training before the August 22 race day. To make matters worse, I caught a cold staying up all night on August 14 to make sure our triathlon series was prepared properly and a wonderful memory for those racing our event on August 15.

*****

After a long drive to Camarines Sur in Southern Luzon, we arrived safely Tuesday night. Wednesday morning, we drove over to CWC (Camsur Watersport Complex), the site of the upcoming triathlon event. Once we saw their wonderful wakeboard park, we as a family, decided to spend the next couple of days wakeboarding and relaxing. Since my accident in 1992, I had stayed away from two things I used to love, snow skiing and waterskiing. My children again encouraged me to try wakeboarding, and to my surprise and joy, I was able to get up on a wakeboard and enjoy wakeboarding for two days.

In spite of the great time relaxing with my family, I had an unsettled feeling about the impending race of 70.3-mile and the challenge it presented to me on Sunday. I was nervous after almost no training for two weeks and certainly none of my normal race preparations for Camsur. I knew I was in for a rough time but somehow was looking forward to seeing how my body would hold up on race day. Before I hurt my hamstring, I had been feeling great.

Everyone was hoping for cloudy weather with rain to keep the heat away from the previous few days. On race morning, it became apparent that mostly clear, sunny, hot and humid weather was in store for all who came to challenge Camsur August 22, 2010. Every triathlete seemed almost hyper as race day was in full swing when I arrived. I had only swam once since I arrived but was still looking forward to the race getting under way. Those my age in transition seemed to think I would be unbeatable, but I wasn't so sure.

The elite triathletes went off at six thirty, then the twenty to thirty-nine age group two minutes later, followed by my group forty and older five minutes later. Being the second oldest triathlete in Camsur, I couldn't wait to get underway and see if my swim would give me a good start, ahead of many younger triathletes.

When the hooter went off, I immediately tripped and fell flat on my face in about a foot of water. Once I awkwardly stood up and started swimming, I felt fine. Starting last, I eventually began passing quite a few who had entered the water ahead of me. It felt good to be racing again, and after the first lagoon swim ended, I actually felt good running to the wakeboard lagoon for the last part of the swim. As with everyone else, it was difficult to navigate the second lagoon with sun directly in our eyes. Finally exiting the swim with the twenty-third fastest swim among the one hundred eighty or so over-forty group. I was excited to have done so well.

My transition was okay as I headed out for the ninety kilometer bike course. The course was inspiring with multitudes of school children screaming, "Go, Ironman, go," at every school along the route. As always, I enjoyed the bike portion of Camsur. Even with marshals yelling "stay to the left," then "stay to the right" then back again "stay to the left" over and over, it didn't take away my enjoyment of being out there feeling the wind in my face again. After knowing God was doing it all, I could relax and enjoy the moment.

The excitement of cycling started to wane at around 70k, as I began thinking about the upcoming run of 21.1 kilometers. This foreboding just got worse the closer I got to transition. For some reason I had to work extra hard to keep my pace up the last 10 kilometers. When the bike dismount finally came, I was determined to jump off my bike and sprint to my bike rack, only to find both legs totally cramped, hardly holding me up. If it hadn't been for my bike to hang onto, I would have fallen flat on my face. Looking down at my bike, I discovered why the last ten kilometers had been so hard. I had been riding on a low tire and had become completely flat by the time I dismounted my bike.

For the first time ever, I walked through transition and decided to put my shoes on in the tent they provided. I was so cramped up, I knew I couldn't bend down as I normally would to put on my shoes. When I entered the tent, there was another much younger triathlete struggling to put on his running shoes with cramping muscles making it almost impossible. We both looked at each other and laughed as we struggle to put on our shoes. Five minutes later, I was able to straighten up and head out for the run. A much longer transition than I had planned, but I didn't even care.

Another surprise awaited, as I actually felt pretty good after the five minutes sitting down. This good feeling lasted about 800 meters before the inevitable exhaustion set in. When I dropped one of my gels and had to stop to pick it up, I found myself walking. I kept telling myself not to walk, so after a short walk, I forced myself to run again. I thought I was going okay when I felt a hand on my back, and an old friend Michellie Jones ran past and said something like "Come on, keep going." I must have looked pretty bad compared to how she was running, and I had just started my journey. Michellie was already past halfway of her 21.1 kilometers. She looked great heading on down the road. We had caught up earlier and said how Camsur reminded us both of earlier days of triathlon when racing was much more relaxed, almost feeling like a party.

It was then I took a serious assessment of my body and decided at the 4.5k turnaround that I had better start doing a walk-and-run program or someone would find me curled up on the side of the road. With this program, I hoped I would be able to finish this race. Race? It had suddenly become a matter of survival. Forget the idea of racing! When I could run, I would do my best to keep a proper cadence going. It must have worked because a few fellow competitors yell out that I looked strong as I passed by while they were walking.

I also had a few who passed me while I was walking who inquired about my condition. They said I was wobbling around as I walked. I kept telling myself, it must just my spinal cord damage causing my imbalance. Whatever it was, I was not in good shape, but I also knew after going that long and hard, I had to complete the journey. I had finished every triathlon I had started and wasn't about to give up.

David Charlton said I looked so bad coming around the first 4.5k turnaround, that a medic started to come out to help me. When the medic saw us talking and walking together, he left me alone, hoping I was okay. It is amazing how good it feels to have a friend at the aid station to encourage you and provide the banana and orange slice at the exact right time to keep you going. My family was there at the lagoon to cheer me on and tell me it was okay to walk so I could eventually finish. I really wanted to finish strong for them, but I knew it would take all I had just to get across that finish line. To make a very long story short, I eventually found a way to finish. Everyone at the recovery pool asked me how I had done and did I win my race again? I told them probably not as I barely made across the finish line. To my dismay, two hours later, I found out I had won my age group by over nineteen minutes. Obviously, I was not the only one who had experienced a difficult day in the heat of Camsur.

I DO IT ALL

70.3 Half-Ironman Champion at 62 years old

Am I glad I took up the challenge? Absolutely! Do I care that some spectators criticize those of us who had to walk? Not a bit. Their day will come, if they decide to enter and complete a long-distance race themselves. They might even find themselves crawling to the finish line, as some of the greats of triathlon have done. As always, I was able to catch up with some of the greats of triathlon like Cameron Brown and Michellie Jones.

Camsur...it was long...it was hot...it was humid...it was most of all a challenge shared by those who came and raced but, most of all, those who "finished." God was still blessing me as I was able to thank Him for allowing me to continue racing.

As Jason Shortis said after being really sick in Hawaii but still able to finish, "Triathlon is not a sport just to win, but most of all, to finish." If we forget that, we lose the real joy of the sport of triathlon.

LIFE AND WISDOM: EXPECT THE UNEXPECTED

How has life turned out once God taught me these numerous and valuable lessons? Has everything been like riding down a smooth freeway with no pothole in sight? Have I avoided mistakes that seem so easy to sidestep? You would think with age and the wisdom accrued through the years, there would be no thoughtless words or actions that make it necessary to ask for forgiveness. Knowing the truth and living it consistently are two different stories when being blindsided on our life's journey.

Unexpectedly receiving a job offer, we decided to relocate back to the States, and our life completely changed. Being back in the States felt like I was living in a foreign country after living overseas for twenty-seven years. I had a difficult time finding my foothold. My job should have made me feel right at home, being the director of tennis and head professional at a prestigious tennis club, where I taught tennis when this club first opened years before. But it was just the opposite, as the States had changed dramatically since I left twenty-seven years earlier. Or maybe it was just me who had changed. The fast-paced rat-race "look out for yourself" mentality of Silicon Valley I knew from years before had only increased. It was evident everywhere we went. The suburbs had spread miles south, almost to Morgan Hill.

In spite of this obvious change, we were determined to make a success of our move halfway around the world. We immediately got in step with this fast-paced whirlwind society. I ended up working sixteen hours a day to make sure my new program was a success for the club. I wanted to prove to the owner, whom I thought was a good friend, that he had made a great decision, begging me to come back to his club.

My entire family was always involved in our adventures, and it was no different at this club. Daniel and Crystal took up tennis, and we as a family, practically lived at the tennis courts. I had a five-year contract and a five-year plan to rebuild the deteriorated tennis program. I jumped in full speed ahead.

Immediately, I faced opposition from the adult members who were given little or no notice of my arrival. The court time required for my expanding junior program received opposition from the adult members. Most of the former assistant coaches thought my new plan would fail and also resisted these changes. The young coaches were just plain belligerent, refusing to follow the simplest instructions. Every day was a fight to make lessons happen correctly and my attitude started to sour. Once firing the young teachers who couldn't or refused to teach properly, I hired quality, upbeat tennis staff. After that, my spirits started to lift. The junior program expanded quickly as parents of these young tennis players also got excited about their children's improvement.

I got up early as I had for years, only this time I headed to the club in the morning dark to make sure there was order to the day and handle any disruptions that seemed to occur daily. I sacrificed my early-morning exercise routine for the good of the club program. It seemed like every day I would receive caustic e-mails from sour adult members who tried to find fault with the growing and vibrant junior program. They were also upset that the previous head pro had lost his position. They had basically controlled him when he was tennis director. With him in charge, the adults would have court time available for them at a moment's notice. They had been allowed to break club rules, like drinking and smoking on the courts, before I arrived. I had been asked to stop all these activities by the owner. Of course, I had to personally face the members' repercussions.

In the process of this happening, I got lost in the daily fight to keep the program successfully moving forward. I forgot the lesson God had taught me on that early morning run in Australia. God had clearly said to me, "I do it all." Instead of spending time talking with my Creator, I was relying on my past experiences, ideas, and knowledge to turn the tennis program around. That is not necessarily bad, but cutting the wisdom of God out of any equation will eventually leave you hanging by a thread. There are only two ways to look at life's adventures. You can do them man's way or do things God's way. God's way takes faith; man's ways takes effort and, hopefully, the right experience. Now back in the States, I was relying on my vast experience of operating clubs and tennis programs. I knew what was supposed to work and stubbornly forged ahead, forcing my will to make the tennis program a success.

Financial success did come, as in one year, we were able to increase the tennis program profit for the club tenfold, and attendance of the junior program increase threefold. My remaining and new experienced coaches were excited, seeing the results of a quality approach to teaching. They were surprised and excited at how quickly the juniors were improving. The club had seen years of little if any improvement using a babysitting approach with young juniors. These students were now learning how to play tennis and enjoyed the experience. The excitement was contagious with the juniors and their parents. The parents expressed their appreciation weekly with our new teaching approach.

In spite of this obvious success, the relationship with the adults remained toxic and increased no matter how much effort was put in to improve the relationship. The adults were upset with the increasing number of juniors playing tennis and hanging around the club. Juniors were taking away some of their precious court time. I was sacrificing time with my family to make sure my efforts to revitalize the tennis program produced positive results for the adults as well as the juniors in the club.

I DO IT ALL

Sacrificing family time is never a good idea. You would think, I would have known better than to forfeit my family to make my occupation a success. My first year back to the States, I earned $114,000 and substantially increase the tennis profits for the club and my assistant teaching pros. As a reward, the owner called me in one morning and informed me he was reducing my salary by one-third and cutting another 10 percent from my tennis lesson revenue. Wow, was that the appreciation I was expecting? His excuse was simple. The limited partners would not let a tennis teaching pro earn that much money. Even with this huge insult, what was I to do after moving my family halfway around the world? I had signed a five-year contract that I was obligated to fulfill regardless of the situation. I was determined to make the tennis program a success to honor my friendship with the owner.

We had made a huge and expensive move back to the States, so I felt I had no choice but to accept these new terms. I wasn't really worried, as the lesson program was booming and continued to grow every month. The demand for my private lessons had, as with other clubs, produced a waiting list. I worked even harder to organize a new high-level summer tennis camp for juniors who wanted to excel in competitive tournament play. The camp was looking hopeful when students as far away as Asia started signing up three months in advance.

January, February and March are traditionally the slowest months for lessons and income with only outdoor courts in Northern California. By April 1 my personal income was around $45,000. All my assistants were making more income and were excited. What was the owner going to do when in the first three months of the year I had earned that much? If it was true that somehow the limited partners wanted to put a limit on how much I should earn, there could be a problem moving forward. These three months were historically the slowest three months, and I had an expected income of $200,000 or more for the coming year. I hoped this wouldn't be another excuse for the owner to reduce my percentage further. The success of the program and huge increased revenue for the club should be enough incentive to leave things as they were.

My assistants and I had spent many hours organizing a new adult program rollout. This had been planned to energize the adults at the club, hopefully being as successful as the junior program. My assistants were excited about the new program, and I had spent many hours personally putting it together. It was encouraging to see my staff excited and energized to get the adults onboard and involved alongside the booming junior program. With a new general manager in place and his apparent positive review of my plans for the next three years, everything was beginning to look hopeful.

The Friday Family Nights I had introduced were a huge success. Families would bring potluck items and join together to play tennis and eat on the viewing deck until closing time at 10:00 p.m. The energy was building for the entire tennis program. My family was heavily involved with all the new activities, and Daniel and Crystal would come straight to the club after school to study. I would get to be with them and they would have a chance to hit a few tennis balls.

By the beginning of April, I felt the adult, as well as the junior program, had turned the corner. Saturday, April 1, was a cloudy morning with threatening rain. Finishing the morning junior lessons, the clouds finally opened up, and it began to pour. Coming off the courts, the new general manager left a message in my office to meet him in the conference room with the head of HR (human resources). The atmosphere was somber and quiet as I opened the door and found my way into a chair. With no hesitation, the GM introduced me to a California law I was unaware of called At Will. At Will allows employers to cancel contracts at any time without cause. I felt like the air had been sucked out of the room, just hours before my assistants and I had talked excitedly about what the year was beginning to look like.

My five-year contract, which brought us back to the States was worthless, if what he said was true. This young first-time general manager let me know he was bringing back a good friend of his to the club, the former director of tennis and head pro I had replaced. Without any notice, I was informed he had already hired a new director of tennis and head pro. I was given one hour to pack up and leave. I was shocked, feeling I had been betrayed by the owner, who was at that moment in France getting married. It became obvious that it was never God's will that I be put under that kind of pressure and be immersed under that daily negative environment.

The huge number of hours I dedicated to the club to make sure it was successful was starting to tear my family apart. Without me even realizing, my family was taking second place to my work. I had been working seven days a week to make my friend's club successful while neglecting God's amazing gift to me, my family. Only an hour after leaving the club, I felt the weight of negativity lifted from my shoulders. Knowing I wouldn't be required to wake up to any more negative e-mails was wonderful. I had a clear conscience as I had done over and above my responsibilities to make my former friend and owner successful and proud of his club.

God is always good and faithful as a large number of my students contacted me and asked me to continue teaching them. I hardly skipped a beat with my teaching schedule, only this time without the pressure keg put on me by the club. I was my own boss again, allowing me to enjoy my passion of only instructing my students. I had been doing things my way and the world's way for eighteen months even though I knew better! Where was all that wisdom I had gained over the years? My mind had been clouded by the desire of recognition and success, so much so that I had let God again slip into the background and shadows of my life. The wakeup call of losing the job allowed me to put God back into proper perspective. I had gained weight and lost fitness in this worldly approach of making money and being successful. There is a saying, "You don't stop running because you get old, you get old because you stop running." I had stopped running to help my friend and owner achieve his dream, not mine or even God's dream for my life.

We stayed in San Jose for two more years, successfully teaching my junior program. We then had the opportunity to make another move. This time to San Diego, California, for Crystal and Daniel. Daniel was starting university at Point Loma Nazarene University, and Crystal was headed to Point Loma High School. Once in San Diego, I completely stopped running and saw my weight balloon even more. Seeing a picture of myself with my son Brian at the beach who was visiting from North Carolina really woke me up to my ballooning body.

A Facebook post announcing the twenty-fifth anniversary of the Subic Triathlon in the Philippines was my inspirational wakeup call to train and get back into shape. I made the decision to enter the Subic Triathlon. I had raced and won my age category in the inaugural event and many more Subic races over the years. The race was scheduled for the twenty-second of April, which coincided with the twenty-sixth anniversary of my bike accident. Starting out forty-five pounds overweight and not able to run for more than a minute without gasping for air was not encouraging. Since I entered, I had no choice but to stay with my new training program. Each day, I did my best to get back into shape so I could complete the 1,500-meter swim, 40-kilometer bike, and a 10-kilometer run. Big aspirations, but I was determined to finish even though many people thought I was too old, at seventy-one, to do another triathlon.

The big problem facing me was the knowledge I had gained over many years of competing in triathlons. There is a balance of being fit enough to train properly for an event. In preparing for an event, you must take a look at your overall fitness level to ascertain what training is even possible. From past experience of racing around Asia and the world, I knew it took about a year to become fit enough to go all out in your training regimen to eventually achieve maximum results. With this information available to me, I was still hoping to somehow shortcut the process and have a respectable finish in Subic.

There are no shortcuts! Pulled and strained muscles, ligaments, and tendons were my weekly problems while trying to replicate my training program from past years. Information doesn't necessarily make you any smarter. I only had four months, and no matter how hard I tried to cut corners, it only provided more frustration.

My goal needed to be adjusted if I hoped to finish the race. Attempting to race fast was no longer my goal. I told friends in Hong Kong years before how to start training by running "one light pole at a time." Then keep training smart and as best as you can stay with your program. Now I was doing my best to keep my advice to keep going and let God "do it all."

I DO IT ALL

Joy of Living Life to the Fullest

Life is a gift we all tend to take for granted in our ever busier world. That is until the unexpected smacks us straight between our eyes. I have learned a lot through the years but have found staying positive is one of the most important and difficult factors in living a full and productive life. We also hear how to live positive lives from the many self-help books and blogs traveling the literary circuit. With all these ideas floating around, positivity is probably one of the most misunderstood characteristics. Most of us live with the idea that positivity primarily comes from being successful or positioning ourselves around positive successful people. Although people who are successful tend to look positive, real positivity comes from a deep belief that transcends our circumstances. The very idea that we can be positive regardless of the factors bombarding us daily seems a little far-fetched. I believe true positive character traits transcends the eventual ups and downs in life and will truly affect our ability to stay positive.

If this is true, what are the traits which unknowingly keep us positive? Primarily, I believe positivity is a by-product of keeping our eyes on God and what God puts right in front of us to accomplish daily. This simply means staying focused on doing our best in the moment. As Christians, we should never forget that He is in control of the final results. This is if we really believe God is who He says He is and completely trust Him.

Belief and trust are big words. "Easy to say, hard to do." Does this mean we never get frustrated or angry as unexpected occurrences thwart our plans and pop up unexpectedly in our lives? Of course not! The only way to keep frustration and anger at bay is to stay closely focused on our relationship with God, who created us and this entire universe. Believing He is in control, we then do the little items needing attention right in front of us. I have tried to develop a running dialogue with God each day about everything going on in my life. When I am conscientiously in conversation with Him, the unexpected situations don't seem to disturb my life like they do when I try to take on everything by myself or "do it all."

Nobody is perfect by any means, but I am doing my best to step back and let Him "do it all." Stepping aside and trusting God allows me to relax more and enjoy the moment. With this type of approach, my life becomes an exciting adventure. I can expectantly look forward to God's intervention, working things out according to His purpose, not mine. This frees me up to enjoy those around me instead of having to be in control. I am then able to follow God's ways, not mine. Does this mean I stop trying so hard when striving toward a goal? Of course not. It means doing our very best with whatever goals we find in front of us. This helps us to not get frustrated while trying to reach these goals. Taking care of the important achievable small tasks tend to lead to success. With the success in the little items, I then let God do his part, directing me to what he wants me to accomplish next.

This gets back to the idea of positivity. If we approach our lives this way, we appear to be positive to those around us. They see us always moving forward, attempting to achieve one goal after another. We are viewed as fun to be around as we talk about positive ideas instead of what isn't right and how things could be better if only this or that were not always thwarting our plans. When we are negative, it becomes easy to start finger-pointing, looking for what circumstances or individuals to blame for life not being wonderful and smooth. This is assuming life was ever meant to be so easy and idyllic. Sure, like everyone else, I love spending time at a tropical resort lounging around, enjoying sunsets or sunrises across a picture-perfect ocean. I have been more fortunate than most during my life remembering myself in the middle of that picture many times.

As much as I would like to live an idyllic lifestyle, we all know it is only temporary—a blessing we should never take for granted but to enjoy and remember with fond memories. Having wonderful people in our lives can produce these same feelings of warmth and joy. Sometimes a simple gesture of thanks can fill a moment with joy and suddenly lift our spirits. These moments can be as wonderful as those tropical moments recharging our lives.

When these simple experiences take place, God is allowing me to understand and live out the definition He gave me years ago:

I DO IT ALL

"Simplify my life, focus on Him, so I have the freedom to live life creatively." This produces an incredible freeing feeling. I become more relaxed, and the stress of our modern life tends to melt away, even in the face of adversity. With athletic endeavors, it is usually the little things that end up deciding the eventual outcome.

For a tennis player, it is the ability to stay in the moment. Watching the ball correctly usually makes the difference in who wins when both players have prepared the same. A runner trying to run faster will often tighten up when striving to reach their maximum speed, rather than remembering to stay relaxed and balanced correctly. An athlete may know this to be true, but with the finish line so close in the distance, it is easy to start leaning too far forward, causing him or her to tighten up and actually slow down.

I still play tennis with a good friend who is one of the better players in Southern California in his age group. I usually do fine with my attitude on the court until I arrive with high and unreasonable expectations. Suddenly, frustration bursts out because I have tried to "do it all" by myself. Forcing my will on the court usually leads to disappointment and frustration. Anger starts to well up inside me, taking me by surprise. I can easily be out of control instead of staying relaxed, letting God take charge. Feeling awkward on a tennis court can easily bring on frustration for me. I am no different from anyone else. When I relax and let go of my ever-present will, I can enjoy the moment more and play better tennis. Remembering the old phrase, "Easy to say, hard to do." Maybe that's why the Bible says, "Pray without ceasing!" God knows how life's trials can easily sneak up on us when we least expect it.

The Bible gives us clear instructions on how to gain peace and joy by following some simple guidelines. The problems we face are easy to recognize but can be difficult to deal with or change. We get our eyes on other people, asking why they are this way or that way. Why don't they change, so our life would be better or easier? The truth is, what other people do or don't do has nothing to do with who you are on the inside or how you react. God makes this crystal clear in His Word: "Stop comparing ourselves with others." (Galatians 6:4–5)

We need to stop blaming everyone else for our problems and realize we have a choice in life to live the way of peace and joy God promises or do everything our own stubborn way. Focusing on what is right in front of us, then leave the rest to God will free us up to live a joyful life of peace. We then find irritating situations will be less of a problem and, at times, hardly noticeable. We will find more sunshine in our life. Even if it only shines deep and warm in our hearts. That warmth will show in our everyday attitude. Those around us will wonder how we appear to float through intolerable hardships, hardly noticing the tumult and stormy conditions surrounding us.

With many travels through third-world countries, I have found contentment, happiness, and joy from those living with very little. These people are the very ones who encourage those of us who have, an abundance of the world's goods and successes. They have learned to be content in the moment while still doing their best each and every day. They get up early every day, work hard, and spend time with family, sharing whatever they have available.

My latest adventure of trusting God happened after spending four months getting back into shape to compete again in Subic Bay Triathlon. Race day happened to coincide with the twenty-sixth anniversary of my horrific accident. Trying to be consistent with my training while eating correctly and adjusting my schedule was difficult, to say the least. There was always the constant reminder of how hard it was to train with spinal cord injury and grossly overweight. The niggling little pains and strains on my body was enough to make me wonder if I shouldn't give up on my race goal. However, I had entered and did my best to stay with my training schedule. I was hoping to see some sign that my body would accept this new disciplined lifestyle, like it had been when I was younger. I was hoping to be reshaped into a fit-looking figure of an athlete by race day. I had never competed in a triathlon or a cycle race in the Philippines without looking healthy and fit.

Ten long weeks into my decision to train, I started to see small amounts of unwanted fat melt away. I already knew I would be the oldest competitor but certainly didn't want to be the fattest. By the time I was to leave for the Philippines, my body had reshaped enough to allow my tight-fitting shorts to now loosely hang on my hips. Of course these were the shorts for a very large body. I was still overweight but had lost twenty pounds. I thought that would never happen again when I began this journey three-and-a-half months earlier. I was finally able to swim, bike, and run the Olympic distance in training necessary to finish the race. I was beginning to be excited about lining up for the Subic triathlon.

Arriving two weeks before the race to acclimatize to the oppressive heat and humidity, which is always present in the Philippines, would give me just enough time to acclimatize for race day. Struggling to be strong and feel some speed weren't my main concerns for Subic. I wanted to look healthy and have a respectable finish. *Finish* being the operative word. Most of the Philippine triathletes had known me when I was fast and fit. I didn't want to disappoint them or embarrass myself. To my surprise, eight days before the race, I had a stellar workout. My swim felt strong and fairly fast, but most surprising were my bike and run. Both bike and run felt the best they had since I began training in December. Even with the oppressive heat and humidity, I felt good. Maybe I would have a good race after all, not just finish.

Now I was excited! Could I actually race this triathlon instead of just finishing it? High expectations again were tickling my ego! Was I looking to myself to "do it all" again? I was now looking forward to a good finishing time, not just crossing the finish line.

Life never gets boring, as we drove over to Subic with a couple of friends following my great training day. I wanted to check out the race course and enjoy the warmth and view of Subic Bay. While getting something to eat at a seafood restaurant late in the day, both my wife and I ended up with food poisoning.

How could this be happening? I had committed four months getting into shape and now this. For the next five days, I could hardly leave the house or the bathroom. My wife kept saying, "You don't need to race after being so sick." Thankfully, on Thursday evening, I began feeling a little better. My body felt incredibly weak, but at least the symptoms of food poisoning were gone. In only five days, I had gone from feeling strong and ready to race to wondering if I could get to the start line or hopefully finish the race.

I knew God had wanted me to sign up but also realized my big ego had started to play a role in my attitude again. When will I ever learn to get out of the way and let God truly be in control? God states clearly in the Bible, he wants us to humbly walk before men. I don't believe getting sick was an accident.

For some reason, just when I was feeling my most vulnerable, I was singled out for a feature TV human-interest story for the twenty-fifth anniversary race. There was now even more pressure on me to finish. I can't say I had the best attitude on Friday and Saturday before race day. Thoughts kept racing through my head like the months and time I had committed to training, only to find myself sick and weak. "Why me?" I was still determined but fighting back negative thoughts, which were forcing their way into my head. Now the race organizers and a TV program were singling me out as a positive role model. They wanted me to be an encouragement for the other triathletes, wanting to live a healthy vibrant lifestyle.

When race day arrived, I was apprehensive stepping out into the early-morning dark. Waiting for sunrise to peak across Subic Bay so they could start the race created even more apprehension. TV cameras were there, as well as race announcers, again letting everyone know I was one of the original participants in the inaugural race twenty-five years earlier. Only a couple of us racing had been there to experience the first Subic race.

When the gun sounded for my race, all apprehension disappeared as I raced into Subic Bay and settled into my swim stroke. My swim felt surprisingly good as I pulled away from those around me and most of those in our large wave of age groupers. I knew I was in a good position at the end of the first lap of 750 meters. However, slipping twice trying to get to my feet and falling down, I awkwardly found my feet. Running up the sandy beach in front of the large crowd of spectators felt humiliating. I thankfully disappeared back into the bay for the second lap. But what could I do? I was happy to be racing again in Subic, giving it my best effort. Starting the second 750-meter lap, doubt crept in, wondering if I had enough energy in my body for the entire race, much less the next 750-meter swim? I knew the previous week's food poisoning would affect my race, but how much, I wasn't sure.

I was encouraged when finishing the swim running up the beach without slipping and falling down. I was also surprised at how good I felt running up the 500-meter hill to the transition bike racks. *Wow*, I thought, *I might have a great race after all.* However, I was only five minutes into the forty-kilometer bike course when my body began feeling the toll of being sick all week. There was no power in my legs to allow me to ride hard on Subic's long uphill portion. I had successfully ridden strong up this hill many times in the past. Cycling fast up this hill, hoping to pass many other cyclists was what I planned to repeat in this race. Realization suddenly hit me that this Subic Triathlon had suddenly become about finishing, not racing. My ego needed to take a back seat, if I was going to eventually cross the finish line.

This idea of backing off my effort in a triathlon just to finish was foreign to me. But I had no other choice. I needed to be wise if I was to have a remote chance of crossing that finish line forty-five kilometers away. Watching cyclist after cyclist cruise on by was hard to accept. After trying to pick up speed to follow those passing me, I relinquished any idea of racing fast and settled into "survival mode." I found a cadence, which would allow me to get to the top of this long hill and hopefully arrive safely to the transition area. One triathlete after another was surprised to see me cycling so slow, but they all yelled out their encouragement for me to keep going as I had done for many of them in the past. These encouragements were just what I needed to finish the forty-kilometer bike portion.

Coming down the main road toward transition, I was hoping to have enough energy left for the run. I was exhausted, arriving at the sports oval where most of the spectators were gathered and the transition was located. Thankfully, I was able to finish the forty-kilometer bike. Now running the final ten kilometers in the increasingly oppressive heat and humidity was my entire focus. Somehow I needed to find a way to finish the race.

The 6.2-mile run on hot pavement was going to be a test of mental fortitude as much as physical effort. Everything in my body said, *Stop, crawl away, lay down and fall asleep somewhere.*

My mind said, *Keep moving;* my body said something else. Watching one slow runner after another slip on by was difficult for me to accept. I refused to stop running, if you could call it running? I would grab a quick drink at every aid station thinking it would be just enough fuel for me to survive. I was praying I could reach my goal of crossing that ever-elusive finish line. My fastest ten-kilometer run in a triathlon had been under forty minutes. Now it was going to be well over an hour if I was to finish. The run was three laps, where you could see the finish area right in front of you at the end of your first and second lap. There it was, right there, but you had to turn and head out for another three-and-a-half-kilometer lap.

Just when I thought I was mentally strong enough to finish, one of my eerily familiar spinal cord sensations kicked in with a sharp fiery pain. The sensation almost collapsed my right leg three times in the last mile and a half. A number of other triathletes witnessing my stumble slowed down to check on me. This sharp sensation feels like hitting your crazy bone, making your muscles go numb and weak. After a brief stop and a stretch, I was able to force myself to continue. Off in the distance, I could finally see the finish line. With relief, I could hear the announcer and see the huge crowd milling around the finishing arch on the far side of the running track. Only then did I feel assured of finishing and know God had done it again. He always "does it all!" We just need to be reminded of it again and again. Twenty-six years earlier, doctors said I would not be standing up again, much less finishing another triathlon. Twenty-five years ago, I won my age-group race in Subic looking strong. This time, I may not have looked good, but God was getting the glory. I was seventy-one years old and still standing, winning my division. That is actually funny as I was the only triathlete over the age of sixty racing, so I won the sixty-plus and seventy-plus event for just being alive!

I DO IT ALL

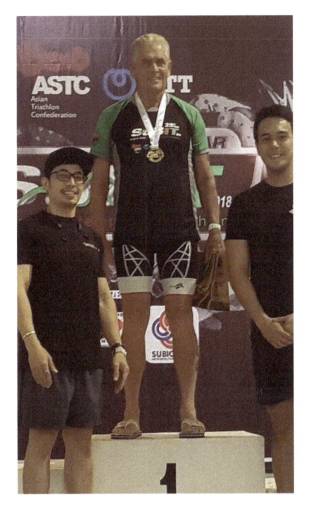

25th Anniversary Subic International
Triathlon, Age Group Champion

Maybe not easy but I am living life to the fullest, even when things don't turn out exactly as I hope and plan for. What an experience, watching how God works as He continues to bless me daily. If we humbly walk before men and God, then they will be able to see God in our lives and glorify Him instead of us. Only then will they ask us for the hope we have within. We can then easily share with them the hope of Jesus that only God can produce.

Faith, Hope, and Love

Many people have asked about my ability to stay positive and keep moving forward with expectations of continued new and bright tomorrows. This was more than a little surprising to me as I knew myself too clearly and my own inner feelings of frustration and strivings, as I dealt with my damaged body and sudden reversal of fortunes. Everyone goes through doubts and uncertainties when unexpected occurrences happen in life. These uncertainties even happen when life just gets bogged down in a rut of mundane jobs and daily routines. Questions easily arise, "Is this the way it is always going to be?" "Where has the excitement and joy gone when looking to an uncertain and unforeseeable future?" This rut only gets deeper unless we make an effort to look for creative ways to climb out.

Even when we recognize a change is necessary, climbing out is not easy unless we have a positive perspective. Three important words were key for me to climb out of a possible dark depression of hopelessness. These words are *faith, hope,* and *love*. Simple words, but how they are intrinsically connected makes a definitive difference in how our lives play out. I believe in a biblical perspective regarding these words. Faith is the essence of my belief in God. Faith that God means what He says in the Bible. When Jesus died on the cross, He said, "It is finished." Our sins or past mistakes were taken away and buried in the deepest sea. No more time spent in the debilitating arena of regret, feeling like our past is controlling our present and future. Jesus said we are forgiven, then set free from our past. This faith allows us to cut the negative bonds that strangle many around us. Have I made some horrific mistakes in my life? Yes, but with the faith that God has forgiven and taken on my mistakes, I will not be forever weighed down by sin. The weight of our past errors and mistakes is too much for anyone to bear for long. You can quickly see the strain of this weight etched across people's faces as they rush madly through life.

Once we know for certain that our past has been taken care of, we can begin to relax and deal with important issues in the present. What about that second word, *hope*? What is hope? Hope, in simple terms, is wishing for something good to happen. True hope is not placing a bet and hoping you are somehow going to win the jackpot. Sure there are hopes which say, "I hope I get that job or promotion." Or "I hope somehow the traffic will be less tomorrow so I can relax getting to work." Or "I hope my boss somehow changes his personality and becomes a positive individual like the hopeful movie, *A Christmas Carol*. These hopes are not really hopes at all, just wishful thinking. Wishful thinking includes, "I hope I have the willpower to start eating correctly, get on a diet which I can really stick with or start and stay with a good exercise program." The true meaning of hope is easily misused and misunderstood. Hope has somehow lost its true meaning and power in our lives through wishful thinking.

True hope is knowing who or what you are putting your complete trust in. Hope is always related to future events and your view of that future during present events. When hope is gone, getting out of bed can be a chore. Keeping your head up and walking with a spring in your step becomes difficult. It all eventually comes back to the truth written down in the Bible. There are so many promises written down through scripture promising a bright future. God has promised His presence will always be there to guide us, protect, and lead us through the most difficult times and situations. This is true hope, trust in God's promises. Does this mean that we will be forever on easy street in this life on Earth? Certainly not. It does mean as the Bible says, "His grace is sufficient!" This grace is freely given for those willing to receive it. This is where hope comes in. If we truly believe these promises, we have a hope no matter the events surrounding us. Worry that suffocates so many in our ever-maddening world cannot hold us down. We can be released from worry and the inevitable depression, which can envelope us like a heavy impenetrable fog.

I know about this kind of fog after living in Medford, Oregon. Sometimes fog would roll in for a month, leaving the simple task of driving, a paralyzing experience. To make it worse, it was tule fog which often makes it possible to see the sky above but only a few feet in front of you. Driving home could only be done by looking out of the side window to hopefully see the center line and stay on your side of the road. After experiencing this impenetrable fog in person, I don't want to experience this in life by letting worry control me and make me blind to what God wants for me. He promises to direct our path but only if we let go of worrying about the future and live in an energized present.

Hope is the essence of energy and excitement that can propel us through each day as if we are floating effortlessly through life. Jesus came that we might have faith and hope, leading us to love and this wonderful gift of life. Without faith and hope, there can't be any real love.

Love for others is the realization that Jesus died for everyone around us. People we come in contact with and tend to irritate us are still loved as much by Jesus as we are. Our faith can spill over into their lives if our faith is grounded in Jesus and not our own feeble ego. When God's faith and hope envelop our lives, we can truly love those around us. Not only that, but we can love each day and live life with a vitality we didn't know possible. The Bible says we are to love others as we love ourselves. When we have real faith and hope, we can begin to love ourselves and therefore love others. Only then can life truly become a wonderful adventure.

We all need to come to the deep realization that God and only God truly "does it all." Give our best, then get out of the way and let Him lead, guide, and direct our paths as He knows best for our lives and those we come in contact with. With Him in charge, there are no accidents or chance encounters. Living life with positive expectations is glorious, wonderful, and only leads to more loving and living each day to its fullest.

I do my best to always remember, "GOD DOES IT ALL!"

Life Continues to Be Blessed

Since my adventure in the Subic International Triathlon race, I have had the opportunity to work with my son Brian, introducing a triathlon training program for people of every age and level. I have also continued coaching tennis to a talented junior tennis player. I have watched him begin to mature and have some success at the local, regional, and national level.

My son Brian's talent with triathlon racing and training has become a source of joy and energy for me to witness. The sheer joy of watching triathletes of every age be inspired by Brian and our Altabrio.com program makes me look forward to getting up each morning. How fortunate for me to have a variety of activities to keep me inspired at my age.

With my youngest children, Daniel and Crystal finishing university in San Diego, I am looking forward to another sea change.

Is my weight where I would like it to be? No, but I am still active, pretending I can still do the things I have done for years. I am getting the seven-year itch again and look forward to relocating back to the Philippines where things are beginning to boom. Even with all I am doing, I am at peace, as I firmly believe

GOD DOES IT ALL.

Asian Triathlon Championship, Singapore

Exiting swim while winning Clearwater

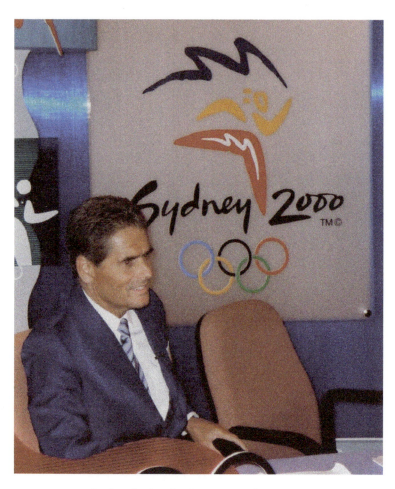

In Studio for Sydney 2000 Olympics

ITU World Championships, Montreal, Canada

USTA National Age Group with partner Rich Hills

Philippine Triathlon

friday focus
South China Morning Post

27 ★★

Courage and a survivor's will to win

Don Bozarth broke his back when his bicycle slammed into a minibus. **Patricia Young** chronicles his miraculous recovery

It sounds like a rip-off. A man who can still run marathons and out-swim people half his age is this week awarded a near-record-breaking $10 million personal injury payout by the Hong Kong courts.

The overall picture is not helped by the fact that he's from the United States, a nation of people with an almost religious zeal completed an Olympic-distance triathlon in Thailand.

But it is his exceptional fitness and spectacular recovery that has drawn flak from critics about the size of the lawsuit payout. If he is strong enough to complete a 1.5-kilometre swim, 10km run and 40km bike ride all on the same morning, then he's faking it and should give back the cash, they say.

pect a three-month convalescence in bed. But he told doctors he would leave when the 30-day in-patient medical insurance package from his employer, The Aberdeen Marina Club, ran out.

They agreed to discharge him only if he could walk without a walking frame.

His stomach muscles were so damaged he could not sit up without a brace to hold him upright.

South China Morning Post

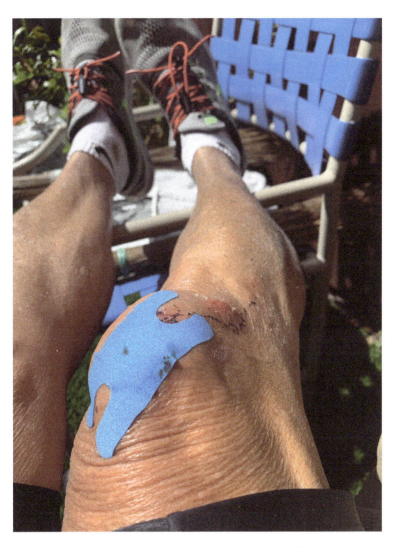

Spinal cord impairment causes many falls

Winning another race on the Gold Coast, Australia

Two years/one month to enjoy running again

ABOUT THE AUTHOR

Don Bozarth is a Christian athlete who has had the opportunity to own numerous businesses and run worldwide companies, traveling and living around the world. He loves embracing different cultures and the wonderful people he encounters. His love of God supersedes his active lifestyle and job opportunities. Whether playing tennis, competing in triathlons, doing Olympic commentary, or relaxing in the surf, his desire is to share God's love and compassion with everyone he encounters. His never ending youthfulness continues to inspire both young and old.

CPSIA information can be obtained
at www.ICGtesting.com
Printed in the USA
JSHW022110090221
11724JS00006B/215